BY PERSONS UNKNOWN

GEORGE JONAS AND BARBARA AMIEL

BY PERSONS UNKNOWN

The Strange Death of Christine Demeter

Macmillan of Canada
Toronto

Canadian Cataloguing in Publication Data

Jonas, George, date
　By persons unknown
ISBN 0-7705-1437-5

1. Demeter, Christine, 1940-1973.　2. Demeter, Peter, 1933-　　3. Uxoricide — Ontario — Mississauga.　4. Trials (Murder) — Ontario — Mississauga.　I. Amiel, Barbara.　II. Title.

　HV6535.C33M58　　364.1'523'09713535　　C77-001218-3

Printed and bound in Canada
by T. H. Best Printing Company Limited
Don Mills, Ontario

The Macmillan Company of Canada Limited
70 Bond Street
Toronto　M5B 1X3

Contents

Acknowledgements

In our research we have received generous co-operation from the Honourable Justice Campbell Grant of the Supreme Court of Ontario; from Deputy Assistant Attorney General F. J. Greenwood, Q.C., of the Province of Ontario; and from Chief Douglas Kenneth Burrows and his staff of the Peel Regional Police. We are grateful to Messrs. Joseph B. Pomerant, Q.C., and Edward L. Greenspan, solicitors to Peter Demeter, who have given us every assistance consistent with the requirements of duty to their client. For additional information on facts and the law our thanks are due to Judge W. L. Durham, and to L. J. McGuigan, John David Watt, and Bruce Affleck, Counsels for the Crown for the Province of Ontario.

Dr. Steven and Marjorie Demeter have given us the benefit of their hospitality and reminiscences. Dr. Peter Rowsell, Dr. Andrew I. Malcolm, and Dr. Joseph Marotta have kindly reviewed some medical matters. Ms. Norma Pullen of the Supreme Court of Ontario has provided invaluable help. We have also received assistance from a number of others who would prefer us not to thank them by name. No one assisted us for any consideration except assurance of fair reporting.

We have tried to make sure of the facts. The conclusions are our own.

Picture Credits

A number of the illustrations used in this book come from private sources and from the Peel Regional Police Force.

Numbers 17 and 40 are from Alex Kalnins.

Numbers 20, 21, 32, and 33 are from *The Mississauga News*.

Numbers 18, 27, 28, 29, 34, 42, and 45 are from *The Toronto Star*.

Number 19 is from *The Canadian Press*.

Number 30 is from George Blumson and *The London Free Press*.

Numbers 37 and 43 are from *The Toronto Sun*.

Grateful acknowledgement is made to all those who supplied the photographs or who assisted in any way.

Books have been written on ambitious and vindictive prosecutors sacrificing the life and liberty of the innocent.

Books have been written on cunning and desperate criminals brought to bay by vigilant guardians of the law.

Perhaps books of either kind can and will be written on the Demeter murder. But this book has no such ambitions. It attempts, instead, to describe how a complex case is investigated and tried in a reasonably good society by honest and competent people. It pursues the question of how well our system is doing when it is doing its best, and how close it comes to justice when doing justice is its aim. It pays some attention to the role of fate and coincidence in human affairs. It casts at least a passing glance at evil. It tries to compare some of the personal and cultural cradles that shape our sympathies and give us our diverse ideas of fairness and truth.

Most of all, it is a book about the story of Christine and Peter Demeter.

Cast of Characters

The Demeters

Christine — The victim, a thirty-three-year-old glamorous Austrian-born model

Peter — Her husband, the accused, a prosperous Hungarian-born Toronto property developer

Andrea — Peter and Christine's three-year-old child

Steven — Peter's cousin, a psychologist and marriage counsellor

Marjorie — Steven's wife, a teacher

Friends of the Demeters

Dr. Charles Bende — A dentist and mutual friend

David and Dr. Sybille Brewer — Friends from Connecticut

Lilian Dayaran — The Demeters' maid from Hong Kong; known as "Gigi"

Philip Epstein — Peter Demeter's civil lawyer

Nicholas Esso — A distant relative of Peter Demeter

Viveca Esso — Nicholas Esso's daughter, at the Demeter house on the night of the murder

Mr. and Mrs. Henri Galle — Friends of the Demeters. Peter suspected Henri of involvement with Christine

Gerald Heifetz — Peter Demeter's business lawyer

Marina Hundt — Peter's Viennese mistress, a much-admired model

David and Alice Mailath — Peter Demeter's former architect and his wife

Klara Majerszky — The Demeters' former housekeeper

Judy Markovitch — Christine's friend and confidante

Konrad Patzenhofer — An old Austrian friend of Peter's

Leo Ross — Private detective and a social acquaintance
Helga Treitl — An old family friend
Nicholas Van Berkel — A management consultant and, briefly, Christine Demeter's lover
Leslie Wagner — Peter Demeter's architect

Neighbours of the Demeters
Rose Papastamos — Christine's fourteen-year-old baby sitter
David and Joan Tennant — Next-door neighbours of the Demeters

The Police
Chief Douglas Kenneth Burrows
Superintendent William J. Teggart
Detective-Sergeant Roy Crozier
Detective-Sergeant John K. Forbes
Detective-Sergeant Christopher O'Toole
Detective-Sergeant Joseph Terdik
Detective Barry V. King
Detective William Koeslag
Detective James R. Wingate
Patrol Sergeant John A. Murray
Police Constable Bernard J. Burns
Police Constable Craig P. Malcolm
Police Constable D. Wayne Pollitt

The Judiciary
The Honourable Justice Campbell Grant of the Supreme Court of Ontario — The judge presiding over Peter Demeter's trial
Judge G. L. Young of the Provincial Court (Criminal Division) of Ontario — The judge who presided at Peter Demeter's preliminary hearing
Ontario Court of Appeal Members
Chief Justice George Arthur Gale
Justice Gregory Thomas Evans
Justice Lloyd William Houlden
Justice Arthur R. Jessup
Justice Goldwin Arthur Martin

The Prosecution
F. John Greenwood, Q.C. — Crown Attorney

Leo J. McGuigan — Assistant Crown Attorney
David Watt — Crown Counsel during the appeal before the Appeal Court of Ontario

The Defence
Joseph B. Pomerant, Q.C. — Attorney for the Defence
Edward L. Greenspan — Assistant Attorney for the Defence

The Others
Laszlo Eper — A cop-hater, small-arms expert, and escaped convict
George and Helen Fancsik — Friends of Mr. and Mrs. Duck
Paul Horvath — A sometime enforcer killed in a car crash on July 16, 1976
William Illerbrun — A guard at the Guelph Jail
Rita Jefferies — A girl who used to date Csaba
Joseph Robert "Foxy" Jones — Brother-in-law of Gaby Kecskes
Gaby Kecskes — A friend of The Duck
Magda and Laszlo Link — Friends of Mr. and Mrs. Duck
Gabor Magosztovics, a.k.a. Joe Dinardo, a.k.a. The Tractor — An underworld enforcer, heavyweight boxer, and friend of Laszlo Eper
Arthur Maloney — One of Ontario's most respected criminal lawyers, first Ontario ombudsman, and Joe Dinardo's lawyer
Imre Olejnyik, a.k.a. Kacsa, a.k.a. Cutlip, a.k.a. Jimmy Orr, a.k.a. The Duck — A shifty small-time criminal who left Toronto suddenly to return to Hungary
Ferenc ("Frank") Stark — A small-job contractor and ex-Foreign Legionnaire
Csaba Szilagyi — Peter Demeter's closest friend in Europe and later in Canada
Julius Norman Virag, a.k.a. Flower, a.k.a. Mr. X, a.k.a. Tom Smith — An informer and the hooded witness at the trial
Maria Visnyiczky — Common-law wife of Imre Olejnyik
Henry Joseph Robert Williams — "The Streetsville Killer"

x

1. The Day Itself

When Christine Demeter opened her eyes that morning the first thing she saw was Beelzebub's head on the pillow. Beelzebub was awake too, and Christine could feel his tail brushing against her thighs under the covers. On the other side of the pillow Peter lay with his face half-covered by the spaniel's hair. He seemed still asleep. Sleeping cheek to cheek with a dog was Peter's idea of domestic bliss, and in her disjointed waking thoughts Christine wondered if it was something vaguely Hungarian. She didn't exactly mind, but in her native Austria most people would have regarded it as unhygienic. Beelzebub stirred, yawned, and started pounding his tail against Christine's leg. She slipped out from under the covers quickly to put the dog outside, and stood for a second watching the spaniel waddle into the garden with great dignity. It was not yet eight o'clock and the morning sun cast the shadow of the house obliquely across the back yard almost as far as the ravine. In the swimming pool, just beyond the line of shade, the water lay still and sparkling. The sky was blue, not crisp but soft and shimmering, and the haze made the distant buildings of Erindale campus on the other side of the ravine appear out of focus. July 18, 1973, was going to be a warm day.

Christine looked back at the house with a little catch of pleasure. This kind of suburban living, she often told friends, seemed to her the best of all possible worlds. Here in the bedroom community of Mississauga she was scarcely fifteen minutes away from busy downtown Toronto, but that Wednesday morning in July Mississauga seemed far off somewhere in the country. The house at 1437 Dundas Crescent was the last but one on a dead-end street. Its garden sloped back to a ravine that extended nearly a mile to the west and several miles to the north. Busy

Highway Number 5 was less than forty yards from the circular drive-way fronting the Demeter residence, but a strip of trees and bushes provided foliage dense enough in July to completely obscure the view and all but muffle the sound of passing cars. Even the narrow footpath leading from Dundas Crescent to the soft shoulder of the highway was nearly obliterated by vegetation during the summer months. Thank God for the part-time gardener, Christine thought, looking at the shrubbery rimming the garden. It was getting as dense as the rest of the ravine. She turned back into the house.

Andrea hadn't made a sound yet and the house guests seemed still asleep, but Peter's eyes were open when Christine returned to the bedroom. Some men retain a boyish softness around the mouth and eyes, even when they are forty with grey threads in their hair and faces fully set. This was the case with Peter, and it suited him. He looked at her and she got back into bed. They made love, quietly and quickly; after all, they had a houseful of guests and important things to do later in the day. Soon Christine felt the familiar change in rhythm and thrust of her husband reaching climax, which always reassured her. It was worth eating no lunch and hardly touching dinner. It was worth swimming forty lengths of the pool every evening and lying in the sun for much longer than was comfortable. As long as a woman could arouse and satisfy a man she might be safe, and she might even have her own way. Peter hadn't kissed her, of course, but Christine didn't expect him to. He had never kissed her since the birth of Andrea three years ago.

The house guests were all Peter's friends, really, not hers. Dr. Sybille Brewer even shared certain habits with Peter, like the alarming punctuality and energy she constantly displayed. By nine o'clock that morning Sybille and her two teen-age nieces from Germany, Katja and Silja, had been working out in the pool with Teutonic zeal. Christine could see them through the kitchen window while she prepared the breakfast necessary to maintain such energy. The other two guests were teenagers as well: a Canadian friend of the German girls, and Viveca, the sixteen-year-old daughter of one of Peter's distant relatives. The house had the atmosphere of a girls' summer camp.

It was eleven o'clock when Peter assembled them in front of the garage and choreographed the day's activities. Moccasins had to be purchased for Sybille's nieces, who could not show their feet back in Germany without them. Peter had some business errands to do in Toronto. Viveca opted for bed and bumming around, but Peter much preferred doing his rounds with an audience and so Viveca was conscripted. They all stood ceremoniously in front of the house admiring the New World booty. In front of them was a double garage furnished with Christine's oyster-coloured Mercedes 300 SEL and Peter's gleaming grey Cadillac. The only jarring note was the broken garage door in front of the Cadillac. "It's the hardware, not the electric part," explained Peter, automatically expropriating Christine's car on account of the crippled technology. The Mercedes, its six passengers, and one dog sped smoothly away from Mississauga in search of moccasins.

Cleaning up the dishes and debris of five house guests can be as relaxing for a hostess temporarily off duty as shucking off a tight girdle. Christine worked fast, fuelled by the prospect of a lazy afternoon in the sun. By the time next-door neighbour David Tennant had changed into his swimsuit, the pool at the Demeters' was filling up. Three little Greek girls from farther up the street were already happily splashing around. Christine looked vaguely out of place in this suburban setting. The blonde streaks in her long dark hair glinted in the sun. Her smooth tanned skin boasted of constant care and emollients. She was a tall girl, 5'9", with long slim legs and a matching figure. After two children (one left behind with a former husband in Europe) and at thirty-three years of age, her body was as firm and supple as a teen-ager's. Swimming in the summer, riding in the fall, and skiing in the winter had kept the inevitable sag of tissue and skin at bay. In her pale-blue bikini she seemed an exotic creature who had through some curious misunderstanding been transplanted to Mississauga from the terrazzi and lemon groves of the Italian Riviera.

Tennant always thought of the Demeters as "over the fence" neighbours, and no more. It might have been the difference in their ages: at fifty-seven, David Tennant was nearly a generation older than Peter. All the same, he was enjoying Christine's invitation to a quick swim before leaving to join his wife up at their summer cottage. As he munched the open-faced Austrian sandwiches Christine offered him, he reflected on how well she was looking. Later he would tell the police she seemed in much better spirits than before. Still, he couldn't get her to depart from the strict dietary regime she followed: she wouldn't touch the sandwiches. "I never eat lunch," she explained. The most she would do was have a sip of David's beer. "It's really bad for my weight," she said guiltily, accepting the inch or so he poured into her glass.

As the Greek girls left the pool, Christine asked the eldest, Rose Papastamos, if she could babysit next Friday. Rose quickly agreed. Later she revealed that a further date was made. "What about coming over tonight," said Christine, according to Rose. "Not for Andrea, but just to keep me company. You could come any time after five. Say between five and eight." Rose happened to have a baby-sitting job for the evening, but for some reason she didn't feel like explaining the situation to Christine. "Okay, Mrs. Demeter, I'll be over," she said, knowing she couldn't. (Rose's memory of this conversation made her a significant figure in later events. It must have been a heady experience for a four-teen-year-old to have brushed so close to so sensational a crime. It might, indeed, have been the sort of headlines that could easily stimulate a little girl's imagination.)

One of the things Dr. Sybille Brewer liked about Peter Demeter was his evident concern for details, coupled with an almost military precision. He'd never say Andrea was three years old, for instance; he'd say her age was exactly three years and four months. Sybille, being a rather precise lady herself, found this appealing. When Peter brought the Mercedes to a stop on the corner of Front Street and Bay, the two of them immediately synchronized their watches. Sybille and the younger girls got out of the car and headed for the Yonge Street Mall.

The Mall was an experiment in an alternate style of community living, and it enjoyed the support of progressive members of the Toronto City Council. The idea consisted of closing the downtown portion of the city's main street to automobiles for the summer months and turning it into a haven for pedestrians, sidewalk cafés, soft-drink vendors, and strolling troubadours. Unfortunately, at night it had also become something of a haven for the city's few addicts, pushers, and prostitutes. Toronto didn't yet have the urban sophistication to avoid this, or to be philosophical about it when it couldn't. A year later the Mall was declared a failure and closed down. On that Wednesday in July, however, it seemed the perfect place to buy Canadian souvenirs for German teenagers, and Sybille began propelling her charges through the crowd. The day was turning very hot, and the smell of frankfurters and pastrami mingled curiously with the aroma of eau de cologne and incense drifting from doorways across the street. Old men sat dozing on the benches along the Mall or watching the tilted figures of black teen-agers, dazzling in their peacock colours and extravagant bodies. Under different circumstances Sybille herself might have enjoyed sitting down in one of the Mall's ersatz beer gardens and watching the parade. But Silja's eagerness propelled her to the shop windows.

The Mercedes was very much more comfortable now that only Viveca, Peter, and Beelzebub were sharing it. Beelzebub in particular seemed happier to have the back seat to himself. Peter had insisted the spaniel come with them that day — apparently he wished to familiarize the dog with those holdings of Eden Gardens Limited that provided his daily biscuits. The company had a number of properties and construction projects in town, and it appeared to Viveca that Peter was bent on showing her all of them. She had the interests of any normal sixteen-year-old, and real estate as such held no particular fascination for her, but searching for moccasins along a strip of steaming asphalt with three younger girls and a middle-aged lady wasn't much better. If Peter wanted company, as he seemed to, it was simpler to stay with him in the Mercedes.

Viveca had known the Demeters casually for some time. The family ties between them were distant enough so that any friendship was by choice rather than obligation, even for Europeans who tend to attach importance to even the most tenuous family connection. Having been born in Toronto, Viveca didn't really think of herself as European, at least not until her parents separated and her father went back to Austria, taking Viveca with him. Just before the trip Peter had told her that if she was unhappy in Europe she could come and stay in Mississauga with them. Perhaps she did miss some of her Toronto friends at first. High school in Don Mills wasn't much like school in Borgenland, Austria. But being a North American in Austria had more glamour than being of immigrant European parents in Canada, so the transition wasn't so difficult after all. Anyway, there were always her Toronto-based grandparents to flee to if the sturm-und-drang got out of hand. As it was, Viveca was simply lazing away her summer vacation in Canada.

She was a wholesome-looking girl with an appealing freshness that is exclusive to sixteen-year-olds but not necessarily shared by all of them. It seemed important to Peter that he explain himself to her. The confidences tumbled out as the Mercedes eased its way through the busy Toronto traffic, its dark-brown rosewood and leather interior cushioning the passengers. But perhaps because air-conditioning doesn't show, the unit in the Mercedes wasn't very good. The windows had to be rolled down, and the sound of a dozen car radios and engines of a lesser breed vied with Peter for attention. Viveca noted with some amusement that his converstation was full of unexpected twists and turns, as though he were trying to find a way out of the labyrinth of his own mind. Any one of his words could lead him to a different association and he would change topics in mid-sentence. It was a habit which often exasperated Peter's friends, but the girl found it fascinating. It was like watching a nervous tic on someone's face and counting the seconds in between.

He began with an account of the vacation he and Christine had taken to Acapulco last spring. Friends who were to accompany them had backed out at the last minute. Alone with one another under the white Mexican sun, surrounded by mountains and tiled villas, Christine and Peter managed to have a hideously boring time. Their marriage, they discovered, was "on the rocks". At this point Peter's conversation skipped abruptly back to Vienna. When he first met Christine, he explained, he was in love with another woman. This "other woman" refused to marry him. Now Peter looked fondly at Viveca and started talking about her father. "You resemble Andrea so much," he said to the puzzled girl for no apparent reason.

At City Hall there was a brief respite. For twenty minutes Viveca sat in the Mercedes listening to nothing but the staccato breathing of Beelzebub and the steady thunder of downtown traffic. Then Peter was back and it began again. "I'm sending some money to a Hungarian immigrant in Austria," he announced as the car pulled away from City Hall. "I'm going to send 1300 schillings, that's between sixty and seventy dollars." "Mm-hmm," consented Viveca, apprehensive of a long lecture on exchange rates. But the project was short-lived. Peter couldn't remember the unlucky immigrant's name or address and neither could Christine one telephone call later. This occasioned a caustic remark to Viveca. Putting down Christine seemed to be a ritual with Peter; Viveca reflected that he seemed curiously disorganized himself for a man who was so fierce about accuracy and detail. His papers were scattered about the house and he used a cereal box on his desk for a filing cabinet, while Christine was expected to be perfect. He's a sadist, Viveca thought, employing the casual hyperbole of her generation.

The hopscotch continued. Now Peter was talking about his first love again. Apparently she had come to Montreal only a few weeks ago, after Peter sent her money and a ticket. They had spent five days together and Peter pronounced it "good". Mercifully this was not enlarged upon. When they said their airport good-byes Peter had been a little worried that "someone might see them". Then, abruptly, he turned to Viveca.

"Do you have any problems?" The question was posed as if Viveca's equilibrium had been the thread of their conversation all along. "Do you need anything? How do you like Europe, living there I mean?"

It was like a romantic movie, played with the wrong sound track. Peter himself would have made an appropriate leading man. The cut and understatement of his clothes played well against his 6'2" frame and easy, charming looks. Viveca glanced at him and felt a little ungracious as she shook her head. It was kind of Peter to inquire about her, but somehow coming right in the middle of all this talk about his old girlfriend and the inadequacy of Christine, it made her feel a little uncomfortable. It was as though he wanted her to owe him a favour, to be on his side, although Viveca was sure he didn't mean it like that. It was just the way his mind jumped from one thing to another. "Isn't it time to pick up the Doctor and the kids?" she asked.

The great moccasin hunt had not been an unqualified success. One of the nieces was still without a pair and her unhappiness was quite evident. As they drove away from the Mall, Sybille reassured the girl. "Don't worry," she said, "I'll take you to the Yorkdale Plaza after supper tonight." Peter responded quickly.

"I'll drive you," he offered. "I've got some shopping to do anyway." Viveca recalled this exchange but thought it occurred later in the day, during the drive back to Mississauga. The difference, though not crucial, was important.

It was early afternoon now and the prospect of an afternoon swim back at the house seemed inviting. But Peter had one more thing to do. He wanted to speak to one of his contractors. The group drove to a house under construction near the old and smelly Riverdale Zoo and waited, jammed together in the hot car, while Peter searched unsuccessfully for him. As they drove for a bite of lunch to a sidewalk restaurant shielded from the afternoon sun by blue awnings and tall apartment buildings, Peter seemed unperturbed. If he was anxious, it showed only in his eagerness to get to a phone and try again to locate his man. "I haven't got him yet," he reported to the table, "but I did talk to Christine. She said the little Greek girls came over for a swim."

Only yesterday, thought Viveca, Peter had sworn he would kill the Papastamos girls if he ever caught them in his pool again. He blamed them for a plugged filter system and was quite livid about it, screaming abuse at Christine. When he wandered off at the end of his tantrum Christine sighed, then said to Viveca, laughing, "Wouldn't it be nice if I could knock him off and get all his money? Then you could come and live with me here." Of course it was only a joke, as Peter's threat to kill the girls was just an outburst. Christine certainly didn't take it seriously or she would have barred the girls from the pool, or, at the very least, not mentioned their presence to Peter. But Viveca knew all about bitter jokes, dark moods, and outbursts. She paid little attention to them. In more than one marriage they seemed to be par for the course.

Before the escape to the cool chlorinated waters of Mississauga, Peter wheeled the car back to the Riverdale house, leaving his passengers to relive the stuffy moments they had spent earlier waiting for Peter's contractor to show. Their host disappeared into the construction site, hidden behind mounds of earth and raw red heaps of bricks. When he returned, his business was finished, whatever it may have been. Before four o'clock Beelzebub was able to scuttle out of the Mercedes onto the firm land of the home driveway.

About the same time, an old friend of Peter Demeter's was driving along a small, elegant street of townhouses and boutiques. Toronto's Yorkville district specializes in the handsomer variety of urbanite, and Csaba Szilagyi enjoyed glancing at them as he crawled along in the bumper-to-bumper traffic. Suddenly he recognized an ex-girlfriend whom he hadn't seen for months. Their parting had been traumatic and unequivocal. In fact, the well-bred English girl had felt impelled to toss a glass of Coca-Cola over him in a restaurant. Still, on seeing her unexpectedly, Csaba felt a twinge of nostalgia. Since it was obvious that the girl had seen him too, he made a point of waving at her in a cheerful, no-hard-feelings fashion. After a split second of hesitation, Rita Jefferies waved back at Csaba in much the same way. There is at least an outside possibility that, but for this chance meeting, Peter Demeter would never have been tried for murder.

It was a day full of unremarkable events: a chance meeting, shopping at the Mall, a swim in a backyard pool. So it was nothing unusual when, at four-thirty that afternoon, a contingent of real estate people parked on the street outside the Demeter house. Nor did Mr. Rick Varep, the vice-president of a Mississauga realty company, consider it of any great importance when, just a few minutes later, a beige Volkswagen with at least three men in it pulled past him into the Demeter driveway, stopped for about thirty seconds, backed out, and turned around again. There was no reason to pay any special attention to the beige bug: Dundas Crescent was a dead-end street and Varep supposed the driveway of one of the last houses would often be used for turning around. Since he was a little early for his afternoon appointment to evaluate the house at 1437 Dundas Crescent, Varep waited politely outside.

Inside, Viveca was helping Christine in the kitchen. Supper was to be an elaborate meal reminiscent of the menu at a German summer resort: *Rindsrouladen*, or rolled beef with mushroom sauce, potatoes, cucumber salad, and home-made apple strudel for dessert. Peter was hovering around the garden, picking away at odd jobs, first cleaning the pool, then attempting to fix the garage door in front of the Cadillac. He was trying to force the door down, but he couldn't do it alone and called for Christine to help him. She came to the garage from the kitchen with flour on her hands, and together they finally managed to slam the door shut, but not before the spring jumped off, cutting Peter's hand between the thumb and forefinger. It was a small wound, just enough to draw the first blood of the day.

Caroline Wight, the next member of the real estate team, arrived at the Demeter house a few minutes after Rick Varep. Ms. Wight was a top saleslady with a shrewd eye for talent in the business. At the beginning of each financial year, like spring bulbs pushing tender green shoots into the March chill, a new crop of developers surface. They have a little money and plenty of sure notions, and few of them last longer than the first corporate tax return. But Caroline Wight had spotted Peter as a survivor from the beginning. She had sold real estate for some time and knew that his combination of drive and good business sense could make him an important developer. As it was, his holdings were edging up around the $400,000 mark. On this occasion, Caroline thought, glancing around the living room of the Dundas Crescent house, Peter shouldn't miss the chance to sell it and move into the Toronto property he wanted to convert to condominiums. By establishing the Toronto development as his own principal residence he could avoid paying capital gains tax later. It was a method he had often used in the past, and it saved a fair amount of money, even if it did turn life into something of a caravan. It was evidently worth it to Peter, although Caroline wasn't so sure about Christine. It was Christine who had wanted to move to Mississauga originally, and Caroline knew she thought of 1437 Dundas Crescent as their first real home.

Rick Varep was enjoying his gin-and-tonic bargaining with Peter. His people had appraised the house at around $120,000. Peter wouldn't hear of it. Caroline watched Peter edge the price up, and when it reached just under $140,000 she drew up the listing agreement. But when it came to signing, he balked.

"You know how Christine feels about leaving here," he said. "Give me a chance to talk it over with her."

Caroline would have preferred to settle matters immediately, but she had no argument against the display of consideration Peter seemed to be showing for his wife. Instead, she decided to wander into the kitchen and chat with Christine. Christine turned to her in obvious agitation.

"Has he signed anything, Caroline? Has he signed anything?"

For a second Caroline couldn't help feeling sorry for her. The Demeters' marriage appeared amicable enough, but they really didn't seem to have much in common. For instance, Christine couldn't possibly appreciate Peter's plan to designate ten townhouses with eighteen-foot frontages as condominiums by connecting them with communal sewers, which to Caroline's way of thinking was a brilliant idea. Christine may have liked money as much as her husband, but she viewed it from the opposite side of the cash register.

"No, dear, he hasn't signed anything yet," she said to Christine, patting her reassuringly on the arm.

In spite of the elaborate preparations, supper was not a happy meal. Christine seemed a little edgy as she shuttled back and forth between the kitchen and the dining room. Peter blamed the tension on the realtors, who had overstayed their welcome, sipping their drinks and leaning back in the down-filled, stuffed velvet furniture. It was 6:30 P.M. when they finally pulled themselves up and left. It was hot, too, in the kitchen and dining room, where there was no air-conditioning and hardly any ventilation. Viveca felt that Peter hadn't helped cool things down with his constant sniping all through the meal. Sybille recalled only that Christine seemed a little tired and complained of a pain in her back. When the girls brought up the subject of moccasins again, Sybille decided it would be inconsiderate to drag Peter out of the house that evening.

"How far is it to Yorkdale?" she asked. "I'll take the girls in my car." Sybille had made the 500-plus mile trip from her home in Connecticut to the Demeters' by car and enjoyed her mastery of the internal combustion engine.

"No, I'll drive you," insisted Peter. "It's no trouble, and Viveca can help me choose a gift for Christine's name day." Among European Catholics it is customary to honour one's saint's day with a small gift, and Saint Christina's day was less than a week away. Christine was not placated by Peter's sudden public generosity. She preferred Viveca to stay at home with her. But Peter intended to choose a gift without resort to concealment or secrecy and with an audience.

"Aren't we going to have dessert first?" asked Christine, who had laboured over the strudel.

"A good dessert should be enjoyed, not hurried," said Peter somewhat grandly. "If we're going, let's go now before the shopping centre closes. We'll have coffee and dessert when we come back. And look at Andrea; she has bags under her eyes. I think you should put her to bed."

Viveca glanced at the child. At three years of age she was by any measure a beautiful little girl. With parents as attractive as both Christine and Peter it wouldn't really have mattered which one she took after, but her resemblance to Christine was quite striking. Her tawny blonde hair had the same luxurious wave and texture as her mother's, and the afternoon hours spent next to the pool in serious conversation with her sea serpent and spotted Mr. Mouse had given her skin the same golden glow. To Viveca, at least, she appeared no more tired than usual.

It was at this time, 7:45, that Ernest Kosonic, a full-time mailman and part-time gardener, got a can of weed spray from his car and ambled over to the Demeter garage. He expect to find the key, as usual, in the garage door and to walk through the garage to spray the weeds in the back yard. He was mildly surprised when the key seemed missing, because he recalled seeing it in the lock on all previous occasions. The Demeter property was surrounded by a fairly high fence and the gate leading to the back yard was padlocked. Now, being unable to get through either the gate or the garage, Kosonic was faced with the choice of climbing the fence or knocking on the front door. Just at this moment Peter solved his dilemma by emerging from the house. He didn't seem to notice the gardener right away.

"Mr. Demeter, I came to spray for the weeds."

Peter looked puzzled.

"Oh, geez, Ernie," he said, "can you come back another time? I've got eight guests in the house."

Kosonic found the request perfectly natural. The smell of weed spray was not pleasant, and it was likely to linger for more than a day. He put the spray back in his car and left for his next moonlighting job at the Erindale Medical Centre. He had married off two girls on his postman's salary and had four more children at home to support.

As the guests got ready to leave for the Yorkdale Plaza there was one last moment of tension when Peter picked up Beelzebub.

"You're not taking the dog along too, are you?" asked Christine.

Peter replied in German too quickly for Viveca to catch, then said rather sharply, "Do you mind?"

Christine shrugged and didn't answer. When Sybille also expressed surprise over the canine company, Peter became almost belligerent. Only Beelzebub seemed indifferent to the squabbling and clambered into the Mercedes after the six passengers had squeezed themselves in.

It was exactly 8:15 when Peter brought the Mercedes to a stop in front of the Bagel King on the immense parking lot of the Yorkdale Shopping Centre. As the passengers and the dog spilled out of the car, Sybille Brewer and Peter Demeter synchronized their watches for the last time. This accomplished, Sybille and the girls disappeared into the crowds.

Yorkdale is the ultimate extension of the North American urge for everything-under-one-roof. Flanked by Canada's two major department stores, it contains 110 shops and is accessible only by car. This geographic condition weeds out the idle shopper. On any of the six shopping days of the week the plaza throbs with an urgent consumerism. Even the expensive Holt Renfrew store has a branch here, although the merchandise is tamed for suburban pocket-books and figures. On the seventh day the plaza dozes but never sleeps. Its cinemas and restaurants carry on.

Yorkdale is convenience shopping. Easy stuff. Perhaps it doesn't have the best, the most unique, the most original, but its shoppers know it always *has*. So Peter Demeter walked towards Henry Birk's Jewellers and Silversmiths, confident he could find something perfectly passable there.

"What do you think?" Peter asked Viveca. "A silver locket maybe?"

Viveca was non-committal. Her own tastes didn't run to silver things from Birks. Maybe ivory or even tortoiseshell. But Birks wouldn't have that unless it was imitation. Then Peter saw the sign. It was gold-lettered on the glass swing doors leading into the plaza: No Dogs Allowed For Sanitary Reasons. This seemed to exclude even Beelzebub.

"Just as I thought — the dog can't get in," said Peter, according to Viveca's recollection. "Well, you go into Birks and look around. I'll put the dog in the car."

Viveca had been away from Canada for a while, but all that is immutable in the Anglo-Canadian spirit can be found in the ambience of

Henry Birk's & Sons. The restlessness of the sixties passed Birks by as if the chain of jewellery stores were all wrapped up inside a time lock. The rows of glass counters displaying sets of matched engagement and wedding rings were still under the surveillance of granite-tempered salesladies with eyeglasses secured by gilt neck-chains. In the showcases, green and pink china bouquets were displayed as centre-pieces for tables sporting silver-plated pickle dishes and butter servers on feeble little legs ending in claws. They could have served as symbols on suburban flags.

Viveca wandered about looking half-heartedly for silver lockets. When Peter joined her she thought he had been gone for about five or ten minutes, but Peter himself estimated it at less than a minute. In any case, it was the only time he spent alone since they'd made up their minds to go shopping that evening. None of the lockets Viveca had picked out impressed him. This one was too ornate, that one not big enough. As a gift shopper Viveca clearly hadn't worked out. She wandered off into the nether regions of Birks. When she next looked up, Peter was talking on the store phone. She began walking towards him but stopped when he appeared to be waving her away. A few minutes later when she approached again Peter extended the receiver to her.

"Christine wants to say something," he said.

All Christine wanted to do was put Andrea on the phone. "Hi! Mommy and me want you to come to our house soon," she lisped. Christine laughed as she came back on the line, and Viveca said they'd see each other later. Peter replaced the green push-button receiver which some enthusiast from the silverware department had decorated with an ugly piece of embossed silver. The time was around 8:35.

By the time everyone had finished shopping it was 9:15. Night was falling rapidly, and the cars pulling out of the parking lot looked like clumsy fireflies in the changing light. The Mercedes drove west along the highway, stopping just once for a newspaper at the corner box. Now it was completely dark and Peter switched on the vertical headlights of his wife's coupe. They cast rich yellow beams on the dense foliage around the double garage doors as the car swung into the driveway of the house.

Peter looked at his watch. "It's exactly 9:45," he said. "We're just in time for coffee."

He reached for the remote control which activated the door in front of the west bay. The door rose slowly and silently like the curtain in a theatre before the first act. The vertical beams crept along the garage floor, turning from yellow to bright red. "Oh, my God," said Peter. After a second of stunned inaction Sybille Brewer jumped out of the car, trying to avoid the blood which now was seeping out of the garage and into the driveway.

REGINA VS. DEMETER
CHARGE: NON-CAPITAL MURDER

WITNESS
Detective Sergeant John Forbes,
Mississauga Police Department,
80 Dundas Street West,
Mississauga, Ontario.

- WILL STATE -

. . . On entering the garage I noticed that there was the body of a female lying face down, on the concrete floor of the garage, with her feet towards the north and her head towards the south. Her hands were folded under her breast and not visible. She was wearing a long, ankle-length, brown plush gown and silver slippers, one which was still on her right foot and the other lying on the floor, west of her left foot . . .

. . . On closer examination, I observed she was wearing a pair of white bikini panties with black and brown polka dots. These panties were in apparent good condition and were in place on her hips. She was not wearing a brassiere. The gown she was wearing was backless and tied at the back of her neck.

. . . On examination of the body it was noted that there were numerous small bruises on both thighs, shins and right knee. There was a large massive wound to the skull of the body caused by a crushing action. It was apparent that brain matter had emerged from this cranial wound.

Christine was crumpled on the garage floor face down, her arms folded under her like a tired child. The Cadillac was spattered with the blood which flowed in two broad pools away from her head. The thick hair was matted and clumped with congealed blood and tissue. All that seemed untouched was her bare back. The even tan which she had worked so hard to get was having one last hurrah: her lean muscled shoulders gleamed under the garage lights.

Inside the house, dressed in her pajamas, 3½-year-old Andrea Demeter was quietly watching television, alone in a darkened living room.

2. Peter

The Red Army reached the outskirts of Budapest in the early days of December, 1944. Instead of laying siege to the city right away, it went around the ancient Hungarian capital, as if carried by the impetus of its own immense weight. During the month of December low-flying Russian planes dumped thousands of leaflets on the surrounded city. The leaflets showed a lean, cowering canine creature with Hitler's face, trying to escape three bayonets held by hands that might have belonged to the Jolly Green Giant, except that one wore the Union Jack on its sleeve, the other the Stars and Stripes, and the most muscular of the three the Hammer and Sickle. The caption underneath this piece of socialist realism read: *We will destroy the fascist beast in its lair!*

The artwork of the Soviet military may have been camp, but its artillery wasn't. The ring of the 2nd and 3rd Ukrainian Fronts around the city grew tighter, while nearly a hundred miles to the west the Red Army's vanguard was already crossing into Austria. It was in the face of this classically hopeless encirclement that Hitler ordered his troops to defend Budapest to the last man. Just to put the Russians in a good mood, the Germans began by machine-gunning the two Soviet envoys, Captains Steinmets and Ostapenko, who were sent to demand their surrender under a flag of truce. This happened on December 29. Twelve hours later, around 5 A.M., Marshal Malinovsky unplugged his field pieces.

From that morning until February 13, the earth shook under Budapest. For one million civilians huddled together in their basements or air-raid shelters, without food, water, or electricity, the next six weeks were a continuous nightmare of shock waves, flickering candles, and jars and glasses dancing on makeshift shelves, while the fine dust of shaking brick and plaster shimmered in the air. In each neighbourhood, as the Russians drew closer, the roar of siege guns would be replaced by the clatter of automatic weapons and the sharp explosions of hand grenades. For tens of thousands there would be no memory of any sight or sound, except perhaps an instant of blinding flash and searing pain. By the end of the siege an estimated ten per cent of the population lay dead under the rubble, not counting military casualties or thousands of Jews summarily executed by the Arrow Cross Guard, Hungary's own greenshirt version of the brownshirt Nazis. In the ghetto district of Dob Street and Klausal Square the frozen bodies were piled on handcarts like cords of wood.

On the fifth day of the siege, January 2, 1945, twelve-year-old Peter Demeter was sitting under an arch in the shelter beneath their old, luxurious apartment building in Buda, on the west side of the Danube. There was a momentary lull in the cannonade, but a dogfight seemed to be developing across the river over the Parliament Buildings on the Pest side. The characteristic low-pitched whine of a Russian bomber was shattered by the sharp staccato of a Messerschmidt fighter's machine guns. Suddenly the planes seemed to be right overhead. Peter glanced apprehensively at his mother, who was sitting next to him, then at his father, who was standing near them with a group of neighbours. The screech of the propellers reached a crescendo and receded as the planes headed harmlessly away. Then the explosion came.

People said later it wasn't even a direct hit but a nearby munitions train. It blew two storeys out of the eight-storey building, causing the rest to collapse inward over the shelter. Two and a half days later rescuers dug out twenty-three survivors, including Peter and his mother. His father was among the nearly four hundred dead.

When the walls of the elegant, upper-middle-class Buda apartment building collapsed over Reserve Cavalry Major Andrew Demeter and his family, Europe was already in ruins. Although Dresden and Hiroshima were still some months away, Rotterdam, Leningrad, and Coventry had passed into history. The smokestacks of Auschwitz were not yet museum pieces, and Dachau was still hell on earth instead of just an exit sign on the Autobahn en route to Munich. On the other side of the globe, twenty-year-old Marines from Maine and Milwaukee were pinned down by Japanese machine-gun fire on tropical islands in the Pacific. Across the Danube, the headquarters of the multi-national Trieste Assurance had been levelled to the ground. Andrew Demeter, as managing director of Hungarian operations, might have reflected that it was a good thing insurance companies were not responsible for damage caused by acts of war. In spite of its considerable holding, *Assicuracioni Generali di Trieste* would have been wiped out many times over if it had had to pay for even a minute part of the holocaust. But it is a principle of insurance law that people can't profit from their own wrongdoing, and there were few nations or individuals in Europe entirely innocent of the catastrophe that ultimately destroyed them. Mrs. Demeter's cousin Admiral Horthy, for instance, didn't come to his senses until the fall of 1944. At that late date cousin Horthy, the hapless Regent of Hungary — nicknamed "the mounted sailor" by his subjects — tried to steer his ship of state clear of his sinking Nazi allies and offered a separate peace to the British if they would come and occupy the country. Churchill told him, rather coldly, to make his offer to the Russians: they were closer. It was an understatement, since by that time the Red Army had already crossed the border into Hungary. In the end, the Germans got wind of the Admiral's belated flirtation with Western democracy and rather unceremoniously replaced him with a local quisling named Szalasi. It was this gentleman who then maintained the alliance with Nazi Germany for three more months, until the final collapse of Hungary. Although the old Admiral would probably never have had him at his table, Szalasi carried to its logical extreme the policy Horthy had begun many years earlier.

At twelve, Peter may not have fully realized, of course, that the Russian bomb exploding over his home covered in rubble not only his father's body but his whole world. Gone were the exclusive boarding schools, the country estates, the invisible threads of privilege connecting people of the right accent, income, family ties, and race. Gone were the heavy silver, the brocade tablecloths, the fine leather-and-walnut armchairs, and the chauffeur-driven 1.7-litre Mercedes taking father to the office every morning. Quite incidentally, gone would be also the last vestiges of taste, decorum, wit, charity, *noblesse oblige*, and even common decency that may have been part of Demeter *père*'s universe. Peter's legacy would be nothing but the rubble; to survive he would have to claw his own way out of it to reach the top.

A day before the fighting ended in Pest — the newer half of the capital, on the east side of the Danube — Peter's twenty-one-year-old brother was killed, possibly by a German bullet. This was on January 17. In mountainous old Buda the fighting continued for nearly another month as the Germans, determined to give their lives for the Fuehrer, hung on to strong defensive positions. "That's typically Hungarian thinking," said a smooth-cheeked German sub-lieutenant when urged by a veteran Hungarian officer to surrender the bunker he was trying to defend with one soldier against a Russian company. "We Germans have a different perspective." Peter's brother may have been shot in one of the clashes over perspectives that were becoming more and more frequent between the Germans and their Hungarian allies.

The Nazi resistance, " . . . the most fierce of any defensive fighting in 1944", according to the official history of the Red Army, did little to put the occupation forces in a charitable mood. When the building in which Peter and his mother took refuge was eventually "liberated" on the last day but one of the siege, the Russian soldiers raped several of the women and shot some of the men on the spot. They did that in Peter's presence. One of the violated women was the lady who gave Peter and Mrs. Demeter shelter after their own house had been demolished. She was raped in front of her sons. ("We're fighting Hitler," said Stalin, when told about the behaviour of some of his soldiers. "Our boys may die before the day's out. Do we expect them to kiss a woman's hand and ask her for a date?" It was clear the Soviet High Command expected nothing of the sort.)

The weeks of street battles were followed by months of frost, darkness, and hunger as Budapest slowly dug itself out from under the ruins. People were less surprised by the corpses of their friends and neighbours than by the relatively high number of survivors. It seemed impossible that anybody could have stayed alive in a city in which every wall left standing bore the symmetrical perforation of machine-gun bursts. But people did stay alive, and began nailing sheets of plywood over their gaping window frames and spreading tarpaper across the broken beams of their roofs. The winter of '45 was mercifully long and cold — the coldest on record in nearly a century — and there were no epidemics, in spite of the dead bodies in the streets and under the ice of the Danube. At least the ice was thick enought between Buda and Pest to permit some communication, since not one of the nine bridges was left standing. Pedestrians crossed with ease, horses and wagons at their own peril. The peril of the horses included the risk of being walking protein in a starving city, to be slaughtered and cut up by women and even children if left unattended for a minute. A gold Swiss watch was a fair market price for a slab of marmalade in the months following the siege. Many people were saved from starvation by the occupying soldiers, who seemed as unpredictable in their kindness as in their cruelty and would often distribute their bread rations among children whose parents they had just robbed or herded off for an undetermined period of forced labour. Certain expressions crept into the vocabulary of victor and vanquished, an occupation hybrid, a linguistic no-man's-land between German, Hungarian, and Russian. Things that didn't work were "kaput", as were people when they stopped breathing. "Kleba" became, from the generic Russian for bread, that special mud-like substance the soldiers carried in their knapsacks, as in "Are you selling kleba or bread?" Some expressions carried a connotation of terror. The words "malinko robot" — literally a little work — coming from a Russian soldier might mean years in Siberia for a Hungarian civilian. For a man, the thing to do was to look too old or too young, and for a woman, too ugly.

So the old, the young, and the ugly survived in greater numbers, as did the shrewd and the unscrupulous. Somewhat like a marine disaster, the war took its toll primarily among the brave, the strong, and the chivalrous. All survivors may not have lived by this lesson, but all survivors learned it.

Peter had been close to his father. A late child — Major Demeter was over fifty when Peter was born — he received the special attention middle-aged parents often bestow on the last sibling. This doesn't necessarily make a child spoiled and soft, but it does give him a sense of importance. His well-being, which seems to matter to everyone around, may acquire some intrinsic significance to him. Quite innocently, a child may even equate it with the natural order of things: the world is arranged to give him pleasure and satisfaction. Taking their cue from the values of mature adults, such children are often precocious, which in turn may convince them of their own superior intelligence. In later years Peter would sometimes describe himself as "the clever product" of his elderly parents.

He needed every ounce of cleverness to survive in a post-war world that gave him no advantages. Indeed, the very advantages of his past — his family connections, his civilized and sheltered childhood — became handicaps of the gravest kind. The inflation that soon swept Hungary — the worst in recorded history — saw housewives exchanging shopping bags full of paper money for food that hardly filled their purses. In such a world a child needed parents who could deal on the black market, or at least fix things with their hands, grow corn, or raise chickens. White-collar workers on fixed salaries were just about useless. Executives from the old regime were worse than useless: they were dangerous. By dying when he did, his father perhaps did Peter a favour.

As one of the émigré archdukes remarked in Paris after the collapse of the Romanovs, aristocrats have only the skills of masters or servants. Mrs. Demeter, widow of the insurance executive, cousin of the Regent of Hungary, became a domestic in Budapest. Peter was sent to live with relatives in the country.

It's highly unlikely that a teen-age boy under these circumstances could serenely contemplate the abstract justice of the Nazi defeat or the new social order. He would only know fear, cold, and hunger. He would only see a world which had told him he was valued and loved, and then had suddenly turned on him for no apparent reason. It would suggest an existence all the more cruel for being totally capricious, a world in which rewards and punishments seemed to follow no recognizable pattern. And if it was impossible to tell enemy from friend, it was safer to regard all people as enemies to be cajoled, intimidated, manipulated, and outwitted.

Had Peter drawn such conclusions from his experiences, he would not have been alone. Individuals may vary a great deal, but history does leave an imprint on national character. The psyche of a whole generation growing up after the war in countries such as Hungary was informed by much cynicism and bitterness. This revealed itself in a certain style, a turn of phrase, a sense of gallows humour that was quite common to everybody. It was a mannerism picked up by even the warmest, kindest people, although in some it went much deeper and became an attitude. But whether it meant what it seemed to mean or not, Westerners would often be shocked by, or arrive at the wrong conclusions about, the sardonic graduates of Eastern Europe's school of defeat and humiliation. To North Americans especially they might appear cold, unfeeling, and arrogant in some situations, or smarmy and obsequious in others. Their responses would seem inappropriate to people nurtured in an atmosphere of relative goodwill and stability, and along with their thick European accents they would forever be sending out the wrong cultural signals.

In 1946, of course, Peter would not have given a thought to how North Americans would come to view him later, but in his style he became very much a product of post-war Budapest. In that city of survivors many people had a glib tongue, a suspicious mind, and an eagle's eye for loopholes. The mind-numbing hypocrisy of party-line Communism imposed on their country at the point of Soviet bayonets was countered by razor-edged jokes and lightning ripostes. In a grocery store a customer offered the standard clenched-fist Communist greeting: "Freedom!" The grocer looked up and replied, "Pineapple!" "What do you mean, pineapple?" asked the puzzled Party faithful. "It's also out of stock," answered the grocer, and his reply became the underground watchword of the period. More perhaps than the actual terror, it was the chilling euphemisms, the necessity of not only feeling the whip but kissing the hand that held it, the constant pressure to describe the naked Emperor's clothes in colourful terms, that finally impressed upon many Hungarians that not only words but concepts had lost all meaning. What one could get out of life for oneself at any cost to others remained the only reality.

It didn't happen all at once. For a little while after the war things looked promising. The worst devastation was cleared up with surprising swiftness. In only a few months it became possible to switch on the lights once again, and before the end of the year a temporary bridge connected Buda and Pest. Soon even some of the streetcars started running. By the end of 1946 the currency was stabilized, and Mrs. Demeter began receiving a widow's pension from Trieste Assurance. The two-room apartment into which she moved with Peter seemed at least adequate, and Peter was doing well in school. It slowly became safe to walk the streets at night without being "stripped" — during the inflation muggers never took their victims' money, only their clothes. Free elections were held, in which the Communists received only seventeen per cent of the votes in spite of the Russian presence. Szalasi and some members of his Arrow Cross government were extradited from the American zone of Germany, to which they had escaped during the last days of the war, and after a brief trial, five of them were garroted in the courtyard of the Marko Street prison. Newsreels carried the execution in the movie theatres in Budapest, and audiences broke into applause when the hangman twisted the knot and a clonic shiver ran through Szalasi's face. It seemed that most people wanted nothing more to do with the fanatics of either racial purity or class warfare.

Then the Russians stopped competing for the hearts and minds of East Europe and grabbed it by the throat. Democratic politicians were arrested and thrown into prison. Some were killed, like Czechoslovakia's Jan Masaryk, whose murder reintroduced the word "defenestration" to the language. Companies, including small private businesses, were nationalized without compensation. People who patriotically (or stupidly) invested their savings not in hard currency or gold but in their own country's economy lost everything. Those who did invest abroad were jailed for being "economic criminals". Simple transactions, such as trading in carpets or eggs, became "crimes against the working people". So did, eventually, making a remark to a friend or attending a service in church. Censorship over everything printed or spoken was complete. Before he died, Stalin established his special, Oriental brand of terror over half of Europe.

International companies like Trieste Assurance were expropriated shortly after the others. By 1950 Mrs. Demeter's pension had stopped. Peter, who had grown from a pudgy boy with glasses into a lanky, handsome youth with dark curly hair, was trying to finish his last year in high school while working in the evenings for a company machine-knitting ladies' underwear. Mrs. Demeter took in a lodger, and Peter moved into his mother's room. The money he earned went for food, and it often wasn't enough. If Peter wanted to go someplace, he walked. Public transportation was relatively cheap in Budapest, but it was more than the Demeters could afford.

It wasn't a question of hard times only, but of hopelessness. Under the grey tyranny of totalitarian Socialism a boy couldn't pull himself up by his bootstraps. Ambition, hard work, top grades wouldn't help. Drive, sacrifice, achievement would count for nothing. As a scion of the former élite, a "class-alien" according to Marxist mythology, Peter was barred from any kind of advancement. Stalinism introduced its own kind of affirmative action in employment and education, prescribing fixed percentages for each social class. Sixty per cent of all openings would go to the children of industrial workers, thirty-five to poor peasants. Five per cent would be reserved for the offspring of the "intelligentsia", meaning any white-collar worker from history professor to accountant. The sons and daughters of former aristocrats, executives, big businessmen, would get none. Not only ability but even *desire* became immaterial in face of the quotas. Those who didn't belong to the new order couldn't get an education, and those who belonged pretty much had to. The results, predictably, were unhappy people, inefficient production, shoddy merchandise, legendary red tape, little scholarship, and no art.

Naturally, Hungarians looked for loopholes. In job applications requesting information on class background, parents were speedily demoted from school principals to janitors. A four-star restaurant became a "greasy spoon" in a candidate's *curriculum vitae*, and the feed and grain depot grandfather had struggled for a lifetime to build was reduced to a humble country windmill. Middle-class urbanites were desperately affecting regional accents and working-class manners, some managing to convince even themselves. It was not only students: a newspaper editor, trying to hold on to his job, would transform his overseas aunt into a dishwasher in the Montreal hotel she owned. Like thousand of others, Peter had made the attempt to get into university. He had top marks and his school's recommendation. He was interested in film, theatre, and journalism, but these faculties were especially closely monitored for infiltration by the "enemy". With his late father's position and his mother's family connections, Peter didn't have a chance. He was "unmasked" and expelled in 1953.

A mere 150 miles west of Budapest lay Vienna, the old capital of the one-time Austro-Hungarian monarchy. Although still under joint occupation by the British, American, and Russian forces, Vienna was a gateway to the miraculous West. The incessant anti-American propaganda and the hermetically sealed borders between the Soviet colonies and the rest of the world had a curious reverse effect on the imagination of most young people: they believed the West to be a Garden of Eden. In this forbidden paradise there was to be no pain, sickness, struggle, or disappointment. There, people could become whatever they wanted to become, own whatever they wanted to own. They could go wherever they pleased, generally in their own cars. They could listen to Western music, dress in colourful, casual clothes. The less hard news the people of Prague, Warsaw, or Budapest were permitted to hear, the more the legends grew. A stick of gum, a pair of cheap nylon stockings, a Gillette razor blade became a symbol of status and riches. To go West became the impossible dream of a cheated generation.

In 1954 Peter got himself a job as a truck driver with a company building roads in the western part of Hungary, not far from the border. Twenty-one, tall, quick-witted, ambitious, his only hope for any kind of future lay on the other side. In December he would be called up for his two years of compulsory military service, but being branded as "bourgeois" he would have to serve it in a special forced-labour unit. In Hungary, even ordinary military service was bad enough — hair cropped to a quarter-inch, black coffee in the morning, soup and a piece of bread for dinner — but a punishment unit was worse than prison. Like thousands of other twenty-one-year-olds born to the wrong set of parents, Peter was guilty of no crime. Unlike most others, he was not willing to submit to any punishment for it. Escape, however, was possible only for those willing to risk their lives.

Viewed from the wrong side, the Iron Curtain was more than a piece of Churchillian rhetoric. The section between Austria and Hungary was a nearly impenetrable strip of ploughed land between mined approaches, watchtowers, and sets of barbed wire. Although during the relative thaw after Stalin's death the minefields were mainly deactivated, in the winter of 1954 nobody knew that, and in any case some sections were still not safe. The border guards would shoot to kill anyone not responding to the first challenge. On the Hungarian side a special pass was required even to enter a zone fifteen to twenty-five miles from the actual border, while a person crossing into Austria would at that time still find himself in the Russian-occupied sector. Between 1949 and 1956 — the time of the Hungarian revolution — only a handful of people were desperate enough to try.

Peter and a friend tried twice and succeeded the third time, in December 1954. They spoke German well and passed through the Russian sector without attracting notice. Compared to crossing the border it was relatively easy to have themselves smuggled into the American zone. Two weeks before he was to have reported for service at his punishment unit, Peter applied for political asylum at the American Embassy in Vienna.

On the surface it was all there: the neon lights, seeming all the brighter after the austere darkness of socialist Budapest, the private cars, the incredible variety of merchandise in the shop windows. Young men with healthy appetites on their first trip to the West tended to linger in front of delicatessens, looking with reverence at huge Westphalian hams, pyramids of Portuguese sardines, mounds of Brazilian coffee. On streetcars, instead of the tense, suspicious expressions of exhausted, frightened people with hair-trigger tempers, the *gemuetlich* Viennese would look at their neighbours with shy friendliness. When a bus stopped suddenly and passengers stumbled against each other, they would laugh and apologize, not spit and threaten like overcrowded rats in a cage. The blue Danube would seem somewhat grey and narrow for a person used to seeing the old river in her full majesty at Budapest, but the dresses of the women were elegant and sophisticated, and the cafés on the Graben were full of men discussing business. In the evenings on Mariahilferstrasse even some of the prostitutes would cruise by in their own Volkswagens, scanning the sidewalks for customers. In this town a person might make a deal, get a chance, recapture some of the birthright that only a little while ago seemed lost forever. Perhaps the snows of yesteryear had not melted completely. Peter was greeted by the American Consul General himself at the Embassy in Vienna. "So you're young Demeter, eh?" he said. "Used to know your father and your uncle before the First War." It must have seemed to Peter that his name, instead of closing doors, might just open them again.

But Europe was teeming with refugees after the war. Unlike Canada or the United States, European countries were not used to dealing with masses of immigrants. It wasn't just lack of space or job opportunities; for a Belgian or a Swiss the very *idea* of a whole group of foreigners settling in their midst would seem unusual and threatening. A refugee probably wouldn't starve, but unless he succeeded in emigrating to the New World (which would take only the cream of the crop), he would forever remain a "displaced person", isolated and kept at arm's length by his host country. Europe has never been a Canadian Mosaic or an American Melting Pot.

Little, vulnerable Austria had to be especially careful. The Russian occupation forces were still on Austrian soil. Although it was protected by the secret provisions of the Yalta agreement, being too friendly with Czech or Hungarian refugees from the People's Democracies might have invited retaliation. The Austrians had no wish to provide the Soviet Union with a *casus belli* in case it wanted to slice off another piece of the globe.

For a while Peter lived in a camp with other refugees from behind the Iron Curtain. For stateless persons a work permit was almost impossible to get. Austria would grant asylum for humanitarian reasons, but no encouragement. The inhabitants of the camps would lounge around, stand in line in front of consulates, wait (sometimes for years) for the embossed envelope that might bring them their American visas, or maybe take casual jobs hoping nobody would find out. Luckier than most, Peter spoke German and had some training in journalism. He also had some connections. The Cold War propaganda stations Radio Free Europe and Voice of America were not part of the Austrian labour market or subject to its regulations, although some of their offices were situated in Austria. After receiving his security clearance from the Americans, Peter became a reporter for Radio Free Europe. At night he also helped unload coal from freight cars at two dollars a shift. Mrs. Demeter was in Budapest, and naturally penniless. Peter sent his money home. It was better than the military punishment unit in Hungary.

But not much better. After a little while many refugees discovered that it was perhaps more frustrating to walk freely in a Garden of Eden where all the luxurious fruit was out of reach than to be barred from it altogether. They were like the hungry man of the Arabian fable, invited to the feast but not served. It was an economic strip-tease, with a glittering life-style displaying its unattainable charms at the gaping outsiders across the footlights. A few of the refugees had risked too much, sacrificed too much, wanted it too badly to be able to restrain themselves now that it seemed within reach. They couldn't wait any longer. Some banished the vision by returning home. One or two killed themselves. Another small minority turned to crime. The frustration was even greater for those who, like Peter, belonged to a privileged stratum in a distant past and might have expected, however vaguely, the sudden restoration of a lost paradise. But even the West seemed to favour the new social classes. Sons of peasants and Jewish shop-keepers with marketable skills had a distinct edge over the descendants of titled families with their crests and patents of nobility inside their battered suitcases. A plumber's certificate counted for more than a classical education from the finest parochial school in old Hungary, like Peter's Cistercian Gymnasium. The West offered no special rewards for gentlemen. They were greeted politely, of course, handled with bemused curiosity, and might at best be offered some ill-paid, insignificant sinecure far removed from the mainstream of Western life. In the Hungarian sections of Radio Free Europe, first in Vienna, then in the smaller Austrian cities of Linz and Graz, Peter would meet some of these relics of a bygone era.

They were helpless, bitter people for the most part, often living in tiny furnished rooms separated from their families. Joseph Szilagyi, for instance, once a career diplomat under one of Peter's uncles in Horthy's foreign ministry and the Hungarian *chargé d'affaires* in Zurich at the end of the war, was now receiving a tiny salary in Graz to write Hungarian reports for a radio station that was jammed in Hungary and of no interest to anyone outside. For a while Peter would see him every day at lunch and dinner. The older man evoked mixed feelings of pity, contempt, and attraction in him: so that's what it was like, that world he never really knew. A disappointed man, repeating phrases that even to Peter sounded reactionary, complaining about his daughter marrying out of her religion (he was a staunch Protestant), or his sixteen-year-old son, Csaba, coming under Jesuit influence in his Austrian school. At the same time Dr. Szilagyi seemed lost in the world without the props of his former position, hardly capable of making a living. He wanted to drive a car but Peter found it difficult to teach him. All strength, all vigour had gone out of the past, not to be resurrected even by nostalgia. The old world with its sins as well as its virtues seemed irretrievably lost.

Power, wealth, and privilege hadn't disappeared, of course, but had passed into different hands. The new rich had a harder, more blatant style, a more practical system of values. Having no pretensions to *noblesse* meant that they were obliged to nothing. They asked not where a person came from, but where he was going. Nothing was too vulgar for them as long as it was successful.

Peter hesitated. There were a few fortunate people like the young Patzenhofer, an Austrian student Peter met through some old family connections, who could combine the style of the old world with the riches of the new. The Patzenhofer holdings — a castle, a sugar factory — remained intact after the war. Konrad Patzenhofer would have no need to seek his fortune overseas, in an alien language, among alien people. Peter admired Konrad and saw him as often as he could. In fact, early in 1956 he had himself transferred to Graz because Konrad was there. Driving his Radio Free Europe car and going out on double dates with his wealthy young friend, Peter lived, in his words, "as a Western human being, for the first time in my life".

But it was a borrowed lifestyle, and Peter wanted his own. At twenty-three he had no desire to spend his life broadcasting stories back to his homeland about the wonders of the West in which he himself had no stake. He had relatives in Canada who even sent him bits of money when he first arrived, penniless, in Austria: he received twelve dollars from Welland, fifty from London, Ontario. They were obviously not wealthy people, these ex-officers, ex-lawyers, now working as salesmen or factory hands in that curious, faraway country, but they might give him a leg up. For a young man of military age there was also the important consideration that Canada, except in wartime, had no compulsory military service. The American GI's fatigues had no more attraction for Peter than the rough khaki of the Hungarian infantryman: going to the United States might mean just a few more wasted years of his life. He also wanted to bring his mother out of Hungary, and by quitting Radio Free Europe he might exercise some leverage on the officials in Budapest. Such deals were not uncommon. They might let an unproductive older woman leave the country (which would also free a valuable apartment for the state) if her son undertook to broadcast nothing more against them. In the early summer of 1956, Peter had a bad accident when his car blew a tire on the highway to Munich. For forty-eight hours he lay in a coma, and it seemed like an omen. Austria was not the right place for him. Less than two months later he was on a ship bound for the port of Quebec City.

Peter Demeter got off the train at Toronto's Union Station with eight dollars in his wallet. Except for the downtown area with its few drab skyscrapers, he saw nothing but wide streets bordered by low, nondescript houses. The cars seemed to be the size of river-boats, and in most districts a person could walk for blocks without seeing another pedestrian. In 1956 there were few signs of the urban boom that would, in less than twenty years, transform Toronto from an immense industrial village into a chic, expensive, sophisticated city. To a European, everything seemed somehow raw, makeshift, impermanent. Squirrels and chipmunks were running up and down the sides of houses built more of wood than stone and brick, and at night even skunks or racoons might be seen ambling across Yonge Street. Animals that in Toronto lived under the porch would, in Peter's part of the world, have withdrawn into their ever-dwindling forests more than a century ago. At the same time, incongruously, there were ultra-modern fixtures attached to the walls of primitive buildings. The temperature in tiny, uncomfortable living rooms could be controlled with the flick of a finger on a thermostat. Photo-electric cells would open the doors of a supermarket plunked down in the middle of nowhere between ravine and the bush. The whole country resembled nothing more than a nuclear-powered log cabin.

For a stranger in this intriguing land, time seemed truly out of joint. The brightest neon displays would glitter, not over supper clubs or cabarets, but over used-car lots. Hamburger stands, selling next-to-inedible food, would be equipped with gadgets not to be found in the most up-to-date restaurants in Europe. Handkerchiefs were purely decorative: people wiped their noses on bits of paper. Everything seemed disposable, used once or twice, then thrown away. As in a hastily erected gold town, there was a smell of success and quick riches in the air, but for a greenhorn the secret of the payload was hidden under vast stretches of alien rock. Funeral homes would play soft music and light up in shimmering blue at night, as if to entice the living to avail themselves of their services.

On the corner of Bay and Cumberland, Peter greased the axles of huge American cars for seventy-five cents an hour. He would have preferred working the pumps, but he couldn't speak English. Peter might have thought that he had learned in Austria what it was like to be an immigrant, but it was only in Toronto that he understood what it meant to be deaf and mute. Canadians seemed to take a number of words into their mouths, chew them, then spit them out again. It was impossible to understand them.

The future might have been in Canada, and Peter no doubt realized that every start is difficult, but his mother was in Austria now and it was a relief when Radio Free Europe offered to pay his way back to that country. It was October 1956, and the Hungarian Revolution was making headlines around the world. Peter's services as a reporter were needed, and he responded with alacrity. His first sojourn in Canada lasted just about four months.

Back in Graz, Peter took an apartment with his mother. The events of the last years had taken their toll on Mrs. Demeter and soon she had to enter a hospital. Peter was doing his duty as a son, even though it was clear that a dependent sixty-year-old lady in poor health was not going to make things easier for him. Such things are always ambivalent. Many people have a compulsion to look after relatives and friends and at the same time resent the burden it imposes on them. Certainly Peter always seemed to be doing things for others, even when he himself had very little. The reason, as he sardonically remarked more than once, was that grateful people were "as flattering to one's ego as a cocker spaniel". It would have been very un-Hungarian to admit that fear and insecurity might have played any part in it.

One such "cocker spaniel" Peter encountered in Graz was young Csaba, the Jesuit scholar, Joseph Szilagyi's seventeen-year-old son. With his excellent memory for detail, Peter would recall that they first met on October 28, but it would have taken a prophet to foresee the role they would later play in each other's lives. Quite naturally, the younger boy seemed to be in awe of the travelled, sophisticated twenty-three-year-old who drove a car, had escaped through minefields, and had a girlfriend of his own. His very name — Demeter — was that of a Greek goddess, the goddess of fertility. In contrast to Csaba's feeble, embittered father, Peter seemed full of vitality, strength, ambition. Even the fact that he spoke Hungarian appealed to Csaba, who, being raised in an Austrian school, could hardly understand the ancestral language. Peter did nothing to discourage his admiration, and while he was in Austria, Csaba would contrive to see him nearly every day.

To keep his status as a landed immigrant, Peter had to return to Toronto at the end of six months. He still had no English or money, and 1957 turned out to be a year of bad recession in Canada. Peter managed to get a job as a janitor, and later as a car jockey at the Granite Club, an exclusive bastion of the city's WASP establishment that might have served as a model for Stephen Leacock's Mausoleum Club. The wealthy members and their elderly wives liked the handsome, well-mannered Hungarian, but they naturally had him dismissed for putting a scratch on the door of a lady's brand-new Pontiac. By that time Peter probably needed no lessons in realizing that millionaires didn't get to where they were by being considerate of other people's existence. He worked as a Fuller Brush salesman for a while — Cabbagetown, Toronto's skid row, was the only available territory — but couldn't make enough money to send any to Mrs. Demeter in Graz. Then he took the plunge, got himself a real estate licence, and like many novice salesmen with a circle of acquaintances, sold a few houses to some fellow Hungarians. With his earnings he bought himself a small used car — his first — and at the end of 1958 brought his mother to Toronto. In the meantime his Austrian girlfriend married someone else. It didn't matter much: his English was becoming more fluent and he had started working for himself. He was now twenty-five.

For the next seven years Peter would try any business, take any job going, that might bring him closer to his goal. When tight money made the real estate market slack, he would drive a cab. For a few hundred dollars he'd buy a small collection agency, then sell it as soon as it had served its purpose. He'd work as a skip tracer — a collector of bad debts — and as a chauffeur for the American Consulate. Every once in a while he would take some of his savings and nip over to Europe, as if to assure himself that the real world, his own world, the world of his friend Konrad Patzenhofer, was still there — and one day he could become part of it on equal terms if he only struck it lucky in Canada. On such occasions he would stay with relatives in Switzerland or acquaintances in Italy, or in Konrad's castle at Siegendorf. He would also visit the Szilagyis, do them small favours, and bask in young Csaba's admiration. Even though he hadn't yet made it, in Europe he might seem the glamorous traveller, the international man of business. (Not that he would spend much money doing it: Peter was always very prudent in financial matters.) Also, in Austria there were girls, pretty and sophisticated, better than any his circumstances would allow him to meet or impress in Toronto. Unfortunately, none of these affairs would work out; between one visit and the next the girl he selected would get engaged to someone else. A gambler might have said that Peter had more luck at cards than at love.

Because Peter's luck at cards — in his case, business — was getting better. In 1962 he and a partner registered a company, Eden Gardens Limited, to build one apartment building close to Edenbridge Street in Toronto. This was the beginning of Peter's career as a developer, and Eden Gardens would remain his company until the end. He had to put about $20,000 into the business to start it, and the source of this capital became the first question-mark in Peter's story. At this time Peter was still working as a chauffeur for the American Consulate at a modest salary. But a couple of years earlier, according to some reports in Hungarian-language papers, a company named Continental Collectors had enticed a number of people, through handbills and advertisements, to send sums of money to relatives in Hungary. In return the senders received receipts; the relatives got nothing. The papers named Peter as the man behind Continental Collectors. The police investigated, but no charges were laid. Ontario Attorney General Wishart, replying to a Member of Parliament who turned to him on behalf of one defrauded constituent, could only write: "I can assure you that the Metropolitan Toronto Police have made every effort to gather evidence against Demeter, but as you are aware criminal prosecutions cannot be commenced on suspicion alone. . . . The people who did pay money to Demeter did receive receipts from a Post Office in Budapest but the police are unable to prove that these receipts are forgeries since they are not able to gather evidence in Hungary." About two years later Eden Gardens Limited was incorporated in Toronto.

The following year Mrs. Demeter died. Peter happened to be in Europe at the time. He had last seen his mother alive when, some months earlier, she had said good-bye to him at the bus station. Although he could not have foreseen it — she died suddenly — Peter felt guilty about her dying alone, and would often mention afterwards that she had been well provided for, had more than $300 in her savings account, and was actually calling his name with her last breath. Peter flew back for the funeral, returned to Vienna, then came back to Toronto again when construction work began on his first development. Some time later a Viennese girl came out to live with Peter for about six months. It was something of a trial marriage, and it didn't work. But there were compensations: Eden Gardens sold its first apartment at a decent profit and Peter bought himself a brand-new car, a red Pontiac. Then, after another year of work and travel, Peter found himself in Vienna again.

It was at a party to which he went with his friend Konrad that Peter was introduced to a young girl named Marina Hundt. The year was 1965. A little over twenty years had passed since Peter had been dug out from underneath the ruins of his parents' home in Budapest.

3. Marina

She didn't know what to make of this man. The second time he saw her, just a week or so after that cocktail party at Karl's, he actually proposed to her. And the things he chose to impress her with, too, all these deals, mortgages, fortunes to be made in Canada. Canada! Well, really! He might as well have said the moon. Who cared about money, anyway? Possibly all these earnest, older men, these real boring types. He said himself he was thirty-two, didn't he? (Marina had just turned twenty.) Well, she had tried to discourage him, God knows. Whenever he called she'd tell auntie to say she wasn't in. The few times he absolutely *insisted* on seeing her she'd make sure he'd hear all about her fiancé George, and her boyfriend Wolfi, and the other old friend she was going to meet in Salzburg. She'd write him chatty letters about how her exams were going and how her stepfather expected her to marry soon and they had a big argument but he had lent her a car anyway. She'd mention the house in Spain they were all going to stay in during the summer and how she had counselled a girlfriend not to go to Paris to forget about her big love because it doesn't work and how *she* would never go if she had anything to forget about but (oh, how he must have hated this) as it happened she had nothing to forget about, thank heaven.

But the man was not to be discouraged. Annoyed as she was, Marina couldn't resist picking up his letter again.

> My dearest little Marina, last November 26th, Konrad's birthday, the evening of the party, was an unforgetable experience for me, one I could never ever in my life not to be able to reconstruct, revisualize, I remember every word said, most of them, what I said you found rather cheeky — you were right I was sort of feeling you out,

try to find out are you real or are you a forged one? And the following week, on the 2nd of December last year, to be exact, I looked and looked at you and I knew, as clearly as I know I am to die, that I loved you; I loved you more than anything I have seen or imagined on this earth or hoped for anywhere else. . . .

Well, it was nice to be able to excite such passion, very flattering really, but what kind of a person would write such things? People just didn't talk like that any more. What exactly did he expect her to do, fall in his arms?

> . . . *would you or would you not consider* to come overseas this summer to see it for yourself how life is here in North America in general, in Canada specifically, how you like or dislike the Toronto area, its people, my relatives and friends, and last but not least me, working hard, being busy most of the time . . . making corporation tax returns, trying to pay less income tax with all the tricks in the books and still not to get in jail for tax evasion . . . see your own ideas grow into real projects, your dreams as a penniless immigrant into every day reality, to be in short your own boss, self-employed, the president of your own limited company, being envied by the less daring and hated by the less fortunate, living life 24 hours a day. . . .

Oh, who cared about his crummy companies. Marina found her wandering eyes making the edits. Yes, this man did expect her to fall in his arms, then spend the rest of her life checking figures on building materials in his office. In return he might take her to Mexico or the Côte d'Azur once a year. No, thank you. She could get there on her own, and more often, with people who were much more fun, had more money to spend, and would spend it more freely. That perfume he bought her, or the serious talks he would have with her stepfather — of all people — as if this were the way to her heart. Why, the man simply didn't know her at all, had no idea what she wanted. Stretching her limbs, settling more comfortably her thighs and buttocks (by no means thin, but with muscles taut from swimming and tennis in a body she liked to think of as "crunchy"), Marina looked at Peter's letter. What other goodies did he have in store for her?

> . . . I could open doors for you, you never thought about. I could offer you security, emotional as well as financial. . . . having the

necessary age and experience to be able to be happy with just one woman I love and cherish the only one, I would like you to be the mother of my children, the one I am willing to share everything I have, I accomplished till now and will amass, having finally found the right partner for it — only the sky is the limit. . . .

The book I once started to write, I probably spoke to you about it, I was going to dedicate "to the memory of my mother — and to the countless thousands of men and women entangled in a nightmare jungle of loneliness . . . " "Through no fault of his own a man may lose time, the essence of life; or money, without which dignity is impossible; or health, which alone gives real joy to living; he may lose his sanity too: and he may even forfeit his life to the right cause, but going through life alone is being dead alive. . . . "

Think about all this, Marina, and in the meantime please don't forget that loving you and being in love with you is not a crime!!!

Your Peter

Well now, the poor fellow. She would have certainly had him where she wanted him if she had wanted him at all. The trouble was, she didn't. Life was so unfair, really. This Demeter was actually quite handsome, very tall and impressive and all that, but so earnest and intent, so preoccupied with *making it* over there among the grizzly bears. He had a sharp tongue too; he would pretty much expect everything to go his way. Well, in that department she could give him as good as she got. He must still carry the parting sting of what she had said to him when he flew back to Canada, after he had said, "I'm leaving because of your cold and cruel attitude," and she replied, "I hope the navigator falls asleep." But this letter now, how should she respond to it? Should it be something breezy and cheerful, should it be dramatic and dark, or sort of whimsical to keep him dangling on the hook a little longer? With fine instinct, Marina decided on a mixture:

Dearest Peter,
Thank you very much for the nice letter which I received long time before, please do not be angry that I did not answer at once but I have such a lot to do. And the weather here is so beautiful I am not able to sit at home. . . . Winter is over, it is spring. When I walk down Kaertnerstrasse, I meet all my friends, they say hello, they talk to me, they laugh with me and I know they like me. Can you understand that I never want to go to a country where nobody

knows me, where I am a stranger, nothing, people around me are strange, things around me are so big, I could not stand it.

When I like to go home and see mommy, daddy, and my little dog Whisky, I go to the station, go in a train and I am home in a few hours. Where else in this big world could I do this? Nowhere, Peter. Austria would be a country far away from me. It would be a country to visit, not my home any more.

And there is another thing which makes me insecure, which forces me to stay, and you know what it is. I told you very often, it is a person, yes. You know it.

Forgive me, I can never leave this land, never give away my freedom. Never. I will stay here, learn a lot and be alone. I will wait for a long time.

There is a thunderstorm coming, I love weather like this, I must go for a walk. I must smell the lovely clean air and see the fire in the sky. . . .

I send you my love and all my good wishes, and ask you to forget about a silly little girl.

Marina

She was glad she wrote the letter in English, it was good practice. Still, before sealing the envelope, she decided there was something missing. It was a very good letter but it was too final. Things should never be left as final as that. She picked up her pen and added a few lines to the typescript, in German.

Now it's raining cats and dogs, there's thunder and lightning, and I sit here listening to records and writing, although I have nothing more to say. Life is a game of chance like roulette. . . . You bet small, you win —you stake everything you've got and the wheel turns — you lose, everything. It's childish to believe we ever get anything back. But we don't give up, I know. Because hope is the most beautiful thing human beings possess. But again, these are just commonplaces. Forgive me. For today, goodbye

Marina

There, that was better. That ought to keep the mad Hungarian at bay without scaring him off altogether. One can't see into the future and there was no point in closing doors completely. Marina was a Viennese girl, and while the Viennese appreciate the beauty of thunderstorms, in stormy weather they generally carry umbrellas. It's not that she was calculating, far from it. Peter had nothing she particularly wanted. Her stepfather, Ivan von Rubchich, a manufacturer of plywood who employed nearly 300 people, might not see eye to eye with her in everything but would deny her nothing. Besides, she could probably make it on her healthy, suntanned, robust good looks alone. In the late sixties the world of modelling — which meant New York — was just beginning to discover "the German look". For quite a few years delectable beauties from Hamburg would be all the rage, and not only in milk commercials. Dozens of top photo models, looking just like Marina, would flash rows of perfect teeth set off by alabaster or golden-brown skin from the cover of every magazine caught up in the trend. Break Free with Max Factor. Dare to Put On the Ritz. Splash Out with Aqua Manda. Take the Flag in a Triumph. Marina had her eyes on the Winners' Circle herself in that company. What was more important, like many twenty-year-olds with a taste for freedom she saw little profit in exchanging parental shackles for the bonds of marriage, especially with a moat as wide as the Atlantic around her marital castle. The New World might have exercised a magic attraction for the huddled masses of Europe, but Marina was not one of them.

All the same, he *was* an attractive man, and Kaertnerstrasse had seen many changes of heart and fortune. Who could tell how things might go with Wolfi and the others? If Peter wanted her as badly as he sounded, he'd stick around.

Marina was right. Less than three months later Peter reported in with a light-hearted little note that she could answer in much the same vein:

Really, Peter, it was very nice to hear from you after such a long time. I thought you are dead or madly in love with somebody. Anyway, did I tell you that I am so upset, because my little poor silly dog Whisky is dead? They shot him when he was chasing a little bambi. And I told him often and often, Whisky, do not kill little animals, they will shoot you one day, when they see you. . . .

My mummy is against me, she will not buy me another dog, because I want another Whisky and not a stupid dog like poodles or dachshounds. I want a dog like my dog was. A bastard. She cannot understand me, because she is a lady and I am not.

I am looking forward to see you again, although this will be in September. In August I am on holiday in Italy and after that in

Velden–Worthersee. Around the 15 of September I am back in Vienna. But I am sure your time is filled with Miss Ettingshausen in the meantime. She is waiting for you trembling with desire. Only sometimes she forgets about you, when she makes love to her poet. There is not much to tell you. I drive a Volkswagen now, collecting tickets, because the Austrian police thinks I am too fast.

Be good and do not work too much, as I already told you: I do not like work, and I do not like people who work or pretend to work much.

Thank heaven my poor father does not hear me. He would kill me. My love to you,

Marina

Would that keep him on the back burner until September? Maybe. The reference to Miss E. was a nice touch, just to remind him that she cared enough to notice. Also, perhaps, that other women had their little indiscretions, too. She certainly wasn't the only one to play both ends against the middle, not by a long chalk. Such a lot of things could be accomplished by a couple of short sentences. Still, to make sure there was a personal touch, Marina added a few handwritten lines to the typescript:

P.S. My English is terrible, it has been much better, ages ago. When I was young and beautiful. I am still beautiful, but not young.

Their date in September turned out just fine, from her point of view. Peter called, as she expected him to, and took her to a night club in the country, and she enjoyed herself chatting to him about her holidays, her stepfather's office where she was now working, and her boyfriend Wolfi. It was a thrill to feel the glance of a mature, handsome man rest on her all evening. With the unconscious selfishness of extreme youth, Marina might even have thought Peter was having a good time too. After all, she hadn't gone out with him under false pretences. She had told him plainly Wolfi was number one on her list.

Marina had no way of knowing the shattering effect her whole being and behaviour had on Peter. She couldn't guess that, for him, she happened to correspond in every detail to that elusive, inexpressible mental picture all people have of the perfect mate. She didn't realize that everything, from her deliciously crunchy figure to her family's social position, from her popularity with other men to the soft submissiveness present in her voice even when saying no, and perhaps especially the challenge of resisting him, added up in Peter to a desire equal to the one that, twelve years earlier, motivated him to cross the line behind which history tried to confine him. Marina didn't know that she became, at least for the moment, another Iron Curtain to be conquered. Had she realized it, perhaps she wouldn't have called Peter in the course of the next few months whenever her affairs with other men hit a snag, only to neglect him as soon as she had better things to do. But like most human beings, Marina had more capacity for feeling than understanding, which is how we all convince ourselves of the seriousness of our own passions and the remarkable frivolity of the passions of others.

On December 2, 1966, on the anniversary of the day he had first proposed to her, Marina let Peter take her to "their" restaurant. The sentimental journey altered nothing: she spent the following weekend with Wolfi. When Peter found out, he appeared on Marina's doorstep in a fine rage. The scene that ensued was described in a lawyer's note in the following terms:

> Dear Mr. Demeter,
> On the 5th of December in the course of a visit at my client's home you have slapped and choked her and also threatened her with a revolver. . . .
> My client suffered a nervous break-down and several medically certified and visible effects from your choking and beating. She also feels much threatened especially by your having menaced her with a revolver, and still suffers from a severe shock. . . .
> Considering the fact that bringing criminal charges against you would ruin your social and business position my client is willing to refrain from taking a punitive stand provided that you shall, within 8 days, make a declaration that this has been a once and only occurrence that will under no circumstances be repeated, and at the same time excuse yourself for your behaviour.

The credibility of this ominous letter was considerably reduced by the fact that the initials of reference on it belonged to Wolfi, who happened to be an articling student in the law office that sent it. In any case, less than a month later Marina exercised her woman's prerogative again. The handwritten note she sent to Peter ran:

Dear Peter,

If you still want me then take me far away from Vienna, but do not ask why.

I'd understand it very well if you kicked me now, I certainly deserve it. But still.

Marina

In the time-honoured tradition of all stricken men, including shrewd, hard-bitten, practical men, Peter ran to the call. On arrival he found Marina in Wolfi's arms. They had had a tiff and made up. So sorry. All's fair in love and war.

Less than a month later Peter asked a friend to introduce him to a girl he had seen some time earlier in a theatre. She was very much in the news just then, as a model and as the fiancée of a well-known motion picture producer. She was very tall and blonde, with a showgirl's striking figure and face. Her name was Christine.

4. Christine

By the time Christine was born in 1940, the double-headed imperial eagle on the stamp of the registry office of the city of Innsbruck had lost one of its heads but acquired a swastika in its claws. Seven years later, when her parents applied for a copy of Christine's birth certificate, both swastika and eagle had been replaced by a mythical beast resembling no known animal, just as occupied Austria of 1947 resembled no known country. Russia and her western allies glared at one another from their zones of occupation, channelling enmity into bureaucratic harassment of their Austrian wards. Innsbruck, though, was in the western zone. While the occupying forces would linger until 1955, life for little Christine Liselotte Maria Ferrari was not so very out of the ordinary.

She was an only child born to middle-aged parents who, as practising Catholics, sent their daughter to be schooled by the Ursuline nuns. Whatever else the good sisters managed to instil into their charge, some of their strictures seem to have made little impression. After four years of vocational school, on a dull, grey day in February, Christine abandoned her advanced studies in sales and married Helbert Honliger. Less than two months later baby Martin made an appearance. At seventeen Christine was a mother.

Helbert, the son of an Innsbruck doctor and an engineer himself, might have been able to narrow the gulf in interests that developed between his bride and himself, but when it came to the relentless logic of the pituitary gland, he was powerless. At seventeen Christine still had some growing to do, and soon the young bride was an inch or two taller than her husband. This, of course, would have presented no problem to some of her contemporaries, and none at all to a generation conditioned by the longitudinal miscegenation of the Kissingers. But in the late fifties the ideal couple was always a She looking adoringly up at Him. Christine, whose interests were now turning to fashion magazines and their recommended lifestyles, might well have honed her values on such considerations of style and appearance. Her husband was not an accessory of the right proportions. They were divorced on April 11, 1963. Helbert got Martin and Christine got her freedom.

Christine, as many of her friends said later, was not an especially bright girl. What she had were striking good looks and, by her own admission, a taste for the Good Life. She decided to use one to gain the other and turned to modelling to achieve it. She had a stunning figure. The large raised mole on her forehead gave her face piquancy, the flawless complexion interrupted by a dark velvet spot. All the same, modelling, while it may have little to do with cerebral functions, has a great deal to do with instinct and intuition. An ability to convey the uniqueness not only of couture but (more frequently) of a pair of oven mitts requires a talent that can be honed but not created out of thin air. Christine's career, which began before her separation, never really developed into much more than the occasional small assignment. At first she might have put that down to family responsibilities and the time-consuming business of raising a child. But with *Kinder, Kuche,* and *Kirche* long abandoned, Christine still found herself subsidizing her modelling by working as a waitress and once even as manageress of a small snack-bar attached to a gas station.

Still, though her talents were leaving fashion editors unimpressed, her presence in Munich and Vienna was not passing entirely unnoticed. Pretty girls were common enough on the Kaertnerstrasse of the sixties, but Christine, with her curving figure, long blonde hair, and height of almost six feet in her stylish boots, combined the impact of a high-fashion model with a woman's sensuality. Soon she had worked her way into the fringes of the newly identified Jet Society. She was not yet a name in her own right, of course. One had to come into the world tagged Onassis, Berenson, or Crespi for that, or be blessed with the luminous talent of a Mick Jagger, Yves St. Laurent, or this week's hairdresser. Still, she was seen dating auto heir Gunther Sachs and, as she liked to tell admiring Canadian friends later, once he had asked her to marry him. But Gunther was so close with one of his men friends and so overwhelmingly *gentle* with her that she felt marriage with him would be too tame an affair. Perhaps, she speculated, that was why Brigitte Bardot had left him. It was nice, though, to be flown to Rome by private plane in order to pick out a dress for the next party, or to be one of the privileged few waiting in the pits when a member of the set was racing in a European Grand Prix.

By 1967 Christine had moved on to film producer Franz Antel. She had been working now for seven years with very little to show for it. At twenty-six she was at the peak of her attractiveness, and her life seemed built entirely around that happy circumstance. (Later, in Canada, friends would tell the police of a thirty-two-year-old Christine, paralysed by fear of aging, her actions governed by her skin tone, a wrinkle acting as a caution sign. Certainly her one bold gesture, the exit from her marriage and the relinquishing of her son, had been made when youth guaranteed her the security of several more years of beauty.) As Franz Antel's fiancée, or at least special girlfriend, Christine had no need to strain for attention or worry about her appearance. This time Franz was producing a musical, and though Christine's part was not very big, she could walk onto the set with the proprietary confidence of a star. It was early February when, during a break in filming, she was introduced to the visitor from Canada.

Peter's courtship struck the right note with Christine from the beginning. The tall, bespectacled Hungarian had none of the softness she had disliked in Gunther, or the tiresome fickleness of the film set. He was a businessman, planning a future in subdivisions, not sandcastles. Moreover, he seemed to move in the right circles. The day after they met, Peter took Christine swimming at the château of his good friend Konrad Patzenhofer. But Vienna in February was not the most appealing climate for a romance, and anyway, Christine's desertion of Franz for an unknown émigré from *Toronto* might have left her currency shaky. Peter and Christine took off for the Canary Islands late in February.

If Peter had been asked to make a list of Christine's assets, he would probably have begun with her fluency in French, Italian, and German, all of which augured well for her ability to learn English. Ability in languages was highly regarded by Peter, perhaps because his own verbal skills were limited. (Crown Attorney John Greenwood, reading translations of Peter's conversations in Hungarian and German, would later claim, somewhat unkindly, that Peter was "illiterate in three languages".) But that missed the problem. Peter's vocabulary in English was very decent, and in Hungarian it was that of a well-educated man. It seemed to be the thought-process itself that tripped him up. His mind appeared unable to get a firm hold on an idea and think it through:

half-formed thoughts swallowed themselves up, reappeared, and sprouted a dozen irrelevancies. In English, German, or Hungarian, the problem would be the same. No matter how hard Peter tried, a simple idea plainly expressed seemed beyond him. It was as if through some ghoulish circumstance Peter's mental processes had been rewired, leaving his thoughts trapped in circuits that fed constantly upon themselves.

Christine had no such problem. Her language was adequate to express thoughts which rarely ranged beyond the perimeters of her immediate situation. She seemed to have no need to dominate a conversation like her new fiancé, and at first this accommodating personality might well have been soothing to Peter after the altogether too barbed and independent ways of Marina. Peter paraded her through Austria and Germany, presenting Christine Ferrari to his friends, including of course the Szilagyis, *père et fils,* and winding up with an engagement party at Siegendorf. It seemed a happy time. Christine's beauty, set off by the public knowledge that she had jilted a well-known movie producer for him, was balm to Peter. Perhaps now his bedroom skills were beginning to pay off like his business accomplishments. After a quick trip to New York and a visit with the Brewers in Connecticut, Christine Ferrari arrived in Toronto.

Afterwards, when it all ended on the floor of the garage on a dead-end street, there would be shocked conversations about how ill-matched Christine and Peter were. But Christine seemed to take a certain pride in a subjugation that began almost from her first days in Toronto. Friends didn't know what to make of it. The pair were to be married as soon as all the necessary papers were forwarded to Canada, and in the meantime the couple were existing in a state of armed warfare. Christine took to showing Alice Mailath — the wife of Peter's architect — bruises that she had received from what she described as "Peter beating me up". The Mailaths, who had known Peter for a dozen years, were so concerned about Christine's unhappiness that at one time they offered to loan her the money to go home. But clearly they didn't understand the nuances of the situation — or else Christine was exaggerating for her own reasons — because, in spite of their offer to lend her the money to go home and leave Peter, Christine chose to go right on living with him.

Then there was the matter of Christine's career. Peter had noted Christine's "ambition" with approval. Ambition for him was more than a quality: it was evidence of moral worth. Christine herself was quick to point out to new acquaintances how ambitious she was, but she seemed to equate the meaning of the word with wanting to have things rather than wanting to go out and earn them. Eventually it came down to Christine's hoping to do some modelling and Peter's expecting her to run their home and help him at his business.

From a strictly financial point of view, Peter's perspective made more sense. Christine's future as a model was limited. She was nearly twenty-seven and had never had any professional experience. That may have accounted for the way she got herself up for auditions and interviews. Her make-up was heavy and precise, with a careful matte finish like a well-to-do European matron's. Even her hair was elaborately coiffed, wiglets and tendrils galore, just at a time when the easier American look was asserting itself. She signed up with the Judy Welch Modelling Agency who did their best to temper her look, but Christine had her own idea of what would propel her to commercial success. "Her problem," explained her hairdresser tactfully, "was that left on her own she did look a little tarty." She leaned to plunging necklines, tight clothes, and heavy eye-liner. Though friends knew her as a warm and vulnerable woman, her professional photos showed her with a sullen look and a hardness around the eyes. She didn't understand that the image she was trying to create was almost an anachronism: in the late sixties the seductress was being replaced by the breezy sophisticate. The few jobs she landed were ads cashing in on the tail end of a trend. Dolled up in a leopard skin and carrying a spear, hair teased and tumbling over her bare shoulder, Christine was posed in a field next to a new-model car whose lifespan would turn out to be longer than hers. "The Great White Hunter Is Loose/Animals Beware!" was the tag line for the Javelin ads that splashed the scantily clad Christine across newspapers and billboards. It was the biggest job she ever had. Most of her "working" time was actually spent fixing up elaborate hair styles for herself and posing for still more photos and snapshots to file away in the massive portfolio she kept. She did some professional photography for the local *Toronto Life* magazine, which paid next to nothing on the questionable premise that it was good for a model to be seen in their pages, and occasionally she did a bit of work for her hairdresser, allowing herself to be used as a model for his latest hairdo at a Hairdressers' Guild demonstration. But these were rag-tail jobs. She appeared to have, in fact, precisely the same commitment to modelling as an attractive, wealthy wife of a successful businessman might have to charity work.

For Peter, the sight of his leopard-skin-clad fiancée standing up full-page in the Toronto *Telegram* might not have been quite the same proud and happy experience it was for Christine. Complaints to the Mailaths were more numerous now. Peter's behaviour was reported as increasingly possessive and sometimes downright bizarre. The lifeguard at the swimming pool and the cashier at the grocery store both became targets for Peter's jealousy. There were daily inquisitions about the men she met. How long had she taken to park the car and buy the groceries, and what had she said to the butcher? On one occasion, according to Christine, Peter scooped up her underwear and precious photographs and dragged her by the hair to the apartment incinerator, threatening to drop her most valued possessions into the fire one by one unless she told him the truth about all the men she had seen, and what they had been talking about. It was enough to drive anyone to distraction, wept Christine.

The summer of '67 dragged on. Canada was bloated with tourists coming to enjoy the Centennial celebrations. For Europeans, this one-hundredth birthday was a thing of wonder. They had almost forgotten that a country could be so raw-boned and young. Cameras focused on the sleek highways, overpasses, and shopping plazas in much the same way that Canadians snapped pictures of Europe's old and peeling antiquities. Peter revelled in the opportunity to play host to his out-of-country friends. This time his country was the centre of attraction and he responded generously: the Brewers came in from Connecticut, and even Konrad Patzenhofer turned up sporting a new girlfriend. Christine was impressed by the celebrations but kept her enthusiasm restrained. One visit to Expo, with its sticky crowds and shortage of facilities, seemed to her to be enough. When Peter wanted to make a second trip to Montreal she refused and stayed home alone in Toronto.

Of course her refusal may have had less to do with her indifference to the geodesic fantasies of Mr. R. Buckminster Fuller than with her natural interest in less esoteric matters. Life in Canada may not have worked out quite as satisfactorily as Christine had hoped. It was one thing to lie around the pool at Konrad's château and listen to Peter's construction plans but quite another to live them out among the shabby middle-class apartments that lined Toronto's Lawrence Avenue. She had no doubt that he would achieve the success of which he spoke — after all, he worked hard enough at it — but getting there was not half the fun *being there* might be. And it wasn't her fault if she attracted attention when she went to the supermarket. Toronto was cleaner than New York, more casual than Vienna, brasher than London, but its women were, well, just no match for her. What else was life about anyway? All she had to offer, she explained to her friends, was her body and her beauty, although sometimes she wished men wouldn't use her just for *that*. Whatever these vague longings might have meant, when left on her own in Toronto without the inhibiting presence of her fiancé, Christine did not flee to the nearest library or employment office. Instead, she found consolation in the friendship of a soccer player.

When it came to matters of sexual stratagem, the imagination Peter showed in his business dealings seemed to desert him. His natural advantages of height and good looks were neutralized by an unpleasant aggressiveness in behaviour. An embrace refused was a personal insult that had to be disputed, sometimes even combated with a painfully literal arm-twisting, or a refusal to let the unwilling companion out of his car. Such heavy-handed tactics did not always appeal to his dates: Peter more often than not seemed to be on the losing side. Perhaps because he seemed so desperate in his advances, women quite naturally tended to take advantage of him. It was the cool, indifferent lover they had to worry about, not the ardent, possessive Peter. Not without some reason, Peter developed a deep suspicion of women. Marina's sexual flexibility was a great provocation to him, but she was his ethereal love, and anyway she had never made a public commitment to him. Christine, though, was quite another matter. There could be no forgiveness for any humiliation she caused him.

When Alice Mailath opened the front door she was confronted by a weeping Christine, bleeding slightly from the mouth. Word of the soccer player had reached Peter on his return from Expo. This time, said Christine, she was through with Peter Demeter. In the confusion it was not quite clear whether Peter had kicked Christine out after giving her a few slaps, or whether she had left him. Christine, in a state of evident hysteria, referred to the incident as "a beating", which implied a more serious encounter than the back of a betrayed lover's hand. All the same, it was only a matter of a few days before the two of them were sitting together in the plush Imperial Room of Toronto's Royal York Hotel, planning the date of their wedding.

Friends were astounded. They looked at Christine's decision from their own point of view. To the Mailaths, middle-aged and settled, it seemed to make no sense at all. Christine was young and beautiful. These were qualities that could surely command a higher price than a moody, surly Hungarian given to jealous tantrums. Anyone could understand the irrationality of an overwhelming passion, of course, but Christine — let alone Peter — exhibited none of the most rudimentary symptoms of that particular state.

Christine's own perspective was far more modest. She did not suffer from the contemporary malaise of inflated expectations. On the contrary, every day brought her further confirmation of her own limitations. A social encounter with the school-teacher wife of Peter's cousin or one of his real estate friends would throw her own inadequacy into sharp relief. Peter was a clever businessman, anyone could see that, and he could also talk at length about current events and matters of literary and historical interest. He had opinions on everything. Christine, as she ruefully explained to friends, couldn't really bring herself to read much more than the fashion and furnishing magazines she loved to look through under the hairdryer. Of course men had always wanted her, but in spite of her claims of European romances, Canadian friends suspected there were far more propositions than marriage proposals. Christine was not rich, well connected, or accomplished enough to ever really escape her demi-monde position among the château set. Now her only card was her beauty. Men praised it, women envied it, and she devoted herself to its maintenance.

And it trapped her. For at twenty-six she was haunted by the knowledge that the kind of allure she had was only temporary. Cosmetics and exercises could not prevent aging, the shifting of tissue beneath the skin, the blurring of the firm contours of her face and body. Without the protection of her beauty she would be helpless, of no possible interest to anyone. Behind her, far away in Austria, she had left a son she no longer knew. Now she wanted to build a home for herself in this new country, where she could start afresh, where people seemed to care so little about the past. She would create a warm and supportive climate for Peter, taking her responsibilities seriously, for now her youth was almost gone. This handsome, self-confident, aggressive man would shield her from a world that would soon have no use for her. This Peter Demeter, he could do anything.

On November 14, 1967, nine days after Christine's twenty-seventh birthday, Christine and Peter were married at City Hall in Toronto. The two witnesses were real estate lawyer Gerry Heifetz and Peter's cousin, Steven Demeter. Less than six years later they would also be among Christine's pall-bearers.

5. Csaba

In February 1969, a young man sat on a plane droning its slow way, via the Icelandic route, from Vienna to New York. He found the flight uneventful. There was no turbulence. He always slept well while travelling, and shortly after take-off he started dozing. He stayed over in Reykjavik for a day and did some sightseeing. Although he was nearly thirty he hadn't travelled much, and he had never been on the North American continent before. He had attended university for six years, switching from engineering to law, but hadn't got a degree in either. After university he had spent nine months in the Austrian Army. When he got out, at the age of twenty-eight, he took a job servicing vending machines for a friend and slept in his converted office above a bowling alley. The friend's name was Konrad Patzenhofer and the job had been arranged through Peter Demeter. Before that he had never held a job of any kind.

He was now coming to North America because he felt he had a mission. The mission, as he would tell a hushed courtroom five and a half years later, was to prevent Christine Demeter from being murdered.

The family from which Csaba Szilagyi (pronounced Chaba Silahdy) is said to have descended was one of the most illustrious in East Europe. To this day in Catholic churches around the world the bells are rung every day at noon to commemorate the victory of a nobleman named Hunyadi, whose armies prevented the sword of Islam from slicing into the body of a Christian Europe some five hundred years ago. It was Hunyadi's wife, Elisabeth Szilagyi, who gave birth to the great Renaissance ruler King Matyas of Hungary. (True, it was Matyas's first act as king to throw Mihaly Szilagyi, the uncle who had helped him to the throne, into a dungeon where he eventually perished, but this was done for reasons of state.) Of course, by the time the Szilagyis descended through the ages into this century, they had no rank or holdings any more. Csaba's father had barely made it into the higher echelons of the diplomatic service.

Csaba himself did not claim descent from the family as such. As far as he knew, it may have been just a similarity of names. Csaba claimed very little; it simply wasn't his style. He might admit to knowing something about guns, for instance, but he would never claim to be an expert. A slightly built, cautious, polite, unassuming young man, he would seem to be a weak second fiddle, a pleasant fifth wheel, a content shadow around the light of stronger personalities. If he had an intensity, a temper, a pride touching on haughtiness, it would be all inside, carefully hidden not only from superficial acquaintances but even from close friends. To the rest of the world he would be little Csaba, that nice boy.

Growing up is a difficult process for everyone, and for Csaba it seemed to take especially long. A child's life is filled with daydreams and fantasies in which one might become a princess, an aeroplane, or a secret agent. For an eight-year-old, lumps of porridge on a plate could be a moonscape or an important naval battle in the Second World War. A teen-ager's fantasies, more realistically, might involve conspiracies, revenge, or owning fast sportscars and being admired by beautiful women. The less a boy enjoys the real world around him, the more he may withdraw into this kind of private world. In the end his real achievements may matter very little to him, reality being drab and disappointing compared with the brilliance of his dreams.

For a short time perhaps most young people go through a mild variety of this syndrome, and in a very few it may persist until it reaches full-blown clinical psychosis. But in some it simply engenders a lassitude, a seeming lack of concern with the practicalities of existence, or a certain polite indifference to other people or their own future. Such people often seem lazy and unreliable. They tend to attach themselves to strong patrons who'll do the needful for them — paying the rent, getting jobs or breakfast or visas — and in whose shadow they can continue dreaming undisturbed. Their effort to prolong their childhood a little longer makes them appear irresponsible spongers in the eyes of strangers, and devoted, faithful, weak-willed pawns in the eyes of those who take them under their wings. In fact, they may be neither.

Peter was waiting for Csaba as the turboprop settled on the runway and taxied past the sleeker jets at Kennedy International in New York. "Papitschek" (Csaba's affectionate nickname for Peter) may have had his own reasons for paying his way to the New World, but "Csabaschek" had his own reasons for accepting it. Still, there was no talk of reasons, then or for a long time afterwards, as Peter dragged the exhausted young man through the sights of the "Big Apple". For a couple of days they rested in Connecticut — in Hartford, at David and Sybille Brewer's, where Christine was also staying — then drove in Peter's car back to Toronto. For the next eighteen months, from the spring of 1969 until the fall of 1970, Csaba lived with Peter and Christine in their house on Fairfield Avenue.

Their relationship seemed, as it had seemed in Austria before, that of a protégé and his benefactor. Although Csaba took a job in the first week of his arrival at a firm making spectacles (which Peter arranged for him), he paid nothing for his room and board for nearly a year, and only a modest amount thereafter. Somewhat in the way of a poor relation he'd be a member of the family. Once in a while he would take out the garbage or cut the grass on one of Peter's properties. In the mornings he'd plug in the percolator. He'd help Christine carry the laundry to the nearby laundromat, feeling no need to contribute his own coins. Occasionally he'd go to the movies or drive Christine around town in Peter's car. He might take the cocker spaniel, Miro, for a run. When the Demeters were invited to a party, Csaba would tag along.

If this was an unusual relationship between a married couple and a grown man, it was not exactly unique. Among Europeans the idea of distant relatives, or even mere friends, living together under one roof is perhaps not quite as rare as it is among North Americans. Peter and Christine seemed especially fond of staying with friends or having friends stay with them, almost as if being by themselves bored them beyond endurance. The Brewers would spend many weekends in their house. On various occasions nieces and cousins-by-marriage would come and stop for months at a time. (Once, in a villa rented from a friend in Europe for the season, Christine had to entertain over forty house guests for weeks, including Peter's old mathematics teacher, who was visiting them from Hungary.) Certainly none of the Demeters' acquaintances — themselves immigrants from Europe for the most part — found anything remarkable about Peter's providing a temporary home for another newcomer, the son of an old family friend.

If it was a *ménage à trois* in any sense, it seemed quite free of the emotional tensions that often go with such relationships. Christine didn't appear to mind whatever special bonds may have existed between Csabaschek and Papitschek. On the other hand, though Csaba spent quite a bit of time in Christine's company, there seemed to be no hint of jealousy from Peter. This was all the more noteworthy because Peter was normally suspicious and possessive, and Csaba appeared to have no outside interests. Christine herself was both exceptionally attractive and not entirely impervious to the attentions of other men. Still, with only one exception, the usual abrasions of three sexual beings under the same roof seemed not to exist in the Demeter house.

The one exception had to do with Andrea, the child who was born of Peter's and Christine's marriage in the spring of 1970. Peter had been looking forward to having a child — he named her Andrea after his own father, Andrew — and as a reward for fulfilling his dream he ordered for Christine, before the girl was born, a white Mercedes 280 SL coupe. However, on looking at the child, he decided that the resemblance between Andrea and himself appeared insufficient.

Peter's experiences with women had not been happy. He recalled with dismay what seemed to him the absence of any sexual contact between him and his wife during the crucial period in the summer of '69. He also remembered that it was in the same period that he had seen Christine embrace an acquaintance by the name of Henri Galle, and in fact he had made a scene about it at the time. The lack of resemblance preyed on his mind, and he even suspected a distant relative, Nicholas Esso, the man who had sent him a small sum of money when he had first arrived in Vienna. (In fact, on the very day of Christine's death three years later, Peter would be telling a puzzled Viveca Esso how much she looked like his own daughter Andrea.) Lastly, Peter remembered that in the summer of '69 Csaba took Christine for a drive, and their car broke down somewhere in the country in the small hours of the morning. Could Andrea, in fact, be Csaba's child? The suspicion that he might not be his girl's natural father had never left Peter from that moment, and he would voice it with such abandon that it became common knowledge among their circle of acquaintances.

If his old friend's suspicions disturbed Csaba, he gave no evidence of it at the time. He continued living in Peter's home through the spring and summer of 1970, quietly doing his job at the optical firm, cutting the grass, babysitting Andrea, and putting on the percolator in the morning. On a couple of occasions he would have a heart-to-heart talk with Peter, just as in the old days in Austria when he was a bright teen-age boy in a depressing home and Peter the sophisticated young Caesar about to arrive, see, and conquer. On these occasions Christine would be upstairs, out of earshot, and in any case they'd be talking in Hungarian, a language she did not understand. They might talk about cars during these conversations — both Csaba and Peter were fascinated with automobiles and collected magazines about them — but most likely they would also discuss far-fetched and daring plans, celebrating their own cleverness, their superior brains unfettered by conventional scruples and morality, the qualities that lifted them high above the common herd. Peter was an avid reader of mysteries and detective stories, and if he liked a suspense movie he might go to see it two or three times. Touching on these subjects, Peter might remark that *their* intelligence, of course, would far exceed the combined brain-power of all the policemen in the land. He'd always include Csaba in the distinction of his own smartness in spite of the evident difference in their achievements. Whether or not such magnanimity would bring home to Csaba all the more clearly his own dependent position, his being a non-starter, a houseboy in the home of his successful friend, he would say nothing about it to Peter. If he had any resentments, he'd nurse them quietly and alone. If and when the time came, he could prove who was the smarter of the two.

Peter had a different way of dealing with *his* resentments, whenever he had any. He'd quarrel, censure, grumble, make caustic remarks, or fake an argument with Christine to get a message across to a third party. Csaba always believed this was what Peter did when he got Christine to ask him, after a year, to contribute something to the expenses of the household. The request came from Christine but on Peter's instigation. He would also let it get to Csaba that he disapproved of his purchase of a used Cutlass convertible when a Volkswagen might have done just as well. There he was, practically subsidizing him, and Csaba was just throwing money away. Like many parsimonious people, Peter seemed afflicted by alternating bouts of generosity and regrets. He would lend his car, even urge it on people, then make a note of the gas gauge when it was returned. He would throw lavish parties, then keep tab of what his guests consumed. There seemed little point in possessing things unless one could show them off; money locked in a vault did nothing for a person's ego, but for someone like Peter, compared to whom (in his cousin's words) Jack Benny was the last of the great spenders, every penny disbursed was a drop of his life-blood. Yet, almost masochistically, he would continue to buy, give, bestow, and invite. He seemed to want Csaba around and resent the expense of having him at the same time. As the months went by, the situation became more and more awkward.

Finally, whether of his own volition or at Peter's request, Csaba moved out of Peter's home in the fall of 1970. The Demeters were away in Europe when he moved, and by the time they returned he was gone. For the next few months they had no contact at all. Csaba would call Peter only once, at a friend's place, to wish him a Merry Christmas. His own Christmas was not particularly merry: soon after leaving Peter's house he'd lost his job, and he was now eking out a living delivering pizzas. It wasn't much to show, at the age of thirty-one, for a good family, six years of university, and a superior intellect.

For the next two years, as far as appearances were concerned, Csaba and Peter seemed to drift apart. They met once in a long while, mainly on Monday evenings when Csaba was off work, at all-night restaurants such as Fran's on St. Clair. The cooling off of their friendship appeared to be logical: Peter was becoming a successful developer with properties, foreign cars, European holidays, while Csaba remained a deliveryman. (He did — against Peter's advice — try to start a gardening business with a friend for one summer, but he soon went bankrupt and even lost his Cutlass in the process.) Under the circumstances it was less surprising that they saw little of each other than that they continued meeting at all. Of course, they still had their interest in car magazines in common, and some nominal real estate deals.

And years later Csaba would maintain he also had a mission.

6. The Spring of '73

The Boeing 727 was comfortably on course less than ninety seconds after taking off into the February overcast from Toronto International. The passengers bound for the sunshine of Mexico via the snowy skies of Canada settled back into their narrow foam-rubber seats. For a sizeable man like private investigator Leo Ross, the next five hours would be uncomfortably cramped. He was glad that his neighbour in the aisle-seat, at least, happened to be an attractive woman. A very attractive woman, in fact. When he heard her say something in German to the man on the other side of the aisle, Ross couldn't resist speaking a few words to *his* wife in the same language. That took care of the introductions between the Rosses and the Demeters.

Peter was taking Christine for a holiday down south, as had been their custom in alternate years when they were not going to Europe. Christine was not a demanding wife, but she rather expected this. The previous year they had gone to Barbados even though they were going to Europe as well, and it hadn't even been such an outstanding year for real estate. Not that Peter had any difficulties: the difficult years seemed to be past forever. He had even been able to acquire the house in Mississauga that Christine had her eye on — two acres of land, a pool, a double garage — next to a ravine on a secluded dead-end street, Dundas Crescent. It cost Peter a pretty penny to make the 150-year-old former farm-house habitable. He had considered it a bit of a sacrifice to move there, his own living habits being more attuned to the centre of town, but he decided to do it for Christine's sake. He also got her some ocelot skins for Christmas — they cost thousands — even though one major deal, a deal he had counted on, hit at least a temporary snag.

Nineteen seventy-three was promising to be a bumper year for business. The land-boom that would eventually send real estate prices in Toronto galloping off the top of the chart was getting into full stride. Soon after the New Year Peter's properties began moving at unexpected profits. Having sold Christine's old Mercedes before going to Europe, Peter bought for her the oyster-coloured 300 SEL in January. At $15,225 (tax included) it was a bargain; since it was a discontinued series Peter had managed to get it at a 15 per cent discount, possibly the first discount Mercedes-Benz ever gave to a new car customer. The car was Peter's "almost" gift to Christine: he got financing for $12,000 and she was supposed to come up with the rest. However, when the time came to put the money down she couldn't, much to Peter's chagrin. According to Peter, money was simply flowing through his wife's hands; he had no idea what she did with it all. Her allowance was $240 a month in addition to $600 for household expenses, and of course Peter paid for everything else from mortgage to utilities, even the Chinese maid, Gigi, the live-in help they'd had since September. Peter couldn't stand carelessness and waste: Christine was supposed to pay him a one dollar fine for each cigarette she smoked, and once he demanded from her a $25 deposit for a new set of house-keys after she had lost the original. She had to account for household items in excess of her allowance with sales slips (although Peter didn't learn until after her death that she had often been picking them up from supermarket floors). At any rate, she was supposed to have the down payment for her car from the sale of the old Mercedes and she didn't. In the end Peter co-signed a loan for that amount, too, but only after long and bitter arguments, some of them in front of the astounded sales people in the Mercedes showroom.

By the time the jet-engines reversed thrust on the Acapulco runway the Rosses had heard it all. When it came to talking about some aspects of his own affairs, Peter had never been reticent. Christine herself, though not remotely as loud or sarcastic, was not above striking the odd note of marital discord in public. When the Demeters were unhappy with one another most of their friends and many of their chance acquaintances would know about it. Not just in general, either, but often in minute detail. Most people would instinctively take Christine's side: she seemed a well-mannered, vulnerable, beautiful woman who had made the mistake of marrying a boor. Leo Ross was no exception.

For the next eight days he would watch the Demeters making the worst of a bad marriage around the pool of the El Matador Hotel. Their quarrels were the kind to elicit sympathy for Christine without the need for active interference, though on occasion some people would itch to punch Peter in the nose. If Leo Ross felt so inclined, he kept it to himself, but the retired owner of a Toronto construction firm, W. J. Richards, didn't. Like the Rosses, the Richardses met Peter and Christine in Acapulco and were soon treated to one of Peter's tantrums over a 50-peso item in a restaurant bill. Peter would see red whenever someone tried to do him out of something that was his. On this occasion he even accused one of Mr. Richards' Spanish-speaking friends, who was kindly acting as interpreter, of being in league with the Mexican waiter. It was a bad scene, with Peter shouting at the top of his voice amid the embarrassed silence of the other guests. Finally Richards offered him the $4 at issue to keep him quiet, but Peter kept talking about the subject all evening, managing to use it as a springboard for pointing out Christine's inadequacies. It was at this point that Richards told him, "Shut up or I'll punch you in the nose." To everyone's surprise, Peter immediately settled down.

If Peter appeared manic about people taking things away from him, it may have been more than the usual reaction of a person from whom many things *had* been taken away. Beyond the incalculable combination of his nature and experiences, Peter had another reason for appearing unusually abrasive on that last holiday in Acapulco. There he was, watching his second-choice wife spending his money in Mexico, just when at the other end of the world the elusive Marina had surfaced once again.

For nearly four years after their last traumatic meeting in the winter of 1967 Peter had resisted all temptation to get in touch with the Viennese model. He had been busy with his business, his marriage, the birth of his daughter, and had not even contacted Marina on the one or two occasions he visited Vienna. Finally, in the fall of 1970, he more or less impulsively sent her twenty-five roses for her twenty-fifth birthday. Marina immediately acknowledged the gesture in a letter:

Dear Peter,
I believe my English has become so miserable that I prefer to write in German.

First of all many thanks for the beautiful roses. They are magnificent and I was really happy especially because you didn't forget my birthday. Where on earth did you get my address?

For the last year I have been travelling so much for professional reasons that I hardly ever get a chance to keep house. In January-February I was in the States, mainly in New York. I found it wonderful, fascinating and exciting. Now in November I will be going to Mallorca and then Tunisia. When I come back, I'll go skiing with my girlfriends at St. Anton. It's always very beautiful there before Christmas. Marvellous powdery snow, few people and very cold.

Otherwise there isn't much happening here in Vienna. Most of my friends got married which turned them old. And boring. I don't know why; I'm always getting younger. And there's so much ahead. In the summer I want to go to Japan. . . .

You have a little daughter, don't you? She must be nearly a year now. Is she good? I'm sure you're a proud father. Can't you write to me how you are and what you are doing? . . .

I want to thank you once more for the wonderful surprise and hope very much to hear from you again.

Bye, bye and thank you

Marina

She did hear from him again, in less than six weeks. It was not roses this time but a crocodile handbag and a card for Christmas. Marina waited just a week or two before responding:

Dear Peter,

. . . When this letter reaches you the New Year will have started already. . . . Nevertheless I wish you have had a nice Christmas Eve with your little family. . . .

Anyway, I have to ask you something. What did you mean by sending such a present to me? I should thank you very much, because I always wanted a handbag like this. . . . But I can't say a word until you explain what you mean by it. . . . I know you don't give costly presents just to show what you're able to do. . . . What are you trying to tell me?

Well, I'm not going to give myself headaches, you'll tell me the truth. . . .

In this Marina was mistaken; it wasn't like Peter to come right out with the truth, even assuming there was a truth to come out with. Still smitten but wiser, Peter was not about to make a fool of himself again. Quite understandably he was in no hurry to let quicksilver Marina ruin his marriage, and then lose her to a Wolfi, a film producer, or a South

American millionaire. He ignored the bait in Marina's letter that her upcoming trip to Kenya was "perhaps a good-bye present" from her current boyfriend. This was a game at which two, et cetera. Now Peter would simply wait, content to do no more than keep the channels of communication open between them with the odd letter, postcard, or gift. Whether it was simple prudence or a clever ploy, this time Peter was playing it right just by playing it cool. Now it was Marina's turn to get impatient and show more and more of her hand. Peter had always known the tactics of business, but finally it seemed he had mastered a few of the strategies in the battle of the sexes which, until now, had always found him the loser. In her second campaign the crunchy Fräulein would not get a commitment from him without giving one in return.

Marina tried. When Peter sent her a gold bracelet in the summer of '71 (he got it for Christine, originally, but she didn't like it) and Marina wrote, "you should not make any presents to me again . . . because there is not one reason for me to get such gifts from a married man," Peter didn't reply, "Fine, I'll get a divorce," but simply ignored her remark and sent her a cheque for Christmas. Between her trips to Africa, Russia, Hamburg, or the French Riviera she would try to cut him down to size by coy little hints, or long, ominous silences, but she couldn't. Lifting her little finger did not seem sufficient any more. Unlike the man she knew in the winter of '66–'67, he didn't seem ready to give up house, home, family, business just to rush to Vienna and throw himself at her feet. In fact he did not even look her up in person until the summer of '72 — that is, five and a half years from the time they had last met.

It worked. Whether it was by design or by accident, his attitude intrigued her and, like many women, she was drawn to conundrums. Being intrigued, she could be won. She still had the presence of mind to be casual with him, to talk to him about her trips, her boyfriends, and to make sure he saw her surrounded by smart young men in photography studios, but the subtle change in their relationship was evident in their exchange of letters after Peter had returned to Toronto in the fall.

Toronto, November 30, 72

Hi, could you force yourself to write me a few lines? How is everything — (please write in German) — I'm working hard trying to get my houses under roof and behind glass before frost comes, will have more time soon. Best regards, your

P.

Vienna, December 7, 72

Mon Amour!
1) My name is not Hi.
2) I have as little time as you.
3) Did you forget my birthday?
4) Did you overlook December 2, and
5) Before I write another word to you at all you *must* tell me where you plan to spend your Christmas holidays and it had better be with me.

Marina

There was Marina, reminding him of their "anniversary" of December 2! Still, Peter couldn't be sure. Sitting in the bone-bleaching sun of Acapulco, he fretted, fought with waiters, quarrelled with Christine. Needless to say he *didn't* go to Vienna for Christmas (now it was his turn to write coy little letters: "Thank you for the invitation . . . but you seem to overlook the fact that happily married men usually spend their Christmas and New Year with their families") but he did send her an $800 cheque for a present. He had to play her very carefully now, not too eager, not too cold. But it wasn't just a question of playing: it was a genuine puzzle. Perhaps for the first time in his life Peter might not have known what he really wanted. He wasn't happy with Christine, but was Marina really worth jeopardizing his whole life, his business, everything he had accumulated or was about to accumulate? Divorcing Christine would be costly and disruptive. For a married man it might be much simpler to have an affair; after all, that's what other married men did all the time. An affair with Marina might just get her out of his system. For the time being he sent a postcard:

Hi . . . It's my first time in Mexico — just unbelievably beautiful. From the airport you pass one day after another with beaches of extreme beauty — but rather unsafe water with under-currents and full of sharks, honest (!) one accident after the other according to the Toronto newspapers! More later. Your

P.

Whether the curious punctuation with reference to accidents — "honest (!)" — had any special meaning or not, the subject of sharks must have fascinated Peter, for he returned to them in the second of three postcards he sent to Marina from Acapulco. ("Still having a rather masculine voice, or the sharks didn't get me yet. . . . ") Of course there *were* sharks in the Pacific and it was not unnatural to write about them. Christine, especially, was an inveterate swimmer. But the eight days in Mexico passed without incident, and when Leo Ross said good-bye to the Demeters in the ten-below frost of Toronto (they had the same seating arrangements on the way back), he had little reason to think they'd ever see each other again.

Back home Peter was looking forward to an unusually busy spring season. He had sold six of his houses since the beginning of the year, and he had to make sure the deals closed without a hitch. This left little time for socializing, even with close friends — "the inner circle", as Peter liked referring to them — who at that time consisted of people like Peter's cousin, the psychologist Dr. Steven Demeter, and his schoolteacher-wife Marjorie; Peter's architect, Leslie Wagner, and his girlfriend Yvonne; the Markoviches; the Meders; business friends, like real estate lawyer Gerry Heifetz or chartered accountant Danny Salzberg; and more recent acquaintances, like the Richardses from Acapulco. Once in a while old friends from Europe or the United States, like Dr. Sybille Brewer, would come for a visit. The "inner circle" shifted and changed over the years; Henri Galle was no longer part of it, ever since Peter had started to have doubts about Andrea's paternity, though Mrs. Galle was still friendly with Christine. In much the same way, Peter's former architect, Peter Mailath, and his wife had little friendship left for Peter, but would talk or spend some time with Christine once in a while. Peter's one-time greatest friend, the Viennese Konrad Patzenhofer, had not been on the list since 1968. According to Peter their friendship cooled because of Konrad's gossip and indiscretions during the Marina-Wolfi affair, and his later rudeness to Christine. Konrad saw the matter in simpler terms: he claimed that Peter cheated him on several business deals.

Csaba Szilagyi was no longer a member of the "inner circle" either, but Peter would still turn to him in confidential affairs. Whatever their differences, Peter felt he could trust Csaba completely in money matters and perhaps even in other things. This was extremely rare for Peter, who, being a shrewd and aggressive businessman himself, automatically expected to be shortchanged by most people. Csaba might have been the only human being in whom he had full confidence.

The deal, for instance, for which he enlisted Csaba's assistance in March was to be a simple but effective piece of psychological bargaining. They met briefly to discuss it at Mr. Pizza, the restaurant where Csaba had in the meantime been promoted to night manager. It was just a favour Peter wanted, really, and Csaba immediately agreed. At the time Peter was trying to acquire a property on Russell Hill Road and had already put in an offer for $200,000. The owners, hoping to get more, hesitated. Peter now wanted Csaba to pose as a rival developer and make an offer of $190,000. This might indicate to the owners that Peter's offer was actually higher than the current market price. He gave Csaba a cheque for the $10,000 required to accompany the bid, and Csaba submitted his "offer" through a well-known real estate firm the next day. Whether or not this influenced the vendors, Peter's offer was accepted and Csaba got back "his" $10,000, which he then returned to Peter. Neither of them could know at the time how this figure of $10,000 would crop up in later events. They had done a few such deals in the past and would do one or two more in the remaining months of their friendship.

For Csaba things had not become much easier in the intervening years. His promotion to night manager at the pizza restaurant might have been a slight elevation in status from deliveryman, but it came at the price of a reduction in income. Now, at the age of thirty-four, he still hadn't quite made up his mind what to do. For many people being co-manager of a pizzeria would not necessarily mean failure. Csaba, however, in terms of his background and education, couldn't possibly view it in any other way. His lack of worldly success might have been especially galling to him since in the course of the last year he had become very attracted to a certain girl.

Csaba, of course, had had relationships with women before, but Rita Jefferies was different. A tall, well-bred, serious girl, she seemed attracted by Csaba's evident intelligence and good manners but found his lassitude and lack of ambition frustrating. It wasn't a question of money or social position for Rita, but one of attitude. If Peter (whom Rita hardly knew) was the archetypal immigrant, hustling, making it, trying to beat a new world at what he took to be its own game, Csaba seemed more like an *émigré* sitting out a palace revolution on the Left Bank in Paris. Life in this century seemed somehow temporary for Csaba, a kind of bothersome wartime condition which would soon pass, to be replaced by normal existence. Then, in that rebirth of his old world, Csaba might start living again. In the meantime he would handle a ten-inch pizza as though it were a gas-mask or a blackout curtain, something one had to put up with for the time being until the barbarians were thrown back and one could return to the ancestral seat.

Although their differences would not be spoken of in these terms, what Rita felt all along was that Csaba lacked *reality*, while she was nothing if not a realistic girl. His ideas, dreams, schemes, fantasies all ran counter to what she understood the real world to be. She might also have glimpsed a hardness under the indolent politeness of his mask which she found frightening. Their on-again, off-again affair lasted for several months, until it finally flared up in a bad scene in which she walked out on him. Csaba was bothered by the loss — enough, in fact, to threaten her with violence, though it was only a threat. After their last meeting he would see Rita one more time, purely by chance, on the day of Christine's death.

Peter was too busy with his own affairs to pay attention to Csaba's love life in any detail, but when he heard about the break-up he offered to introduce his one-time protégé to Christine's pretty Chinese maid, Gigi, who had no boyfriend in the country. That was just fine with Csaba, who was as used to having Peter arrange things for him as Peter was to putting Csaba under an obligation. It seemed to suit the nature and purposes of both.

Peter was working hard. During the months of March and April, as the snow was turning to slush in the unseasonably warm spring of '73, he would deal with buyers, architects, real estate people, or tradesmen like the sub-contractor Ferenc (Freddie) Stark, a slight middle-aged man of sharp features who did some building and demolishing jobs, liked painting watercolours and writing poetry once in a while, and had served in the French Foreign Legion. Stark was not only a tradesman but a peripheral acquaintance, having met the Demeters and Csaba at a party some years before, although they never socialized. In the spring and early summer of that year he was working in the area of the old Riverdale Zoo, where Peter also had some properties.

Every so often Christine would help out in the business, holding open house for prospective buyers, showing them properties, or turning the lawn sprinkler on or off in front of Peter's virtually unsalable town-houses on Dawes Road in the east end of Toronto. Once in a while Peter would take her along to a Planning Committee Meeting: being lovely and feminine, just by sitting there she might put in a more receptive mood some alderman who would otherwise look askance at Peter as a developer. (That was the start of the period when the city's

"Reform" Council tried to save Toronto from the fate of some American cities by stopping all development that didn't coincide with their vaguely socialist ideas of urban planning.) One day that spring Christine did double duty: she sat in at a Committee Meeting with Peter; then, while the meeting was still going on, she drove out to Dawes Road alone to show the house to someone. After that she came back to the meeting to pick Peter up again. This was on April 2. Later a witness would testify at Peter Demeter's trial that Christine was not supposed to return from the house on Dawes Road alive.

Marina's decisive letter was dated April 16:

> Dear Peter,
>
> Two days ago I was in Zurich. It was snowing furiously and was bitterly cold. I was at the cinema: The Last Tango in Paris. It was so hopelessly boring that I could hardly sit. And then the whole Europe was talking about the film.
>
> In Vienna it is winter with all annoyance. Snow, wetness, cold. Just disgusting. . . .
>
> My business-like mind throws me out of bed at seven each morning. I have a sleep deficit like Napoleon. Because of this reason I'm looking as if I were 70. . . .
>
> To end this terror we have decided to relax my restless mind. And what can lastingly relax a person like me? . . . In one word — I am being married. To make everybody happy! This delightful event will take place in summer. . . .
>
> Write to me once again. Until then
>
> > A merry Easter and a happy sex-life
> > yours forever
> > Marina

The letter arrived around April 19, Peter's fortieth birthday. He was expecting to have it celebrated in a big way, and the absence of preparations suggested to him that Christine was planning it as a surprise party. Some surprise; when he got home that day, Andrea was at the neighbours', Christine had already eaten, and a cold supper was waiting for him on the table. This was the final blow. Both women seemed to be rejecting him at the same time. He didn't know if Marina was bluffing or not (she was, as it happened), but he decided to take no risks. If he let the affair of his life slip through his fingers now that it finally seemed within his grasp, he'd never forgive himself. He got on the telephone to

Marina and made the arrangements for a Big Fling. Later he followed it up with a letter in questionable German:

Hi, Dearest!

It was nice to hear your voice again after five months!!! Monday, June 4, as discussed, I will call you again briefly and I hope to see you again on the 6th or 7th. Nine months have rushed by since the beginning of September when I parted from you in Vienna.

Now do you see why I *never* write to you in German?

Handkisses from your
P.

(P.S.: Please find enclosed Can. $750.00, it's an international money order; like *cash*.)

Casual as he was in his business dealings, Peter seemed curiously cumbersome in his personal affairs. He wasn't so old-fashioned as not to cheat on his wife at all, but neither was he sufficiently sophisticated to do it with an easy conscience. He felt compelled to make a big deal out of trying something — possibly for the first time in his marriage — that some men try, if not at every lunch-hour, at least at every out-of-town convention. When he finally decided to spend a week with Marina he had to tell absolutely everyone about it, as if purging himself of a guilty secret. Leslie Wagner knew about it. Steven and Marjorie Demeter knew about it. Even Gigi, the maid, knew about it. Csaba knew about it as a matter of course, since Peter made some of the arrangements on the telephone from his apartment. (Csaba stepped out, discreetly, on the balcony while Peter was talking to Marina, but Peter informed him about everything anyway.) It was almost inevitable that by the time Marina landed in Montreal Christine would know about it too.

May was not a happy month for Christine to begin with. Peter seemed unusually edgy and depressed. Christine, who wasn't particularly close to her parents (they would often let months go by without exchanging letters), was now very much looking forward to her mother's projected visit in the summer. It was on May 1 that she wrote these lines in a letter:

Dearest mommy and dear papa,

Please forgive me for the long silence, but I have been very busy with my work for Peter and the housework, guests and swimming pool. All these things have to be done and Gigi is very slow in everything. Work makes her fall asleep. The whole house has to be polished, drapes cleaned, etc., and Andrea also needs some time. . . .

I feel up and down these days, and I'm glad mommy's coming. Sometimes I get this terrible *anxiety* that I'm not going to live for long. I'll be so glad when I can talk it all over with mommy, maybe the whole thing is just in my imagination.

I'm trying to pull myself together and overcome this fear but sometimes it's too much for me. . . .

Chilling as this premonition was, the rest of the letter contained no hint that Christine would have associated her fears with her husband in any way. On the contrary, she talked about her parents' birthday telegram making Peter very happy, or how Andrea seemed to have inherited Peter's "golden sense of humour". This, incidentally, showed either that Christine appreciated her husband's sharp, macabre, jabbing wit more than most outsiders, who found it cruel and unfunny, or that she felt the need to be defensive about it. (On a previous visit to Canada Mr. Ferrari was somewhat shocked to hear his son-in-law announce in company: "If I die some day, everything I own will go to my dog, then to no one for a long time, then to my daughter, and lastly to my wife.") Whether or not Christine was hurt by such remarks, they certainly didn't have the sting of novelty for her. Jokes at his wife's expense were as much part of Peter's routine as they are of certain stand-up comedians', and, while no more tasteful, they might have been just as harmless. The events of June, however, were qualitatively different.

Peter didn't actually *tell* Christine he was off to Montreal for an affair but what he did say about needing a week or so by himself "to sort things out" was almost as bad. It seemed as if, instead of wanting to allay her suspicions, he had been trying to arouse them. They argued, Peter bringing up *her* solo skiing trips and Cape Cod holidays, and the fact that in more than six years *he* had never been anywhere alone. Christine might have wavered; after all, Peter had been working hard and — as she told Mrs. Markovich a few days before her husband's departure — he really deserved a vacation. But everything changed when, a day before he was due to leave, she found a hotel reservation for two in the pocket of one of his jackets. The inevitable blow-up followed.

The next morning Peter left in his old Cadillac (she wouldn't let him take the Mercedes), and Christine went through all the shrill, desperate motions betrayed spouses usually go through. She took her car for an aimless drive on the Queen Elizabeth Way, hitting the suicidal speed of 110 miles an hour until a policeman stopped her and, seeing her distraught state, bought her a cup of coffee to calm her down. She called mutual friends in Vienna to find out Marina's whereabouts. When she was told that the crunchy photo model was off somewhere to an unknown destination, Christine searched Peter's files of business documents and correspondence until she found all of Marina's letters. Naturally, they confirmed her suspicions. She phoned her friend Judy Markovich and told her she wanted to deposit photo-copies of the documents with her. She herself, Christine said, was off to Montreal to confront Peter and Marina. Judy Markovich talked her out of this and suggested she leave the documents with a third party. The next day, on June 8, Christine phoned private investigator Leo Ross.

Since their Acapulco trip Ross had already met Christine once, quite by accident, on the corner of Dawes Road and Danforth. They chatted for a while and the private detective gave Christine his business card. Now, on hearing her story, he recommended a lawyer Christine might consult and leave her documents with. On June 11 Christine had an interview with Toronto attorney Ronald Biderman. She wanted to know what her rights were if she decided to leave Peter because of his adultery. Would she be able to get custody of Andrea (she had lost one custody application in Europe after her previous marriage) and would she get any alimony? Could she share in some of her husband's property? She appeared anxious, but quite contained and rational. She spent about three-quarters of an hour in the lawyer's office and left a sheaf of documents with him. After that Biderman never saw her again.

Christine's calmness in the presence of the solicitor was in sharp contrast with the mood in which Judy Markovich saw her during the same period of time. In Judy's home, which she visited with Andrea, Christine was hysterical with anger and fear. She said that what she knew about Peter's business dealings, along with some documents she found, would be enough to put him away for fifteen years. For this reason, she said, he would never divorce her but would try to get rid of her in some other way. On one previous occasion he had tried to push her in front of a car on Bloor Street. (This was a story Christine had also told Mrs. Galle a year or two earlier.) Now she repeated it, adding that her marriage had been sheer hell all along. "You'll see, they're going to get rid of me," she cried before Judy Markovich succeeded in calming her down and sending her home.

Meanwhile in Montreal Peter and Marina were spending the first nights of their seven-year-old liaison in the same bed. Even though he had to pick her up at Dorval Airport in the 1968 Cadillac rather than the brand-new Mercedes, she still seemed impressed and happy. In the next few days Peter showed her a bit of Canada: from the Bonaventure in Montreal they drove to the Frontenac in Quebec City, then to the Château Laurier in Ottawa. Since Marina had only purchased a one-way ticket in Vienna, in Ottawa Peter bought her a *return* ticket to Vienna and back. The forty-five-day excursion fare was only a few dollars more than the regular one-way ticket back to Austria, but to use it Marina had to return to Canada no later than July 26. As far as she was concerned, it was a date.

They drove back to Toronto for the last day of Marina's visit. Peter called his cousin Steven, and he dropped by to have a drink with them at the Inn on the Park. Evidently Peter couldn't resist displaying Marina to the closest member of his family. On the last afternoon they took the air-conditioned coupe with the eight-track stereo tape-deck for a spin to Niagara Falls. On the way they talked about Peter's divorce, which seemed a *fait accompli* to Marina, with only the details and time-table still to be worked out. The same evening at nine o'clock she flew back to Europe. He drove home. It was June 12.

The first confrontation between Peter and Christine had the usual trauma of all such situations. She began by showing him Marina's letters. Denials being pointless, Peter attempted none. The argument continued throughout the night. After putting Andrea to bed, Gigi quit on the spot: she had had enough of the "demented Demeters" as she had come to call them in her own mind. (By that time she had more or less started going steady with Csaba, and it was he who picked her up when she finished packing her suitcases.) But, as usual, the scene between Peter and Christine did not remain private, as Leslie Wagner's mother arrived to spend the night at Dundas Crescent.

Peter's defence was simple. "In six and a half years I had no indiscretions, no flirtations, nothing," he shouted. "You have had them all the time. Now that I did it, you can either put up with it or leave." Christine's reply was equally to the point: "I'll leave but I want my share. You won't throw me out without a penny. Mississauga is mine!"

In a way it seemed almost as if Peter had *wanted* Christine to find out about his fling. His actions and statements, as ever, had the inexplicable ambiguity of a person whose motives and desires are so mixed that he has difficulty sorting them out himself. On the one hand he had made some nominal efforts to use an assumed name in *some* of the hotels he had checked in with Marina, and had asked a New York friend to send a misleading telegram to his home so Christine might think he was away on a legitimate business trip. On the other hand he had bragged to so many people about his affair that it would have been almost impossible for Christine not to find out, even if he hadn't kept all Marina's letters in unlocked files at home. One clue to his real feelings might have been something he yelled at his wife at the height of their argument that night: "You always said to me 'not even a girl like Marina would want you'. Well, it looks like you were wrong!"

The change, however, that took place in the Demeters' relationship immediately after that night was so complete that it seemed to justify the views of those who would never take sides in marital disputes. From the next day on Christine was all smiles, slippers, and favourite meals. To acquaintances like Judy Markovich or next-door neighbour Joene Tennant this only went to show that one shouldn't put too much weight on things spouses say to or about one another in the heat of the moment. Judy was especially glad she didn't take Christine's "they want to get rid of me" at its face value, for she called her a day or two later begging Judy not to mention anything to Peter. It was clear she had decided to attempt a reconciliation.

The reason for this *might* have been a conversation she had had with Peter's cousin. Psychologist Dr. Steven Demeter, a former lawyer and army officer, and at six foot six a very impressive figure of a man, happened to be a marriage counsellor by profession. His advice to Christine was based on Emerson's dictum "the only way to have a friend is to be one" and also perhaps on the traditional European view of how a good wife ought to behave. He suggested to Christine that if she really wanted to save her marriage, *she* should take the first step. Forgive everything. Expect no penitence and no deals. Always show her best side.

Possibly this was sound advice and possibly Christine took it to heart. In any case, for the next six weeks she and Peter entered the friendliest phase of their relationship, at least to all outward appearances. They entertained, they went to dinners and dances together. They actually held one another in public. Peter even attempted to curb the sharp side of his tongue, and although it was an ingrained habit, he stopped putting Christine down so often and making jokes at her expense. At a party someone overheard him say that she "looked like a million dollars" — a phrase kindly meant, even if unfortunately chosen in light of later events. But at the time it looked as though Peter's Montreal trip had had a purging effect of some kind and might actually save the Demeters' marriage.

All this would have been bad news for Marina, had she known about it. For throughout the month of June she was writing letter after letter to Peter, all sounding the same note of complete devotion. " . . . I miss you very much and I love you and I need you."(June 13) "Now I go to sleep — without you? And how in heavens shall the time pass till end of July?"(June 15) "I hope to find a letter from you in Vienna," she wrote from France on June 20, "as soon as I get back. . . . I had an ugly dream two days ago, that is that you left me and returned to your wife. . . . When shall I see you at last again?" And on June 27: " . . . I come home totally exhausted and there's not even a 'Hi!' from you. . . . My darling, the days without you are long, however bearable, but the nights are grisly! Do you think I can stand it until July 26?" Finally, on July 3, this note:

Dear Peter

Since I came back from Toronto I wrote to you at least 10 times. Until now you never found it worth answering me.

I only got a telegram. Thank you!

I have at least as much to do as you. But it seems I can arrange my time better. Of course, one has to give you credit that you are also very busy at night. So, I can also start that here again.

Your lack of interest frightens me a lot. I draw the consequences. Adieu.

Marina

Whether Peter's silence throughout June was due, as he later claimed, to a genuine quandary about his own feelings, which at the time inclined towards Christine, or to his preoccupation with other business, this latest note finally prompted him to reply. In his long letter, handwritten in passable German, he assured Marina of his love and his desire to be with her. Everything would be all right, he wrote, if she only had a little patience while he made the necessary arrangements. The last two paragraphs of his letter were quite specific:

Ch. makes rather big demands which I am, however, rather ready and also able to fulfill. Everything turns around her present standard of living and the child, education and future. She is not an enemy of mine, but quite the contrary, — please understand this, — I want to arrange everything for her friendly, elegantly, and gentlemanlike — in the long run you would also not expect it any different from me!!! Right?

When I *always only* loved you, all I could give her for so many years (6½) was friendship and understanding — I don't want to lose her friendship because of her herself and especially because of Andrea who really is not to be blamed for anything. . . . I want a *friendly divorce* with prearranged financial agreement, no fight with each other and even less about the child, — that is as much important to the *two of us*, I hope, you will also soon see that!? I am awaiting the 26th with so much pre-happiness and love that, once you are here, you will be satisfied with me. . . .

P.

This letter was dispatched on July 9, and Marina replied to it exactly a week later, on July 16. By that Monday Sybille Brewer, her two nieces, and Viveca had already arrived for their visit to Mississauga. Early in the afternoon that day Christine met Gigi at the doctor's office where they exchanged some prescription pills, then drove in the Mercedes to Dawes Road, where Christine had to shut off the sprinkler system. They talked on the way and, as Gigi recalled, Christine was saying that Peter had been very nice to her lately, too nice, in fact, for Christine to trust him. She also said Andrea missed Gigi, and only the other day had said: "Beelzebub belongs to Pappy and I belong to Mummy." On Dawes Road they were unexpectedly accosted by two men who seemed interested in looking at the property. The men were Chinese and Gigi exchanged a few words with one in the Cantonese dialect. The men examined the house and left; Christine drove home, and Gigi took the subway to Csaba's apartment, where she was staying. It was around this time that Marina was writing her last letter to Peter:

. . . I quite agree if you do everything to keep a more or less bearable relationship with Christina. Fights and hatred cost a lot of energy and nerves and should not be necessary by all means. Among grown-up and halfway intelligent people.

Only one thing worries me — now I really don't know her — but since I count myself among the thinking people and have some experience with women like Christina — I am very much afraid that she will cross your plans. . . .

The following day — Tuesday — was spent sightseeing at the Science Centre and at Ontario Place. The little German girls loved it. The evening turned out to be less successful because the Czech garden restaurant had only one table available, which was in the scorching sun, and afterwards they couldn't even have dessert because the Hungarian Sweet Shop was closed. They drove home, where Christine gave the children some ice cream. Peter had to drive back into town again to inspect some properties, and by the time he got back he was too tired to join Christine in the pool, so he went to bed.

Christine did her forty lengths alone that night in the chiaroscuro of the dark water illuminated by the sealed swimming-pool lights. It was after eleven o'clock. She had about twenty more hours to live.

7. Cat and Mouse

In 1962, when twenty-nine-year-old Peter Demeter registered Eden Gardens Limited, a thirty-two-year-old suburban policeman got the first big break of his career. It all came about somewhat accidentally, for William James Teggart had no desire to become a detective. The son of a market gardener who had emigrated to Canada from Northern Ireland, young Teggart dropped out of Grade 11, worked for his father, then drove his brother's tractor-trailer for a while. It wasn't that he lacked discipline or determination — he never smoked or drank and would work out in the boxing ring to keep his 200 pounds well muscled on his six-foot-plus frame — but for quite some time he couldn't find a focus for his interests. Then his younger brother Stan joined the police force, and when Bill saw him in uniform driving his big yellow car he thought Stan looked "really slick". It was the uniform more than anything else that made Bill Teggart follow his brother's example, and it was a let-down for him to be transferred from traffic to the detective branch one summer to help out while the "hotshots" were on holiday.

It took him no more than a month to realize that he could do it better. Most of the time it was just a question of going the extra mile, and Teggart was never a man to put in his eight hours then settle down with a beer in front of the television set. If he hesitated before deciding on a career, it was precisely because most callings didn't seem to ask for that additional effort, that little edge over the ordinary, that bit of self-discipline or one drop of adrenalin by which you could tell average men from the ones who get the blue ribbon. In his own mind Teggart had never any doubt which group he belonged to: he was the man who stayed at his desk when all the others had gone home, who was willing to think hard and fierce, who would turn on his radar, put out his tentacles, and wear his golden slippers all the time. He was the man who would wait until the smoke had cleared, until they all thought he had given up, except he'd be knocking at the door and putting the bracelets on. He was the man who would talk to people, cheerfully, relentlessly, in a flat Canadian voice but with a rich Irish turn of phrase, until people began talking to *him* and telling him everything he wanted to know. The trouble with some good detectives was they were not incurable optimists. They could solve "smoking gun" cases all right, but not the whodunits. Teggart would be an incurable optimist and climb those high mountains.

None of the senior detectives wanted the case in 1962: a couple of boys, aged twelve and thirteen, missing from the Malton area just north-west from Toronto. What's the point, they told plainclothesman Teggart, it's obvious the boys are dead. But both kids had meticulously burned their I.D.'s before they disappeared, and Teggart knew one of them wanted to be a private investigator like The Saint. It took him nine months, much of it his own time, to trace the boys to Greenwich Village in New York, where they had become part of a homosexual ring. The case made the headlines, and Bill Teggart hit the jackpot. Let other men put up their feet, smoke a cigarette, or have a bottle of beer. Teggart was heading for those snow-capped summits, with no time for leisure, self-indulgence, or self-doubts.

By the summer of 1973 he was more than half-way there. Full detective in '63, detective-sergeant in '68, inspector in '72, and superintendent in charge of criminal investigation on January 1 the following year. Now he was top cop, boss of all detectives, in the sixth- or seventh-largest police force of the land. Married to a handsome blonde wife (though not until his thirty-seventh year; time just didn't permit it) and the father of two children. A member of St. Andrew's Presbyterian Church, but modestly, occupying no special position in spite of his high standing in the community, joining simply as Bill Teggart, sinner. Not bad for a high school drop-out, a first-generation Canadian whose Orangeman father had got off the boat just the year before he was born. From probationary constable at twenty-six to superintendent at forty-three — not bad.

Of course, to go far in an organization it helps to get on with the boss. Through their joint careers with the Toronto Township (later Mississauga) Police, Bill Teggart and Douglas Kenneth Burrows got on extremely well. Perhaps they were so different that they complemented one another: big, hearty, loquacious Bill, who looked like a policeman though he didn't talk like one, and trim, neat Doug Burrows, not exactly taciturn or humourless, but as careful and measured in speech and appearance as an actuary or a chartered accountant. Always a rank or two ahead of Bill (*he* made detective-sergeant in '67), Burrows had a build that seemed only average for a civilian and rather slight for a cop. In the openly macho world of police-culture, Burrows would make a virtue of what he couldn't help: not looking big in a confrontation (he'd say) gives you the advantage of surprise. Certainly the bandits who shot two men and kidnapped another two in the course of a bank robbery in 1963 must have been surprised to see Burrows barrelling after them, alone, at a hundred miles an hour, in a commandeered white convertible. They might have understood him better when they had a chance to look into the slim policeman's pale-blue eyes as he pulled up beside them and brought out his gun. The steady, unblinking gaze that even in casual conversation had the sub-zero temperature of liquid air must have seemed like a glimpse from outer space when, for a split second, Burrows' finger tightened around the trigger. But then a sense of law and order prevailed. The instinct to kill was there, but so were years of police training and the earlier discipline of the Canadian navy. Doug Burrows would not gun down even escaping murderers in cold blood.

What he would do is go to school, school, and more school at night. Just like Bill Teggart, Burrows sensed that in the degree-obsessed world of post-war North America having what it takes when the guns go off was not enough. Nor was instinct, patience, common sense, or insight into human nature sufficient; a spotless record and even impeccable results did little for a policeman's career unless he had some framed certificate to hang beside his arrest-and-conviction sheet. Seasoned cops who would see through any con-game became perfect marks for the doctrine of liberal education. It was no longer just a question of specialized training in such sensible subjects as fingerprinting, photography, firearms, or basic law, but courses in psychology, sociology, management, and communications. Doug Burrows received his baccalaureate degree from the University of Toronto, then went on to study Police Management at Northwestern University in Illinois. (Teggart ended up in the same course, having first gone through the adult-education mill in such subjects as "Communications and Human Relations" and even "Effective Communications".) Northwestern had become *de rigueur* for every policeman with aspirations, and middle-aged pillars of society with rank and many years' experience would compare grades the way undergraduates did (at one time, but no longer) at Harvard or the Sorbonne. Teggart never got under ninety on an exam. Burrows averaged 93.5 and 96 per cent. In 1972 (when Teggart was an inspector) Burrows became Deputy Chief of the Mississauga Police. A year later the reigning chief retired, Doug took his place, and Bill moved up the ladder immediately to superintendent. They thought of themselves as others thought of them: a good team ready for big things, should big things ever happen in Mississauga.

The call Complaint Officer Constable Glen Lumber recorded at 9:51 P.M. on Wednesday, July 18, 1973, didn't sound like a big thing at first. The male voice, garbled by excitement and a strong foreign accent, talked about an accident in a garage and his wife who was bleeding. Then he calmed right down in response to Lumber's matter-of-fact, professional questions and gave his name, address, and telephone number in a slow, clear voice. This was helpful, and the Complaint Officer only wished all distressed people behaved in such a sensible manner. It was standard practice to assess the nature of a call to give the first officer on the scene some idea of what he might be walking into, and the constable jotted down "Mr. P. Demeter, 1437 Dundas Crescent, 279-0738, Possible Attempt Suicide" on a slip of paper he passed on to Dispatcher G. A. Derochie. Lumber was used to handling emergencies on the midnight shift, and this call sounded like a P.A.S. to him.

The case seemed less routine barely an hour later when Bill Teggart's phone rang in his Streetsville home. Members of the superintendent's team were aware he didn't usually go to bed until after 1:30 or 2:00, but when he heard Detective Sergeant Christopher O'Toole's voice on the other end of the line Teggart knew that his star investigator wouldn't call him for any frivolous reason. Chris O'Toole was not a frivolous man, and there weren't many things he'd regard as too big to handle alone. Now, even as Chris was outlining the scene they had come upon in the garage on Dundas Crescent, Bill Teggart started putting on his golden slippers.

By 11:55, a little less than two hours after Peter Demeter's call was logged at the Mississauga police station, Teggart was standing in the garage looking down at Christine's body. The first thing that struck him was that her blood, collecting in two large pools under the doors along the slightly sloping cement floor, was still bright red. Teggart was no doctor, but he had seen a great many dead bodies. It seemed to him this woman must have been killed very recently, possibly only minutes before she had been discovered. He also suspected, as did several of the other policemen on the scene before him, that however this extremely attractive, well-groomed, athletic-looking lady met her death, it was neither by accident nor by suicide.

It was easy enough to understand how experienced policemen might have come to this conclusion right away, long before it was indicated by a plethora of medical and physical evidence. The damage to Christine's skull seemed just too extensive to have been received in an accidental fall inside a garage. (Pathologist Dr. Hillsdon-Smith would later say that if she had fallen, she would have had to bounce seven times to receive injuries like these). She *might* have shot herself, of course, in the mouth for example, and one of the first policemen on the scene, Patrol Sergeant John A. Murray, actually spent a few minutes looking for some tell-tale signs of blood-splattering on the walls, such as might be made by an exiting bullet. But there was no weapon to be seen. They even tried turning the body carefully to one side (in the presence of the coroner, but before Superintendent Teggart arrived) to see if there might be a handgun underneath it, but there was nothing. So while later in court it would take many days and long volumes of testimony to confirm that Christine had met her death at the hand of another human being, the police assumed homicide practically from the first few moments.

It would be much more difficult to explain why suspicion focused on Peter Demeter almost as quickly. In one sense, of course, a husband is always a natural suspect in the violent death of his wife, but as a matter of practical experience the police would know that while the rich are no better than the poor, they commit fewer blue-collar crimes. The degree of self-control and intelligence required to master a profession or keep a business going generally goes hand in hand with a personality less impulsive, less likely to lash out in sudden anger, and in any case much more wary of the consequences. The police go by the facts of life. They know that the owners of Cadillacs and swimming pools, whatever their character, tend to deal with their frustrations and achieve their desires by other means than physical violence. Without some compelling evidence, the owner of a $100,000 home would not be quite as natural a suspect in the death of his wife as a slum-dweller or even an ordinary working man. The police might protest — and even honestly believe — that they treat everyone equally, but that simply means they apply common sense and look at each case according to the logic of its circumstances.

There was nothing in Peter's circumstances that would have made him an immediate suspect in Christine's death, but according to the Mississauga police there was something in his *behaviour*. It would be hard to pinpoint it exactly, because the appropriateness of a person's behaviour depends to some extent on the interpretation of the observer. The natural reactions of a chorus girl, for instance, would appear totally inappropriate to a suburban matron. Similarly, the convoluted workings of a haunted Hungarian's mind might seem very strange to a straightforward Canadian detective of Anglo-Celtic ancestry.

To the policemen on the scene Peter appeared curiously calm and inexplicably aggressive in turn. He upbraided Constable Pollitt, the first one to pull up in the circular driveway in his marked cruiser, for cancelling the ambulance he had called. (Pollitt hadn't; he merely confirmed it with the dispatcher.) A few minutes later he demanded to know what "right" the constable had to say Christine was dead. (Pollitt did say, having looked at the grievously battered skull and after gingerly trying to take a pulse from the right ankle, "I'm sorry, sir, it's my feeling your wife is dead.") While waiting for the ambulance, Pollitt observed him standing next to Christine's body in the garage and demonstrating to Sybille Brewer, with his arms outstretched and his knees bent, how Christine must have fallen while reaching for something in the storage area in the rafters. (This would be a recurring theme, for in the course of that night and the following few days Peter would repeat this demonstration, speaking never exactly to, but always in the presence of, the investigating officers, who eventually came to view this as an attempt to influence their investigation.) When Pollitt invited him to sit in the cruiser and answer a few questions, Peter gave him his name, age, and address, and when the constable asked for his wife's name he replied: "Christine, with an 'e' at the end of it." Then suddenly he said, "Could we do this later, there's too much excitement." Pollitt replied, "Certainly," but later he would say this was not the type of reaction that he expected to see from a man. In his view Peter ought to have shown more "remorse" and he expected "perhaps even to see him cry".

Whether Peter felt no grief or merely failed to display it in a manner acceptable to the local authorities, there was no doubt he seemed irritated with the police, who continued to arrive in ever-increasing numbers, in uniform or in plain clothes, then stood around and (as it seemed to him) did nothing but ask for his age or address. Right from the beginning Peter insisted that his wife's body should be immediately removed to a hospital and "an operation or something" performed on it, but of course neither Pollitt nor Plainclothes Constable Crosson (who arrived just seconds after Pollitt in his unmarked car) would permit the two ambulance attendants who pulled up a few minutes later to touch the body in the garage. Patrol Sergeant Murray, arriving just after the ambulance, heard Peter ask plainclothesman Crosson: "Well, who's in charge here, officer?" Looking around, Sergeant Murray told Peter that for the present he seemed to be the senior officer at the scene.

"Why aren't you doing something?"

"I'm doing something; I'm instituting an investigation," said Sergeant Murray with appropriate dignity. In reply Peter nodded his head towards the interior of the garage.

"Well, can't you get her out of here?"

Sergeant Murray would later testify that he was so much taken aback, not just by the request, but by the calm, deliberate tone in which he thought it was delivered, that he drew Constable Pollitt aside to ask him if the man was aware the lady in the garage was dead. Hearing that he had been so informed, Murray decided it was one more reason, along with what he could see of the nature of the injuries, to treat this death not as a case of suicide but as one of possible homicide.

Still, up to this point, the husband was just a man who didn't happen to break into tears, seemed somewhat irritated by the police's penchant for routine questions while his wife lay bleeding in the garage, or wouldn't necessarily accept their diagnosis that she was already past assistance. However, by the time Bill Teggart was briefed an hour or so later, there was more to it than that. It seemed, somehow, that Peter *expected* to be suspected and was defending himself long before anyone accused him of anything. At least, this was the way the investigators came to view the conversation Peter had with a certain police constable, B. J. Burns.

Constable Burns knew Peter slightly from a previous investigation when someone did some damage to one of Peter's properties and he was one of the officers assigned to the case. Now, apparently, Peter called the police station again and requested Burns's presence, perhaps just to see a familiar face among the representatives of impersonal officialdom. (Although understandable even to a North American, having a friend at court when dealing with the authorities would seem a *must* to someone of Peter's background.) In any case, when Burns arrived just a few minutes after the other officers, Peter thanked him for coming and they exchanged a few words standing next to the ambulance in front of the garage. By this time — 10:20 or thereabouts — the first detectives from Identification and Homicide had arrived, having been requested by Sergeant Murray. Detective Koeslag began taking photographs, while Detective-Sergeant Forbes made notes, took measurements, and started dusting for fingerprints. The scene had been officially "turned over" to Detective-Sergeant Crozier, who had been dispatched by Chris O'Toole to start the initial investigation.

Recollections were somewhat conflicting on just whose idea it was to take Peter down to the police station within the next ten minutes. Sergeant Murray thought he requested Constable Burns to do it, but as Burns remembered it, it was his own idea because he knew the detectives would want to talk to Peter. Chris O'Toole's recollection was that he told Sergeant Crozier to separate the two people at the scene — Peter and Sybille Brewer — and send them back to the police station, after Crozier phoned him to say it was a probable homicide. (This mattered only because Murray and Crozier were already suspecting homicide at that point. Constable Burns, who had hardly glanced at the body in the garage, would still have assumed it was a suicide, and if he had taken Peter of his own volition, there could have been nothing in his behaviour to make Peter go on the defensive.) In any case, when Burns asked him to accompany him to the police station, Peter said: "Am I under arrest?"

"No, I'm asking you as a friend to return with me," replied Burns.

During the eight-minute drive to the Erindale station, Peter recounted his movements that day without having been asked to do so. At the station Burns told Peter to take a chair in Superintendent Teggart's office, and as they continued their conversation Burns asked Peter about his marriage. He replied that after six and a half years he and Christine seemed "drifting apart", though they had no violent arguments to speak of. They had, in fact, had sexual intercourse that very morning. Then Peter said he felt he was going to be sick, and Burns left the office to get some coffee.

When he returned with the two Styrofoam cups of indeterminate brew dispensed by a machine in the main detective office, Peter was on the telephone talking to his real estate lawyer, Gerald Heifetz. "Hello, Gerry," he said, "this is Peter. Christine is dead. Would you call Steven, he lives on Old Yonge Street. My cousin Steven. I'm down at the Mississauga police station."

Having finished his phone call, Peter drank his coffee, and it seemed to Constable Burns it was at this point that his attitude changed. He became agitated and a bit belligerent. "What's going on here?" he kept saying to Burns. "Who is in charge? Why aren't they out looking for him?"

If Burns was still assuming suicide at this point (as he later said he was), this outburst must have surprised him, as it was the first indication there might be a "him" the police should be "out looking for". Of course Peter might have simply meant looking for the officer in charge; after all, he had by this time been kept at the police station for more than a hour without seeing anyone in authority. Being asked to wait with no explanations, especially after such a trauma, might make anyone impatient. But after Burns succeeded in calming Peter down a bit, he surprised him once again. "Why aren't you writing this down?" Peter said, then immediately answered the question for himself, "It doesn't matter, you can't use anything against me in court, anyway." (In this Peter happened to be wrong: voluntary statements, even to persons in authority, are generally admissible in Canadian courts as long as they are made without intimidation or inducements.) Then he said something about having recently purchased some insurance on his wife's life. Burns thought he even mentioned the amount, but he couldn't quite understand it. The next thing Peter did was to ask Burns if he thought he had killed his wife.

"I don't know," said Burns, surprised.

"Well, how do you think it happened?" asked Peter, then immediately answered himself, saying: "She must have been climbing up on the rafters for something and fell."

Meanwhile Teggart and O'Toole were on their way back to the Erindale station. Everything they saw at the scene seemed to confirm their initial impression of homicide, even after a cursory examination. Although they would have to wait for the autopsy the next day to determine the exact cause of death, they felt certain Christine had been hit over the head with a crowbar-type object, probably several times. It was not only that the wounds didn't look self-inflicted or accidental, but they could see droplets of blood on the Cadillac, inside, outside, and even on the roof, some of which seem to have been deposited with an *upward* flow, the classic sign of a bloodied weapon being raised and swung repeatedly over a victim. But, if it was a bludgeoning, it had some unusual features. Teggart could recall few cases where the bludgeoning instrument would not have been left at, or very close to, the scene. Escaping killers ditch their crowbars, hammers, or tire-irons immediately; such weapons, being next to impossible to trace, can incriminate a person only if found in his possession. Still, Teggart preferred not to jump to conclusions. His men were just beginning a thorough search of the garage and the grounds.

Taking over-all charge of the investigation himself, Teggart quickly assembled his team. Detective-Sergeant Chris O'Toole would be in charge of field operations and act as Teggart's alternate. He would be assisted by two of the best younger detectives on the force, Jimmy Wingate and Barry King. Detective-Sergeant Forbes, the senior I/D (identification) man, would be in charge of the physical evidence. Detectives Koeslag and Malcolm would be part of the team, which would soon be joined by a young detective named Joe Terdik, a man of Hungarian parentage, who, as intelligence officer, would perform some of the most important functions of the investigation.

Unknown to them all, Chief Doug Burrows would drive by the Demeter house a few times that night, debating with himself whether to put in an appearance or not. Having heard about the mysterious slaying over the police radio in his private car while driving to a civic function with his wife, he was tempted to look at the scene, but then decided his men might feel he didn't have enough confidence in them. Had he decided otherwise, being an experienced criminal I/D man, he could have given his people some pointers about the preservation of the scene and the gathering of evidence which might have saved them a few embarrassing moments in court.

It was at 12:50 A.M. when Chris O'Toole and Barry King took Peter to another office and seated him in front of a desk. By this time Peter had been waiting at the police station for almost two and a half hours and might well have had some reason to feel that he was under suspicion. O'Toole had looked at the garage and had talked to some of the other officers. Unlike Teggart, who was capable of dissembling in a good cause and pretending to sympathies he didn't have, O'Toole was a man of more straightforward attitudes. An ex-miner of Irish background, with thirteen years of experience on the force, he was devoted to routine and self-discipline. He would work out for an hour and a half every morning to keep his muscles in condition, and read for the same length of time to keep his intellect in shape. As a result he had a marvellous physique, and as good a mind as can be developed by building it with the same determination. As an investigator he was quite aware of his own abilities, though saved from pomposity by a natural, self-deprecating sense of humor. Very much his own man, he was as good to have on one's team as a Bobby Hull, in spite of what some of his team-mates viewed as a preference for carrying the puck all by himself.

Regardless of the circumstances under which they met, the direct, well-ordered routes of Chris's mind would have had few intersections with the coiling serpentines of Peter's. Chris would genuinely regard himself as a friend of the public, and would expect animosity only from crooks, or maybe very ignorant persons. Since Peter was clearly not ignorant, his antagonism would have suggested other causes to Chris and his colleagues. They would not consider the possibility that someone like Peter might turn resentful and uncooperative just through the indignity of being kept waiting at a police station before being interviewed by a pair of middle-echelon suburban policemen, who were his social inferiors yet would make no gesture of obeisance in recognition of this fact. Having the combined hierarchical consciousness of old privilege and new riches, Peter would expect to be treated with due deference, and the officious impersonality of police procedure might well humiliate and provoke him into a defensive attitude.

This, then, was the mood in which the first interview began. "I'm not a black-jacketed motorcycle punk," shouted Peter. "I may be wearing casual clothes but I'm a well educated man worth $400,000. Now, am I under arrest? Can I make a phone call to my lawyer?"

"Yes, you can call him now," Chris replied, handing him the telephone. Peter, however, declined.

"No, no, just as long as I know I can call one," he said. "Now how are you going to conduct this? Am I going to be treated as a man who just lost his wife or as a suspected murderer?"

"We are investigating the death of your wife and we want to know the truth and the circumstances surrounding her death," replied Chris. "Where have you been this evening?"

"First, I want you to answer a question for me," said Peter. "Tell me how she died. Surely the coroner must have told you how she died."

Although Chris would not have found it much easier to tell an outright lie than George Washington, his long police training enabled him to keep a poker face and give out as little information as possible. He explained to Peter they'd have to await the results of the autopsy in the morning (which was true) and that there seemed to be severe injuries on her head (which Peter had seen for himself anyway). He said nothing about his private conviction that Christine had been bludgeoned to death. *If* Peter's question had been designed to keep a step ahead of the police and arrange his answers according to whether they suspected accident, suicide, or murder, he would have learned nothing from Chris's response.

"Now, Peter . . . " the detective began, but then he stopped, possibly because he noticed something in the other man's eyes. To call a stranger by his first name may be just friendly informality for a North American, but for a European it would be undue familiarity at best, and coming from a policeman it might seem a deliberate insult. Even those Europeans who have lived on this side of the Atlantic for a long time and are well acquainted with local customs might, on being unexpectedly addressed by their first names, give vent to a flicker of annoyance or surprise. Sensing this, O'Toole continued: "Can I call you Peter?"

"Yes, yes," Peter conceded as though it didn't matter to him. "Is it Mr. or can we call each other by our first names? My name is Peter."

Having passed this minor cultural hurdle, the interview continued for nearly three hours. As the conversation progressed O'Toole's suspicions grew, although he couldn't quite put his finger on anything. He was less concerned with Peter's seeming lack of emotion — after all, some people may be dazed by events or don't have that great a relationship with their wives — than with what he viewed as his continuous "digressions". Peter would go into minute details about what Christine cooked for supper or the exact route he took from Yorkdale back to the house, but whenever Chris would ask him a straightforward question, such as "Do you think your wife was murdered?", instead of answering he'd go off on another tangent. Once in a while he'd say, "You're not writing this down, are you?" or take off his glasses and roll his eyes. He would jump back and forth in time and not relate events in sequence. He'd say "Our marriage was not the best," then follow it immediately with, "We made love this morning when we woke up." O'Toole thought this was strange behaviour for a bereaved husband, and might be designed to evade and obfuscate things deliberately. (O'Toole may have been right, of course, but those who had known Peter well would have found his method of conversation less unusual. They'd say digression was as natural to Peter as gills to a fish, and he'd never consider a straight line the shortest distance between two points. With a defensive convolution typical of his mind, he might also have thought that displaying much grief over the loss of a wife with whom he was known to have a bad marriage would be the very way to make the police suspicious of him. He might have feigned indifference so that people wouldn't think he was feigning grief.)

While O'Toole was talking with Peter, Superintendent Teggart was interviewing Dr. Steven Demeter and his wife Marjorie. He also tried talking to Andrea, who was brought by Steven and Marjorie from the house to the police station, but the little girl saw and heard nothing. She did say something about a doorbell ringing, but since the Demeters had no doorbell she might have meant the telephone. (Andrea's English was rather uncertain at the time since Christine tended to talk to her almost exclusively in German.) Teggart found Marjorie a "totally honest person" and it seemed to him that, unlike Peter, cousin Steven was quiet , sensible, and co-operative. He told Teggart that Peter and Christine had had their difficulties in the past, but lately everthing had been fine between them. Teggart liked Steven and, as he'd say later, "I wasn't suspicious of him at all." He suggested that Steven and Marjorie should go home and take little Andrea with them.

It was at three o'clock that morning that Bill Teggart and Peter Demeter met for the first time. Teggart was amazed. For a man who had just lost his wife, he was certainly unlike any other the superintendent had ever seen before. Arrogant, tall, handsome, he was strutting around the office in a circle. Teggart observed that his clothes hung well and his hair seemed neatly groomed. As they shook hands, he also noticed that Peter had a bad cut on his rather small and delicate right hand. "Superintendent, did my wife have an accident? When will the coroner's report be in?" This was certainly not the broken, bereaved husband one would put one's arm around, Teggart thought. Their first conversation was very brief, with Teggart asking nothing and saying nothing, except to promise that they would investigate who killed Peter's wife. This, of course, would have been enough to indicate that the police regarded Christine's death as homicide. Teggart believed in putting suspects under pressure: in his experience it was then that they started making mistakes. (The only drawback of the theory was that pressure might cause even innocent people to act in strange ways.)

At 3:30 A.M. Barry King and Chris O'Toole drove Peter back to 1437 Dundas Crescent. By this time Christine had been removed to the morgue of the Mississauga Hospital, her hands and feet "bagged" in four small sacks of protective plastic, her body zipped up inside a clear plastic body pouch. On arrival she was put on a stretcher and wheeled into the refrigerator room. For the next eight hours she lay there guarded by Constable Michael Ambrosio, the stains in her thick, healthy hair slowly turning from bright crimson to rusty brown. As gravity settled the uncirculating blood in her body, small dark blotches appeared on her tanned skin that could be mistaken for bruises quite easily. Her withdrawn lip, exposing her upper teeth, hardened her features into a snarl of defiance or a grimace of unendurable shock and pain. Only the colour of her painted toenails remained unchanged, a pair of well-cared-for feet that might be lying on the warm, sandy beaches of Acapulco or the Italian Riviera.

Looking out from the fortieth-floor windows of Pomerant, Pomerant and Greenspan, Attorneys at Law, one could see private planes letting down over Lake Ontario and settling on the concrete ribbon of Toronto's Island Airport. Perhaps it was this view that made Joseph B. Pomerant, Q.C., think of his suite of offices in the Toronto-Dominion Centre as a control tower with a traffic of new cases stacked up over it awaiting permission to land. Although there were many in the holding pattern on that Thursday, July 19, the case of the Mississauga developer seemed to merit priority. The initial call had come to Pomerant's partner, Eddie Greenspan, but the younger lawyer was on holiday and Joe Pomerant agreed with the attorneys who referred the case to his office that the Demeter affair might require immediate handling.

On the face of it there seemed little reason for Peter to think about acquiring legal counsel on the first day following his wife's death. Even assuming Christine *was* the victim of homicide, Peter was clearly twenty-two miles away at the time she was killed. The police, not being aware of this fact, might have questioned him closely for the first few hours, but they had released him the minute they determined through Dr. Brewer and Viveca that he had been hunting for silver lockets and moccasins in their company during the critical time. Peter himself thought that as soon as the police understood this, their whole tone changed and (as he reported to his cousin Steven) they were all handshakes and sympathy from that point on. But there was one additional factor, and when Peter's civil lawyers, Gerry Heifetz and Phil Epstein, became aware of it, they agreed that a criminal lawyer ought to be consulted immediately. The additional factor was this: Peter and Christine had over one million dollars' worth of insurance on each other's lives.

Like many experienced lawyers, Joe Pomerant thought the precaution of legal counsel was justified. Laymen with high-school ideals of justice and naïve assumptions of the law often do not understand how little evidence is needed to charge, and sometimes even to convict, someone of the most serious crimes. The authorities do not, as a matter of law, require a strong case to bring a person to court: if, on the balance of probabilities, there is a chance an accused may have committed a crime, the matter can be brought to trial, and the rest is up to the jury. A jury, of course, could always go either way. Twelve good men and true have often been known to acquit or convict a defendant on nothing much more than their own sympathies. In fact, Pomerant was mindful of a fairly recent Australian decision where a man was convicted of murdering his wife with the Crown offering *no* evidence of his guilt except motive.

When it came to motive, as Joe explained to his client at their first meeting a day after the murder, Peter had three classic Victorian ones: a bad marriage, another woman, and big insurance policies. Innocent people have been hanged for less throughout the history of English common law. If your wife was killed and you had a good reason to kill her, you *could* be convicted of having done so without any proof that you actually did. The fact that such cases were rare would not make you feel any better if yours happened to be one of them. It wouldn't even be incumbent on the prosecution to find the man who actually did the killing: you could be charged with having someone murdered by a person or persons unknown.

Peter seemed somewhat dubious of all this at first, and for that matter so did his cousin Steven. The latter especially doubted if Peter was doing himself any favour by going on the defensive. The thing to do, he told Peter in the course of a long telephone conversation, is to offer a substantial reward and co-operate with the police. No point in letting a bunch of lawyers scare you half to death, then charge the earth for having "rescued" you from the gallows.

Peter hesitated, but not because he had a less jaundiced view of the legal profession than his ex-lawyer cousin. It was the insurance companies, Peter thought, that would be loath to shell out a million dollars without putting up a hell of a fight. Insurance people may have had less authority than the police, but they were smarter. They would find out about the difficulties in his marriage; they'd find out about Marina. She was supposed to be arriving back in Toronto in less than a week's time: even if they cancelled her ticket, the airline computers would still have her record in their memory-banks. The insurance companies would not hesitate to frame him ("sew me in" was the Hungarian expression Peter used) to avoid payment. The one subject Peter happened to know about ever since he was a boy was insurance: after all, it was his own father's business. If there was a suspicion about a beneficiary's role in an insured person's death, the insurer might escape the obligation to pay. Such civil cases did not require as high a degree of proof as criminal trials: a person wouldn't have to be proved guilty beyond a reasonable doubt. If a jury thought it *probable* that he had something to do with his wife's death, it would be enough. Surely, from the insurance companies' point of view, it might be worth a try.

It was for this reason that Peter seemed to believe he had to have lawyers, and this was why his business attorney, Heifetz, called in civil litigation man Epstein, who in turn called Greenspan and got Pomerant. The question in Peter's mind at this point was only whether they were the right team.

There was certainly one thing in their favour: they were Jewish. In Peter's part of the world anti-Semitism came in two varieties: vicious and genteel. Vicious anti-Semitism was the standard, old-fashioned approach, popular chiefly among the petite bourgeoisie and the working classes, and at its worst it was expressed in pogroms, atrocities, or the gas-chambers. The anti-Semitism of more up-to-date people and the upper classes was different. The genteel version was best put by a well-known actor in 1944: "I can hardly wait for the Nazis to drop dead," said he, "so that a gentleman can be an anti-Semite once more." Anti-Semitism as practised by gentlemen often found expression in the belief that Jews were incredibly clever. Moreover, this was supposed to embrace *all* Jews, who were thought to come by their cunning as naturally as blacks by their rhythm. "You're as smart as ten Jews," Steven would say to Peter in the course of their discussion on the phone. There was, of course, a grain of truth in this prejudice (as there is in most prejudices), but it mistook a statistical tendency for an immutable law. Thinking in generalities has a built-in penalty, which at times seems like poetic justice. A genteel anti-Semite might turn to a Jew for his brains even when he has very little.

Whether or not this was true of Peter (he certainly never stated it explicitly), the fact was that many of his important business friends, such as his real estate lawyer or his accountant, had always been Jewish. On a later occasion he would mention, with a certain pride, that his lawyer

1. Christine Demeter (1940-73)

2. Christine, Peter, and Miro, Beelzebub's
   predecessor

3. Peter and Beelzebub

4. Christine and Beelzebub

5. Christine and Beelzebub sharing
   sleeping accommodation

6. As a model, Christine specialized in a look that was already out of date.

7. Christine's major coup as a model—this ad appeared in the Toronto *Telegram* shortly before her marriage to Peter Demeter.

8. Off guard

9. Christine in contrast to her professional image—warm and vulnerable

10. Christine in a more voluptuous pose

11. The Demeters' home at 1437 Dundas Crescent in Mississauga: "the best of all worlds"

12. The living room in which Andrea Demeter was watching television on the night of her mother's death

13. Christine

14. 9:45 P.M., July 18, 1973

was coming to his house from Jewish Forest Hill in his chauffeur-driven limousine, as if to indicate he was in good hands. In the beginning, though, he had some doubts about this "Bogotov" — he couldn't remember Pomerant's name at first and kept making various stabs at it until he settled on Bogotov — because he seemed to treat him like a child. He even asked Steven to voice these doubts to Gerry Heifetz (but under the pretext they were Steven's own doubts) to see if Gerry *really* thought they had made the right choice. Peter wondered if there was something wrong in their chemistry, with this lawyer assuming he was some kind of a retarded boy who could be patted on the head and told to let Uncle Bogotov handle it all. Not bloody likely; Peter rather fancied his own grey matter. Steven cautiously concurred: the trouble, as he saw it, was that both Peter and his lawyer liked talking and disliked listening. But there were more important things at stake than chemistry.

Steven might have thought that the danger of criminal accusations against Peter was over the minute the police realized he was miles away from the scene at the time, but the lawyers knew better. According to Joe Pomerant, what with the million-dollar insurance and the Marina affair, Peter might be put through an ordeal compared to which Kafka's *Trial* would seem like a traffic court hearing. Said Pomerant when Peter handed him his retainer: "You gave me a cheque for $15,000; let me give you $15,000 worth of advice. *Say nothing to anyone*." (One of Peter's old friends murmured something different under his breath when he learned about parsimonious Peter handing over the sizeable cheque without protest: "He's guilty.")

Pomerant's advice might well have been worth fifteen thousand, but in certain respects it had already come too late. Shortly after eleven o'clock that morning, the police had requested Peter to go and officially identify his wife's body at the Mississauga Hospital. Peter was somewhat suspicious of the request, since Detective-Sergeant O'Toole had told him the previous night that a formal identification would probably not be necessary; after all, Peter had identified his wife when he found her in the garage. Peter felt the police were now arranging this as a quasi-confrontation, maybe to see his reaction on being shown Christine's remains. Perhaps it was his determination not to appear emotional in case it might be interpreted as a sign of guilt that led him to identify the naked corpse on the autopsy table with the somewhat callous sentence, "She's very much my wife, Christine."

To make matters worse, when he noticed the name tag on the

pathologist's lab coat — Dr. John Fekete — he recognized a compatriot and addressed him in Hungarian. As the autopsy surgeon was to tell it later, Peter asked if his wife died as a result of an accident or homicide because it would make some difference to the family, which he was sure his fellow-countryman could appreciate. Finally he told the doctor that he had had sexual intercourse with Christine the previous morning but he "had a licence to do that." This sample of Budapest gallows-humour would lose quite a bit in translation when repeated in English to a solemn courtroom eighteen months later.

Meanwhile Superintendent Teggart, whose fondness for metaphors was matched by a nonchalance in employing them, was getting ready to put his tentacles into second gear. Teggart believed a good detective should always look for the unusual and felt that in a husband who behaved like Peter they had found the unusual right at the start. All the same, the routine checks had to be made: a grid search of the area right down to the ravine (no weapon found), and a tracking dog borrowed from the Ontario Provincial Police (which, as Peter said later, was having the time of his life picking up Beelzebub's old scents). Mindful of the fact that most of his men, well-trained and conscientious as they were, had never investigated a murder before, Bill Teggart was resolved to stay on top of everything personally. The truth was the superintendent preferred the pilot's seat to flying a desk anyway. Wanting to be sure of his facts — and also anticipating a possible line of defence — he got top pathologist Dr. Hillsdon-Smith from Toronto to look at the scene and assist the local man at the autopsy. (The superintendent never forgot one of his early cases where an inexperienced pathologist wiped the nitrate stains off a gunshot wound.) There were no such problems in this case: Dr. Hillsdon-Smith agreed with Mississauga's Dr. Fekete that Christine's death resulted from at least seven separate blows to the head, six on one side and one on the other, administered by some kind of blunt instrument. She had also suffered a deep gash on her left thumb, the kind of injury a person might sustain when attempting to ward off a blow. There was no evidence of sexual attack at all, the small, bruise-like discoloration on her legs observed by some detectives on the scene being due to post-mortem causes. Her blackened left eye, in the doctors' opinion, was not caused by a separate blow — such as being punched in the face — but resulted from internal bleeding.

The cause of her injuries being an accidental fall was completely ruled out. The only accident one doctor could recall producing injuries of this kind happened to a person whose head was caught between a loading ramp and a moving truck.

If the autopsy findings seemed to eliminate accident and showed no evidence of a sexual attack, the condition of the house and garage on Dundas Crescent made burglary just as unlikely. There was no sign of forcible entry anywhere, and Peter himself confirmed there were no valuables missing. Bill Teggart was a practical man, not given to the elaborate fantasies of detective fiction. If Christine wasn't the victim of an accident, a burglar, or a rapist, her death was likely to be caused by things closer to home. When, at noon, Detective Barry King reported that Christine had been complaining only a few weeks earlier to over-the-fence neighbour Mrs. Tennant about her husband's infidelity and certain letters she had found, as far as Teggart was concerned "things started to darken for Mr. Demeter." About an hour later he ordered intelligence officer Joe Terdik to place a wiretap on the telephone at 1437 Dundas Crescent. By 7:00 P.M. on July 19, roughly twenty-four hours after Christine finished serving the family's last meal, the electronic surveillance of Peter Demeter had begun.

A tape recording of a telephone tap sounds like a badly tuned radio for the first few seconds, with snippets of music and a debris of voices spilling over from the surrounding telephone wires and airwaves. This is because of the "line automatic" which starts the reels of tape turning as soon as the receiver is picked up on the monitored instrument. No one needs to stand by and listen in: at the end of the day, somewhat like a trapper checking his lines, a detective comes and removes the captured conversations before baiting the trap with a fresh reel of BASF electro-magnetic tape.

Had Christine died a year later, the police would have had to ask for a court order before they could legally eavesdrop on Peter's telephone. Probably no judge would have refused them — after all, they *were* investigating a homicide — but some judges would come to require solid grounds for suspicion before authorizing any invasion of an individual's privacy. In 1973, however, the police still had jurisdiction to act on their own gut-feelings. The only thing they had to be careful about was the Bell Telephone Company. Even though a wiretap authorized by a police chief or his delegate was quite legal, Ma Bell took a dim view of anyone interfering with a subscriber's service. The company's linesmen would often remove the bugs as quickly as the police could put them on. That, too, was quite legal, and when sophisticated crooks suspected their phones might be tapped, they would alert Bell and watch the company and the police engage in a battle of wits. A veteran of such battles, Joe Terdik had learned to make his bugs virtually undetectable. Two men, borrowed from the Royal Canadian Mounted Police and dressed up as telephone repairmen, spliced a direct wire from a box less than a mile from Peter's house to a tape recorder locked in a suitcase and deposited in the residence of a neighbour, who happened to be a policeman on the Mississauga force. From that moment Peter could say nothing on the phone to his friends, relatives, business acquaintances, or lawyers without saying it to Bill Teggart as well.

In a curious way it seemed as though Peter had wanted precisely that. Being under strict orders from Joe Pomerant not to talk about his case with anyone — and no doubt understanding the wisdom of the advice — he nevertheless appeared to be seized by a longing, amounting almost to a compulsion, to talk about practically nothing else. Of course he couldn't be sure that his conversations were being monitored but it was a pretty good guess, and he was warned about it by all his lawyers. In fact Joe Pomerant wouldn't even discuss the case in Peter's car for fear it might be bugged. (It wasn't.) But having come under this unjustified, unaccountable, nightmarish suspicion, Peter seemed to feel his only hope for salvation lay in convincing the police — and specifically Bill Teggart — that they were making a horrible, incomprehensible mistake. Why would they concentrate on him in such a churlish, obtuse manner, and without a shred of evidence too, when there were dozens of far more plausible theories? While they were interviewing *his* friends, searching *his* house, going through *his* business files and bank accounts, the real killer, that Peeping Tom, bum, hitchhiker, madman, was getting farther and farther away. That first night, while O'Toole and the rest were wasting their time questioning him, somebody covered to his eyeballs in Christine's blood had to be walking, driving, bicycling around the streets. By now, of course, even an idiot would have taken a shower and put on a clean shirt. And it wasn't *his* idea to go out that evening at all. Poor Christine had to die because of a little German girl's seven-dollar moccasins. He would like nothing more than to help the police, but his lawyer had forbidden him to talk to them.

Of course as far as Bill Teggart and the rest of the officers were concerned, Peter *was* talking to them, through the medium of Steven Demeter, Leslie Wagner, or other friends and acquaintances. If he was talking, the more he talked the more he managed to fix the idea of his own guilt in the policemen's minds. Every one of his utterances seemed self-serving, every one of his theories an attempt to mislead. His perform-ance reaffirmed Bill Teggart's faith in wiretaps: if a person doesn't sus-pect he's being tapped, you can catch him in the truth, and if he does, you can catch him in a lie. As the superintendent would say later, "Demeter's weakness was his need to convince me of his innocence." And Joe Terdik: "Peter thought we were the Keystone Cops. He thought we'd sit around the table with him and listen to his theories." But if Peter's protestations would have been enough to convict him in the eyes of the police, they knew they needed much more to convict him in a court of law. It would take another twelve hours until, at 11:15 A.M. on Friday, July 20, the police would receive that bit of outside information that provides almost every investigation with its first real break.

Since Rita Jefferies barely knew the Demeters even while she was see-ing Csaba Szilagyi, she would have had no reason to think about them months after she had stopped going out with Csaba altogether. True, the Toronto papers carried the news of Christine's murder quite promi-nently right from the first day, but it's possible that Rita's eyes might have skimmed over the item if it hadn't been for that coincidental meet-ing with Csaba on Yorkville Avenue on the very day of Christine's death. Unexpected meetings have a way of bringing back memories, and Rita remembered something Csaba had said to her at a much ear-lier point in their relationship, while they were having a drink in the fashionable Hyatt Regency Hotel. Rita certainly didn't take it seriously at the time — people say all kinds of things — but in light of what had happened, she thought the police perhaps ought to know about it. Lis-tening to the tall, blonde, earnest girl, Chris O'Toole and Barry King agreed. By 4:35 that afternoon they were talking to Csaba at Mr. Pizza. They had no warrant for his arrest and he could have refused to go with them to the police station, but he didn't. The afternoon rush-hour had just about begun as they started out for Mississauga, and it was hardly over when they had Csaba's signed statement in their hands. It was easy; almost too easy. Bill Teggart decided to take no chances.

If what Csaba Szilagyi was telling them was true, it was confirmation that in suspecting Peter they had been after the right man all along. In spite of the superintendent's faith in his "radar", he must have had flashes of uneasiness during the day and a half that had elapsed since Christine's death. If his sixth sense deceived him and he started his team up the wrong track, it might be too late or too difficult to turn them back and start all over again. Once an investigation gathers momentum it can become as committed to a certain course of action as an airliner to a take-off: half-way down the runway is a hell of a time to find out there's no gas left in the tank. But, if true, Csaba's story could be the fuel to lift their case soaring up in the air. But now Teggart had to be certain. In the evening he took Csaba over to a local Justice of the Peace and had him sign his statement again. This had little legal value, but it might have a psychological impact, and Teggart had known people who'd make up a story for the police but wouldn't lie to someone they took to be a judge. But Csaba signed, and also agreed to take a lie detector test in the morning.

Canadian law takes a properly jaundiced view of the polygraph machine. If an accused fails the test or simply refuses to take it, the prosecution can't offer it as evidence, though if he takes it and passes, it can be evidence for the defence, at least according to one recent Canadian decision. But if Bill Teggart shared one thing with Peter Demeter (other than a habit of saying a lot to tell very little), it was a respect for the ability of the little electric wires to arrive at the truth. Though Bill Teggart would readily admit that a polygraph machine is only as trustworthy as its operator, he felt, perhaps rightly, that a lot can be deduced from a person's willingness to take the test. (Cool, sensible Steven Demeter said to Peter when the latter was agonizing over whether or not he should take a polygraph test with his war-shattered nerves: "If you fail, you get a lawyer, if you pass, you tell the police to go fly a kite." In fact, Peter would eventually refuse even the Crown's generous — and confident — offer to have himself tested by an expert of his own choice, in spite of the prosecution's assurances that they would not use such a test against him if he failed, but would consent to the defence's offering it as evidence to the jury if he passed.) But when Csaba passed *his* lie detector test administered by John Jurens of Transworld Investigators (and later a second test by an expert imported from the United States), Superintendent Teggart was sold.

As a shrewd, experienced policeman, Teggart knew that being sold is one thing, but selling something, first to the Crown and then to a jury, is quite another. Csaba's story sounded fantastic enough not to be credited without corroboration, and there was only one person to corroborate it: Peter. Convinced that Peter would never talk, the superintendent hit upon a different idea.

It was a bold, unorthodox idea, and Bill Teggart discussed it at length with Chief Doug Burrows, sitting by the river in the Chief's country house, surrounded by the lush summer foliage of oak, aspen, and sumach trees, being served lemonade and sandwiches by the Chief's stylish wife, Roberta. The location had great natural beauty, but Doug and Bill chose it for a much more down-to-earth reason: "It was the only place," as Burrows said, "we were sure we weren't bugged." Spending a lifetime in the surveillance of others, both officers had great apprehensions of being surveyed themselves. They wouldn't talk to each other on the telephone, for instance, without using a personal code of some kind. Now, listening to his superintendent's plan, Chief Burrows agreed it was their best and possibly only chance. By 3:00 P.M. on Saturday, July 21, Bill Teggart was briefing intelligence officer Joe Terdik, the man who would execute the operation.

The Skinner and Middlebrook Funeral Home in Mississauga is located close to the intersection of Highways 2 and 10. It is a respectable, standard establishment of the shimmering blue-light-and-soft-music variety that newly arrived Europeans find so quaintly North American. Peter, of course, having spent almost twenty years in Canada by that Sunday evening in July, would have found the vaguely modern, broadloomed, impersonal chapel quite unremarkable. When Csaba walked in at 6:45, Peter was sitting on one of the chairs lined up in the still empty rows facing his wife's casket. For a moment, as in the years when they were all sharing the same home, Peter, Csaba, and Christine were alone.

Then Peter took his old friend outside for a brief chat, just walking up and down in front of the funeral home on Lakeshore Boulevard before the services began. He didn't know that underneath Csaba's appropriately dark suit there was a Motorola transmitter, complete with batteries and a thin aerial extending seventeen inches down along his leg. There was a microphone taped to his left breast, just over his heart, and the transmitter itself, swaddled in bandages, was placed over his pelvis because, according to Joe Terdik, "even police officers don't check a man there." If he had noticed a parked delivery van with the word "Macdonald's" painted on the door, Peter wouldn't have known that inside the dark, airless, narrow space, Hungarian-speaking Detective Terdik and German-speaking Constable Blume had already pressed the start-button on a low-speed UHER tape recorder.

The conversation on the tape (in the stilted English of the eventual Court translators) began this way:

PETER: Now very quickly, as if we were talking about some thing or other. For what reason did they come to you and when?
CSABA: Nothing, they just came.
PETER: You know this is interesting since you arrived there with the two Chinese women at that most unfortunate time. And when was this?
CSABA: What do you mean, unfortunate time?
PETER: Well, look . . .
CSABA: This is a normal reaction, isn't it?

The references here were clear enough: on the evening of the day after Christine's death, Csaba, accompanied by Gigi and her sister, drove out to Peter's house. It was total pandemonium, of course, what with the police still checking the grounds, and Peter, his civil lawyers, and Joe Pomerant having their first conference inside. (Pomerant interviewed his client on the scene instead of in his own office at their initial meeting. Although he might have had good reasons for doing so, it added to the suspicions of the policemen, who were not used to seeing bereaved husbands surrounded by a battery of lawyers.) Now Peter was saying to his friend that the reason the police "came to you" was because Csaba had put in an appearance at that "most unfortunate time". Csaba was countering that this couldn't be the only reason for the police wanting to talk with him since such a visit would be "a normal reaction" from a friend. Continuing, he told Peter the police went to his apartment, seized clothes, bed-linen, papers, and bills from him, and had already been asking him about some of the real estate deals he had with Peter. True, he had been working on the night of the murder, but he had had to go out to make a few deliveries, possibly around the same time that Christine was killed, and might not be able to account for every minute.

Peter didn't seem much concerned with this; it could be checked out. Nor was he too upset when Csaba said the police were asking him if Peter had ever come to Csaba to ask "whether you couldn't kill Christine". That, said Peter reassuringly, was just a routine question they'd ask from everybody. But then Csaba said something that elicited a different reaction:

CSABA: Why do they want me to take a whatchamacallit, a lie detector test? And what the hell should I say there?
PETER: (stammering) Csaba, for God's sake, refuse it, for that, that

they have to charge you with something. First of all let's hire a lawyer, a very good lawyer.

CSABA: But I haven't got any money for that.

PETER: But I have plenty. Csaba, just take it easy. I don't take a lie detector test because I work here, I was not away from here for more than an hour, it is not even sure that it was at the same time, I cannot drive that fast out there and back.

There was Peter, obviously sharing Superintendent Teggart's faith in the marvels of modern technology. Of course, there could have been any number of things having nothing to do with Christine's death that Peter would not wish Csaba to divulge to the miraculous machine. There were deeds, contracts of all kinds, even things that might relate to that arch secret of so many businessmen, income tax. But Csaba pursued the point, his voice as well as Peter's occasionally obscured on the tape by the roar of passing trucks:

CSABA: Listen, old chap, it is their logic that if I wanted to be absolutely clean in the future too, then it is such, that they say if I have nothing to hide then . . .

PETER: (inaudible) ———— your whatchamacallit, your nervous system, to go through such a war with them when you know very well that you are the only one, who . . . knows . . .

CSABA: Yes.

PETER: Now then, you, you know that you are perfectly innocent. Don't you?

CSABA: Well, yes, I know.

PETER: But now then consequently . . .

CSABA: You know it too.

PETER: I am the one who knows best. And you know even better how innocent you are, don't you? Consequently please don't get excited about it.

The line "you are the only one, who . . . knows . . . " certainly sounded ominous. But Peter and Csaba were talking in Hungarian, and while words and phrases are easy enough to translate from one language to another, inflections that may change the meaning of a sentence are not. "You are the only one, who . . . knows . . . " *could* be translated, using exactly the same Hungarian words but giving a different interpretation to the stress on the last one, as "you are the only one, who . . .

you know." The difference between a guilty or an innocent reading would be even more pronounced in an exchange a few minutes later, when Csaba pretended to wonder why the police would take certain items of clothing from him:

CSABA: Not watchamacallits, not undergarments but blue jeans and things and the like.
PETER: On what it would be, don't you understand? He who left the scene left it of course covered in blood from head to toe because she was hit on the head seven times. I don't know who this is.
CSABA: You don't know yourself.
PETER: Csaba, the hell I don't know. But it was done in such, so, such a terribly primitive and barbarian way that ———

A heavy truck on Lakeshore Boulevard swallowed up the rest of the sentence, but what was clearly audible seemed very damning to Peter. But again, the incriminating line "Csaba, the hell I don't know" *could* have meant the exact opposite just by assigning a different value to the inflection: "Csaba, hell! I don't know." On the other hand, there were no possible problems of inflection in the next bit where Peter advised Csaba to get in touch through "Pista" (Steven Demeter's nickname) in case there were any further complications.

CSABA: Pista is out of the game?
PETER: Yes.
CSABA: How . . . ?
PETER: Pardon?
CSABA: How . . . ?
PETER: Because there is no third person involved.
CSABA: How could it be that there is no third person involved?
PETER: He doesn't exist, ah . . .
CSABA: But you told me that . . .
PETER: I don't know him.
CSABA: You don't know him.
PETER: That is, he doesn't exist, because he is not here.
CSABA: Well how in hell . . . ?
PETER: Yes, this ——— (inaudible) there is no such person.

The conversation meandered on for some minutes, then ended as the first group of mourners arrived at the funeral home. There were a few more dubious lines on the tape (such as Peter's advice to Csaba: "Let's try and always stay with the truth with the exception of the vital point"), but in the end all Peter's statements amounted to the same thing: quite suspicious, not quite conclusive. They certainly seemed to be the words of a person who had *something* to hide, but they contained no admission of a murder plot and supported only obliquely, if at all, Csaba's statement to the police. However, Superintendent Teggart was satisfied. Where there's smoke, and so forth. The fox was in the bush all right, even if it might take a few more stones to make it fly straight up.

On Monday Christine was buried in her elegant dark Tyrolean suit over an immaculate white blouse. It was a brief ceremony, with Christine's chiropractor, Dr. David Drum, giving the eulogy. Two days later, on Wednesday, July 25, Csaba was driven to 1437 Dundas Crescent by a policeman disguised as a taxi driver. It was after 2:00 A.M. and Csaba pretended to have been interrogated by the police at the Mississauga station since five o'clock in the afternoon. A lot of people have their defences down late at night, but Peter seemed alert. Although their conversation lasted long enough for the batteries to go flat on the police tape recorder, his statements were no more conclusive than before. He kept repeating that Teggart and his men had no evidence of any kind, and their only hope was in finding a person who could be pressured, tricked, or scared into saying that Peter had discussed "such things" with him. Said Peter: "Yes, in short old chap, the whole war of nerves is aimed at, that you tire of it and remember that, that possibly I had such a topic." He reiterated that Csaba should not take a lie detector test, gave him reasons he could give the police for refusing, and begged him to let him know the minute they tried to squeeze him into a corner. What Peter did *not* say was that he had been planning, plotting, or setting up any murder.

Perhaps the most damaging thing Peter did say came when Csaba asked him if "that person" — meaning the murderer — knew him because, as Csaba said, "I'm terribly frightened of that."

"Whether that person knows you?" replied Peter. "Well, in short, Csaba . . . if that person doesn't know me — and just for once believe me, old chap, and remember that one and a half, more, in short one and seventh tenth of a decade that we know each other — if that person doesn't know me and doesn't even speak our language, and there is no, we don't even have contact; I couldn't, even if my life depended on it, pick that person out of two or a hundred . . . "

"That means that person doesn't speak Hungarian," interjected Csaba.

"Uh . . . then, then how could this person possibly know you? This, in short, you see, with this . . . "

"Peter, I don't know out of what circle you chose this person, you cannot find one in a newspaper ad."

At this Peter changed his tone.

"I didn't choose . . . Oh, now, now you see, see the thing, how skilfully they are trying to watchamacallit you? . . . "

If Peter's suspicions about *who* was being "watchamacalled" were slightly off the target, little Beelzebub's weren't. The cocker spaniel smelled the body-pack under Csaba's clothes and kept sniffing and jumping on him in friendly excitement. Peter noticed this, and asked Csaba if the police had "put something on your clothes". Csaba replied with a casual aplomb that seasoned informers might have envied: "No, I had them on all the time." It seemed as if after many years he had finally found the one profession for which he had a real aptitude.

But Bill Teggart decided it was time to relax the tension for a little while if he didn't want his fish to break the line. After all, the hook seemed firmly set; there was no point in taking chances by trying to reel it in too fast. There would be no body-pack conversations with Csaba until Peter was played out a little more. A gentle, even pressure would do the trick, and it seemed to the superintendent he might have the help of two personalities in this strategy: Peter's own, and that of his lawyer.

Joseph Pomerant had all the trappings of a big, establishment attorney. His fortieth-floor suite of broadloomed offices was filled with junior partners, articling students, and bustling secretaries. Whether or not he had won more cases than any other good criminal lawyer, whether or not his fees were ever unusually high, he had the *aura* of being very successful and expensive. He even had the vaguely impatient, distracted manner of an immensely shrewd and experienced person who is five jumps ahead of everybody at all times. Listening to people seemed to him an unwelcome chore: Steven Demeter remarked, after one of their early meetings, that Joe developed a nervous tic, with sweat pouring down his face, if anybody else held the floor for more than a minute.

For some reason the word "sweat" was also used by others when talking about Joe Pomerant: one Toronto attorney, who liked and respected him, described Joe as a man who could change shirts five times a day and still create the impression of sweating. Even a girl who dated him once or twice in college remembered him as the young man who didn't actually have clammy hands but who somehow looked as though he would. This was clearly less a physical quality — Pomerant was always immaculately groomed and wore understated suits of excellent cut — than a feeling of a man pushing too hard. Although Joe's office had just the right touch of casualness, there seemed to be a hint of effort behind the effect that reminded people of a movie set. His armchair was set not behind a desk, but next to a telephone with banks of flashing lights, on one side of a low coffee table facing a slub-textured ivory tuxedo couch. This was not in the least wrong, only *too* right in some undefinable way. Never ungracious, Pomerant still had the preoccupied, somewhat aimless intensity of an actor playing a part in which he didn't feel fully comfortable, needing the props of success to convince himself of the reality of his role. It was interesting that he would be called arrogant, self-confident, and aggressive mainly by people who didn't know him very well.

Because not far underneath that surface there seemed a much more vulnerable and hesitant person, a man who, far from being able to enjoy his success, was made uncomfortable by it. Joe's highly literate parents would have placed less value on rich lawyers and businessmen than on writers and thinkers. In the home from which he came, as in many traditional Jewish families, lines of wisdom in a book would command more respect than figures in a bank account, and a man of action would count for less than a man of reflection. Of course, besides a reverence for the things of the spirit, boys from such backgrounds might also learn about the bitterness of unrealized dreams. This would often induce them to go after worldly success, but almost never with an easy conscience. Joe himself, at times, would prefer to talk about art, literature, philosophy, and social justice rather than his law practice or money. In the middle of a conversation he might even lapse into a long, introspective silence, as though he were reviewing the values and priorities of his whole existence. Even his initial choice of criminal law was unusual for someone eager to make it in conventional terms, for glamorous as criminal work may be, it doesn't offer the steady, reliable income of a commercial or matrimonial practice. Except for the few at the top, crime doesn't really pay on either side of the dock. When Joe opened his office in 1959, there wasn't even legal aid to pick up the tab, and only a dozen or so counsels devoted their entire practice to criminal law in Toronto.

Not only that, but in his first year Joe took on the nearly hopeless case of a man named Fisher, dubbed the "Moon Killer" by the local papers because his frenzied, mutilating attacks always took place at night under a full moon. No lawyer whose main object in life was money would ever seek out cases like that, though one with an eye on the headlines might. So might one who believed that even the most atrocious criminal caught dead to rights deserved a spirited defence. Whatever Joe's reasons, he put up a good fight that took him from a split decision before the Ontario Court of Appeal all the way to the Supreme Court of Canada. In the end he did lose his client to the hangman, but losing a bleak case after a hard fight is no disgrace in professional terms, and after the Moon Killer, Joe won *all* his murder cases right up to Demeter. In any event, Joe would say, a spotless record of acquittal isn't a real indicator of ability in a lawyer. When it comes to murder, it's more a question of choosing your cases wisely. If so, Joe's own spotless record between Fisher and Demeter might have reflected a development of that wisdom which never deserted him from 1960 until that phone call on July 19, 1973.

A lawyer is under no obligation to crusade for his client's innocence. His task is to win an acquittal or prevent a charge from being laid, but not necessarily to vindicate a suspect or defendant in the eyes of the world. The presumption of innocence the law automatically extends to each person accused of a crime frees his attorney from any such burden, at least in theory. He can't tamper with the evidence, of course, but he doesn't particularly have to co-operate with the police. He doesn't have to prove his own good faith or his client's. He can say, in effect: *If you have some proof, lay a charge, and we'll answer you in court. If you have no proof, leave us alone.*

But the other side of Joe Pomerant's personality, the side that had nothing to do with high fees, elegant offices, big Forest Hill homes, or other stamps of worldly success, militated against the cold meticulousness of this approach. As far as Joe could see, here was an ordinary businessman who came home to find his wife brutally murdered, then through a combination of circumstances found himself under the nightmarish suspicion of having arranged her death. Joe may not have been under an obligation to address himself to the question of Peter's innocence in his own mind — it's simply not a defence lawyer's job — but there was every indication that he believed in it. He saw an injustice perpetrated before his very eyes. An immigrant who had pulled himself up by his bootstraps (much like Joe himself), and in the process might have cut a few corners (who didn't?), and had the additional misfortune of a bad marriage (whose marriage was perfect?), was now being run over by the Establishment's impersonal wheels.

Joe may have been *in* the Establishment himself, but was certainly not *of* it. His was the perspective of a boy growing up in the pressure cooker of Toronto's Spadina district. His Yiddish poet-father had married his schoolteacher-mother back in Poland, but he had to pretend he was single to be admitted to Canada. A year later Joe's mother was also admitted as a single woman, and eventually they got married again in Quebec City. From this perspective, everybody coming into conflict with the Law of the Gentiles was an underdog. For such outsiders, owning ritzy houses with swimming pools and big cars would just be an added handicap, engendering not only the normal distrust but the envy of the WASP majority. Real life wasn't like a government pamphlet showing glossy pictures of happy ethnics in some multicultural paradise. Real life was prejudices and injustice, enough to put away a good man for life unless other good men stood up to be counted. Real life, as often as not, was a bungling small-town police force unable to solve a murder, then pinning it, under community pressure, on the first likely suspect.

Joe Pomerant may have had a strong drive to do well for himself, but his Yiddish intellectual parents had also passed on to him the peculiarly Jewish tradition of wanting to do well for the world. It's possible that the passionate, intense, socially conscious side of Joe's personality perceived the Demeter case, at least in the beginning, as something of a cause, an opportunity to transcend the lucrative but spiritually empty existence of a hired mouth and speak with the voice of justice. Beyond mere money, beyond simply doing one's job as a defence lawyer, here was a case that might offer the once-in-a-lifetime opportunity of raising seminal questions about an individual helplessly carried by the currents of suspicion into the steel nets of the State. Such a drama, spotlighted by the centre-stage attention of the whole community, would be worthy of the talents of a Clarence Darrow or an F. Lee Bailey.

Consequently Joe did not say to Teggart: *Look, I'm busy, do your investigation and stop bothering me and my client.* Instead, he kept in touch, "communicated", maintained a co-operative, high-profile attitude. True, he had some good reasons for doing so. First, there was Peter himself, chafing under Joe's "no talk" orders, pressuring his lawyer to "help" the police by all kinds of ideas, some quite plausible and some very far-fetched, such as certain half-naked photographs of Christine he found in a closet, or suspicions about Christine's chronic lack of funds in spite of the good allowance he had always given her. There was also a telephone call Peter said he received from someone with a "heavy immigrant's accent", saying only, *"Your daughter is next!"* As a result of this call, Peter wanted to withdraw the $10,000 reward Joe had persuaded him to put up earlier the same day. Joe had no way of knowing, of course, that this threatening call, which his tearful client told him about late at night, was *never recorded* on the police tapes. Nor could he be certain that the photographs of Christine in the nude that Peter "found" in a closet had been around for a long time, and that in the opinion of the police Peter had even taken some of them himself. All Joe saw was a difficult, jumpy, indignant client, who trusted neither the ability nor the good faith of the authorities to *really* investigate his wife's death, and unless Joe carried his messages to the police he'd take the bit between the teeth and start talking to Teggart on his own. To Joe it seemed the lesser of two evils to maintain a liaison with Bill Teggart himself.

Pomerant's other reason was that an acquittal, though obviously desirable, would only be second best to no charges being laid against his client in the first place. Like many a good lawyer, Joe had won more cases by keeping them out of court altogether than by triumphing in front of a jury. Joe was a good negotiator — Bill Teggart called him a real "people person" — and believing (as he seemed to) in Peter's innocence, he might well have considered it his duty to convince the police they had simply no case against him. This would have been a highly ethical and unselfish approach on Joe's part, since there's clearly more glory — not to mention more money — in a courtroom victory than in a negotiated truce. Nevertheless, the net result of Joe's strategy was that it enabled Teggart to maintain his gentle pressure on Peter.

Unlike Joe, Teggart *knew* certain things at this point. To begin with, he had in his hands the statements of Rita Jefferies and Csaba Szilagyi. He had Peter's own suspicious words to Csaba on tape. When Pomerant brought him Peter's stories about nude photographs and threatening phone calls, which Teggart had reason to believe were false, he had to assume an attempt to mislead the investigation. Naturally he was all for maintaining a friendly, informal contact with Peter and his lawyer: let them make up new stories, let them bring him new leads, all of which he could eventually use as evidence. But most important, he could employ Joe to spook Peter. He could feed back through this slick, smart lawyer (who Teggart was convinced thought of him as a thick-headed small-time, small-town cop) certain information that might keep Peter on edge, and eventually make him jump right into the superintendent's waiting tentacles. If they wanted to con him, well, conning was a game at which two could play. "Joe," said Teggart later, "was dancing along very nicely and doing his job."

From Teggart's point of view they both were dancing along, Peter and his high-priced lawyer. One example was Peter's conveying to the superintendent what he said was Joe's request to put a tape recorder on his own telephone. This enabled Teggart to say that he, personally, didn't believe in recording devices and that his chief was utterly opposed to them, but if Peter gave him written permission to install it, he would let him have one. This might well have suggested to Peter that the police were *not* tapping his phone after all. Or the time Teggart was poking around the scene (which he did once in a while, even taking Chief Burrows along with him on one occasion, not in the hope of finding some new evidence, but just to "psyche" Peter out a little more) and Peter couldn't resist in engaging him in conversation:

"If you were to question me, Superintendent, " he said, "what would you most like to question me about?"

"Your lawyer asked me not to question you, Peter," said Teggart, looking at the raw, pink rashes the other man seemed to have developed around his neck in the last few days. Peter smiled enigmatically.

"I have my friends."

This was quite true, and by that time Detectives O'Toole, King, and Wingate had talked to most of them. Teggart remarked that some weren't very friendly to Peter.

"I don't care about my so-called friends," said Peter. "We have an expression in Hungarian: you have to separate the shit from the kidney."

This kind of talk was right down Bill Teggart's alley. "You mean the wheat from the chaff, Peter," he said, "that's what we call it in Canada. Well, don't worry, this case is solvable. We will solve it."

It was a hot day and Peter invited the superintendent into the house. Teggart accepted a cold drink, and sat for a while on the velvet chesterfield looking at the photographs in the family album Peter opened out on the glass coffee table. He kept talking about Christine and her family, often using the adjective "poor" when referring to his late wife. Pointing out a snapshot of Christine at the age of three, he said: "This makes me hope Andrea will be as beautiful one day as poor Christine."

"She's beautiful now," Teggart replied.

"Come now, Superintendent," said Peter, which Bill Teggart regarded as a "goof". The inviolability of one's own children's perfection is axiomatic for a North American, and a caustic Hungarian could breach it only at his own peril. Then Peter said:

"How do you know when a man is guilty, Superintendent?"

"If I didn't know you, Peter," Teggart replied, "I'd say one of the things would be your saying 'Poor Christine' all the time."

All these things were not evidence, of course, but they served to confirm Teggart's suspicions and, more important, to keep Peter on his toes. It was an entirely different question whether the police were not misreading certain signals — to call any deceased person "poor" would be a common expression in Hungarian, and Peter's English, though fluent, was far from idiomatic — and pressure could be a self-fulfilling prophecy, causing people to say or do foolish things in the mistaken belief that it might clear them of suspicion. But there's little doubt that by this time the authorities were committed. It was no longer a question of *whether* Peter was the guilty man, but how to make it stick in court. It was only human that it should involve the egos of the police officers as it later would the egos of the lawyers for the Crown. While talking with Peter, or drinking coffee with him by the swimming pool, Bill Teggart was mentally measuring him for the handcuffs. "He looked so distinguished," Teggart would say later. "I knew it would be the most important arrest in my life because he looked so distinguished."

(The curious thing was that during this period, while the police were waiting with bated breath for Peter to give the game away, he did say two things of considerable significance, both of which were missed at the time and never became part of the evidence for or against him. The first thing was something he said to a certain Constable Shaw, who was doing guard duty in front of the house on Dundas Crescent. It was a casual remark about how the police ought to have *blocked off the Burlington Skyway* right after the murder because an escaping killer could easily have dropped the murder weapon off that bridge into Lake Ontario. The second remark was made in a long, rambling telephone call to Pomerant's partner, Eddie Greenspan, and it concerned a nest-egg of a few thousand dollars Christine got from the sale of the old Mercedes and used to keep *inside a roll of architect's plans* rather than the bank. Whether or not either of these remarks could have altered the outcome or duration of the trial, they might have made some difference had anyone realized their significance at the time or remembered them later.)

On July 27 Joe Pomerant called Bill Teggart on the telephone, and the superintendent decided the time was ripe for a little more spooking. (Teggart often taped his conversations with Pomerant, which was not considered cricket even in police circles. When Joe learned about it later he wouldn't talk to Bill for days, but as far as Teggart was concerned, "this was a murder investigation, not a Jewish social club.") In any case, they agreed that Peter would go to Teggart's office the following day, in Joe's company of course, to assist the police by giving them his detailed recollections about the events of the week preceding Christine's death. Joe's only condition was that his client wouldn't be interrogated and treated as a murder suspect. At this point Teggart said:

"There'll be no questions like 'Did you kill your wife?', because we know he did. . . . "

After a long pause Joe replied with a faint, rasping catch in his voice, something between a chuckle and a gurgle of despair.

"Because — we know — he did —"

"We don't ask questions we know the answers for," said Teggart.

Pomerant was evidently not sure whether to treat this seriously or as an example of the Mississauga police's sense of humour. Having made the appointment for 3:00 P.M. the next day, Teggart opened the subject again:

"I think at this point we'd be out of order to put any questions like 'Did you have anything to do with this?' "

"I don't mind the single question put, 'Did you authorize anyone to kill your wife?' " said Joe, trying to sound reasonable.

"I think if we get to that, I'll put the question," replied Teggart, with a hardly disguised purr of satisfaction in his voice. Later he would comment: "Joe's trouble was he wanted to sell me his client as a good guy. He should have told me to go to hell. Eddie Greenspan would have."

Whether or not the superintendent was right in this, Eddie Greenspan's involvement in the case was still marginal at this point. Joe's younger partner did not really enter into the picture until early in August after Joe himself left for his summer holidays. He was going to Israel and, as Greenspan would recollect it later, he didn't expect anything momentous to happen while he was away. It seemed as though Joe felt the police had no real evidence against Peter, and considered Teggart's ominous remarks on the telephone as nothing more than a bluff.

With Joe Pomerant temporarily out of the way, Peter seemed to behave somewhat like a puppy who'd been let off the leash. Joe left on August 8, planning to be back on August 29. By August 10 Peter was on the telephone to the police, reporting to Inspector Rowland that the tape recorder he got from them wasn't working, and asking if they had a Hungarian interpreter on the force. Later that day Teggart would amble over to Dundas Crescent, "fix" the little Philips cassette recorder attached to Peter's phone by plugging it back into the wall, then irritate his quarry by chatting pleasantly about every subject under the sun except the murder. (During this phase of the investigation many of the higher-ranking officers were reading or re-reading Dostoevsky's *Crime and Punishment*, with Teggart and O'Toole quoting to each other some of the exchanges between the axe-murderer Raskolnikoff and the police inspector.) Then, on the afternoon of August 14, Peter appeared in the superintendent's office. His story, according to Teggart's recollection, was that he had new information about his wife running around with a soccer player.

"Superintendent, when can we talk man to man," said Peter, "so I can help you with this investigation?"

"I would just love that, Peter," Teggart replied, "but your lawyer hasn't permitted it."

"When will I be cleared as a suspect?" asked Peter.

It was at this point that an idea came to Teggart. Maybe the fish was tiring; maybe it was time to start pulling in the line. In any case, a little spooking couldn't hurt.

"I'm very concerned, Peter," he said, "about the private detective your wife hired to investigate you up to her death. I am very concerned."

"When did she stop investigating me? Was it a month, two weeks?"

"Peter, I can't tell you that," said Teggart slowly, "but we must talk about it soon."

When Peter and Csaba Szilagyi had their next conversation two days later, Teggart struck pure gold-dust.

With an induction coil fastened to a public phone at one end and attached to a tape recorder at the other, Csaba called Peter, who was having dinner at his friend Daniel Meder's place. It was obvious that Peter couldn't talk in front of the other dinner guests, so Csaba suggested he call him back later. In half an hour the pay phone rang on the corner of Yonge Street and Pears Avenue.

CSABA: Hullo.

PETER: It's me.

CSABA: Hi, old chap.

PETER: Old chap, don't you think that because we talked so much about this number in Hungarian they have since checked it out very thoroughly, or is it that they can't keep the Meders so much under surveillance?

CSABA: I wouldn't think so. . . .

PETER: And don't you think they are watching where you are going or something?

CSABA: Look, Peter, I drove around for at least half an hour and I know when I'm being followed.

PETER: Then tell me, why did they take you in today?

Csaba's story to Peter was that he had been brought to the police station for another round of questioning earlier in the day, and had been warned to watch what he was saying because all his meetings with Peter before Christine's death *had been observed by a private detective*. This, naturally, coincided with the remark Teggart let drop to Peter two days before. This bit of news apparently disturbed Peter very much (as the superintendent had hoped it might), and he had even worked it out in his own mind that the private eye in question had to be Leo Ross, the male half of the couple with whom they holidayed in Acapulco.

PETER: No, no, no, I want you to know that a . . . a huge hairy Jew by the name of Leo Ross . . .

CSABA: Yes.

PETER: . . . he very much made friends with, fell in love with my wife, exactly like in the film "Heart Break Kid", I want you to know . . .

CSABA: Yes.

PETER: . . . I'm just telling you the story . . . she spent all her seven days in Acapulco in the hotelroom . . .

CSABA: Yes.

PETER: And, and the man sat there beside my wife, and just like Henri, adored her and hated me.

Peter had evidently still not forgotten Henri Galle, one of his prime suspects in the case of Andrea's paternity. The next ten minutes of the conversation were spent with Peter trying to reconstruct the exact period Ross was supposed to have had him under surveillance. This, as he told Csaba, was terribly important. It obviously had to be somewhere between March and the middle of July, but when? It couldn't have been the *whole* period because that would cost too much; Christine didn't have that kind of money. With mounting excitement, Peter concluded it had to be prior to the time of Marina's visit in June, about which Christine knew anyway.

> PETER: Now then, I want you to know, because this, I mean, I'm very sorry old chap, sometime in the future if I can't show my gratitude, then I'll show it now, but . . . uh . . . uh . . . for these things, but do you know how terribly important this is to me, because the guy for a short time, I mean Christine had me watched for a short time until she found out that I have no girlfriend here in Toronto.
>
> CSABA: Yes.
>
> PETER: And now I know when this was and not in the vital last days . . .
>
> CSABA: Yes.
>
> PETER: . . . but in the completely neutral first days.

Then, a minute or two later, he returned to the subject with great elation, though without losing the aristocratic stammer he cultivated in Hungarian.

> PETER: . . . Csaba, you don't know what a dreadful thing fell off my uh . . . uh . . . watchamacallit . . .
>
> CSABA: And how do you know, Peter, that they haven't watched you in the last days?

At this Peter started to chortle.

> PETER: Because I am at large and free. Such a . . . a . . .
>
> CSABA: And what if they are only waiting for you to make a mistake? Or some sign . . .
>
> PETER: No, I don't, I don't . . .

In fact, he just had. The irony of the whole situation was that the private-eye story had been entirely Teggart's invention; Leo Ross never had Peter under surveillance for a minute. But now the superintendent felt they had enough evidence, and informed Assistant Crown Attorney Leo McGuigan that he wished to make the arrest. Teggart was flirting with the idea of doing it at midnight, as soon as Peter returned home, but McGuigan demurred: holding a prisoner incommunicado overnight might not look very good in court. Gold-slippered Bill Teggart didn't quite see it like that (there was one very dead lady, after all), but he agreed to play it the Crown's way. All the same, that night was a little like the night before Christmas for him and Detective-Sergeant Chris O'Toole. At seven o'clock the next morning they knocked on the front door of 1437 Dundas Crescent. The date was August 17. A month less a day had passed since Christine's death.

Peter came to the front door in his brown pajamas, carrying Beelzebub under his arm. He asked the two policemen to step inside. Teggart, who wanted the biggest arrest of his career to go perfectly, had written his lines out on a clipboard which he carried in his hand.

"Peter Demeter," he said, "you are under arrest on a charge of non-capital murder in connection with the death of your wife Christine on July 18, 1973. You are not required to say anything unless you wish to do so, but whatever you say will be taken down in writing and may be given in evidence."

"I have been expecting you, gentlemen," said Peter. "Can I phone my lawyer?"

"Yes, back at the police station."

"Can I get my clothes?"

"Yes."

Very quietly, Peter put on a dark business suit. O'Toole searched his pockets and took away a comb and a nail file. Watching him dress, Teggart noted that his thighs were quite thick but his upper arms seemed soft and flabby. The superintendent would have expected him to look different, somehow.

8. Death on the Campus

Slightly less than a month after Peter Demeter was arrested, a short, rusty-haired girl walked across the Erindale campus of the University of Toronto. Of all the university's scattered campuses, Erindale was by far the prettiest, set in a pleasantly landscaped area of Mississauga. The location, though, had its disadvantages. The affluent Mississauga residents were not inclined to let rooms to students, and low-rent apartments and rooming houses were few and far between.

Nineteen-year-old pharmacy student Constance Anne Dickey was not discouraged. She had come from Prescott, Ontario, a small town some forty-five miles away, and the excitement of being away from home at university made the crisp September day sparkle with newness and anticipation. She was scouring the local newspapers, had her name down at the student housing bureau, and for the time being could put up with a room at her brother-in-law's place in Toronto. Something, she was sure, would turn up.

Something did. Just a few days after she had enrolled, a friend called with fabulous news about a vacancy in a rooming house not ten minutes away from the campus. By Tuesday, September 11, Constance Dickey was all set to move into her own place. It would be her first real grown-up lodging and although it wasn't exactly an apartment, it was still a room to which only she would have the key. But before moving she wanted to open a new bank account and then get over to the campus to quickly check up on class schedules and plan her timetable.

It was late afternoon when her brother-in-law began to wonder. Constance had planned to make the move that day and was to telephone about the arrangements. Soon her parents were concerned, too. Their daughter was not like some of their friends' children. Constance could always be relied upon to keep her word, and she had promised to telephone them that evening and let them know how the new room was working out. Three days later, with no trace of the missing co-ed, Mississauga police filed a missing-persons report.

The search began immediately. On the following Friday, September 14, Detectives Dan Banting and Craig Malcolm, who had been temporarily taken off the Demeter case, began methodically working their way through the wooded section of the Erindale campus about three hundred yards south of the main college building. Under some bushes the two detectives found the nude body of Constance Anne. Her head was slumped forward, partially concealing the crude discolouration that indicated she had been strangled. Later they discovered that she had also been raped.

Anyone looking southeast from the spot where Dickey's body was found would see the back door leading to the Demeter garage about three-quarters of a mile away on the other side of the ravine.

9. The Improper Left Turn

Metropolitan Toronto and the small communities that ring it are known in North America for a tranquillity that is the envy of many an urban police force. Toronto citizens, for example, who number just over two and a half million, were outraged to discover that in 1972 their city had 41 murders. This figure seemed only slightly short of paradisaical to their beleaguered fellow urbanites in cities of comparable size, such as Detroit, faced with 615 murders, Philadelphia with 413, or even Canada's own Montreal with a total of 92 homicides for the same year. The homicide shortage may account for the attention each one receives. Just about any murder rates a few lines in one of Toronto's major dailies, even if it is only another dreary domestic quarrel with an outcome that might as easily have been a few smashed dishes but turned into a broken neck. And most of the time that's what Toronto homicides are — family quarrels that go too far and end up as manslaughter verdicts once the defence lawyers are through telling the jury about the misdeeds of the dead spouse. But in the summer and fall of 1973 there were a number of spectacular exceptions to this. First of all there was the death of Christine Demeter, and then the strangling of Constance Dickey. Just a few weeks after that came the disappearance of a pretty Mississauga Grade 13 honour student called Neda Novak. Then on August 29, 1973, five weeks after Christine's death, a police shoot-out took place that could have come straight from the streets of any one of America's steaming ghettos.

It began in an area of Toronto informally known as little Hungary, a short strip along Bloor Street west from Spadina. The whole area is no more than half a dozen blocks of poolhalls, gaudy working-class nightclubs, and a number of modest restaurants serving a variety of goulashes and much frequented by students, who know the food is cheap and filling. August 29 was a sweltering day. The traffic on Bathurst Street was moving sluggishly around the lumbering old streetcars that still run that route, and the delivery trucks that had pulled over for temporary stops. Bathurst and Bloor is a main intersection of little Hungary, and the area is patrolled by cars from number 14 division of the Metropolitan Toronto Police. It was just after lunch, about 1:15 P.M., when the patrol car spotted a brown Chevrolet making a prohibited left turn off Bathurst Street onto Harbord. Illegal left turns were about the last thing the clogged street needed, and the patrol car made a quick left-hand turn of its own to pull the errant Chevy over to the side of the road. Amazingly, the car took off, veering wildly along Harbord and squealing up a one-way street the wrong way.

Very sensibly the men in the patrol car decided that this was more than a bad driver — or indeed anything they cared to handle alone — and radioed for help. But the speeding car had already attracted the attention of another police cruiser. Hemmed in by the two cars, the driver of the Chevy jumped out and began running on foot past rows of working-class homes, past children playing under hoses in the heat, across the heavy traffic on Bloor Street, and down Manning Avenue. Behind him came a posse of plainclothesmen and officers, stumbling and sweating in the early afternoon sun. Now the man was fumbling at the waistband of his pants, where he had a large trucker's wallet on his belt. Inside was a holster, and as he ran he managed to pull out a .38-calibre gun. The nearest policeman was still some forty feet behind him when the man fired the first shot. The policman dropped to the sidewalk, not hit, but unwilling to tempt fate the second time. The others took cover, one behind a car, another behind one of the sturdy old trees that lined the street. The man tried running again but he tripped, fell, and from a sitting position pointed his gun straight at the policeman still lying on the pavement. From behind a parked car another constable took aim. Although his target was about forty-five feet away, the bullet entered the bridge of the man's nose, and as it ripped through his skull his finger jerked the trigger of the .38 again, sending the last bullet ricocheting off a tree. On the verandah directly opposite, a youth, stripped to the waist, sat in a rocking-chair drinking beer and idly watching the shoot-out. It seemed like television to him.

It was easy enough to see that the man was dead but more difficult to know who the dead man was. The plastic folder in his pocket had a driver's licence that identified him as Peter Voosen of Gulliver Road, but that was a stolen I.D. of course. He had been living in a basement on Shaw Street under the name of John Solke, which didn't turn up a thing when the police ran it through their files. Finally, around four o'clock in the afternoon the computers responded to the dead man's fingerprints and the police discovered they finally had Laszlo Eper just where they wanted him — in their morgue.

The feeling was mutual. Since about the age of nineteen, Laszlo Eper had thought — and talked — about little else than killing policemen. He was born in Veszprem, Hungary, just one year before the Second World War broke out, and when eighteen years later the refugees streamed out of Hungary, Laszlo Eper was among them. He landed in Western Canada in April 1957 and was offered employment as a mechanic in Dawson Creek, British Columbia. This was a step up for Eper, who by trade was only a bricklayer's assistant. But perhaps the promotion had come too quickly or Dawson Creek was not quite what he had in mind, because Eper refused the job and settled for Motor Theft instead. By June of that year he was in Lethbridge Jail. He never looked back. From petty theft to possession of stolen goods and repeated charges of breaking and entering, he worked his way through Canada's correctional system. Thanks to a series of suspended sentences, fines, or short jail terms, Eper soon managed to rack up three or four separate arrests and convictions a year. In between prison terms he would hit the streets for a week or two, just long enought to pull a few jobs before being caught again. His first penitentiary stint was completed on April Fools' day, 1964. By April 9 he was back in on new charges. Finally in 1967 he hit the big time. While on parole, he was convicted of the attempted murder of a Hamilton, Ontario, policeman and was sentenced to life. But after six years he was getting restless. Being a senior con "inside" was OK for a time but not forever. So on May 16, 1973, just two months before Christine Demeter would be murdered, Laszlo Eper decided to leave.

He was particularly attentive to his work that day. The guard in the upholstery shop of the Collins Bay Penitentiary noticed that Eper was the last to leave when it came time for lunch, instead of knocking off early like everyone else. He was the first one back, too, just in time to level the revolver he had smuggled in at the guard and take him hostage. From then on the escape had all the complexity of a "B"-movie plot. A gun-toting Eper commandeered a prison employee's car, driving employee and car to Ottawa until the sputtering engine ran out of gas. From there he hitch-hiked. Next day he stole another car at gunpoint and took off for Toronto. He never bothered to change the licence plates of the stolen car, which was the brown Chevrolet he was driving on the day of his death three months later. Logic and forethought seemed to play no special role in Eper's actions.

Bill Teggart was still in his office when the Metropolitan Toronto Police called him. Their search of Eper's room had unearthed some material that seemed directly relevant to the Demeter investigation. Although there was little affection lost between some of the detectives on the two police forces, Metro's men were confident that by now they had pretty much fine-tooth-combed Eper's place, and a regional superintendent tramping through the evidence couldn't do too much harm. Teggart wasted no time with unnecessary questions. His respect for some Metro investigators was about equal to their admiration for the regional police. Teggart wanted to look things over for himself.

The basement apartment at 663 Shaw Street in Toronto's west end was a dingy bed-sitting room with a private bathroom and some communal cooking facilities. When the police arrived, Eper's room was locked — with good reason. However indifferent Laszlo Eper might have been to the finer things in life, he was most attentive to the tools of his trade. Inside the room police found three hand-guns and a .22 semi-automatic rifle. The rifle had been expertly customized: the stock had been modified and the barrel cut down and fitted with a silencer. The silencer was home-made but beautifully tooled and sweated onto the barrel, the work of a man who knew his business. Two of the weapons were Smith and Wesson revolvers, taking large-calibre ammunition. One of them, a 357 magnum, could hit anything, with no danger of it ever hitting back. Eper was no dilettante gun-collector. In a briefcase there was ammunition for all of them: .22s for the rifle, 9-millimetre for the Spanish automatic and for the .38 special he was holding when he died, and magnum ammunition for the two American hand-guns. Sitting next to the bed was a device that had initially sent the Metro police scuttling for the bomb squad: a concoction of transmitter parts, batteries, and a jar full of a thick, viscous substance thought to be nitroglycerin. It turned out to be Hungarian preserves or something similar, but it *looked* lethal enough.

There was merchandise of a different sort in the room, too, an Aladdin's treasure trove of rings and watches, some still with the price tags on them and in little velvet display boxes. Then there were several ski masks, which concealed everything but eyes and mouth, and a list of all the Metro police cars and their numbers. In fact, there was a radio tuned into police frequency sitting next to the quality stereo rig Eper had hooked up for himself after he had expropriated it from an apartment on Gloucester Street. And under his mattress — in a touchingly naïve Old World gesture — were four one-hundred-dollar bills. Still, after the police had pinned down some of the jobs Eper had pulled since arriving in Toronto that May, four hundred dollars didn't seem like very much money. Back at the end of May he had made off with over $13,000 after holding up a Dominion Store supermarket on Bloor Street in broad daylight. Eper, decked out in a green baseball-cap, made his getaway on a bicycle, pedalling like mad through heavy traffic and successfully eluding his pursuers. Then, on July 4 he had taken over $18,000 worth of jewellery from Paul's Jewellery Store on St. Clair in a brazen daytime armed robbery. "Press the alarm," Eper told the terrified staff, "and I'll blow your brains out." Three of the four guns in his room came from a big break-and-enter job he did on Hallam Sporting Goods, one of Toronto's best-equipped gun shops. Within a matter of hours the police had traced most of the stolen property in Eper's possession back to a whole list of unsolved burglaries and armed robberies.

But Teggart was less interested in the fruits of Eper's crimes than in pinning down exactly *what* his crimes might have been. The police tagged Eper as a fringe member of the so-called Hungarian mafia, described as a small, loosely organized group of "rounders" — crooks — sharing a common language and a reputation for brutality. By now Teggart was up to his close-cropped hair in Hungarians, and while he had reluctantly conceded that a mere knowledge of the Finno-Ugric Magyar tongue was not in itself proof of complicity in Christine Demeter's murder, it was beginning to seem grounds enough for suspicion. He began by yanking up the floorboards of the two cars Eper had — the brown Chevy and a blue Volkswagen parked in a garage up the street — and sending them off to the forensic lab in case any bloodstains might be detected. (None were found, but this intrusion into evidence under the control of the Metro Toronto police caused a slight territorial dispute, until a crack Metro homicide detective-sergeant named Walter Tyrell decided it was wiser to accommodate the beefy Mississauga superintendent than to try to impede the progress of his golden slippers. Meanwhile a Mississauga detective was rounding up the neighbourhood kids.

Eper had been on the RCMP's most-wanted list, and Teggart figured he'd be short of company during the day. He was right. As far as the kids on the block were concerned, "John" (as they knew Eper) was "the greatest guy in the world", always taking carloads of them every Sunday to the movies. (He'd also tell them exciting things, like how he'd like to kill a policeman whenever he saw one.) Neighbours in the Shaw Street rooming house also thought very highly of Eper, which may have had something to do with the stolen television sets and portable radios he'd given away, or his handiness in fixing broken-down toasters. Even the Toronto *Star* was moved to run a story the next day, August 30, with the headline "Slain Man 'Great Guy' Pals Say", in which the reporter told about the "Santa Claus of Shaw Street" who, said the neighbourhood kids, had an alcoholic wife in the suburbs and three children he longed to see. But Teggart was more interested in some other stories the kids told about Eper. On hearing of Santa's trips to the corner phone booth, where he would write numbers on the wall, Teggart had his men photograph and dust every inch of the booth. This produced an astoundingly complete list of "fences" — dealers in stolen merchandise — in the city. But he couldn't get that extra piece of information that would link Eper to Peter Demeter. There was nothing other than the evidence the Metro police had initially called him about.

Teggart looked at it again. In his fifteen-dollars-a-week room, Eper had kept a collection of newspaper clippings about people who lived a different sort of life. The clippings were mainly from the business and financial sections of newspapers, and featured interviews with people like N. J. Alexander, Managing Director of Richardson Securities, or C. E. Medland, president of Wood Gundy. The grubby newspaper pages had been shoved in a drawer next to the notebook Eper had kept with a list of gun shops and explosives dealers. Probably planning to extort money from rich people, Teggart thought. He'd scare the hair off their arms with that phony bomb. But what had caught the Metro detectives' attention and now bothered Bill Teggart was a piece of brown wrapping-paper with irregular scissored edges. There were two names written on it. On one side, in what seemed to be Eper's handwriting, was scrawled "Peter Demeter, Eden ACR Associates", and on the other "Police Superintendent William Teggart".

10. The Firebug

The incident on Greenwood Drive in the town of Burlington seemed to have nothing to do with the Demeter case. The 11:00 P.M. CBC National News, still largely concerned with routine Watergate items, had just ended. It was Friday, August 10, 1973, and Charles Walkinshaw and his wife were seated in front of the television set enjoying their leisure, one of the little compensations that retirement brings. The noise of the explosion sliced through their living room, shattering the calm suburban night with a clear, sharp report like a dozen cars backfiring at once. Outside, the Walkinshaws' garage was blazing away with flames already as high as twenty feet.

Across the road the noise sounded like a gas explosion. Pat Murphy raced down his front steps towards the Walkinshaws', then watched as, impossibly, part of the fire began moving away from the blaze. It was a man running through the night. His clothes were burning and he seemed to have a ball of flame playing on his back. Still, he was upright, tearing down Greenwood Drive like some bizarre neon sign. The fellow must be hysterical, thought Murphy, fanning the flames when he ought to have been smothering them on the smooth green lawns bordering the street. With Murphy in pursuit, rattling off first-aid advice, the smouldering man rounded the corner and jumped into the driver's seat of a parked car. That gave Murphy a chance to catch up. "Are you OK?" he asked. The man turned his head, looked at Murphy just for a beat, then without a word pulled quickly away. Murphy stood winded, grimacing, in the middle of the road. The hospital was in the opposite direction.

It must have hurt like hell and the police could never figure out how he did it, but Joe Dinardo managed to drive himself some thirty miles to

St. Joseph's Hospital in Toronto with twenty-five per cent of his body covered in burns, the skin on his arms and hands hanging in shreds, and a chunk of his flesh left behind on the hood and windshield of the Walkinshaws' Chev. It didn't need an expert to explain why a simple arson job had turned into a demolition disaster. After dumping the gasoline all over the garage, Dinardo must have waited too long, and by the time he lit the match the gasoline fumes had risen up around him and the whole place blew up. The police never did find out why Dinardo was torching a decent, respectable family like the Walkinshaws. Maybe it was because they had refused to sell their house (to the wrong party), or perhaps it was simply a mistake. Anyone silly enough to blow himself up, said the police, might be dumb enough to torch the wrong joint. Anyway, Dinardo wasn't talking. His birthdate was May 17, 1943, he said. He was born in Hungary. He understood the warning given to him and had nothing to say concerning the incident, which occurred on the night of August 10, 1973, at 629 Greenwood Drive, Burlington. Anything beyond his name, rank, and serial number would have to be discussed with his lawyer, Arthur Maloney.

On September 20, 1973, he was placed under arrest in room 649 of St. Joseph's Hospital. After an unprecedented twelve months on the outside, Gabor Magosztovics, alias Joe Dinardo, had come to the attention of the authorities once more.

For the first six months after he left Hungary in 1956, Joe Dinardo got by on the twelve shillings a week that the British Red Cross handed out to Hungarian refugees. Perhaps if the donors had known that he was only thirteen years old and had slipped across the border alone without a single relative to look after him, they might have put the boy in a foster home. But Dinardo was already over six feet tall with the build appropriate to his childhood nickname, "Tractor", and so one more waif eluded the good ladies of the soup kitchens. Besides, Dinardo already knew how to take care of himself. He'd had enough of crowded little countries that hold a good man down. In the summer of 1957 he emigrated to British Columbia in time to pick apples in the lush orchards of the Okanagan Valley. But at heart Dinardo was still an urban lad. He drifted inevitably towards Ontario, and at the age of fifteen he was settled in Toronto with a good start on his criminal record. By the time of the Walkinshaw arson Dinardo had a sheet a yard long, with multiple convictions for break and entry, unregistered firearms, and assault with intent. Still, there has to be more in a man's life than work alone. In between his spells in prison Dinardo was building up his career.

Before it changed hands around 1974 and turned into the Lansdowne Boys Athletic Club, the building on Wade Avenue in Toronto's west end was the home of the old Lansdowne Gym. The ground floor was a run-down auto-body shop which never seemed too interested in cars and was rarely open. The boxing ring was set up on the second floor, in the middle of a long, dreary room with a couple of exhausted chesterfields and a battered television set pushed against the wall. Some people thought the whole operation was a front for a bookie joint, and it was an article of faith that the pay phone in the gym was bugged by the police. All the same, some very legit boxers (such as champ George Chuvalo) would always work out in the Lansdowne.

So did Joe Dinardo. Boxing kept him in good shape, and at 6'4" and 220 pounds he could throw a powerful punch. Throwing a powerful punch, however, is not always as lucrative as throwing a whole fight. By his own account, Dinardo's price hovered around $1,000 a fall. But the Lansdowne was more than just a place to do some sparring. It was a place to cool out in when the heat was on at home. Joe often found himself having to change his residence address quickly, like the time two men with shotguns came looking for him. He wasn't sure who they were, but in his racket there were bound to be "people who were pissed off". For besides boxing and stealing, Joe had another sideline — he was an enforcer. He didn't use that term himself. The way he put it to the police was simple. He'd break hands, he said, legs, arms, whatever he was asked to do. If you wanted he could just beat someone up. For an arm he'd get $300, or sometimes as much as $500. Legs, maybe $1,000. It was a way to score.

But even a man like Joe Dinardo was not without friends. He used to meet them in the gym or in the restaurants near by. His closest friend happened to be a fellow Hungarian — a man named Laszlo Eper.

11. Cat and Mouse Continues

Charging Peter Demeter with murder was only the first step in a long journey that could end either in his conviction or in his acquittal, and on the day of his arrest, perhaps even the incurably optimistic Mississauga police would have conceded that their chances for a conviction were far from being assured. As far as the defence (and most members of Ontario's legal community) were concerned, the prosecution's chances were almost nonexistent. The defence's confidence in their own case was not unwarranted at all: on the morning of August 17, when the news of the arrest reached the offices of Pomerant, Pomerant and Greenspan, they had no inkling of Csaba Szilagyi's statement, let alone the recorded conversations between Csaba and their client. Since Joe Pomerant was still in Israel, the task of arranging an immediate bail hearing fell to Eddie Greenspan. As he happened to be attending a conference that day at which Assistant Crown Attorney Leo McGuigan was also present, Greenspan naturally asked him about the charge. He asked in very plain terms, as lawyers usually do in informal discussions.

"Why on earth did you charge him, Leo?" Eddie said. "You're not likely to convict a man on motives. Why did you do it?"

"Trust me," McGuigan replied. "Last night we had a meeting and it was decided to charge him. Trust me."

"I know you, and I have enormous confidence in you," Greenspan replied, "but I certainly won't 'trust you'. Why did you do it?"

But Leo McGuigan wouldn't say, and Greenspan concluded in his own mind that the Crown probably had no real evidence. In a sensational case (and Christine's murder had become front-page news in Toronto) it was not unheard of for the prosecution to jump the gun. Greenspan felt the local community had formed a very early opinion about the guilt of the highly visible Hungarian, based on little more than newspaper photos of Peter walking his dog right after the murder, and similar bits of "evidence" that he was a hard, unemotional man. (Joe Pomerant had, in fact, suggested to Peter the first day that it might be wiser to move out of his house temporarily and make himself unavailable for any but the most necessary official communications, but Peter resisted the suggestion and Joe didn't press it. Had Joe insisted — and had Peter obeyed — the bulk of the evidence against him might never have been acquired at all. But possibly Peter felt that changing the normal habits of his life would only arouse additional doubts about him. He was an innocent man; why should he be hounded out of his house, change his phone number, and go into hiding? It's harder to speculate why Joe didn't put his foot down; on previous occasions he had been known to say: "Either do it my way, or get yourself another lawyer." Possibly in this instance he was afraid his headstrong client might take him at his word.) In any case, it was Eddie Greenspan's view that he was dealing with a Crown going off half-cocked because of vague suspicions and without having any facts against Peter that would support a murder charge.

At the same time Eddie was uneasy, in part because he *did* trust McGuigan, but also because the Crown seemed to put up a suspiciously weak resistance at the bail hearing on August 22. They opposed Peter's application, of course, but they didn't seem to care whether they won or lost and did not even think it worth the effort to send their senior counsel to argue the case. The young lawyer appearing for the Crown seemed to have been briefed in a hurry and knew very little about the whole affair, while Leo McGuigan poked his head into the courtroom only after the hearing was over and Mr. Justice Callon had granted Peter's bail. The top man, Crown Attorney John Greenwood, Q.C., didn't bother to appear at all. While Eddie was naturally happy to get the $75,000 bail for his client, it all seemed very unusual to him. Frankly, he smelled a rat. But then, he reasoned, if the prosecution were holding their fire, it wasn't necessarily because they were waiting to see the whites of their opponents' eyes: it might be that they had no ammunition to shoot with. This alternative became even more plausible as soon as Eddie discovered that John Greenwood had happened to be away in Ottawa when the decision to lay a charge against Peter was made. In his absence Bill Teggart and his boys must have got his assistant, Leo McGuigan — nicknamed "Tiger" for his pugnacity — to agree to the arrest. "I didn't consider it unusual," Eddie Greenspan would say later, "that the police should succumb to public pressure that someone be charged, and they'd pick on the husband as a likely candidate. . . . These things happen."

In any case, as Joe agreed with Eddie after his return from the Middle East, the whole investigation had been characterized by a certain trigger-happiness on the part of the police. The most blatant example had been the "arrest" of Marina in Vienna less than a week after the murder. This came about mainly as a result of the police misunderstanding a taped telephone conversation between Peter and Marina. What actually happened was simple enough: on July 21, having learned about Christine's death, Marina called Peter from Vienna. Towards the end of their highly emotional conversation Peter asked her to go to a certain address in Vienna to give a Hungarian person there 1300 Austrian *schillings*, which he would later pay back to her. Whoever translated the German-language conversation for Bill Teggart failed to indicate that 1300 *schillings* equalled no more than $60 or so, and for a moment Teggart must have been convinced that this transaction represented the pay-off to the murderer. The next morning Marina was taken into custody in Vienna and charged with being an accomplice. She was, of course, released a day or two later. Had the police not missed another phone conversation in which Peter promised a relative in Hungary to give $60 in Vienna to a penniless refugee friend, the blunder could have been avoided; the two conversations were on the same reel of tape. (True, the second conversation was in Hungarian, which might have added to the confusion, and perhaps Superintendent Teggart cared less about the transaction itself than about throwing Peter off balance by the sudden arrest of his mistress.) Whatever the reason, Joe and Eddie must have felt that precipitate arrests and charges were par for the course in this investigation.

For the next number of months Peter Demeter's daily life didn't change much. Though he was now officially charged with murder, the immediate physical inconveniences resulting from his first head-on clash with the law were minimal. He had spent less than six days in actual custody — in the old Brampton jail, where his cell-mates tended to be unsuccessful smugglers caught at the nearby Toronto International Airport — and after his release he had to report once a week to the Mississauga police. He would appear on Mondays, generally between 12:00 and 1:30 in the afternoon, but he wouldn't know that (at least on one occasion) he'd be undergoing a psychiatric examination of sorts at the same time. One of the people waiting in the vestibule of the police station was a well-known Toronto psychiatrist, who was observing Peter at Superintendent Teggart's request while Peter was making his report at the sergeant's desk. Not being able to use his favourite polygraph machine the superintendent, whose faith in modern science was almost touching at times, tried to see if he could find out through this method what made Peter tick. Of course his medical man could only report that Peter appeared somewhat nervous and furtive to him, which, under the circumstances, was less than a surprise.

For someone interested in the workings of Peter's mind the brief exchange he had with Teggart himself right after his arrest would have been far more revealing. Although his replies to the superintendent's questions meant little in terms of guilt or innocence, they told quite a bit about his attitudes. Having booked him on the murder charge, Teggart and O'Toole led Peter to the interrogation room at 7:45 in the morning. The superintendent was in the process of giving him the official caution again — anything you say may be used as evidence, etc. — when Peter interrupted him.

"I don't want to discuss this at all. I want for the second time to call my lawyer. When does the beating begin?"

Teggart was so much taken aback by this response that he had Peter immediately returned to his cell. Although his closest friends could not describe Bill as a bleeding-heart liberal, beating confessions out of people simply wasn't his style. If Teggart had a fictional hero, it resembled Lieutenant Columbo rather than the cop from *The French Connection*. He might go to the very limits of the law as he conceived it — or even cross the line as conceived by others — but beating suspects was outside his boundaries. If nothing else, Teggart was too ambitious to allow any irregularities to spoil the biggest arrest of his career, while for Chris O'Toole the strictures of proper police conduct had the force of religion. They would not have understood that, for Peter, the suggestion was a perfectly natural one. Chris and Bill took more than an hour to cool down and to try putting a few questions to Peter again.

"Did you kill your wife?" asked Teggart when Peter was brought back to the interrogation room.

"No."

"Did you conspire with anyone to kill your wife?"

"No."

"Is Csaba Szilagyi a friend of yours? Or your wife's?"

"Yes, he's a very dear friend of mine," said Peter.

It was an indication that while he had too many suspicions about Canadian policemen, he had too few about Hungarian friends. It was something for the prosecution to rely on in the remaining months of the investigation.

Because Eddie Greenspan's instincts were right: the prosecution did have its reasons for not fighting too hard against Peter's bail application. Although Crown Attorney John Greenwood suffered from some optimism himself, his affliction wasn't quite as incurable as Bill Teggart's. In addition, he knew more about the rules of evidence. Greenwood appreciated the enthusiasm of law-enforcement officers, but he had no intention of standing in a courtroom with egg all over his face. He knew he couldn't delay a trial for too long with Peter in custody, yet he wasn't quite sure he was ready to proceed. Letting Peter out on bail would free the prosecution to prepare at its own pace. But that wasn't all.

Both Teggart and Greenwood agreed that the best evidence they had against Peter so far had come from Peter himself. Whether or not it was enough, he seemed the type of person who, given enough rope, might just do the prosecution the favour of hanging himself. While Greenwood and McGuigan had a properly cautious view of their chances of convicting Peter, they shared with Bill Teggart and the rest of the police the opinion that "he was guilty as hell." This being the case, he might continue giving himself away, or might even try to make a run for it. Presumably Greenwood was also hoping the police might come up with some evidence independent of Peter's own actions or utterances. This, to put it mildly, would have been useful, since the Crown Attorney had at this point some doubts not only about the ambiguity of Peter's statements but about their admissibility in court. "We had less than an airtight case *with* the tapes, " Greenwood would later say, "and without them we had no case at all."

Of course, it was possible to say, after hindsight had put everything into sharp focus, that the defence made its first tactical error when it got Peter out on bail instead of using his custody to press for an early trial. (This suggestion was eventually made by many Canadian legal authorities, including the trial judge himself, the Honourable Justice Campbell Grant of the Supreme Court of Ontario.) But this view left out of the account the fact that Joe Pomerant had no reason for believing he might be defending a guilty man. The Crown was under no obligation to disclose any of the evidence they had against Peter at this point, and of course they didn't. While a lawyer might elect to rush a dubious case through trial before the prosecution has a chance to come up with much evidence, he need have no such worries about an innocent client. If there's nothing to find — as Peter seems to have insisted all along — why not let the Crown and the police search to their hearts' content, taking all the time they want? Besides, there was every indication that Peter would not have submitted to a strategy requiring him to languish in jail as long as there was a way of getting him out. He would almost certainly have fired any lawyer on the spot who suggested it. As a man claiming to be innocent, he might in fact have been quite right to do so. It's a different (and much more difficult) question how far Joe Pomerant ought to have allowed himself to be influenced by his client's opinion of the merits of his case. (The police would say that in trying to con them, Peter only succeeded in conning his own lawyers.) The best view seems to be that the defence, in light of the available facts, acted in the only way it could at the time.

About a week after Peter was released on bail, Eddie Greenspan decided to have a chat with Csaba Szilagyi. The young lawyer couldn't quite put his finger on what it was he suspected about Csaba — dozens of Peter's acquaintances had been interviewed by the police and Greenspan didn't have this uneasy feeling about any of them — but there was something about Szilagyi he didn't like. Perhaps it was because he seemed to be the one person to be questioned again and again — at least this was how Peter understood it — or because he wouldn't come to Greenspan's office to be interviewed. In any case, on August 28 Eddie notified John Greenwood that he was arranging to talk with Csaba Szilagyi at Csaba's place of work the next day.

Bill Teggart found this news very disturbing. Although at this time he had only met Greenspan on two or three occasions, he had developed a somewhat grudging respect for the young lawyer and, in fact, considered him a more dangerous adversary than Joe Pomerant. He was worried that Csaba, who could get past Peter's guard easily enough, might not perform nearly as well against Eddie Greenspan. If Csaba were to give the game away, he would not only expose himself to possible danger but would jeopardize the whole plan of the prosecution. As far as the superintendent was concerned, they were dealing with a cold-blooded murderer who would stop at nothing. As Teggart saw his duty, he had to protect the person of the prosecution's surprise witness as well as the integrity of the Crown's case against Peter Demeter. He gave instructions that Szilagyi should wear a body-pack for his interview with Greenspan.

For the police to eavesdrop on a reputable member of the bar — in fact, an officer of the court — is in no way comparable to eavesdropping on a murder suspect. While Bill Teggart's action might not have been illegal, it had few precedents in the hitherto seemly, decorous, and more-or-less-gentlemanly administration of Canadian justice. Not only was Teggart's decision *infra dignitatem* enough for the Crown to later disclaim all knowledge of it, but it was done against the advice of more conservative police officers, such as Chris O'Toole, who had objected to it very seriously. Honourable as Teggart's intentions were, there's no doubt that by surreptitiously taping Greenspan without censure from either the courts or his superiors, he helped to introduce a new and questionable spirit into the procedure of criminal investigations in Canada.

As it turned out, the police needn't have worried. Csaba held his ground against Greenspan and didn't give anything away — although he came very close to it on one occasion. This happened near the end of their conversation when Eddie inquired, point blank:

"Did he [Peter] ever ask you questions about where he could get somebody to kill her?"

"I can't think of anything of . . . ah, that nature," replied Csaba with little enthusiasm. "Anyhow, you see . . . ah, I mean, I still regard him as a . . . as a friend, so ah, I wouldn't say anything that would anyway incriminate him."

This seemed a strangely ambiguous answer. For some reason Greenspan chose not to pursue it, though once he opened the subject it would have seemed logical for him to say, "Never mind about incriminating your friend, did he or did he not?" If Csaba had replied ambiguously for the second time, the defence might well have had a chance to guess what it was up against. But when Eddie said: "Okay. Well, I think that probably covers it," the opportunity was gone. Neither Greenspan nor Pomerant would meet Csaba Szilagyi again until the preliminary inquiry some six months later.

Still, the interview did little to alleviate Eddie's suspicions of Csaba. On his way out from the Pizza Restaurant (and just out of range of intelligence officer Terdik's microphone) he remarked to his articling student: "If this was one of Peter's friends, I'd hate to meet his enemies." But if he communicated this feeling to his client, Peter elected to dismiss it. In the course of the following months he would have yet another conversation with his old friend Csaba, duly recorded on Joe Terdik's tape machine for posterity. But this would come later.

For the time being Peter engaged in nothing more than a little mopping-up and rear-guard action. His situation, much as Joe Pomerant predicted it, had now become truly Kafkaesque. He existed in a kind of strange limbo, living alone with his cocker spaniel in the empty house where his wife was slain, free yet monitored and supervised at every turn, innocent under the presumption of the law yet publicly accused of the gravest crime known to human society. A few of his friends stood by him, but most had turned away in open hostility or disgust. Some, no doubt, shied away from Peter just because of the publicity. Christine's murder was never a two-paragraph item on the back page, but as time passed the crime seemed to catch the public's fancy more and more. When Peter was finally charged, it became firmly established as the most sensational case in decades. Not only in Canada, either; the murder made front-page news in Italy, Germany, Austria, and the eastern United States. Amid all the headlines, pictures, and television and radio news stories, the alleged wife-killer was walking around the streets, buying groceries, picking up his newspaper from his usual corner box, and even trying to conduct his business — developing and selling properties or negotiating bank loans for new investments. At first it was only eerie, but soon it became clearly impossible. Apart from some loyal friends — such as Klara Majerszky, a lady who had lived with Peter and Christine as a housekeeper when she had first arrived from Europe — or business partners such as Leslie Wagner, only cousin Steven and his wife would continue a regular association with Peter. In the first few weeks a middle-aged German lady, an old family friend, came over to keep Peter company, but after Helga Treitl left there was no one. Not even a cleaning lady could be persuaded to set foot inside the place. Since Peter was never much good at keeping house, Dundas Crescent, Christine's dream-home in the suburbs, was soon given over to decay and neglect. Though Peter would always come home to sleep, he'd pass much of his day consulting with his lawyers or doing odds and ends of business in town before going to dinner at his cousin's, where he could also spend a little time with Andrea. Beelzebub, who was very much used to human company, would now disconsolately sniff around the empty house trying to comprehend it all.

So would his master, in his own fashion. To Peter it still seemed inconceivable that this calamity should happen to him, and that he should be helpless, utterly helpless, to do anything about it. Sitting tight and letting the lawyers handle it might be all very well for other people, but Peter didn't get to where he was by taking a back seat to the events of his life. Had he done that, he might still be a truck driver in communist Hungary, or a brush salesman in bourgeois Toronto. With what he had seen of the ways of the world, how could he possibly depend on the integrity or diligence of lawyers and policemen? Other people had their own fish to fry, and why should they be loath to do it over the flames of Peter's burning house?

He would ponder about this question day and night, by himself and in conversations with Steven and one or two other friends. What could he do to help himself? The police couldn't possibly have any direct evidence against him (he'd tell Steven), since such evidence could only come from an accomplice. If there's no such person, then this is impossible, as even his lawyers agree. In any case, this is Canada; the police can't keep a person in jail here in secret; the newspapers would report it the day an alleged accomplice had been arrested; and surely the police wouldn't send an accomplice home to wait for the trial. Speculations, speculations. Of course, he'd go on, what people don't understand is that the Mississauga police are incapable of finding murderers, ever, and that's why they have to fabricate them. "I don't care about being taped," Peter would say; "I'd tell it right in their faces, and if they put me in the witness box — which I hope they will — I'll explain it clearly that these fellows are not clever enough to issue ten-dollar parking tickets because it's beyond them to find an illegal parker during the rush-hour . . . I'm the victim of the fact they never catch murderers."

As a matter of fact, Peter's impassioned speeches seemed to contain a grain of truth. First there was the unsolved murder of Constance Dickey shortly after Christine's death and only a short distance from the Demeter garage. Then, less than a month later, another neighbourhood girl named Neda Novak had disappeared under mysterious circumstances. The police clearly suspected foul play (though Neda's body had not yet been found) but they could report no leads on her killer. Surely it couldn't have been just a coincidence, three women murdered within three months of each other in this peaceful neighbourhood that hadn't seen a murder in eighteen years before that? There was a maniac on the loose, and the Mississauga police were too dumb to catch him.

Peter didn't confine his suspicions to his friends: a day or two after the Novak girl's disappearance he had the opportunity to talk about them to Superintendent Teggart himself. This happened in a somewhat roundabout way, since neither man was supposed to have any conversations with the other. But when a slightly inebriated neighbour — a man Peter hardly knew — unexpectedly knocked on his door to offer his condolences and then wouldn't leave, Peter called the police for help. Much to Peter's astonishment, instead of some rookie policeman it was the superintendent who responded to the call. Peter immediately assumed that the supposedly drunk neighbour was a police plant, sent by Teggart to "draw him out" in some way, and therefore said: "Nice trick, superintendent, but it didn't work." Then he couldn't resist baiting Teggart a bit further about how the police's case against him must be weakened by all these murders in the neighbourhood. Teggart, however, was not at a loss for a reply.

"You'd be surprised, Peter," he said, "how many people are suspecting *you*."

This answer must have demonstrated to Peter that he could count on no sympathy from the police. Far from beginning to doubt his role in Christine's death, they might soon start suggesting that Peter killed Constance Dickey and Neda Novak as well. "If they ever caught a sex murderer," said Peter to Steven a day after the incident, "Teggart would beat him until he confessed he *didn't* kill Christine." For the superintendent, said Peter, it was a question of prestige: catching a sex maniac who started his career on Christine, after having charged her solid-citizen husband with murder, would be a slap in the face that would cost Teggart his position. (As it happened, some lawyers shared Peter's view, and one was heard to remark at the bail hearing that before this case was over the Mississauga superintendent would be on a paper route.)

But if the police wouldn't yield, perhaps some of the local citizens might. It was bootstraps-time, and Peter wasn't constituted to let even a slim chance go by. The painful surprise was evident in next-door neighbour Mrs. Tennant's voice when she answered the telephone on the morning of October 9:

"Hi, Joene," the male voice said, "it's Peter."

"Oh, hello . . . "

"I'm sorry that you and Dave put me on the drop-dead list in the last few months. I was just wondering, would you have any idea what's going on here in Erindale . . . because for me and my friends it's starting to be pretty obvious there is something wrong as far as the general situation is concerned. . . . "

It was highly doubtful whether Mrs. Tennant knew at this point what Peter was talking about, and it took him a few moments to make it clear it was "this Novak girl" and also "this girl, just a few hundred yards from my garage here, this Constance Dickey". Nothing like this had ever happened in the high-priced Erindale area of Mississauga, as far as Peter knew. "And doesn't that somehow make you think that maybe this charge they laid against me is getting a little bit ridiculous?"

"Well, I don't know, I just don't hear anything, Peter," said Mrs. Tennant in acute discomfort. "The only thing I hear is what I read in the papers."

"Well, it's certainly . . . it's . . . thirty days later, it's . . . well, it's just unbelievable. Unbelievable." Since the called-for indignation wasn't forthcoming from the opposite end of the line, Peter had to double his own to keep the conversation in balance. It was a curious, embarrassing dialogue with one person supplying all the feeling and some of the words he hoped to hear from the other. "I mean I'm not, ah . . . ah . . . I don't know if you read in the paper I'm not charged with killing my wife myself . . . and . . . just . . . you know, getting to be a night-mare. . . . "

Eventually, however, Peter came to the point.

"I'm just wondering if some sort of a citizen's action or something . . . I mean you and your friends are usually very active when somebody wants to build something around here . . . and this is a little bit bigger problem, I guess."

"Hm, yes, well," said Mrs. Tennant, "this is more of a police problem too, you see, there's nothing a citizen can do. . . . "

But Peter wouldn't give up that easily.

"I'm asking you, that's the reason I didn't phone, I met Dave a few weeks back and I was hoping he will show some interest in my . . . my misery," and here for some reason Peter found it appropriate to giggle, "as neighbours, but this was not the case so I didn't want to bother you, but now that things are getting so obvious and so much out of hand . . . that . . . I mean one doesn't need more than four . . . four years public school to understand that there's something . . . fishy in the whole . . . whole thing."

"Listen, Peter, I'd like to talk to you longer but I'm supposed to be over at the church."

"Oh, yeah, yeah. . . . " Peter managed to convey in two words the feeling that, whatever was happening to *him*, for other people of course it was just business as usual. "Say hello to Dave. I'd really appreciate to hear from you . . . and . . . at some time when it would be convenient for you, because . . . I . . . I honestly don't even know if you're aware of the other side of the coin as we say in Hungarian . . . that how ridiculous these charges are and . . . my side of the story or how my lawyers see it . . . and what happened here before the elections or obvious political reasons and how I got charged and how I got into this. But anyhow I'm here next door as you probably noticed," and here Peter giggled again, "and would really love to exchange views now that things are really getting out of hand here. . . . "

From the prosecution's point of view things were not getting out of hand at all. On the contrary, Peter's every utterance was seen by them as further confirmation of his guilt. His conversation with Mrs. Tennant, for example, which to a neutral observer might have appeared little more than a trapped victim's humiliating cry for help, sounded to the police an archetypal Demeter-attempt to confuse and manipulate. Teggart, O'Toole, Terdik, and the others had by this time developed an odd pride in Peter's efforts to escape them, somewhat as hunters might admire the twistings and turnings of a particularly clever quarry. At briefing sessions in the morning it was "Jesus, you should have heard him on the phone last night," and spoken not without a curious note of affection. This wasn't just everyday stuff, old Peter, but real good fishing, hooking into a big one from a fighting species. And one that might yet easily get away; that was how Crown Attorney John Greenwood saw it.

Because in fact the police had come up with absolutely no new evidence since the first few days of the investigation. The motives of bad marriage, Marina, and the $1,000,000 insurance were known practically from the outset: Peter himself never denied them, and Pomerant surrendered Marina's letters to Teggart on the second or third day. The statements of Rita Jefferies and Csaba Szilagyi had also become available a short time later. But since then, apart from Peter's words on the telephone and body-pack tapes, there was nothing.

And Peter's own words, no matter how one sliced them, remained somewhat ambiguous. He certainly didn't seem a very nice man, he certainly seemed to have something to hide, but the charge against him wasn't moral turpitude or income tax evasion. The charge against Peter was murder, and even if he had come right out and admitted to it — which he hadn't by a long chalk — it might still not have been enough to convict him. People can say they have killed for all kinds of twisted reasons. Murder is a very serious charge, and it carries strange emotional overtones which are fully recognized by the law. A person, for instance, isn't permitted to plead guilty to capital murder in court even if he wants to. He *has* to enter a plea of Not Guilty, and it's the prosecution that has to prove his guilt beyond a reasonable doubt. Theoretically Peter could say to Teggart, yes, assume I hired some people to kill my wife, but I'm going to deny it, and you just go and try to prove it in court. Then, if Teggart were unable to offer any other evidence against Peter than this statement, the court might feel obliged to direct a verdict of acquittal. What John Greenwood wanted was some real proof, independent of Peter, perhaps some physical evidence or a witness tying a middleman or a killer to Demeter in some way. Without this, he had reason to fear Peter might not even be committed to trial.

If Superintendent Teggart and his men couldn't come up with any evidence of this kind, it certainly wasn't for want of trying. "Money's no object," Chief Burrows had said, and Bill Teggart had taken him at his word. More than a dozen of his men were investigating, researching, observing, pounding the pavement, but for the time being all to no avail. Peter's telephone continued to be monitored after his arrest, not in the hope of any direct admissions but because he might mention a name, a place, or give a hint of some kind that could possibly provide a new lead for the police. But they could hear nothing except more lengthy conversations, with Peter putting down the local cops, discussing world politics, or managing, on one occasion, to take a few dollars off the floral arrangements at Christine's grave-site because some of the flowers were wilted.

When giving away Christine's clothes, Peter was volubly shocked to discover how many she had, and how much money she must have spent on them behind his back. They were impractical, too, like that white canvas-and-leather outfit stamped with some Italian designer's name that Christine had said she got at a sale for $30, yet here was the bill Peter had just found from Holt Renfrews for $180. . . . These compulsions of Christine's were totally abnormal, Peter would say to Steven; well, a sickness, really. Marjorie's young cousin must have gone to her car at least six times piling in the stuff, yet the closets were still full of clothes. Leather coats, brand-new blouses with the labels still intact! "I should have paid it into taxes," said Peter ruefully; "the money would still be gone, but my situation would be easier." Viewed from a strictly practical angle Peter had a point, as always.

Quite possibly — as John Greenwood had come to believe — the whole point about Peter was that he was a totally practical person, a kind of ultimate, Hungarian version of the Harvard School of Business, who would view life entirely as a cost-benefit analysis, just a series of advantages or disadvantages devoid of any moral content. Indeed, at times Peter seemed so unaware of living in a world of different sensibilities that he would bump into them like a bat forced to navigate by alien sight rather than familiar sound. For example, he couldn't break himself of the habit of making acerbic comments about Christine even after her death. In a way this showed that whatever vices Peter might have had, hypocrisy was not among them. Some of his jibes were quite witty, in a very grim sort of way. Talking about finding his battered wife in the garage he'd say: "I never realized until then that Christine had so much brains." This was a classic, even for Peter, and his friends would remember it for a long time, though evidently Peter saw nothing wrong with it.

But whatever this might have told about Demeter's style or character, it was no proof of murder. Tape after tape after tape would be filled with Peter's telephone conversations, and Joe Terdik would soon start re-using the reels on which there seemed to be nothing of interest from the police's point of view. (While electromagnetic tapes were admittedly expensive, this might not have been the best way in which to save the tax-payers' money, especially in an investigation where "money was no object"; it made the police rather than the courts the arbiter of what was or wasn't significant evidence). But though the rich colours of the gentle southern Ontario autumn were now fading into monochrome under the grey and frizzled skies of November, Bill Teggart's team hadn't managed to turn up anything new.

Late in November another meeting was arranged between Csaba and Peter through the unsuspecting Steven Demeter. Of course, the microphones and wires were all in place, and as it happened Peter parked his car directly behind the familiar "Macdonald's" truck — on Dupont Street, in front of Mr. Pizza — in which Detective Terdik was crouching over his UHER recorder. By this time Peter had been given a "shit-list" of prosecution witnesses to whom he was not supposed to talk, but much to his satisfaction Csaba's name wasn't on it. Possibly Peter didn't trust Csaba completely, but he still seemed to trust him more than anybody else ("ninety-per-cent confidence" was John Greenwood's guess). Though the restaurant in which they met wasn't empty, he'd touch on a number of topics in their sotto voce, Hungarian-language conversation.

"How come you never call me?" was Peter's first question on the tape.

"Well, old chap, I'd rather stay quiet and low ———"

"Your, are your, are your nerves in bad shape or something?" asked Peter, sounding perhaps a little shaky himself.

"No, but as long as they leave me alone, I won't ———"

"I see."

Ostensibly the meeting was set up so that Csaba could sign back to Peter certain properties that were still registered in his name for various obscure business reasons. But first Peter wanted to talk about a number of other things. To begin with, he was wondering why, at the time of his arrest, when the police were asking him only five questions, one of them should pertain to Csaba? As Peter remembered it, or at least as he conveyed it to Csaba, the question was: "Do you suspect Csaba Szilagyi of having had intercourse with your wife?" (Teggart's own notes of this question were simply "Is Csaba Szilagyi a friend of yours? Or your wife's?") Whatever the actual question, it indicated that the police had been sniffing around Csaba very persistently. This, Peter said, coupled with the fact that they seemed to have suddenly stopped investigating Csaba, "this, for me, old chap, is the biggest puzzle, one of the biggest puzzles, because certainly they must have some kind of an idea, where this certain combination comes from. . . . " What Peter meant to ask in plain English was: "Do they suspect you still or don't they?" Superintendent Teggart's brinksmanship was proving very effective.

Peter was "taken aback" by two other things, as he explained to Csaba, during his interrogation by the police. One of them had to do with the pronunciation of a mutual friend's name, which apparently Teggart managed to do in the correct Hungarian way, and he couldn't possibly have done it without *hearing* the name pronounced by a native speaker of the language. Did Csaba pronounce the name in the superintendent's presence? (Though the friend was of no special significance, the question was a good guess, and it showed Peter's fine ability for putting two and two together. Csaba had always made a great point of never anglicizing the pronunciation of foreign words and would often introduce himself as "Szilagyi Csaba", putting his family name first in the Hungarian fashion.) The second thing that "consternated" Peter was that the police used the figure ten thousand dollars, quite specifically and on two occasions, while questioning him. "Why didn't they use twenty-five thousand or fifty thousand or something, you understand?" Peter asked Csaba. It appeared that the figure ten thousand had some special meaning only Csaba and Peter were supposed to know about, though Peter did not elaborate on what it might have been. What he did say was that it was upon hearing these two things that ". . . I believed for a moment that, that they had somehow cornered you." If so, it would have been a bad joke because "the tragicomical thing in the whole situation is that *except for us* they have no chance whatsoever on this earth, is that clear?"

For the prosecution it certainly seemed clear enough. They would also have agreed with Peter that ". . . I couldn't have been it [i.e. the actual killer] therefore on this basis, uh . . . I'd be in the same situation if the sharks had eaten her in Acapulco. . . ." But there was another basis, and later in the conversation Peter spelled that out too when he said to Csaba: "They need one man, like you, who would be willing to prove under oath, that counselled, that's why ———" (The rest of the sentence on the tape was unintelligible.) And finally when Peter said: "the beauty of this charge is that it can't be reduced, you understand, it's either-or, in short . . . it is either premeditated, it is either this or nothing," John Greenwood himself would have agreed that Peter had given a fair enough summation of the case for the Crown.

At the same time Peter also repeated, as any innocent man might, that the police couldn't possibly produce a killer or a middleman because there were no such people "on the surface of the earth". A man knowing himself to be without guilt could certainly say this with full assurance; if Peter hired no killer he needn't worry about the authorities coming up with one. But still, he seemed very interested in knowing if Csaba had been asked by the police about anybody, anybody at all, whose name he didn't recognize or whose name might have made him wonder in some way. Of course, this could have been the natural curiosity of an unjustly accused person who — once bitten, twice shy — was simply trying to figure out where the lightning might strike from next. Csaba said no, and on this note their conversation ended. After a friendship of "one and seven tenth of a decade" Csabaschek and Papitschek would never talk to one another again.

November, December, January. The preliminary hearing was scheduled to begin on the twenty-eighth. There was still no new evidence. Just before they were to appear in court the idea crossed John Greenwood's mind that perhaps he should live dangerously and reveal to the defence that all conversations between Szilagyi and their client had been taped. Sometimes when they think the jig is up crooks choose to make a clean breast of it, there being no percentage in bucking the odds. But Teggart and the other policemen disagreed: Peter was no pro and he would not play by the rules. He wouldn't say, well, you caught me fair and square, I'll go and take my medicine. In the policemen's opinion Peter was an amateur, and amateurs were tenacious and unpredictable. His words on tape were ambiguous, and if he knew about them he could make up a story and wriggle out of them somehow. It was better to take him by surprise.

The next morning Bill Teggart and Chris O'Toole watched Peter's lips tighten as Csaba was led into the courtroom to give his evidence at the preliminary hearing before His Honour Judge G. L. Young, of the Provincial Court (Criminal Division) of Ontario.

12. The Cards Are on the Table

If Christine Demeter hadn't been killed, Rita Jefferies would have dismissed a remark Csaba Szilagyi made to her some time in the spring of 1973 as one of those things immature young men say once in a while hoping to impress their dates. Over drinks at the Hyatt Regency Hotel one day, Csaba, whose career prospects did not look too bright at the time, let it drop that he could of course make a lot of money if he helped his rich friend Peter Demeter get rid of his wife. It sounded like a childish boast, and Rita did not dignify it with any question or reply. Since she did not take it seriously, it played no role in her decision to stop going out with Csaba a short time later. In fact, she might have forgotten it altogether if she hadn't happened to see Csaba driving along Yorkville on the day of Christine's death.

"One thing I remember vividly, " Eddie Greenspan would say later, "was when Szilagyi walked into the preliminary hearing. By that time we knew they had a surprise witness, but we didn't know who it was. The look of shock on Demeter's face, the look of total surprise: I remember it. I remember it very well because the look on him was such that I immediately thought that whatever Szilagyi was going to say was a lie."

Whether a lie, the truth, or something in between, the evidence Csaba gave at Peter's preliminary hearing on January 28, 1974, was the following:

Some time in 1968, not too long after he had been discharged from the Austrian army, Csaba met Peter, who was on one of his periodic visits to Europe. In the course of one conversation, Csaba said, Peter started drawing "parallels between Canada and Austria, specifically about business life, about the methods in business life."

"What did he say about them?" asked Crown Attorney Greenwood.

"For instance in Canada, if somebody encounters a problem it seems to be insurmountable, then he resorts to some other method. It might happen that if a developer finds a holdout in a block he has bought and cannot purchase that house, that all of a sudden in the newspapers appears an article that someone has been run over by a car which would happen to be that owner."

"All right. What else did he say?"

"He went on to say that he had problems of his own," Csaba replied. "They seemed to be insurmountable to him and ruining the prospect of his life. He indicated that if it would be possible for me to co-operate and try to get rid of it . . . "

"Yes?"

"At first it was not apparent as to who or what it was."

But, Csaba testified, in a subsequent discussion about the same subject he gathered Peter must be talking about his wife. He said as much to Peter, but Peter denied it, saying that Csaba must be joking, he had just married her, so what reason would he have to get rid of her? Still, Csaba said, the conversations continued throughout Peter's stay in Austria in the fall of 1968. Though the intended victim was still not named, the first concrete proposal about the method of killing was outlined by Peter in the course of a car trip between Siegendorf and Vienna. Apparently he wanted to know if it might be feasible to direct the exhaust gases of a car into its interior in such a way as to asphyxiate the driver. Csaba replied that it would not be feasible for various technical reasons.

According to Csaba, this was the start of a new relationship between himself and Peter in the course of which they would discuss ways and means of killing Christine over a period of nearly five and a half years. The discussions would always be initiated by Peter, at first in a veiled and oblique manner, and later quite openly. They would continue in Canada after Csaba's arrival, both while Csaba was living with the Demeters and after he had taken lodging of his own. They would talk about many unrelated matters, of course, but murdering Christine would be a recurring theme of their conversations. Peter would want Csaba to comment on the feasibility of his plans as well as carry them out for him. Though no actual payment would ever be discussed, Peter would hint that if Csaba did this, he'd return the favour.

Specifically, Csaba testified, the following plots were discussed during this period:

1) To toss Christine off the top landing in one of Peter's unfinished houses on Burnaby Boulevard which had a three-storey stairwell with no banisters installed. (Csaba demurred, saying the neighbours could observe him doing it through a full-length window running parallel to the staircase.)

2) To toss Christine down the basement stairs in Peter's house on Dawes Road, and should the fall be insufficient, to finish her off with a blow on the head. (Csaba pointed out that the difference between a blow and injuries caused by a fall would be detectable.)

3) To kill Christine or render her unconscious by a blow over the head, then drag her out to the poorly lit Dundas Highway across the road from their Mississauga home, where she would be run over by a passing car, or possibly by Csaba's own car. This plot called for Peter to deliver the initial blow himself, while Christine's presence on the highway would be explained by the dog's getting loose. (Csaba refused once again, saying that the difference between injuries caused by a car and a blow would be quite evident.)

4) To blow up or cremate Christine by spilling gasoline inside the garage, then closing the power door and throwing a match as she was driving in with her car. (Csaba said the mixture of air and gasoline might not explode or catch fire.)

5) To have Christine drive a car with faulty brakes that would heat up and ignite the adjacent gas-line running between the tank and the engine. (The gas simply wouldn't ignite, Csaba said.)

6) A variation of the Dawes Road theme, whereby Christine would be sent to the house with a sum of money on her person and would be thrown down the basement stairs by another man. At this moment Csaba would walk in, "catch the guy, so to speak, red-handed", and demand half the money he took from Christine. (Csaba testified that he objected to this awesome plan by saying "there was no way of assuring that this would work the way he wanted it", which was putting it mildly.)

7) To electrocute Christine while she was in the swimming pool by interfering with one of the circuits attached to it. (Csaba told Peter the flaw in this plan was that the water in the pool contained too little soluble salt to be conductive.)

8) Finally, to kill Christine by shooting her in the course of a fake break-in. This plan called for Csaba to enter the house on Dundas Crescent through a window, bringing with him a .22-calibre rifle of hard-to-

trace Mexican manufacture that Peter would supply. Peter would use this rifle to shoot Christine dead, and Csaba would then shoot Peter in some non-vital area. Then Csaba would disappear, taking certain valuables with him that Peter would previously prepare in a heap in the kitchen. (Csaba objected to this plot by saying that experts could determine from a gunshot wound the circumstances under which it was inflicted — and besides no burglar in his right mind would carry a bulky .22 rifle with him on house-breaking missions.)

Even after he had bowed out of this plot, Csaba said, Peter apparently wanted to involve him in one more. This was on June 16, two days before Christine's death. On the morning of that day Csaba said he received a telephone call from Peter, asking him to prevent his girlfriend Gigi, the Demeters' former maid, from spending the afternoon with Christine. (This was the afternoon when Christine did meet Gigi at the doctor's office to exchange some pills and then drive with her to Dawes Road, where she had to shut off the sprinkler system.) Csaba testified that he told Peter he would be too busy to drive Gigi to the doctor himself and make sure she didn't spend the afternoon with Christine. Though Peter tried insisting, Csaba said, "we parted on the note that there was no agreement reached. I heard from him later on that same day at approximately 4 or 4:30 that afternoon, just after opening up the store. He sounded very annoyed."

"What did he say?" asked Greenwood.

"He said he made the purchase, but how can I not do him this little favour in return for all the favours he had done me, besides what satisfaction would I derive from the fact that he had just lost $10,000 and that he had just received a phone call from a certain man who had told him that *the deal was one and not two.*"

Startling, outlandish, incredible as it might have been, this was the gist of Csaba Szilagyi's story given under oath in open court. It took Crown Attorney John Greenwood less than two hours and only twenty-five pages of transcript to elicit it. Beginning his cross-examination immediately after lunch, Joe Pomerant would take nearly ten days and more than five hundred pages of transcript in an attempt to break it down.

A preliminary hearing, of course, is not a trial. It is simply an inquiry before a lower-court judge, who listens to whatever evidence the prosecution has — or chooses to present — and decides whether or not there seems to be enough of it to warrant a full trial before a court of competent jurisdiction. The *credibility* of a witness is not really an issue at a preliminary hearing, because that is something for the jury to decide at the actual trial. Still, when a charge is based on little more than an accusation levelled by one person at another, the truthfulness of the accuser becomes very material. Judge Young was prepared to be fair, and like any other human being he might also have been curious. Though he was moved to comment that Joe's examination of Csaba seemed to proceed "at an evolutionary pace", he made no attempt to curtail it.

Pomerant was faced with a major dilemma. Unchallenged, Szilagyi's testimony would almost certainly result in Peter's being committed to stand trial for the murder of his wife. On the other hand, challenging a surprise witness without preparation can lead into traps of the most dangerous kind. Pomerant had no time to investigate, to reconnoitre and find out if the enemy facing him was weak or strong. He had to decide whether to risk a frontal assault against Szilagyi on the spot, or to retrench, regroup, and meet his testimony from a better defensive position. Perhaps if he had thought that Csaba's evidence contained *any* truth, he might have chosen the latter course. The action he took seemed to indicate that he regarded Csaba's testimony as a bare-faced lie, a transparent fabrication he could safely meet head-on.

Pomerant began his cross-examination in a tone of undisguised contempt. He pulled out all the stops right at the start, and under his relentless scrutiny the weaknesses in Csaba's story became glaringly apparent. If true, the relationship between Peter and Csaba would have had to be grotesque, bizarre beyond belief! A grown man trying to talk another grown man into killing his wife for years and years, through one far-fetched and childish scheme after the other? A friend refusing to have anything to do with killing but maintaining his friendship with a would-be killer and coming back time after time to listen to yet another hare-brained plot? Why would a husband start plotting in 1968, practically on his honeymoon, maybe six months or so after he had married his beautiful wife? Moreover, why would he do it long *before* renewing his relationship with his mistress (Demeter didn't even start corresponding with Marina again until the fall of '70) and *before* acquiring the million-dollar life insurance the Crown was now alleging to be his motive for the murder? Why would someone agree to be sponsored to Canada by a man he believes has murder on his mind? If he does not wish to be part of any such scheme, why would he not decline it by more forthright means than non-committal silence and feeble "technical" objections? If he believed an open refusal would put his own life in danger because of his knowledge of his friend's intentions, why would he take no alternate steps to protect himself in five and a half years? In any case, if Csaba kept quiet because he was afraid of Peter even before he murdered, why would he stop being afraid of him now that he believed he had? (Szilagyi wasn't exactly *cornered* into testifying: all the police had on him was Rita Jefferies' report that he mentioned to her once, during a social conversation in the spring of '73, that he could make some money by helping Peter to kill Christine. Csaba could easily have denied it, or claimed it was a joke or a misunderstanding.) Conversely, if he wanted to tell the truth as a good citizen, why would he not come forward by himself? (Because Csaba didn't: he went to visit Peter the evening after the murder and came away quite sure in his own mind that Peter had something to do with it, yet even after being picked up by the police he would try, for the first few minutes, to "weaken the import" of Rita's statement, according to his own testimony.) Why would he not warn Christine, against whom he said he had no animosity, that her life might be in danger? (Because he didn't, not even after Peter's alleged call on June 16, which, if true, must have indicated to him that Peter had now passed from planning to action. As it turned out, Christine even dropped by Csaba's apartment for a few minutes the following day, on June 17, the day before she was killed, because she wanted to discuss something with Gigi.) Most of all, why would he say nothing to Gigi, his own girlfriend, the woman he was now about to marry, after Peter's call on the sixteenth? If he thought Peter was serious — as he said he did — would he knowingly let Gigi walk with Christine into a possible murder trap? And finally, why would Peter insist on conspiring with Csaba, a man of no criminal record or experience, who came closest to breaking the law in his entire life back in Austria once when his dog bit the apartment superintendent's wife?

And yet, the raging 200,000-word battle between Pomerant and Szilagyi ended in nothing more than a stand-off. Battered, stripped, and humiliated, Csaba stuck by his story. Joe might have scored innumerable psychological points, might have put in sharp relief the patent absurdity of Csaba's relationship with Peter, might have cast many doubts on his motives or character, but he couldn't catch him in any direct lies or contradictions. At the end of Joe's merciless cross-examination Csaba might have emerged a Benedict Arnold, a Judas, a rat; he might have come across as a person of the most conflicting impulses or ideas; but he wasn't proven to be the one thing that would have mattered: a perjurer. It was obvious he was a man *capable* of lying; after all, when he tricked and misled Peter with the body-pack conversations he had to be lying to him all the time; but, as Csaba pointed out to Joe, on those occasions he wasn't under oath.

While Pomerant, in the given situation, probably had no choice but to essay a few probes into the surprise witness's veracity, his attempt to finish him off right then and there, even after meeting stiff resistance, might well have been a tactical error. The cross-examination wasn't a fiasco, but in the end it was futile and it used up some of Joe's best ammunition with no jury there to appreciate the fireworks. In fact, after having withstood to some extent the defence lawyer's worst blows, Csaba seemed to gather some strength or at least become anaesthetized against the pain of Pomerant's continuing jabs. After two or three days on the stand he would even start jabbing back at Joe himself. Worse still from the defence's point of view, by the time the real test of strength would arrive he could prepare himself and know what to expect. He was given a dress rehearsal.

Peter himself, sitting at the defence lawyer's table by special permission, would get over his first shock and start scribbling note after note, presumably in rebuttal of Szilagyi's statements on the stand. The newspapers reported his expression to be devoid of surprise or anger, only concentration and the occasional smile of disbelief. (The stories in the local press were published in spite of Judge Young's explicit orders, giving a foretaste of what was to come at the time of the actual trial.) As Peter's notes would be passed on to Joe, his questions to Csaba would at times reflect their probable content. It would seem that, as far as Peter was concerned, his one-time friend was taking real events and embellishing them with his story. "I considered Szilagyi's story to be absolutely unworthy of belief," Eddie Greenspan would say later. "As to *why* he said what he did, I think I arranged in my own mind the view that he had had an affair with Christine Demeter, that he knew a great deal more about her death than he was letting on, but that none of what he was saying was true."

Joe Pomerant, who must have had enough of Hungarians around this time, chose a group of Mississauga detectives during a recess to unburden himself of his general views on Hungarian habits and national character. As luck would have it, the group consisted of Bill Teggart, Chris O'Toole — and Joe Terdik, who withdrew in pretended anger in the middle of Joe's exposition. The other two detectives, of course, lost no time in telling Pomerant that their colleague, too, belonged to that dubious nationality. As a good liberal, Joe was aghast at his gaffe and spent the rest of the day apologizing to Terdik and explaining to him that some of his best friends, et cetera. Bill Teggart, for whom baiting the slick counsellor had become something of a pastime, relished the incident. Said Teggart: "The lawyer who's trying to relate, touch, and use people-therapy is a disaster. That's for social workers." The superintendent's irritation with Pomerant, of course, might have had other causes as well: Joe had won quite a number of procedural battles during the preliminary, and among other things had succeeded in getting Judge Young to exclude Teggart and O'Toole from the courtroom during much of his cross-examination of Csaba, so that they had no idea for hours at a time how their star witness was progressing on the stand.

In a brief and rather low-keyed summation, the Crown Attorney asked the court on March 4, 1974, "to commit the accused for trial on the charge against him." Joe Pomerant's summation for the defence on the same day was far more impassioned and eloquent. It not only forecast the difference in style between the two protagonists, but also denoted the likely degree of their personal involvement in the case at that point.

"Your Honour," Pomerant began, "in order to commit Mr. Demeter for trial, your Honour would have to make a finding, in my respectful submission, that there is some evidence on which a jury properly instructed could convict the accused person.

"I think a remote possibility of conviction would not suffice to send this case on for trial. There has to be a probability of conviction in order to warrant the time, the effort, the expense, and the placing of an accused person on this trial in a complicated matter of this sort, which will take months to proceed and produce untold anguish, win or lose, on behalf of the accused person. Certainly lose, yes; and even win in this particular case."

The Crown would have to demonstrate, Pomerant argued, two things. First, that a homicide had in fact occurred, and second, that Peter Demeter was responsible for it. For the purpose of the preliminary hearing Joe said he'd concede that Christine had died "as a result of an unlawful act causing her death". But for the second point . . .

Here Pomerant interrupted himself to make a request. "I have been given a note," he said, "that Mr. Szilagyi is present at this stage, and again, I think it would be best for the administration of justice if, without turning around and noticing if he is, if we kept this witness out of the proceedings at this stage, your Honour."

Greenwood rose, astounded. "Your Honour," he said, "I can see no merit at all for this observation. Surely there is no relevance, and it is not a proper issue of comment that Mr. Szilagyi is present at the argument."

"With respect, your Honour," said Joe. "I *have* turned around. There is one argument that I think can safely be made. Mr. Szilagyi . . . sits with the person who taped the conversations, the senior investigating officer, and undoubtedly a guard. . . . Somehow it strikes me that to offer a well-reasoned discourse with respect to the evidence of Mr. Szilagyi and what your Honour must do, ought not to be coupled with a type of psychological positioning of Mr. Szilagyi here in the courtroom. I personally do not care. Perhaps your Honour does not care. But it strikes me as being, in my respectful submission, it puts it into approximately the same position as if I were to bring Mr. Demeter's three-year-old child during the course of the argument."

Judge Young, normally a fluent and rather witty jurist, seemed to have some difficulty finding his voice.

"Mr. Pomerant, the analogy is certainly not — I cannot see this being direct, and I think — you said you do not care. I certainly do not care."

Indeed, it was difficult to see what Joe would wish to achieve by excluding Csaba from the courtroom. There was no jury present; no one to impress by an emotional appeal. Certainly, if it came to that, Pomerant would not be inhibited by Szilagyi's presence if he wanted to call him a liar. The inquiry, as such, was over; whatever Joe would say in his closing argument could later be conveyed to Csaba in plenty of time to influence his testimony in the next round, if that was what Joe was worried about. True, judges were human beings with emotions of their own, but however Csaba's mere presence might prejudice Judge Young against Peter, it could not have been half as bad as Joe's suggestion — if that's what it was — that it might do so.

It seemed much more likely that Joe, at this point, identified with Peter strongly enough to feel personally outraged by the sight of Csaba sitting in the courtroom. If so, perhaps he couldn't help giving vent to his own anger over what he regarded as a vicious and transparent lie spoiling an easy victory in a major murder case.

The rest of the summation for the defence was very much to the point and quite convicing. Essentially, Joe argued, taking Szilagyi's evidence at its best, assuming for a moment he was telling the truth, it would prove nothing but that Peter had been talking to him about killing his wife on a number of occasions. Peter, however, was charged with the specific offence of actually causing his wife's death on July 18. The Crown offered no evidence to substantiate that charge.

Assuming Szilagyi was not lying, Joe said, the best he could offer was Peter's alleged telephone calls to him on Monday, July 16, to show "possibly there being a party other than Mr. Szilagyi and Mr. Demeter to the death of Christine Demeter.

"In my submission," Pomerant continued, "the evidence, taken at its best, Szilagyi at his best, boils down to this: that Peter Demeter intended to rob a bank on Monday. The bank was robbed on Wednesday. Can we in law infer that because Peter Demeter intended to rob a bank on Monday, and the bank was robbed on Wednesday, that there is a probability that Peter Demeter robbed the bank on Wednesday? In my respectful submission, we cannot, as a matter of law, take that position."

Here Joe had put his finger on the weakest point of the Crown's case, a point that would not cease to plague the prosecution until the very end, and perhaps even beyond. If the jury believed Csaba, it would be proof that Peter had thought about killing his wife, but still not necessarily proof that he did kill her. The Crown, in fact, had no such proof. Whatever the outcome of the preliminary hearing, Bill Teggart could not yet retire his golden slippers.

In the rest of his closing argument Joe quoted legal authorities to point out the insufficiency of motive alone for conviction, then dismissed the body-pack tapes by saying they contained "not a tittle of evidence . . . that would indicate that Peter Demeter was involved with the death of his wife.

"There is enough in there," Joe said, "there is a phrase in there, there is a word in there. . . . If you are trying to build up a momentum of suspicion, it exists; there are 20 hours worth of conversations. One thing that is missing in those 20 hours . . . is one statement by Peter Demeter that 'I did it. I caused it to be done.' " (Though this was true, Pomerant's somewhat cavalier dismissal of the tapes suggested one of two things: either he had no time — or inclination — to analyse them in detail, or he felt they would not be admitted in evidence against Peter anyway.

From every other point of view they were as damaging and as worth meeting head-on as Csaba's testimony. Later the suggestion would be made that the defence was late in receiving the tapes from the Crown. If this was true, Pomerant would have been severely restricted in going through them for the purpose of rebuttal.)

Pomerant ended his submission with some ringing lines of oratory, containing a fair share of plain truth:

"I have never been involved in a case where there is as much rank suspicion. If suspicion were the test, this man would be on his trial in one second.

"There is enormous suspicion engendered from a variety of sources . . . but that is not evidence that ought to cause a person to be committed for trial on a charge of murder.

"Your Honour may come to a different conclusion. It may be a situation where a reasonable man may disagree. In my respectful submission, I think that justice could equally well be served in this case and in this community by demonstrating that in our country people are sent on for their trials based on a probability of guilt in terms of fact, and not conjecture. It reduces our system to one of legal speculation, rather than judicial proof.

"Those are my submissions, your Honour."

Judge Young told the attorneys that he needed at least until Friday, March 8, to consider his decision. On that day at ten o'clock in the morning the judge leaned forward slightly in his chair, cleared his throat, and raised his eyes to meet Peter Demeter's.

"I would say that I have now had an opportunity," he said, "to consider the evidence adduced and the arguments presented.

"In discharging this duty the Justice must remember that it is not his function to determine guilt or innocence, but there must be more than a mere possibility or suspicion that the accused is guilty.

"Generally, in order to commit, the evidence must be such as to cause him to form the opinion that the accused is probably guilty, and any doubt in this regard must be resolved in favour of committal.

"Applying these tests through the evidence I find sufficient evidence has been adduced, and I order that you be committed for trial to the next court of competent jurisdiction."

Suspicion or probability, conjecture or fact, the first round was going to the Crown. Whatever Peter did or did not do, it seemed probable to the court that he had had evil thoughts at one time, and they would now come back to haunt him. " . . . I'd be in the same situation if the sharks had eaten her in Acapulco. . . . " Though justice was supposed to concern itself with deeds, if Peter had focused his eyes on the coat of arms hanging above the judge's head, he could also have deciphered the words on a ribbon encircling two mythical beasts: *Honi soit qui mal y pense.*

13. Interlude

Marina returned to Canada in the spring of 1974. Since the death of Christine her feelings for Peter had teetered between passion and exasperation. She spent the winter of 1973-4 in Vienna, with barely a word from her mysterious lover except a few messages from go-betweens like his cousin Steven Demeter, or elderly friends like Helga Treitl. It really was too much. There she was being hauled in by the Austrian police and asked all sorts of questions about pay-offs to murderers, as if she were involved in that horrible business in Mississauga — all because she had innocently delivered a small sum for Peter to one of the Hungarian mendicants he godfathered. Her arrest took some explaining to her friends and most especially to her family, who had never liked Peter in the first place. And then when he did find time to telephone he would never let her get a word in. It was all explanations about what Christine had been up to, and stories about how the insurance companies and the police were persecuting him. It almost seemed as if he didn't want to let her speak.

Still, there were certain compensations. The Hamburg newspapers were very interested in the gory tale of Christine Demeter, and some of the popular photo magazines in Vienna and Rome had been sniffing around Marina now that she had been identified as the "other woman" in the case. Such things couldn't really harm a model's career, and it was not altogether unpleasant to be pursued by local flocks of paparazzi.

Peter hadn't liked it, of course, and there had been one very unpleasant phone call after he had read the November 5 edition of an Italian magazine. He had accused her of being indiscreet. But in Vienna Marina was a mini-celebrity, and some of the newspaper photos were really quite flattering.

All the same, when Peter paused in his endless stories about this tiresome Superintendent Teggart and became again the confident stranger in charge of her life, Marina felt weak with desire for him. Peter had cancelled her summer visit right after Christine's death, explaining that "it would not be right for you to come now", but surely nine months was a respectable enough period of mourning. Besides, Marina was not celebrated for celibacy, and the strain of being true to her Canadian friend was beginning to show. She was putting on weight and, by her own account, hitting the bottle with increasing regularity. She decided to utilize the old reliable weapons of conventional sexual warfare in her bid to join Peter in Canada. In making people jealous, however, it was important to strike the right balance. Marina decided to admit only to limited and selective infidelity.

Marina's virtuosity in the sexual arena was not a matter of conjecture. Her letters to Peter were seasoned with references to her affairs, or at least to her desirability. In April of 1973, just after she had returned from a holiday with one boyfriend and shortly before her Canadian jaunt with Peter, Marina wrote a letter to Demeter about a film offer she had just received:

> I didn't read a script yet and the suspicion is growing in me that this film does not agree with my taste. Most probably they want me in the nude. . . .
>
> Besides it is customary in Vienna to sleep at least with the producer, then with the stage manager, then with the camera man and then with all the light setters, best with all at once. I don't know how I can get out of this affair without annoying the whole team. Like last time.

But Marina was also an up-to-date girl who was not about to limit her activities to the mere one-half of the population who were male:

> Probably I will be in Paris in middle of April. There the "Pret à Porter" and some other things are going on. You know, Paris in spring is just what I like. A paradise for lovers. I am going with a girlfriend whom you don't know, however, and with whom I am in love. And we will turn the city upside down and paint it pink.

Though Marina's lesbian affairs could scarcely have given Demeter any pleasure, they did not seem to incur quite the same degree of displeasure that her adventures with Wolfi et al. brought on. Perhaps that was why she chose to use her Sapphic encounters as a bargaining card with Peter. During one of their lengthy overseas telephone calls late in 1973, filled with recriminations and bitter tallies of each other's short-comings, Peter abruptly asked Marina if she was still on the pill. It was just the opening she had been waiting for.

"Why," she asked, "when I sleep more with women than with men?"

The logic of this was undeniable. Peter paused only a few seconds, bearing in mind perhaps that the call was costing him about four dollars a minute.

"That is one thing I have never done," he replied. "I would never sleep with another man."

Marina seemed unimpressed by this display of consistency. "Why don't you try it," she suggested helpfully, "with Superintendent Teggart?" Whatever outrage this suggestion provoked in Peter, it is unlikely that it matched that felt by the Peel Regional police officer who was monitoring the call. (Even a year and a half later, Deputy-Chief Teggart could barely mention the conversation without a small blush and un-conscious flexing of his formidable biceps.) But at the time it seemed clear to Peter that a Marina loose and alone in Vienna was a situation capable of a thousand and one permutations. It took only a few more remarks of a similar nature to force the issue. She arrived in Toronto early in April of 1974.

The circumstances of Peter's life were now quite different from those of the previous year when he and Marina had enjoyed their steamy liaison through the bedrooms of the better hotels of Montreal, Ottawa, and Toronto. Now Peter was a worried man under indictment for murder. Not surprisingly, he was concerned only with proving his innocence. His days centred around his convoluted telephone calls with Joe Pomerant, and whatever prognosis on his case he could solicit from friends or acquaintances. His movements were confined by law to Metropolitan Toronto and the boroughs of East York and Mississauga. A trip to as ex-otic a location as Niagara Falls, only seventy-five miles away, would have required police permission. If granted, he would probably have ac-quired a discreet police escort as well.

Marina understood none of this when she stepped off the plane. She was coming to the side of the man she loved to help him in his fight for justice. It was a glamorous feeling, probably enhanced at first by the re-porters camped outside Peter's Dundas Crescent home and the contingent of photographers who seemed to follow her every move. They had not had as photogenic a participant in the Demeter case since the summer of 1973 when the press specialized in digging up early pictures of Christine from her modelling days.

It was not long before Marina discovered that the reality of life with Peter Demeter was quite different from the excitement she had pictured. Often Peter would spend his days lying on his bed, unshaven and unkempt. As his business worries increased and the banks refused to finance his projects, he became obsessed with expenses. In the past going out to dinner had been a matter of course. Now he resented spending the money.

"What difference can a few dollars make?" asked his cousin Steven Demeter. "Take Marina out of the house and enjoy a good restaurant."

But it was not only Peter's mobility that suffered. His circle of friends had shrunk considerably. Peter's moodiness and temper had never endeared him to a wide range of friends, but his generous hospitality had always assured him of a house full of guests who were quite content to drink his liquor, enjoy his swimming pool, and keep any remarks about his unpleasant behaviour *sotto voce*. Now that the parties were suspended pending the trial, it was much more fun for some Hungarian friends to gather at one another's homes — without the embarrassing presence of Peter — where they could discuss what seemed to them his obvious guilt with much relish. Only Klara Majerszky and her young boyfriend remained loyal, and for all her sterling qualities, Klara was a good twenty-five years older than Marina and not especially sympathetic to the restlessness of a young girl.

More and more Marina spent her days wandering about downtown Toronto, familiarizing herself with the merchandise at Simpson's or Eaton's, the two huge department stores, and idly filling in time till Peter's meetings at Pomerant, Pomerant and Greenspan would be finished and they could drive back to Mississauga. Peter had given her the use of the Mercedes, which she enjoyed, and she had charge accounts for her needs, but apart from a pair of $135 boots and some sheets, she rarely indulged herself. It was one thing to spend the money of the boys on the ski and disco circuit or cash the money orders Peter had sent her in happier days, but quite another to be frivolous with the finances of this strange, worried man brooding over his lawyers' fees and his shrinking income.

So the summer dragged on. Even the courts had taken a long siesta, with the brief exception of a two-day session of the Grand Jury which, as everyone expected, returned a true bill against Demeter. That occasioned another little flurry in the press, but then life settled back into the monotony of long, agonizing evenings on Dundas Crescent, with Peter reappraising scraps of information and half-formed theories all thoroughly chewed and reappraised the night before. At times Marina thought she would go quite mad. The only place Peter would visit was the home of Steven Demeter and his Canadian wife Marjorie. They lived in a sprawling ranch-style home on Old Yonge Street in North Toronto with a fine swimming pool and an orderly routine presided over by Steven's mother, who, dressed in a white uniform, ran the household with the same quiet efficiency with which she had run the family estate in Hungary. Her daughter-in-law Marjorie possessed a respectable job as a high school home-economics teacher and a tart commonsense, and had a tendency to count her calories. This was not a combination that endeared itself to Marina, whose tastes ran to "crunchy" girls and hard liquor. Marjorie, for her part, tried to live up to family obligations and entertain Marina, but they had little common ground.

"Her idea of a good time," explained Marjorie, "was to booze it up. That just didn't appeal to me."

Marina began turning up at the Demeters' Old Yonge Street house looking as dishevelled and poorly groomed as Peter. Her shoulder-length chestnut hair, which had once swung silkily in the sunlight, was now washed less and less often. The blouses she wore were crumpled and dirty.

"She thought she was coming to a situation where Peter would be surrounded by friends all eager to help and prove his innocence. She would be the centre of the circle," explained Marjorie. "She discovered that he was, in fact, quite isolated except for us."

Then, late in the summer came a new development. On August 19, a sixteen-year-old girl named Judith Sheldon stayed down at Toronto's Canadian National Exhibition to get one last look at the exhibits before flying back to England with her family that night. She dawdled over the displays till late afternoon and then, in a bit of a panic over the transit strike in Mississauga where she was staying, decided to hitch-hike home. She turned down a number of car rides before accepting the offer of a pleasant-looking young man in his mid-twenties. Gratefully, she climbed in. As the car drove along the highway, Judith noticed a sticker on the dashboard with the name "Williams, Streetsville" on it. When

15. The funeral

REGINA vs. DEMETER

CHARGE: NON-CAPITAL MURDER

THE ACCUSED

NAME: PETER DEMETER

ADDRESS: 1437 Dundas Crescent, Mississauga, Ontario

DATE OF BIRTH: April 19, 1933

AGE: 40 years,

HEIGHT: 6 ft. 2 inches,

WEIGHT: 190 lbs.,

STATUS: Widower,

OCCUPATION: Builder,

POLICE REPORT: Occurrence No. 10291/73.

17. Peter Demeter's Viennese mistress, Marina Hundt, during a recess in her testimony at Peter's trial

18. Marina walking Beelzebub during the trial in London, Ontario

19. Marina décolletée

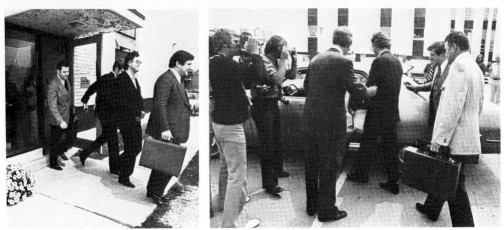

20 & 21. Peter Demeter on the day of the arrest, August 17, 1973

22. "I knew it would be the most important arrest in my life because he looked so distinguished." Superintendent William Teggart

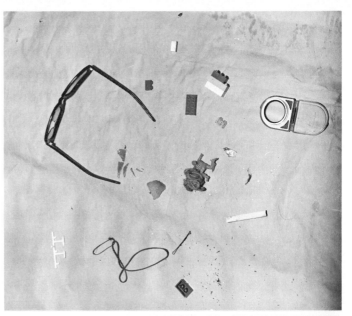

23. A photograph of objects found in the blood-spattered grey Cadillac.

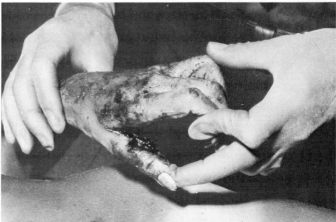

24. This autopsy photo shows the deep gash on Christine's left thumb, "the kind of wound a person might sustain when attempting to ward off a blow"

25. The upward flow of blood on the side of the car, "the classic sign of a bloodied weapon being raised and swung repeatedly over a victim"

26. Crown Attorney John Greenwood and Superintendent William Teggart, and in the rear Detective-Sergeant Christopher O'Toole

27. Peter Demeter is escorted to the London Jail by a police officer on November 4, 1974. Publication of this photo was considered grounds for a mistrial motion by the defence.

28. "Mr. X", the mystery witness

29. Csaba Szilagyi: "If this is one of
Peter Demeter's friends, I'd hate
to meet his enemies."

30. Ferenc Stark, the contractor

31. The Duck

she looked up, the car had gone past the turnoff she had indicated as her destination and was heading away from the main highway. When she questioned the driver, his reply was to hold a knife against her throat.

In a field some distance from the main road, Judith Sheldon was stripped and raped. When that was over her assailant plunged his knife into her back and side repeatedly and began covering her motionless body with rocks. Only the siren of an ambulance passing along the nearby highway stopped him. Quite sure that Judith was dead anyway, he left her partially buried body and drove off. The girl crawled and staggered to the road. The next day, August 20, 1974, Robert J. Williams of Streetsville, Ontario, was arrested. He confessed to the rape and attempted murder of Judith Sheldon, *and* the successful rape-murders of Constance Dickey and Neda Novak. Now the police had the "maniac" of Mississauga in their hands.

As the trial date approached, Marina began to brighten up. Even Peter seemed more confident now that the waiting period was almost over, and he began to talk about how, when it was all finished, they would get married and go away. In the meantime certain preparations had to be made. Since Marina was now a known element in the case, Peter's lawyers decided she might as well be visible from the start. Perhaps they thought the picture of her sitting steadfastly at Peter's side might dispel some of the seamier aspects of her adulterous role. Her wardrobe was discussed and a well-scrubbed look adopted: crisp blouses and a navy blazer with hair pulled neatly back in a pony tail. By the time the trial began, switch-hitting Marina would look like an advertisement for the wholesome effects of drinking milk.

14. The Majesty of the Law

The battle between the Crown and the defence began with a little skirmish that was very nearly won by Joe Pomerant.

The judicial district in which Christine had been murdered would normally have placed Peter's trial in the town of Brampton at the Fall Assize Sittings of the Supreme Court of Ontario. This little community on the western fringes of Metropolitan Toronto was home territory for many of the police officers involved in the Demeter case. It was possible that Peter's right to a fair trial might be seriously jeopardized in a small town where the local newspapers would have occasion to hail detectives like Teggart, Wingate, and O'Toole nearly every week for solving some crime or another. The defence claimed that this, coupled with the sensational publicity Peter's case had already received, might prejudice a jury of local citizens. John Greenwood felt that Joe's chances for succeeding in a motion for a change of venue were excellent, and he had made up his mind at the outset to oppose it only as a matter of form. Much as Greenwood might have liked to try Peter before a Crown-oriented jury, he knew that a show of bloody-mindedness on his part might later reverberate against him. As a good tactician, Greenwood was not at all anxious to win a skirmish and risk losing the war.

If the defence motion was successful, common sense suggested that the venue would be changed to Toronto. Most of the witnesses lived in Toronto, as did the lawyers for the defence. The Mississauga officers and the Crown were based at an easy commuting distance from the city. Although prosecuting suave, sophisticated Peter before a cosmopolitan Toronto jury was the worst possible bet from the Crown's point of view, Greenwood had more or less resigned himself to it. He couldn't, in fact, think of any good reasons for opposing it.

For that matter, simple justice would have found Toronto the most likely place where a man like Peter might be tried by a jury of his peers. Although in a democratic society that no longer recognizes distinctions between citizens "peer" has come to mean anything that isn't a plant, an animal, or a convicted felon, in practice every lawyer is well aware of the lack of sympathy members of one group in society might have for members of another. In the adversary system, lawyers deal with this fact of life by trying to turn it to their own advantage. As long as it is conducted within the proper bounds of procedure, this practice is considered perfectly ethical and legitimate. Since it was in Metropolitan Toronto that Peter might have found his real peers — that is, twelve jurors most closely resembling him in background and lifestyle — it was the obvious place for the defence to seek and for the prosecution to avoid.

That Peter Demeter was not tried in Toronto was due to a couple of casual conversations. The first was between Joe Pomerant and Chief Justice Wells of the Supreme Court. The second was between Joe Pomerant and John Greenwood.

The manner in which cases are conducted ranges from the greatest formality in court to a fair bit of informality in private talks between lawyers and sometimes even judges. Courthouse corridors and cafeterias are buzzing with off-the-record comments, rumours, gossip, and exchanges of confidential information. The court *is* something of a stage, and its corridors of power resemble nothing more than the wings or dressing rooms of any other theatre. Lawyers and judges, just like actors, often exhibit a different side of their being before donning their robes and assuming their legal roles. Such informality is not necessarily improper or even unwise, and off-the-record conversations or negotiations between learned and ethical people can often streamline or make more human the stiff, cumbersome, and antiquated machinery of the administration of justice.

Apparently one day during the summer of 1974 Chief Justice Wells bumped into the head of the Demeter defence team in the courthouse corridor. He had looked at the defence motion for a change of venue, the Chief Justice reportedly said, and had come to the conclusion that Demeter should be tried in Toronto before Justice Haines of the Supreme Court of Ontario. This was good news for the defence, and Joe Pomerant couldn't resist telling John Greenwood about it.

Although Greenwood had more or less expected this decision, he felt that the manner in which it had been imparted might give him an opening to fight it. Of course the Chief Justice had a perfect right to choose Toronto (Greenwood himself conceded later it would have been a logical and fair choice) and there was nothing improper about the Chief Justice's telling a defence lawyer of a decision he had every right to make. Still, the fact that he seemed to have made up his mind even before the formal hearing at which the prosecution could present its arguments gave Greenwood the opportunity to cry foul. He cried it loud and clear, through the Director of Crown Attorneys in the Department of the Attorney General. No doubt his protest reached Chief Justice Wells in due course.

If Joe Pomerant had been less given to tactics of "communications" and keeping in touch with one's opponents, Greenwood might never have found out about the Toronto venue until it was too late. If Chief Justice Wells had happened to be in a more stubborn mood, or hadn't been on the verge of retirement from a long and distinguished career, he might have stuck to his guns in spite of all the hue and cry from the Attorney General's office. After all, it was a good decision and the prosecution had no real arguments against it. As it was, however, the Crown didn't even have to marshal its grounds for opposing Toronto. At the beginning of the hearing, to Joe Pomerant's complete astonishment, Chief Justice Wells announced that courtroom facilities were so crowded in Toronto that Peter Demeter's trial could not be accommodated there under any circumstances. (As Eddie Greenspan was to report later, this was simply not accurate: one of the largest courtrooms in Toronto's new Courthouse ended up being hardly used at all in the fall and winter of 1974.) Then the Chief Justice said he thought St. Thomas might be the best place for the trial.

"With respect, where is St. Thomas?" asked Greenspan, only half in jest. The little Ontario community with its mixture of rural and small-town population sounded like a deadly place in which to defend a case with its cast of international characters. (John Greenwood must have been rubbing his hands with glee at the unexpected success of his intervention. If Pomerant thought he had stolen a march on him, he was certainly returning the favour in spades. "We were losing control of the case," the Crown Attorney said later. "If Joe and the judges are setting up who's gonna hear it where, and having little backroom discussions saying 'this will be it, fellows', then suddenly we become a very ancillary thing. . . . ") In the end, however, it was the man who eventually became the trial judge, the Hon. Mr. Justice Campbell Grant, who suggested the place where Peter Demeter would be tried.

"I was sitting at St. Thomas at the time," Justice Grant recalled, "and I said there's no accommodation for anybody to live in St. Thomas and the courtroom itself is not big enough, it's an old, old building. I said why don't you move it over to London? And immediately he [Chief Justice Wells] said, that's the very place. I said London'll be open the first of September and we'll be in the new courthouse there. There's a lovely view from the new courthouse. He said that's just lovely, that's what we'll do. And so that's how we got to London. Up until then, there hadn't been any suggestion of London and it was rather a surprise to defence counsel to find themselves there. . . . "

Shock would have been a better word. On September 23, 1974, Joe Pomerant and Eddie Greenspan found themselves defending a client, charged with murdering his wife for a million dollars in insurance, in the city of London, Ontario, the self-styled "Insurance Capital of the World". For the defence, St. Thomas and perhaps even Brampton would have appeared desirable in comparison. At this point Joe Pomerant must have wished he had never moved for a change of venue.

It was not so much the prospect of a jury drawn from the London area being biased against Peter. Although London as headquarters for several large Canadian insurance firms was no doubt a company town to some extent, this alone would not have prevented the defence from coming up with twelve jurors who had no connections with the insurance business whatever. Nor were they exactly in the backwoods: the Judicial District of Middlesex is far from being redneck country, and the city itself is a thriving, reasonably up-to-date community of nearly 100,000 people, complete with a respectable university. The average Ontarian, even outside the big metropolitan centres, is a tolerant and fairly well-informed person, not likely to be gripped by blind prejudice at the mere sight of a Hungarian or his Jewish lawyers. So, while the venue was not very desirable, the defence's handicap had less to do with substance than with style.

Demeter had always been an avid reader of mystery stories and was known to return to his favourite Hollywood whodunit movies two or three times. What might have attracted him to Joe Pomerant as his defence lawyer — in addition to his obvious qualifications — was that in his *style* Pomerant corresponded very closely to all the attorneys in those glossy books and movies. While he didn't exactly fly his own jet, he had the personality, the secretaries, the limousine, even the private investigator. For someone comforted by the idea of having retained a Perry Mason, Pomerant appeared to fit the bill. The problem was that this very style, while it might have carried the day in California, New York, or even Toronto, was less than fortunate in the down-to-earth environs of Middlesex County.

Moreover, if there's one law for the poor and another for the rich, this rule doesn't always work in the rich man's favour. To see a well-dressed, cheerful man walk confidently around flanked by several smart-looking lawyers, to watch him get into his Mercedes in front of the Holiday Inn, or seem to give impromptu press conferences amid a barrage of flash-bulbs, while everyone knows he is charged with the odious crime of murdering his wife, is to test the fair-mindedness of solid small-town citizens to an unwise extent. It didn't matter that, by doing all this, Peter did nothing to which he would not have been perfectly entitled. It didn't matter that, as a wealthy and sophisticated man, he had as much right to maintain his own lifestyle under the law's presumption of innocence as though he had been charged with no offence. For while a poor man accused of murder might also have been free on bail, a poor man would not have been so visibly free or seemed so confident of being exonerated. Demeter and his defence team, simply by being themselves, had put themselves at a disadvantage from the start.

Crown Attorney John Greenwood, on the other hand, seemed to fit the Judicial District of Middlesex nearly as much as Joe Pomerant stuck out of it. A large, lumbering man in his late forties, Greenwood exuded an aura of home-spun trustworthiness. In his ill-fitting black robe over his somewhat rumpled business suit, he tended to look like a giant sea-turtle about to take his first hesitant steps on dry land. If Pomerant's strength lay in seeming prompt, impassioned, and incisive even when making a plainly fatuous point, Greenwood operated by appearing slow and dull without missing a trick.

John Monster, as a class wit dubbed him in law school, had come a long way since his first public performance at the Robinette debates in the University of Toronto's Victoria College, where his address amounted to one sentence: "Honourable Judge, my notes are all mixed up." In the very beginning, few people would have forecast a brilliant career for Big John. The aptitude test he insisted on taking after he got out of the army told him he ought to become an engineer. But though he seemed to need the reassurance of tests, when they conflicted with his instincts Greenwood preferred instincts to science. A short time later he entered Bora Laskin and Dean Wright's new law school at the University of Toronto.

The school set up by the future Chief Justice of the Supreme Court of Canada was tough: in the first year only 28 students passed out of more than 120. No one expected the big, good-natured fellow, who always seemed to sit with his eyes shut, long legs stretched out, holding a pencil in his mouth, to be one of the 28. But whenever Dean Wright would call on him, Greenwood would slowly open his eyes and come up with the right answer. Being ponderous might have been his nature to begin with, but eventually it would become his strategy.

It was an effective strategy in a profession that attracts people with nimble minds, big ambitions, and corresponding egos. Unlike a debating society of law students, a real jury of plain citizens doesn't hand out too many points for cleverness; but it can often be swayed by an appearance of fairness, honesty, and concern with the truth. These qualities might well have been Greenwood's own, but whether they were or not, these were the qualities he projected. If a ruling would go against him, if he couldn't get some piece of evidence easily admitted, he was more likely to yield with good grace than to put up lengthy arguments. This would not only please the Bench — and in the long run having the judge on one's own side can be as important as winning over the jury — but would also create the impression that his case was so strong he could afford to give up minor points. Finally, Greenwood seemed to embody a principle that his partner, Leo McGuigan, expressed as "The Crown never loses as long as justice triumphs." This principle assumes that, unlike the defence, the Crown is not interested in winning but merely in arriving at the truth.

Though he might have seemed to embody this principle in court, Greenwood would have scoffed at it in private conversation. The Crown counsel is a lawyer, and in the adversary system a lawyer's job is to *win*. "I have no concept of justice in the abstract sense," he would say. "I think the Crown Attorney is there to get evidence, evaluate it, and get a conviction."

That might have been all there was to Greenwood's philosophy. There was no doubt that the six-foot-three amateur ex-boxer was unsentimental and combative. "He was really proud of his physical strength," remembered his boyhood friend, Family Court Judge W. L. Durham. "Once in a while he'd get into a fracas and want to settle it by 'going outside and fight'. His mother bawled me out once, said I was an ungrateful wretch. Turned out John had been getting handouts of $15 for me and my wife because 'they really need the money'. He had been ripping his mother off." But while he wouldn't miss out on a fight or a trick, John had a shyness and a reserve that were equally genuine, and he would go to some lengths not to appear "emotional". When his parents died he mentioned it to no one, and when his closest friend found out, John merely shrugged: "What the hell, it's a private thing." For such a man to admit — outside the ritual of the courtroom — that he does have an abstract concept of justice might seem unbearably soppy.

But in fact Greenwood was not without a restless and romantic streak beneath the straight, steady, somewhat awkward exterior of WASP understatement and reticence. It was not altogether strange for a man whose uncle was Victor Grayson, the maverick member of the British House of Commons, whose mysterious disappearance in the 1920s had inspired several books and is still a matter for debate among a small circle of afficionados. (Grayson was a mob-orator, something of a poor man's Churchill, sent to Parliament as a left-wing socialist from Yorkshire's Colne Valley in 1907, a year in which being a socialist was not remotely fashionable in Britain.) As a boy Greenwood idolized his uncle's memory, and had visions of modelling himself after the iconoclastic M.P. It was just that his own circumstances and personality seemed to militate against such grandiose notions. His father, though a lover of painting and classical music, was a quiet man who worked in an office for the Canadian National Railways all his life. John, far from seeing in himself signs of brilliance or powers of oratory, had a self-image of gaucherie, and considered speaking in public a terrifying experience. The very qualities that became his big assets in the London courtroom — reserve, a slight maladresse, a hint of rusticity — must have seemed tremendous handicaps to Greenwood as a boy, and perhaps even as a young lawyer.

This might well have been the reason why, in spite of his ambition and excellent early training (Greenwood articled with Roy McMurtry, Senior, then worked with Erickson Brown, the great insurance lawyer), he virtually buried himself for twelve years in an unexciting general practice in the small town of Port Credit, Ontario. True, he had married his high school sweetheart in 1957, and his quiet Port Credit practice would provide him with a good income for his family as well as an opportunity to spend a great deal of time with them. But his basic insecurity was likely to play just as big a part in those barren years between 1959 and 1972. "John wanted to be competitive," said his friend Judge Durham, "but he was afraid he would get his head cut off."

Restlessness and ambition won out in 1972, when Greenwood was forty-six years old. The same summer that Peter decided to have his first date with Marina after five and a half years, John made up his mind to accept the appointment of Crown Attorney for the Region of Peel, which included the Town of Mississauga and the Demeter garage at 1437 Dundas Crescent.

Greenwood's decision was unusual enough to be viewed less in terms of coincidence that in those of fate. The man without whom Demeter might not have been convicted had, prior to his appointment, done no criminal work in his life. At forty-six, he was not only older than the average Crown, but really too old to embark on what amounted to a new career. Though fascinated by litigation, John never had any particular interest in criminal law, and even less in the special vocation of a prosecutor which might compensate other Crown counsel for the relatively low rate of pay. It seemed that Greenwood, in terms of his own personality, was taking a considerable drop in income for no good reason. "My kids were coming along now, so I took it," he'd say later. "It was a marvellous opportunity to practise courtroom litigation." What Victor Grayson's nephew would not say, though it might have played a greater role in his decision, was that the Crown's job looked like an escape hatch from the humdrum monotony of the Port Credit law firm, and maybe even a chance to prove (to himself as much as to the world at large) that plodding old reliable John Greenwood was not yet out of the running.

Not that a regional Crown Attorney's position would assure anyone of such an opportunity: big, precedent-setting cases come along perhaps once in a decade, and a case that would attract as much attention as the murder of Christine even less often. It would have required occult prescience on Greenwood's part to know that after hardly a year in his new job he would be preparing to prosecute perhaps the most notorious case in Canadian criminal history. But when it happened, Greenwood was ready. He quickly declined offers of assistance that came pouring in from other, more experienced prosecutors. "Yes, you can help me very much by taking provincial court while I'm away," he told top Crown Bruce Affleck of Oshawa. John was not far from fifty, and all set to take the big risks that go with the big rewards. To his good friend Judge Durham he said: "You know, this trial is either going to make me or break me."

Greenwood wasn't alone in this feeling: Superintendent Teggart also remembered the threat he'd be "on a paper route before this case was over". Though it was Peter who was facing life imprisonment, some of the others had their careers on the line as Justice Campbell Grant mounted the judge's dais on the morning of September 23.

The fourteenth-floor courtroom in which His Lordship was to spend fifty-one days over the next ten weeks was spacious, though it had no windows from which to enjoy the "lovely view" that was to some extent responsible for bringing the trial to London's new courthouse. The prevailing government architecture of the seventies was much given to gloomy porous-concrete slabs of irregular shape, and would have regarded windows as hopelessly old-fashioned. Instead, it sought to counteract the Victorian pomposity of times past by such modern touches as purple carpets, teak murals, and purple-and-pink tweed pews. The high-backed judge's chair was actually upholstered in an informal shade of plum red. The colour scheme combined with the five single doors along one wall to give the room a somewhat Kafkaesque quality: one couldn't help wondering who would pop out when and from where. The lower benches for the court reporter and the registrar were contained in a sort of plinth, fronted with more teak mural. The walls were covered with a coarse linen-weave fabric. If the architectural style had to be described with one expression, Progressive Inquisitorial would not have been far off the mark.

It was in this atmosphere that the defence fired its opening salvo, which was a formal challenge to the array — the panel from which the jury is selected — on the basis of partiality by the Sheriff. The challenge was delivered with gusto by Eddie Greenspan, who was to handle most arguments about law and procedure in the absence of the jury throughout the trial. (The prosecution did not choose to split its tasks in this fashion; though Greenwood was clearly senior counsel, he and McGuigan argued interchangeably both in front of and in the absence of the jury.) The gist of Eddie's argument was that the jury panel, as returned by the Sheriff and his deputy, did not accurately reflect the demographic makeup of Middlesex County, and that in particular it contained fewer women, unmarried people, and urban dwellers than it ought to have on the basis of the latest census for the region. Presently an expert witness was called to testify that, in his opinion, such a discrepancy could occur only in one case out of a thousand by chance.

This challenge was quickly followed by a number of defence requests: Joe Pomerant asked to be supplied with scientific material pertaining to the murders of Constance Dickey and Neda Novak; police reports of all crimes with sexual connotations in Mississauga between July 16 and July 20, 1973; and a copy of the telex sent by the Mississauga police to the Austrian authorities that precipitated Marina's brief arrest in that country. (The purpose of these requests was clear enough: the defence was obviously going to argue that Christine could just as easily have been killed by a local sex maniac, possibly by the same person who murdered Dickey and Novak, and that the police were so much sold on Peter's guilt right from the start that they never bothered to properly investigate alternate possibilities.)

Then Eddie Greenspan rose to talk about the prejudicial effect it would have if the press were to report the defence's challenge to the local Sheriff. After some talk about foreign papers ("Is that a girlie magazine?" Justice Grant asked about the news magazine, the *Neue Illustrierte Revue*), the defence presented its first motion for the sequestration of the jury. It was to be followed by many others in the course of the next few weeks, as the defence tried to have the jury secluded day and night for the duration of the trial.

These early defence motions seemed to be setting the tone of the proceedings. Although there was nothing remotely improper about them, they might have caused Justice Grant to raise his eyebrows, at least figuratively speaking. The plain-spoken, straightforward, immensely experienced seventy-one-year-old jurist had seen most trial tactics and approaches in his long career, and he might have suspected even before lunch-break that he was going to encounter a defence strategy that would not be to his taste. But if so, he made no mention of it. There was just the barest hint of impatience in his voice when he chided Joe as he was requesting some further particulars from the prosecution: "Mr. Pomerant, you cannot expect the Crown to do all your running for you." Still, he ordered that the scientific material regarding the Dickey and Novak murders be made available to the defence, dismissed Eddie's long-shot challenge to the array, dismissed the motion for sequestration, and asked if he had now dealt with all matters before the arraignment. A moment's silence ensued.

"All right, arraign the accused," said Justice Grant.

Pomerant got to his feet to deliver one more motion about the unconstitutionality of the law under which juries are selected. The motion was as ingenious as it was hopeless, pitting an abstract requirement for due process contained in the Canadian Bill of Rights against the concrete provisions of the Criminal Code. Justice Grant listened in silence as twenty more minutes passed in argument and reply, then said mildly: "I think I am bound by the statute, Mr. Pomerant, and I do not think I have any right to change the section."

It was mid-afternoon when Peter finally stood up to face the registrar of the court. "You stand indicted by the name of Peter Demeter as follows:" the official said; "The Jurors of her Majesty the Queen present that Peter Demeter, of the City of Mississauga, on or about the 18th day of July, 1973, did murder Christine Demeter, contrary to the provisions of the Criminal Code of Canada. Upon this indictment how do you plead, guilty or not guilty?"

"Not guilty," said Peter in a clear voice. It would be the only words he would utter in open court until the last day of the trial. From this moment he would be relegated from central character to the merest spectator. It was not a suitable role for Peter to play in his own drama.

Though Pomerant's gallant attempt to change the law was obviously futile (and therefore not much good for anything except irking a trial judge), there's no doubt that the jury selection procedure *is* weighted in favour of the prosecution. Under the Criminal Code the defence can challenge 12 prospective jurors at will, though of course it can challenge any number for a specific cause. The Crown has only 4 peremptory challenges as such, but then it can "stand aside" 48 more jurors if it doesn't like the colour of their eyes. When the panel runs out of jurors the ones who have been stood aside may be called again, but in practice this seldom happens. In the Demeter case, with 76 potential jurors waiting to be assessed, the rule gave a roughly 4-to-1 advantage to Greenwood and McGuigan.

The practice is that after two jurors have been sworn, they become the "triers of fact". The defence then may challenge the next prospective juror, either peremptorily, or on the basis that he or she is not "indifferent" between the accused and the Queen. In this case the defence and the Crown question the would-be juror, after which the two triers decide whether or not they find him/her impartial.

It has long been a rule of thumb that the ideal juror, from the prosecution's point of view, is a stable, hard-working, lower-middle-class person, with little formal education and a simple, straightforward mind. Farmers, small tradesmen, and blue-collar workers or their wives are generally regarded as the cream of the crop. The defence often prefers people of more imagination, education, or emotional complexity, who might more readily understand the doctrine of reasonable doubt or the Crown's burden of proof. The defence, of course, is also anxious to detect any hidden bias a juror might have against the accused, while the prosecution looks out for prejudice against the victim or the authorities.

The prosecution generally gets its way. Good as the triers often are in weeding out people of obvious prejudice against either side, they never dream of rejecting anyone simply on account of lower education or intellect. Since such people predominate in most random selections of citizens, the Crown can use its forty-eight stand-aside opportunities to screen out the relatively few who belong to a higher stratum of occupation or learning. (It can, of course, similarly screen out anyone who belongs to an undesirably *low* stratum or minority and thus might be suspected of harbouring any resentment against the "Establishment".) In Canada few professionals or socialites (or Indians and non-white immigrants at the other end of the scale) are ever tried by their actual peers. Even more to the point, in an important trial any accused, whatever his own social status, is deprived of the benefit (such as it may be) of being tried by the more enlightened of his fellow citizens.

Joe and Eddie set about their task of selecting a jury with true American zest. Recent practice in the United States has elevated this process — which was never unimportant — to perhaps the most significant single element in a trial. Some authorities believe that a case is won or lost the minute the jury has been chosen, and all the evidence, arguments, and procedure are secondary to having the "right" jurors in the box. According to this theory, most people don't judge but pre-judge everything in line with their background, upbringing, sympathies, and nature, and many of these factors can be scientifically determined and predicted before the trial begins. Some defence teams have actually gone to the length of employing psychologists, statisticians, and demographers to aid them in selecting the "best" jury in a given venue, and in some celebrated cases (such as those of Angela Davis and Joan Little) they have credited their victory at least in part to this method.

Whether or not there is some merit in this approach (and certainly the juror who gave newspaper reporters a clenched-fisted salute after Angela Davis's acquittal is unlikely to have given much weight to any evidence against the black revolutionary lady), it has not become a dominant approach to jury selection in Canada. Of course, it's normal practice for lawyers to challenge and briefly examine jurors about whose fair-mindedness they have some doubts, but a wholesale, searching examination of every potential juror has been rare. Justice Grant certainly didn't think much of the exercise. "Not in Canada, not in Canada," he'd say later. "In the last year or so I haven't had *any* challenges for cause. It's a great mistake to do that sort of thing, you antagonize the witness [juror] against you. I made it a practice for a number of years to say to a jury, now you mustn't take umbrage against anyone because you're asked these questions, defence counsel have a right to do this. . . . But despite that in many cases, when they finally got through with all their questions, they had a jury that was hostile to them."

Whether the Demeter defence team, once they got through all their questions, had a hostile jury or not, they might well have had a slightly frustrated judge. In fact, His Lordship's frustration was not entirely due to the defence. The lengthy game of examination-in-depth seemed to have aroused the Crown's competitive instincts, especially Leo "Tiger" McGuigan's. On the few occasions when Joe Pomerant was ready to accept a juror without any questions, McGuigan would immediately have him stand aside. Juror number 41, a teacher, or juror number 91, the president of a construction company, both of whom would have been unquestioningly accepted by the defence, were in fact unquestioningly thrown out by the Crown. The prosecution seemed determined to have no one on the jury whose social class, bank account, or lifestyle might bear any resemblance to Peter's own. Even the triers came to be infected by the spirit of the exercise, and, bending over backward in their effort to be perfectly *impartial*, would sometimes reject a prospective juror on no other grounds than that he had no "ethnic" friends or belonged to some private club with few Jewish members. (This raised the interesting question of whether, had it been up to the triers, they might not have rejected the trial judge on much the same basis.) Though there's little doubt that Justice Grant regarded carrying the jury selection procedure to such lengths a silly waste of time, he felt that if counsel were going to indulge in it, the triers were also entitled to picking their own nits. When McGuigan objected to the triers' rejecting some prospective jurors on such tenuous grounds, His Lordship snapped at him:

"What do you want me to do about it?"

"I am just wondering," said McGuigan, "if maybe they have lost the original comments of your Lordship to them as to what their purpose is."

"Supposing they have, what then?"

"I think if you repeated it," said the tenacious counsel for the Crown, "it might bring back the original words."

Justice Grant had had enough. While his irritation might well have been directed equally at the defence, it was the Crown's quibble that happened to bring it to the fore. "I have seen jurors stood aside this afternoon, Mr. McGuigan," he said icily, "that I thought would have been admirable jurors. I think the triers have the same right as the rest of us in this to their own views. I am not going to say anything more to them. . . . "

People who knew Justice Campbell Grant well would not have been surprised at his response. The tall, lean, craggy-faced judge, whose mild manners and soft voice gave scant indication of an independent and headstrong nature, had in fact no time at all for the stuff and nonsense that often surrounds legal behaviour. His aesthetics in law demanded spare, clean lines. An eager beaver, or a lawyer trying to be too smart by half, cut no ice in Justice Grant's court. While he was certainly shrewd and experienced enough to be meticulous in granting both sides every bit of legitimate ground on which to manoeuvre, his own sympathies would have been with the lawyer who used the simplest and most direct approach consistent with the requirements of his case. In the Demeter trial this would not turn out to be Joe Pomerant.

Though Justice Grant would no doubt do his utmost not to be influenced against the defence by its strategy, it would require an effort on his part. Sometimes, when the jury wasn't around to see it, the effort would become quite visible. The fact was that the trial judge and the defence lawyer were mismatched, not only in personality, but in their appreciation of how a client ought to be defended under the circumstances.

When sixty-year-old Campbell Grant was appointed to the Bench (in 1962, the same year in which Peter Demeter registered Eden Gardens Limited and Bill Teggart got his first crack at becoming a detective), he'd already had a career of thirty-seven years behind him as a practising lawyer in Ontario. The Grant family's roots in the southwestern part of the province went back a long way, further than those of any of the other major participants in the London courtroom. Grandfather William Grant, one-time piper to the Queen at Balmoral, took up the original family farm in the middle of the last century in Grey County, right on the Guelph–Owen Sound Highway just a few miles south of Durham. His son, also named William, became a prosperous and prominent member of the community, and was in fact the secretary of the united-farmers movement in the area that would eventually take over the Government of Ontario under Premier Drury after the First World War. Young Campbell, one of William Grant's ten children, would be raised and educated in the same peaceful, puritanical, homogeneous district of practical, well-to-do, hard-working farmers. Without being personally acquainted with any of the members of the Middlesex County jury panel, Justice Grant would in effect have known them all his life. For the greater part they would be like his friends, schoolmates, clients, and neighbours.

While Peter's memories as a child, before the war, would have included being dropped off at school in a chauffeur-driven Mercedes, Justice Grant's recollections of his boyhood during an earlier war would have been of a four-mile ride on horseback across snow-covered fields to the high school in Durham. In his law-student days, from the ages of eighteen to twenty-three, Grant would look forward to a spell of hard, physical labour in the summer on a construction gang or a neighbouring farm. During the same period of his youth, thirty years later, Peter, deprived of a chance for a university education, would drive trucks or shovel coal, unwillingly and with loathing. In 1933 — the year Peter was born — thirty-one-year-old Campbell Grant would take his seat as Warden for the County, having already held the position of mayor in the city of Walkerton for two years. He would be at home, among his own people, a prominent citizen beginning to reap the rewards of a straightforward, matter-of-fact existence. Reaching the same age in 1964, Peter would think of life as a game played with loaded dice in which he, "as a penniless immigrant", would have to be "trying to pay less income tax with all the tricks in the books and still not to get in jail for tax evasion" if he were to realize his dreams. From Peter's perspective, a defence could hardly be trusted if it failed to "use all the tricks in the books". The route that took Peter to the London courtroom promised no rewards for directness and simplicity, and it was Peter's personality that put its stamp on Pomerant's strategy.

There was no question that the trial judge, both as a craftsman-at-law and as a person familiar with the particular venue in which the case was being tried, had a far better idea than Peter of how he ought to be defended. As a young lawyer, long before the era of plea bargaining and psychiatric evidence, and at a time when the penalty for murder was death, Grant had saved more than a dozen men and women from the gallows, generally by the simplest, no-fuss, no-nonsense methods. Most often it wasn't a matter of great subtlety or fine points of law. The Crown had to prove its case beyond a reasonable doubt, and a jury of Campbell Grant's neighbours would not put a rope around a man's neck unless it did. ("That night, when you went into the barn where the killing took place, did you get some blood on your clothes?" Grant would ask a local constable, while defending a farm youth charged with killing his grandfather with an axe. "Yes, I did," replied the policeman. "Well, so did this boy, and you even had the lantern," said Grant, and the jury acquitted.) Things weren't always so simple, of course, but the best way was still the simplest way under the circumstances. Making a great to-do would only convince a jury that a defendant had something to hide.

"I didn't want to interfere," Justice Grant would say later, talking of the Demeter case. "I wanted to give defence counsel every opportunity possible to have. At the start of the trial I tried to guide them a bit but my suggestions were not accepted and, I said, it wasn't my business to defend, I was the judge."

In courthouse corridors there's always talk among lawyers about "prosecution-minded" or "defence-minded" judges. This may be more a myth than a reality, but it is a strong myth, and some lawyers do as much judge-shopping as circumstances permit before going to trial. It is not just a matter of finding a judge with a reputation of being favourable to one's own side. When a prosecutor feels he has a strong case, for instance, he may try to avoid a Crown-oriented judge in order to get a conviction without any "help" from the bench and reduce the risk of a higher court's upsetting the verdict on appeal. Though the reliance some counsel place on an individual judge's orientation is probably exaggerated, there's no question that judges are human beings with a normal potential for prejudice. "A judge may go way off on a tangent, you know, or have some very strong, peculiar ideas about matters himself," Justice Grant would say. "It depends, of course; judges are all different."

In this world of different judges, Campbell Grant's own orientation, according to courthouse scuttlebutt, was pretty neutral. He was thought of as a strong, experienced, common-sense jurist, not particularly academic but with a solid grasp on the law, and without a soft spot for either the prosecution or the defence. Though he himself never kept a tab on how many of his decisions were upheld or upset ("You do what you think's right and let it go at that. If you start worrying about your decision, that's what's hard on one. That's why judges get up in the cemetery so much sooner"), his essential fairness was borne out by the record. If anything Justice Grant might have empathized with the defence a trifle more, simply because his own practice in criminal law had always been on the defence side, with one notable exception. (This exception was the Kendall case in 1959, a famous murder trial which Grant successfully prosecuted, securing a conviction in spite of the fact that the crime had been committed twenty years earlier and the body of the victim was never found.) But Grant was never really comfortable in his role as prosecutor. "I hesitated about taking it [the Kendall case] because I'd always been the defence and I was worried about pushing something a little too far," he'd say later. "I didn't worry about that when I was for the defence. The Crown I think owes a greater duty to be absolutely fair. . . . "

Of course, while an ex-defence lawyer might have slightly more sympathy for the defence, he might also take a more personal view on how it ought to be handled. Not that Justice Grant would ever express, then or later, any doubts about the propriety or competence of Pomerant's defence tactics; it was just that they didn't seem the tactics he himself would have chosen. He considered, for instance, the barrage of defence motions trifling. "I had that very distinct impression," he'd remember, "because there were little chance, very little merit in many of them. Most of them were very frivolous." At the outset, the judge did not think of the Crown's case as overwhelmingly strong. He might have seen little point in a scatter-gun, leaving-no-stone-unturned type of defence, which ran the risk of creating the impression that the accused was so obviously guilty he could only be got off on a technicality or some abstract point of law.

But the real problem was that the strategy of crying wolf too often might have brought about a state of mind in the trial judge where he'd find motions or objections of genuine merit more difficult to discern. To some extent a trial is based on trust. Since it would be immensely time-consuming and impractical to have every little point argued out and proven in detail, the officers of the court learn to take one another's word in some things. They are ready to assume that the other fellow is not being merely obstructionist or trivial every time he gets to his feet.

If a lawyer does not enjoy a judge's confidence in this sense, he might have a harder time getting the benefit of his discretion even for valid and significant requests.

Though this would become important only later on in the trial, there was one early indication of the less-then-trusting ambience that developed between the bench and Joe's side of the bar. The matter itself was very small: Pomerant asked the court not to sit on the day of Yom Kippur, the holiest day in the Jewish calendar. Chances are that normally Justice Grant would have acceded to this request as a matter of course. In this instance, however, he wouldn't give an answer without double-checking. Since he knew little about Jewish holidays, he telephoned Abraham Lieff, a highly respected judge and the first Jew ever appointed to the Supreme Court of Ontario.

"I have a lawyer here who says he can't sit on this holiday, Yom Kippur," said Justice Grant. "I think he can sit all right, can't he, Abe?"

"No, he can't, Campbell," replied Justice Lieff, and that of course settled the matter. Abraham Lieff's word was as good as gold, and the tense, crowded London courtroom would remain empty and silent on the Day of Atonement.

Though the jury was now finally selected, three weeks were to pass before they could take their places in the jury box. These weeks were spent with Justice Grant listening to a parade of witnesses on *voir dire* — hearing without a jury — in order to determine the admissibility of certain evidence. While nobody really expected the *voir dire* to take three weeks, the fight put up by the defence in this instance was far from being frivolous. In fact, if this battle had gone in his favour, Peter might have come close to winning his case before it ever got to the jury.

Apart from motive, at this stage the Crown had only two things with which to support a charge of murder against Demeter:

1) Csaba Szilagyi's story, and
2) The body-pack and telephone tapes of Peter's own statements.

What Justice Grant was required to rule on was the tapes. If he ruled that the tapes could not go in, Greenwood would be left with nothing but Csaba Szilagyi to take to the jury. Even if Csaba's story had not sounded as improbable as it did, it would have been highly questionable whether a jury would ever convict a man of murdering his wife on the unsupported word of a former friend that he had talked about such plans with him in the past. Actually in this case Csaba's story, by itself, might have tempted a judge to take the matter out of the jury's hands and direct a verdict of acquittal.

Joe Pomerant had four main grounds for arguing that the tapes should not be admitted:

1) The unreliability of electronic recordings as a true representation of what was being said. (This included a whole variety of points, from the quality of the tapes to the difficulty in rendering into English the accurate meaning of Hungarian inflections and phrases. It also included the fact that some important parts on the tapes were unintelligible, and some critical parts, inaudible.)

2) The integrity of the specific evidence the Crown sought to introduce against Peter on the tapes. (This, too, included many points, from the fact the police erased all the tapes they considered "immaterial", to questions of continuity, voluntariness, and possible intrusions into solicitor-client privilege.)

3) The fact that an amendment to the Criminal Code, known as the Protection of Privacy Act, brought in by Parliament a few months before the trial began (but long after the taping had occurred), had the effect of making the Mississauga police's bugging techniques illegal and their results inadmissible.

4) That even if the tapes were ruled reliable, relevant, and lawfully made, Justice Grant still had the common-law discretion to exclude them for having been acquired in such an offensive way as to negate due process and bring the administration of justice into disrepute.

The three weeks weren't, of course, spent with the arguments themselves but with putting in the evidence on which the arguments would eventually be based. Much of the testimony was technical, and had to do with such things as the making, storing, checking, and safeguarding of the tapes. The main Crown witness was Joe Terdik, supported by a host of other policemen and electronics experts from Bell Telephone, the Department of National Defence, and even the Michigan State Police. Though the defence cross-examined vigorously, they could raise no real doubts about the tapes' having been altered through either malice or neglect.

Joe Pomerant did much better with other aspects of reliability and integrity. Under his persistent questioning, Terdik admitted that he would sometimes be ordered to erase relevant tapes, whether they would be helpful or harmful to Peter. Said Pomerant: "And did your superior officers instruct you to destroy any tape recordings that would tend to incriminate Mr. Demeter?"

"Yes, I think so," answered Terdik. "As I said earlier there is a lot of

information in there that would be prejudicial to him more than beneficial, and those were erased, as well."

"So, that there was evidence," said Pomerant, "that might be material
in this case to the prosecution . . . "

"Yes."

" . . . that you were instructed to destroy?"

"That is correct."

"And there was material, I take it, that would be beneficial to Mr.
Demeter that you were, also, instructed to destroy?"

"That is quite possible, yes," replied Terdik.

Erasing the tapes was unwise, to say the least. In a free society the
police's job is to gather evidence and submit it to a court of law for eval-
uation. They should not decide on their own what is relevant and what
isn't, not even when it's only Peter chatting about the weather or world
politics, but especially not when it involves a value judgement about the
truth or significance of his statements. "I regretted very much," Justice
Grant would say later, "that they hadn't kept all their tapes, every one
of them, so that they would have been available to the defence. But it
was too late, and it served no good purpose to chastise the officers for it.
I think if the police in the Demeter case had done it over again they'd
keep every tape of everything. . . . "

Pomerant also scored strong points with the question of police intrusion into solicitor-client privilege. The record indicated that Joe Terdik's
bugs picked up some hundred and twenty conversations between Peter
and his solicitors, seventy-six of them after he had been charged with
murder. Regardless of whether the police learned much, little, or anything at all from eavesdropping on these talks, Justice Grant had to consider whether the mere fact of their intrusion might not have denied
Peter's basic right to legal counsel.

.The extensive cross-examination of Bill Teggart might have been less
helpful to the defence. Though it was quite legitimate for Pomerant to
bring out what he wished the trial judge to regard as the odiousness of
investigative techniques in the Demeter case, it seemed a bit of an over-
kill to spend more than one hundred transcript pages on police methods
or mistakes which by that time were perfectly obvious to everyone.
There's little doubt that, as a civil libertarian, Pomerant was genuinely
outraged by the leeway the authorities in Canada (relative to the United
States) are often permitted in criminal investigations, and he might
have felt that Peter's trial would be a good forum for raising basic ques-

tions about due process in this country. It's also possible that the sight of Bill Teggart, promoted to Deputy Chief and standing in the witness box a little like a cat who had swallowed the canary, aroused some very human feelings of antagonism that Joe found difficult to control. However, the net result seemed to be a number of polite clashes with a weary Justice Grant who had noted Pomerant's points at the outset and now seemed anxious to get on with the case.

Much more valuable for the defence was the cross-examination of the two Hungarian translators. Initially, after Messrs. Jaczina and Badics had finished rendering into English the contents of the body-pack and the telephone tapes between Szilagyi and Demeter, there remained enough gaps in the transcripts to leave John Greenwood rather unhappy. To make matters worse for him, there were a sufficient number of discrepancies between their two versions — prepared independently — to raise further doubts about their quality as evidence. To resolve these problems, Greenwood hit upon the idea of having Csaba Szilagyi prepare his own version, which would later be double-checked by the official translators. This resolved most of the discrepancies and reduced the number of inaudible or overlapping bits in the conversations, but it underscored the inherent difficulties of translating material from one language into another, and the further problems of transcribing spoken words onto a piece of paper without altering their meaning.

Pomerant's cross-examination of the translators laid good foundation for the argument that if the jury were allowed to hear the conversations in English (and there was obviously no point in their listening to the tapes in Hungarian), they might be asked to reach vital conclusions from less than reliable evidence. The possibility existed that it would be open for Justice Grant to find, on this basis alone, that the tapes ought not to be admitted against Peter. It is possible that if the defence had chosen to make its main stand on this ground, bolstering it with some expert evidence and not dissipating its effect by relying on many other grounds at the same time, Justice Grant might have agreed with them. (Chances are he would not have, since the translations were in fact reasonably complete and unambiguous, yet it was the kind of simple, direct point Grant could listen to without any sense of weariness. It had to do with the merits of the actual case, not with a legal nicety or abstraction.)

Clearly the dissimilarity between Justice Grant and Joe Pomerant went beyond questions of personality or background, though it may have proceeded from them. While their variance in style was a factor, it was less important than the contrast in their feelings about the meaning of justice. Joe believed that justice had to do with a general social idea; Campbell Grant felt it was always about an individual case before the court.

Pomerant, if asked, would have unhesitatingly stated that it matters far less that a guilty man, or a dozen guilty men, escape punishment than that their civil liberties are safeguarded in every possible way. (Like many people, Joe also assumed that others naturally shared his philosophy, and would design his strategy or marshal his arguments to emphasize it again and again.) But Justice Grant, while certainly favouring civil liberties, could not conceive of some abstract good being achieved through individual cases of evil. "It is the truth that the court seeks to find," he'd say later, "and even if [police] officers have to use tactics we don't view in the best light, still if it's an indication that it's the truth, that's probably more important. . . . "

Though Justice Grant would add — and no doubt mean it — that "you must always keep the administration of justice clean, and I'm not here to sanction improprieties", his interpretation of what was proper, at least on the part of the authorities, would have been much wider than Joe Pomerant's. At the same time he might have had a narrower interpretation of what might be fair on the part of defence lawyers. "I think there are many lawyers," Justice Grant would say, not speaking about Pomerant but in general, "who are honestly of the view that the most important thing is to get the client off rather than making certain that he receives a fair trial. He's entitled to a fair trial, and everything that counsel can honestly and ethically do for him, but no more than that."

By the end of the *voir dire* there was the unspoken feeling in the London courtroom that senior defence counsel, at least as far as the trial judge was concerned, might be doing a bit more than simply making sure Peter was receiving a fair trial, and perhaps not going about it in the most appealing way. Justice Grant's expressions of controlled impatience were becoming more and more frequent as Pomerant would embark upon areas in cross-examination that the judge would regard as repetitious, obscure, or irrelevant. Though once in a while Justice Grant would check Greenwood or McGuigan for the same reason, he would have occasion to check Pomerant ten times as often. Still, there was no feeling of things going poorly for the defence in general. On the contrary, while Pomerant seemed to be laying ground after ground for the possible exclusion of the tapes, the essential thinness of the Crown's case was becoming more and more evident. As even Greenwood would admit later: "There we were, hooked into a hundred-pound fish with a six-pound test line." Snagged on an adverse ruling about the tapes, the line was sure to break. It was around this time, according to the Crown Attorneys, that Pomerant took to whistling, absent-mindedly, the theme song from the old Perry Mason television series.

In light of this it was not surprising that Greenwood was in no hurry to get a ruling on the admissibility of the tapes, and did not resist Pomerant's submission that Justice Grant reserve his decision until he could see "the thrust" of the prosecution's case. Although the defence might have had a good reason for wanting to play it this way, on the face of it it might have made more sense for Pomerant to insist that the judge render his decision immediately after the *voir dire*. If the ruling had gone in the defence's favour, the Crown would have been pretty much knocked out right then and there. If not, the defence might have been better off being prepared for the tapes from the beginning. But possibly Joe thought that once the judge could clearly see the weakness of the prosecution's case he might be more inclined to rule against the tapes. Greenwood, for his part, felt that as long as the decision was held in abeyance the Crown was still in the game. (The senior prosecutor resisted McGuigan's suggestion to press for a "tentative" decision. While this clever ploy would have permitted them to make references to the tapes in front of the jury regardless of the eventual ruling, Greenwood was worried it might give the defence grounds for a mistrial later.)

In any event, Justice Grant would not tie himself down to any specific date: he wanted to hear some facts first. As it happened, he would not rule on the tapes until much later, on November 14, or about seven weeks after the beginning of the trial. By that time many things would have changed, and not necessarily in favour of the defence.

On the morning of October 15, just prior to the jury's being brought into court for the first time, Joe Pomerant rose to speak again on the subject of sequestration.

"We have dealt with that, have we not?" asked Justice Grant irritably.

"Yes, my lord."

"Then, why deal with it again, is there anything different, do you have anything more to add than you had before?"

It was clear that the trial judge was not about to lock up twelve working men and women for an indeterminate period, in spite of the continuing barrage of press, television, and radio publicity. In fact, with his considerable empathy with the everyday affairs of ordinary citizens in Middlesex County, he seemed to resent the suggestion. (Earlier he had said to Leo McGuigan: "Don't you worry about me having a jury sitting around, they won't. They will be back home hoeing their potatoes and moving their furniture until we need them.") No fellow farmer would be forced to neglect his livestock on account of the Scottish settler's grandson, Justice Campbell Grant.

And on this note the jury trial of Peter Demeter began.

15. The Leak in the Toilet

A few weeks earlier, just before the trial got under way, a faulty toilet caused a bit of flooding in the basement of one of Peter's properties on Russell Hill Road in Toronto. For some reason, Peter's way of dealing with it was to obtain, through some mutual friends, the home phone number of a small-job contractor in Clarkson, Ontario, some twenty-five miles from Toronto. On the surface it made little sense to ask a Clarkson tradesman to fix a Toronto toilet. Still, plumbers are notoriously difficult to get, and Peter might have felt that his old acquaintance from Clarkson would give him better and cheaper service.

The next day Ferenc Stark pulled up in his panel truck in front of the house on Russell Hill Road. As he was to testify later, he had agreed to drive over during his lunch hour because he had been working on nearby Christie Street anyway. He had warned Peter in advance he would have no time to do any major repairs, but Peter had assured him the job wouldn't be difficult at all. This turned out to be quite true: in fact, Stark found that the "flooding" consisted of nothing more than a trickle of water that, due to a partially open valve, was coming over the top of the toilet-tank. He adjusted the arm of the flotation ball, flushed the toilet, and for good measure cleared the drain of the toilet bowl with a plunger. The job took him about ten minutes.

In spite of the alacrity with which he fixed the disabled water closet, Stark was not just another plumber. A native of Hungary, he had moved to Toronto in 1967, the year Peter and Christine got married. Before that he had lived for years in the town of Wawa in northern Ontario, where he was employed by the Algoma Steel Company. Before coming to Canada in the first place, in 1954, he worked in France as a welder. To begin with, however, he had been an infantry sergeant in the French Foreign Legion.

Stark served in what he'd refer to as "Indochina", getting out not long before the French debacle at Dien Bien Phu. Why he had originally joined the legendary, tough, no-questions-asked mercenary force was not known. Men have traditionally enlisted in the Foreign Legion for adventure, or to escape unrequited love affairs, war crimes, or common murder. Stark's own reasons were anybody's guess — he claimed he was recruited from a P.O.W. camp with promises of better rations — but he's likely to have had even stronger reasons for choosing to lose himself in the dense foliage of Vietnam long before the world's attention became focused on that unhappy country.

As little known as Stark's reasons for joining the Foreign Legion were Peter's for associating with Stark, which he did with some frequency, especially during the spring and early summer of 1973. True, they both made their living building houses, but while Peter was a prosperous developer, Ferenc Stark was a manual worker, doing small jobs with a helper or two. As builders, they were not remotely in the same financial league, nor did they ever have any building projects in common. Still, Peter would often be observed visiting Stark at work and chatting with him on the job site or sometimes in Peter's parked Cadillac on the street. After Christine's death, however, the meetings ceased. Eventually Stark moved from Toronto's Essex Avenue to the nearby town of Clarkson, and (as he was to testify) never heard from Peter until that Setpember day in 1974.

Having fixed the offending toilet, Stark stayed on for a few more minutes of "general conversation". Not unnaturally, one of the topics was Peter's impending trial. This subject reminded Stark of an earlier incident which, he thought, might be of interest to Peter. He proceeded to tell him about it. According to Stark, Peter listened to his story without comment. Then Stark got into his panel truck and drove away.

About a week later, on September 26, when the trial in London was already under way, a car stopped in front of Stark's residence in Clarkson. The man knocking on Stark's door introduced himself as an investigator from Pomerant, Pomerant and Greenspan, and asked Stark if he'd like to accompany him and Peter — who was sitting in the car — to the Toronto offices of the firm. Although Stark replied "Not particularly," he nevertheless got into the car beside Peter. When they arrived in Pomerant's office, Joe asked Demeter to wait outside. As a shrewd and cautious lawyer, he had a good reason for wanting to hear the ex-legionary's story alone, without any chance of prompting from his client.

In 1971 or '72 (Stark's story ran) the contractor was doing some job on a property on Oriole Parkway, practically next door to the house in which the Demeters then lived on Burnaby Boulevard. It must have been spring or early summer, Stark remembered, because he did not have his shirt on. At any rate, as he was working, he was hailed from across the fence by Christine Demeter.

Until that time, Stark said, he had only met Christine twice. The first meeting was in 1969 at a party in the Mailaths' home (Mailath was then Peter's architect), and the second meeting was later that year, or perhaps in 1970, when Stark went to the Demeters' home to see if Peter might be interested in buying a house which he — being broke at the time — was forced to sell. As it happened, Csaba Szilagyi was also present both times. On neither occasion did Stark recall talking with Christine at length. At their second meeting, while waiting for Peter, he remembered discussing with Csaba a topic in which they both had some interest: guns. Christine sat through this discussion, though she did not contribute to it. On this occasion, Stark said, he mentioned to Csaba that he still had a couple of guns he had used for hunting in the northern bush around Wawa before moving to Toronto, a shotgun and a .22 rifle. Then Peter arrived, and the subject changed to real estate deals.

Now calling to him across the fence, Christine wanted to know if Stark was "interested in business". He said yes, not knowing what business she was talking about. He also gave Christine his phone number. About a week later Christine called and asked Stark to come over to her house the next day.

When Stark arrived, Christine seemed to be alone in the house, except for baby Andrea who was asleep in a room upstairs. After showing Stark around and offering him a drink, Christine suddenly came out with what she wanted.

"Are you willing," she asked (according to Stark), "to sell me your rifle?"

"What for?" replied Stark, surprised.

"All I want is your rifle," Christine said, "and proof that someone was with you."

Stark replied that he didn't understand what she meant.

"I want your rifle," repeated Christine, "and for you to say that you were with Csaba. I do have the money, three thousand dollars."

And saying this, Stark said, Christine pulled out a handful of hundred-dollar bills from her purse.

Stark told Pomerant he said thank you, but no thank you, and left. It was his policy never to be "rude" to anybody, especially to women, so he did not protest and asked no further questions. He simply told Christine he wasn't interested. He had no idea why Mrs. Demeter or anybody would make such an offer to him, and he had never mentioned the story to a soul, until he encountered Peter over the leaking toilet on Russell Hill Road.

Pomerant must have felt like a person who is suddenly notified that he has, more probably than not, won the Irish Sweepstakes. Although Stark's story raised as many questions as it answered, it still might be the truth. Stark was a slightly built, neatly dressed, somewhat worried-looking tradesman of fifty who seemed to require glasses for reading. As far as Pomerant could tell, he had no criminal record, at least in Canada, and he certainly didn't give the impression of being a crook. A jury might easily believe him.

Though Stark's story didn't exactly *prove* anything, if a jury believed him they couldn't help concluding that Christine and Csaba were involved in some kind of illegal activity. This meant that Csaba's evidence against Peter had to be taken with a grain of salt — and the Crown had little against Peter except Csaba's evidence. Under these circumstances, the doctrine of reasonable doubt alone ought to ensure Peter's acquittal.

Pomerant asked Stark if he was willing to repeat his story under oath. Stark replied that he was willing. He signed a deposition on the spot and was served a subpoena requesting him to appear in court at a future date.

The prosecution and the police, of course, knew nothing about this development. Still, John Greenwood and Bill Teggart were uneasy. They suspected Joe Pomerant might have a good reason for appearing so cheerful and whistling the Perry Mason theme song so often during the three weeks of *voir dire* in London.

16. Mr. X

There was no rabbit in the Crown's hat. As the trial moved into its second week, nearly a year and a quarter after Christine's death, Greenwood still knew nothing that wasn't known within two days of the murder. There was the insurance, the bad marriage, and Marina; mere motives, never denied. There was Peter's "bizarre" behaviour on the night of July 18, if the jury agreed with the police. There was Csaba Szilagyi's story, possibly true but sounding stranger than any fiction. Christine died on a Wednesday, and all this information, for what it was worth, was in the police's hands by Friday evening. Since that time Bill Teggart's team had been able to come up with nothing but long reels of ambiguous tapes which might or might not be admissible. It wasn't much to show for the biggest, most ambitious investigation of the decade.

All this changed at 3:30 in the afternoon of October 1, when Detective-Sergeant Chris O'Toole received a phone call in the London courthouse.

Since the police solve the majority of their cases through informers, they are rather earnest about protecting the identity of the small crooks who rat on their fellows in hope of a reward or favour. Chris O'Toole's caller was no exception, and he became designated in police records simply as "Mr. X". In fact, his name was Gyula (Julius) Norman Virag, and he was known to be a snitch through the length and breadth of the Hungarian underworld in Canada. How he still managed to come up with the odd tip for the police was a total mystery. Perhaps his own petty crimes, ranging from illegal entry to possession of stolen goods, legitimized him sufficiently in the eyes of his comrades to cause them to drop a careless hint or two in his presence once in a while.

By 10:30 the same evening Mr. X was talking with Chris O'Toole at the headquarters of the Toronto police. It seemed the hint he managed to pick up this time was that Christine's killer was a man nicknamed *Kacsa*, the Hungarian word for "The Duck". Kacsa was said to be living somewhere in Toronto with a Hungarian woman and her child. That, Mr. X claimed at the time, was all he knew.

Small as the lead was, it was a lead. It sounded neither more nor less promising than scores of other leads picked up in the fourteen months of the investigation. O'Toole and Teggart agreed that they couldn't afford to ignore it.

So did John Greenwood. By this time the officers had nicknamed the burly senior prosecutor "The D.A." because his relationship to the investigation was more like a U.S. District Attorney's than the traditional Crown Counsel's, who seldom has any close contacts with the police. (In social terms, for instance, the Crown's lawyer is rather more likely to take lunch with his colleague for the defence than with any of the detectives during a trial.) Greenwood, however, would not only lunch with the police, but would take an increasingly active part in the investigation. Owing to a fortunate coincidence of personalities, Teggart and his men never came to regard this as meddling but, on the contrary, accepted Big John with some pride and affection as a member of the police team. They didn't even resent it when, after an exhausting day, a call would come from Greenwood exhorting the detectives to check out some new clue immediately. "Send them out again, Bill," he would say to an appreciative Teggart, himself a true believer in Going The Extra Mile. "We'll give them a medal later."

In fact, Greenwood's attitude was less due to his fascination with police work than to his anxiety about the essential thinness of the Crown's case against Demeter. Though he noted with satisfaction that the early defence tactics, far from succeeding, seemed to generate a rather uneasy ambience between Joe Pomerant and the Bench, he had no doubt that Justice Grant would base his rulings in the end on what he perceived to be the merits of the case. If he didn't let the tapes in, for instance, the fact that he thought little of Pomerant's style would be small consolation to the Crown. What Greenwood wanted was solid proof, and of course finding the actual killer would be the most solid proof of all. (The possibility that the killer, once found, might turn out to be unconnected with Peter Demeter did not even enter Greenwood's mind. Like the police, he had no doubt whatever that Christine's murder was arranged by her husband.)

In light of this, while the trial in London continued, a team of detectives was dispatched under Chris O'Toole to chase The Duck. They were hoping, as BillTeggart put it, that this Hungarian bird would not turn out to be a wild goose. It didn't, but what it did prove to be in the end was a duck of a different feather: a *canard*, the journalists' traditional bird of false rumour.

For the time being, however, The Duck seemed merely elusive. For weeks Chris O'Toole and Jimmy Wingate lost themselves in Toronto's Bloor-College-Spadina area, but to no avail. The pool halls yielded scant information. They checked practically every hot-dog stand in Toronto following a tip that Kacsa worked in a hot-dog stand. They went through innumerable school records because of another tip that Kacsa's common-law wife had two boys. No luck. At the end of the second week the assignment had achieved only one thing: it reinforced O'Toole's belief that more Hungarians commit crimes than members of any other ethnic groups. (The two policemen on the team who were of Hungarian background, Joe Terdik and Staff Sergeant Hagymasi, gave O'Toole no argument about this. It may not have been true, but on the corner of College and Spadina it certainly *seemed* that way.)

Meanwhile, in London, life settled into a strange kind of routine for all the major participants in the case. At the centre was the Holiday Inn, with its orange tweed carpets and simulated leather couches in the lobby, where card tables would be set up for the lawyers and policemen in the evening so that they could discuss the day's activities over steaming cups of coffee. Everybody stayed at the Holiday Inn: Peter, still free on bail, in room 237, across the hall from Bill Teggart in room 234 and Joe Pomerant in room 232. (On the first day Bill Teggart was handed the key to Pomerant's room by mistake. Joe was unpacking his suitcase when he entered. "Bill, not already . . . " said the lawyer, in mock desperation. Teggart, never at a loss for a swift reply, assured him he was just dropping by to install a two-way mirror.)

Justice Campbell Grant also stayed at the Holiday Inn, though at a prudent judicial remove in the new "tower". John Greenwood, whose respect for the elderly trial judge extended to his know-how about provincial hotels, turned to his roommate Leo McGuigan when he heard about this. "What," asked Greenwood, "could the judge know that we don't?" and immediately transferred the prosecution's room to the "tower" as well. Later Bill Teggart and Chief Burrows also moved to the seventh floor of the new wing. Consciously or not, they all took care to stay a few floors lower than His Lordship.

In late September, as the trial began, Ontario's Indian summer brought a few more warm and sunny days to London. On his first afternoon after checking in, John Greenwood ambled out onto his balcony to cast a longing glance at the Holiday Inn's swimming pool. Looking up, he saw Eddie Greenspan doing the same thing. The lawyers, as well as the policemen, had some very ambiguous feelings about free-time activities during the eleven weeks of the trial. There they were, separated from their everyday lives and their families in the vacation environment of the Holiday Inn, but going for a swim or even taking in a movie somehow didn't seem *right*. The policemen couldn't even have a drink. Being a teetotaller at the best of times, Superintendent (by that time Deputy Chief) Teggart would not have stood for it during a murder trial when his men, even off duty, were on public display. Joe Pomerant was the only person somewhat less affected by such reticence, and while he was a virtual non-drinker, he saw nothing wrong with going for a steam or a swim. In the end he even managed to talk Leo McGuigan and John Greenwood into the sybaritic pleasure of the occasional steam bath, though they would never go together with the defence lawyer.

The police and the prosecution's men had separate rooms, though once in a while the lesser detectives had to double up as more witnesses came into London. The two Crown attorneys tried staying together in a three-room suite at first, but gave up on discovering that Leo liked to have extra heaters going, while John would open all the windows in the consulting room. In the beginning Peter expected his two lawyers to share a room, but needless to say Joe and Eddie refused. Though Peter's tightfistedness was legendary, one could sympathize with his considering that, as a taxpayer, he was picking up the tab not only for his defence but for his prosecution as well.

Living in close proximity, resort-style, had a curious effect on the entire cast of this real-life drama, and brought the differences in their backgrounds into even sharper relief. Personalities would grind against one another in a clash of habits, table manners, and mistaken cultural signals. Except for Justice Grant, who would take his meals alone or sit with the court reporter and his law student, the others mingled freely in the Dutch Coffee House at breakfast or in the dining room at night. Teggart, sitting at the counter with its cheery blue-and-white motif, underneath a wall sporting a heady mixture of English, Scandinavian, and Japanese pottery, would positively *wince* whenever Pomerant approached. He knew that the lawyer, while talking, might absent-mindedly break off a piece of toast or pick a few grapes from anybody's plate. Peter would eat with his lawyers or with Marina, though he would also have some casual conversations with Teggart or Terdik — all calling one another "Bill", "Peter", and "Joe" — especially in the early days of the trial. It all seemed vaguely unreal, as though it were a game or a charade played out by carefree vacationers at a summer resort. Nothing seemed more distant from the Holiday Inn than the pools of blood on the Mississauga garage floor, or the steel doors of a federal penitentiary.

Peter's habit of clicking his heels and bowing whenever he saw Justice Grant in the dining room or hallway became an irritant to the trial judge, who took it seriously enough to go to the unusual length of asking Pomerant to tell his client he "doesn't have to do that". Justice Grant was appalled by what he regarded as a display of obsequiousness. It convinced him that Peter was trying to ingratiate himself with these antics. In fact, it was perhaps the most perfect example of two men misreading one another through a difference in cultural standards. While Peter might have gladly attempted to curry favour with a judge who was trying him for murder, he wasn't so simple-minded as to believe he could achieve this by bowing to him in the coffee shop. But for a well-brought-up East European *not* to acknowledge an older figure of great authority would have been as difficult as for Pavlov's dog not to salivate at the sound of a bell. In all likelihood, Peter obeyed the same conditioned reflex in bowing to Justice Grant that the Scottish-Canadian jurist obeyed when he became annoyed by it. Whether or not it contributed one iota to his conviction, Peter was once again put at a disadvantage just by being what he was: an outsider.

At the courthouse the trial was continuing, with the evidence being finally presented in front of the jury. The Crown was obliged to prove, first of all, that Christine's death was in fact the result of homicide. Conceding little, Joe Pomerant cross-questioned every police and medical witness at length. It seemed possible that he might even rely on the defence of Christine's death having been due to an accidental fall. Certainly if any doubt could be raised in this regard, the benefit of it must, by law, go to the accused.

It was this approach that brought into the open for the first time a split in the ranks of the defence team.

At thirty, Eddie Greenspan was not just the younger partner in the firm, but altogether a very young lawyer, still in the first bloom of enthusiasm and dedication. Though he was a distant relative of Pomerant's, their personalities and temperaments were not similar. Greenspan tended to be cheerful, matter-of-fact, and unpretentious. He was far from being tongue-tied, but he would use words to clarify issues rather than cloud them, and no matter how many he might use he would not seem to use more than necessary.

In business matters he would tend to be somewhat awkward and shy. Discussing fees with a client was not the high point of legal work for Eddie Greenspan. Luckily, the business side of the partnership would be handled with great efficiency by Pomerant. This left Eddie free to do what he really liked, and what even his opponents and elders conceded he showed promise of unusual brilliance in: criminal law. Greenspan seemed to be at home in all aspects of this particular field, from legal research and arguments to courtroom litigation. Very early in his career he showed signs of being one of a minority of lawyers who could be equally successful in an appeal court arguing the law, and in front of a jury dealing with facts and people. This, in fact, was all he ever really enjoyed doing, often up to eighteen hours a day. Though he also liked literature, could go through a meal in a good restaurant with evident relish, and seemed to be happily married to a Moroccan-Jewish girl of striking good looks, his legal work would absorb very nearly his whole life. It certainly absorbed the greater part of his after-hours conversation. The young defence counsel would have found a dinner-guest with no interest in the law a bit of a bore — and possibly his dinner-guest would have returned the compliment.

Pomerant had taken Eddie, whose father died young, under his wing when Eddie was still a law student. He smoothed his way, let him have his early chances, tutored him in many of the finer points of his profession and his trade. Eventually he gave him a partnership in his office.

Even years later, when the partnership dissolved not without the attendant bitterness of all such partings of the ways, Greenspan would acknowledge that for a long time he had felt nothing but admiration for Pomerant. It was more than just a youth being dazzled by a man ten years his senior in worldly wisdom. Greenspan, a born lawyer (as some people are born acrobats or hockey players), had a solid appreciation of Joe Pomerant's legal talents. But, as it sometimes happens, the apprentice seemed to find the master wanting in both attitude and aptitude after a while. The reverence of earlier days lingered, but only out of habit, not conviction. Then habit gave way to bewilderment, and later to frustration. Finally came resentment.

Though this ambivalence about his older partner probably existed in Greenspan's mind before the Demeter case, it was not admitted to his conscious thoughts with any clarity until then. It would have been even harder to tell which specific aspect of Pomerant's defence strategy brought it to the fore, but it might have been the accident theory.

Greenspan felt, along with many other legal observers, that spending any time on the defence of accident was futile to the point of frivolity. It was, of course, possible that Christine died as a result of a mishap, but only in the metaphysical sense that *anything* is possible under the sun. On a less philosophical plane, no accidental fall inside a garage could be envisaged that would produce a roughly four-inch-by-five-inch square on the top of somebody's head in which the calvarium would be literally pulverized into small, broken fragments of bone. Nor would any accidental fall, even from the roof of a parked Cadillac, result in at least *six* parallel lacerations, each about one inch to one and a half inches wide, on the scalp stretching over the broken skull. The same fall, moreover, was not likely to produce a two-and-a-half-inch gash on the opposite side of the head as well, an inch or so behind the left ear.

Most especially, an accidental fall would hardly account for the deep (twenty-two-by-eight-millimetre) cut on the left thumb. Such lacerations are more commonly received by people trying to ward off a blow.

It wasn't so much that Pomerant actually brought forward the accident theory, or even suggested it in so many words to witnesses during cross-examination. It was simply that, right from the preliminary hearing, he had hinted at the reservations he might have about the manner in which Christine's mysterious death occurred. He had made a point of conceding that she died at the hand of another human being *only* for the purposes of the preliminary. Dangling the threat of the accident-defence over the Crown's head, of course, resulted in Greenwood's calling five different doctors: the Coroner, two pathologists, one general X-ray man, and one expert in neuroradiology, to testify at the trial. Though disagreeing on some small details, the doctors were unanimous in saying that, in effect, Christine died because somebody beat her brains out. On the stand the doctors also provided a graphic description of the last seconds of Christine's life, when the young, athletic woman, her heart still beating in spite of brain tissue coming out from the back of her head, struggled for breath so hard that she sucked some of the contents of her stomach into her lungs. Though the jury would no doubt have heard some of this anyway, they might not have heard so much and so repeatedly if it hadn't been for the tactics of the defence.

Greenspan was becoming more and more uneasy about this approach. It worried him to go on and on, raising every doubt possible on earth in the hope that the jury would give the benefit of each to the accused. The law that required a jury to do so also contained the word "reasonable", which the theory of accident certainly wasn't. To Eddie, at least, any advantage was too slim to offset the risk of further frustrating the trial judge, or dwelling on the horrors of Christine's death.

Still, in all likelihood, Greenspan did not voice his misgivings to his older partner about his strategy too vehemently at first. Though by that time Eddie was in no sense a junior partner in the firm, *vis-à-vis* the Demeter trial he was playing only second fiddle. It was Pomerant's case, and Greenspan was there to assist him. Joe was clearly the Commander-in-Chief, and there can only be one commander in the field. The special dynamics that still existed in the relationship of the two men also made it difficult for Eddie to rise in open rebellion against his old principal's plan of battle. Later he would argue, fret, and finally withdraw into silence, not exchanging a word with Pomerant about the case for days on end. But in the beginning he only worried.

Greenspan had a legitimate cause for worry, even apart from the tenuousness of the accident theory. In legal circles it is an old rule of thumb that one does not stretch out a circumstantial case any longer than necessary. The less proof the Crown has, the quicker the defence should get things on and get things over with. There are always exceptions, but generally in such cases delays work only for the prosecution. Every day spent in the courtroom might bring the police closer to some new evidence against one's client.

Though Eddie knew nothing about The Duck (any more than Greenwood knew about Ferenc Stark at this stage), there were warning lights going on in the young lawyer's mind, as though he could sense Chris O'Toole and his team narrowing the circle around the quarry fingered by Mr. X, even while Joe Pomerant was cross-questioning experts on a Styrofoam model of Christine's skull for the hundredth time.

17. The Duck

The Duck was finally tracked to his nest on October 21. As usual, in the end he wasn't found through school records, hot-dog stands, or finger-print-files, but simply through another snitch. "You looking for Cutlip Kacsa the Gambler?" said the informer, unaware of the value of his tip. "Sure I know him, who doesn't? His name's Imre Olejnyik and he lives on 51 Denison."

Joe Terdik and Jimmy Wingate decided to hit The Duck the same day. As they waited for the man assumed to be Christine's killer, their hands did not stray far from the butt of their guns in the hallway of Kacsa's apartment building. In a moment they'd have reason to feel a little foolish. "We were waiting for big-shot Olejnyik," Joe Terdik recounted, "and what we got was Susan, a very sweet twelve-year-old. Polite and well brought up, too — considering her life. She said her mother worked until 9 P.M."

Maria Visnyiczky, The Duck's common-law wife, had worked until 9:00 P.M. on most days of her life. In the self-centred '70s, obsessed with self-expression and self-improvement, it was hard to imagine that such people still existed. There she was, a woman in her mid-forties who had lived in England and Canada ever since the war displaced her at the age of seventeen, yet she was as untouched by it all as if she had never set foot outside her home town in Western Hungary. She could still communicate with ease only in her native language. Her values came from her childhood, and revolved around strict notions of hard work, prayer, and unquestioning endurance of her lot. This seemed to include total submission to her man, but in a curious, stubborn, peasant fashion. She would surrender everything except her own ideas of right and wrong. She would be loyal to her mate, subservient even, without finding it necessary to justify or endorse his ways. He would probably think her simple-minded for that, but she wasn't. She just knew what was good and decent. If her husband didn't, it was unfortunate, but such was the will of God.

Joe Terdik would find himself curiously moved by Maria, whose stock was not unlike the young detective's own. She might have got on quite well with his parents. She most certainly did not get on well with her spouse, The Duck.

"Jimmy was a gangster, a bum," explained Mrs. Duck. "He'd come home and beat me. I said Jimmy don't beat me, I will pray for you. He'd beat me some more."

Terdik and Wingate weren't surprised by the description, but they were surprised by the name. Why "Jimmy"? It turned out that Imre Olejnyik was known not only as Cutlip, or Kacsa The Duck, but also as Jimmy Orr. This proved to be of considerable significance later.

Apparently Mr. and Mrs. Duck had first met around 1960. Maria had a room at the time in a house where Kacsa also shared a room with his friend Gabor (Gaby) Kecskes. Maria's romance with The Duck progressed and soon they shared an apartment. In 1962 Susan was born.

Kacsa never had the reputation of being a particularly pleasant man. He tended to get into fights, especially when drunk. He'd hold odd jobs for short periods of time: a punch-press operator, a baker's helper. In between jobs he'd collect unemployment insurance and go to the races. Once in a while he'd wager greater amounts of money than his unemployment benefits or salary could remotely justify. Maria would never know the source of these unexpected windfalls, nor would she see much profit from them. She'd run the house on her own earnings from cleaning jobs, augmenting the welfare payments she'd been receiving ever since Susan was born.

As far as Maria knew, Kacsa had been married before and had a son still in Hungary with his former wife. He also had brothers, sisters, and a mother living in the bleak industrial city of Miskolc, which also happened to be Maria's native town. In 1969 or 1970 he even took nine-year-old Susan back for a visit, but Maria didn't go with them.

Maria was not very good with dates, but she thought it was sometime around Easter the previous year that she saw Kacsa in a very hush-hush conversation with his friend Gaby Kecskes and Gaby's brother-in-law "Foxy". The three of them were drinking beer and discussing something for hours on that spring day in 1973. In an unusual gesture, Kacsa even gave her forty dollars and told her to go shopping with Susan. They went to Eaton's, but when they returned later in the evening, Gaby and Foxy were still there. Maria never heard what they were talking about, but it must have been something important.

The next morning, according to Maria's recollection, The Duck surprised her by packing his belongings in a hurry. Though Maria was used to sudden arrivals and departures from her mate, she still remembered being taken aback by his unseemly haste. He gave her some long, stiff rolls of paper, muttering something about "the money" having been wrapped in them. "Hide these till I come back," Kacsa said, "and don't give them to anybody. You never know what they might be good for."

While Maria was stuffing the papers down the side of an old chair on the balcony, Kacsa mentioned some further details which made equally little sense to her. He said he got the money because "a rich millionaire husband wanted me to beat up his beautiful Austrian wife." He laughed and said he was going to cheat on the guys and go to Hungary. He said he was going to cheat on someone named "Frankie". He laughed some more and said they'd all forget about the money after a few months. Then the three of them got into the car of a friend named Link and drove to the airport. Maria and Susan waved good-bye as the big jet flew off with The Duck in the direction of the old country.

By the spring of 1973 "the old country" had adopted a no-questions-asked attitude towards her ex-native sons who were visiting with Western passports and Western currency in their pockets. Former defectors, provided they were more or less non-political, had little trouble nipping back and forth across the one-time Iron Curtain. Although visas could still be capriciously withheld, the welcome mat was rolled out for nearly all who wished to spend their dollars, pounds sterling, or Swiss francs in Hungary. But there was just enough of the old Cold War attitude left to make ordinary police co-operation or extradition between Hungary and the West a very complicated and cumbersome business. For instance, there would be no Interpol to telex in Budapest or Miskolc, and no Scotland Yard, Sûreté, or FBI to carry the ball for the Mississauga police. As a result, in spite of its (by Western standards) Draconian criminal laws, the Hungarian People's Republic was often used as a place to cool out by ex-nationals for whom things were getting too hot in other parts of the world.

In the weeks following Kacsa's departure, Maria started receiving some telephone calls and visits that made her feel very uneasy. First it was Olejnyik's old friend Gaby Kecskes who wanted to talk with "Jimmy". Maria told him that her common-law spouse, by whatever name, wasn't around just then. This information made Gaby very unhappy. "Jimmy promised me and Foxy $500 each as our part of the deal," he said, "and he never gave it to us." (Before Kacsa left he told Maria the roll of paper she hid in the old chair had contained some $7000, but now Gaby said it was more like $20,000. Marie believed him because Imre was always lying to her, and the wallet he took with him to Hungary seemed positively bulging with hundred-dollar bills.) Later, Maria said, Gaby phoned again and told her to give information about Imre's whereabouts "or Susan might get hurt by the gang".

But it was when the man named "Frankie" started phoning and coming around that Maria got really scared. Not that Frankie was threatening in appearance; he was just a slight, middle-aged Hungarian with greying hair who talked to her quite politely at first. When Maria told him she didn't know where The Duck was, he left. But the next time he came he was less polite. He wanted to know why Maria was lying. He said that Kacsa had left with all the money, and Maria should phone him and tell him to return it, or his family would be in trouble. He also left Maria his card with two phone numbers on it.

All these events took place in May or early June. This was just around the time when Christine was writing her letter with its strange premonition of impending death to her parents, and Peter was preparing for the fling of his life with Marina. Of course Maria Visnyiczky, having never heard of the Demeters, knew nothing about this. All she knew was that in May flowers started blossoming in Toronto's High Park and one morning she went out to cut herself a bouquet. She was feeling so lonely she even tried to make friends with the policeman who stopped her. He seemed a sympathetic young man and, impulsively, Maria decided to tell him her troubles. She was afraid for Susan, she was afraid for herself. It appeared that her mean, good-for-nothing husband had bitten off more than he could chew for once, got in with some really bad people, then run away and left her family in the lurch. It must have been because of all the money rolled up in that big piece of paper. What paper? If the policeman wanted to see it she would come back in the afternoon and show it to him.

Maria went home, took the long roll with its meaningless squiggles out of the armchair, and brought it back to the young policeman in

High Park. He looked at it, made a note of her name and address, then sent her away with some reassuring words. It's unlikely that the story, told in Maria's broken English, made any sense to him, or that he had followed it up in any way. Had he done so, it might have saved Christine Demeter's life.

The Duck returned to Canada in the fall of 1973: at least Maria never saw him until October. He said he had been in Hungary all this time, but he seemed even more nervous and agitated than before. He left again in a few days, but first he asked Maria to get out the papers from the old chair for him. He looked at them for a while, then told her to find a better hiding place for them. Understanding nothing, Maria stuffed the roll under the mattress in the bed. In the following months she would not see him, though he would telephone her once in a while. On one occasion he told her he was calling from California.

Kacsa showed up at 51 Denison for the last time around February 1974. By then Peter's preliminary hearing was well under way, with Pomerant right in the middle of his cross-examination of Csaba Szilagyi. But Kacsa made no reference to the Demeter case at all. Generally he just stayed cooped up in the apartment, saying and doing very little. "He was very much scared and it got every day worse," said Maria. "He was very mad because he had to get a phone call from somebody and the call was never coming. . . . He was very afraid of Frankie and the gang."

The Duck was so frightened, in fact, that when he decided to return to Hungary again he sent Maria to pick up his passport and ticket because he did not dare to show his face in the street. Maria got his passport and ticket, then went to the bank and took out forty dollars for him from her savings, because by now The Duck was completely broke. Shortly after Easter his friend Link drove him to the airport for the last time.

"Since Imre has gone," said Maria, "I had a letter from him from Hungary. He told me to send all his mail to his mother's house. I think he is now in Hungary. . . . Susan is glad he is gone and so am I."

Maria finished her story around 9:40 P.M. Joe Terdik and Jimmy Wingate had little doubt she was telling the truth, but they couldn't immediately follow every part of her excited, half-English, half-Hungarian narrative. There was the matter of the roll of papers, for instance. "We thought she had thrown them out," said Wingate, remembering the incident. "Then she said: 'Do you want to see them?' We couldn't believe it."

The roll of paper was still under the bed-chesterfield in the second room. It was a blueprint, showing a proposed townhouse property on Winchester Avenue. It bore the designer's name: Leslie Wagner. It also showed the owner's: Eden Gardens Limited, president Peter Demeter.

But this was not the end of Maria Visnyiczky's surprises. While the two detectives were staring at the blueprints, she continued rummaging around until she came up with a business card. "This is the card Frankie left here when he was looking for Imre," she said.

The name on the card said Ferenc Balint Stark. There were two phone numbers on the back of it, 536-2204 and 967-6961. Though Stark's name meant nothing to the two detectives at the time, it did trigger something in Terdik's memory. The next day, October 22, he went back to his office to look at Peter Demeter's address book, which they had been holding since the first days of the investigation. On the last page, written in blue ink, was Freddie Stark, 536-2204.

It took O'Toole's team another week to locate Stark. (Maria couldn't help them any more: she didn't even know the real name of "Foxy", whom the police were also anxious to see.) Finally, on the evening of October 30, Joe Terdik, with three other detectives, rang the bell at 2340 Bromsgrove Road. Like most other members of the team, Terdik by that time had been going on little more than a bowl of soup and maybe three hours of sleep in the past forty-eight hours.

The man who answered the door wore grey slacks and a green turtle-neck sweater. He was slightly built and seemed to be around forty-five or fifty. He glanced at Terdik without any suspicion.

"Are you Ferenc Balint?" asked Terdik, making a deliberate mistake by using Stark's middle name.

"No, I'm Ferenc Stark," replied the man, pulling out his driver's licence.

"You're under arrest."

Stark turned ashen grey and started shaking. He looked like a man about to have a heart attack. To drive the point home, Terdik continued: "You're under arrest for complicity in the murder of Christine Demeter."

"I don't know what you're talking about," murmured Stark.

Terdik put him in the squad car with a detective, then entered the living room with his other two men. Though Stark seemed very neat, the place itself was a shambles. In the middle of the assorted junk a teen-age boy was watching television with his feet on a chair. He hardly looked up when the detectives walked in.

"Are you the sole occupant?" asked Terdik, employing a language that comes naturally to policemen on all occasions.

Stark's son nodded, then went back to whatever seemed more exciting to him on television. The detectives started their search, with Terdik looking through the pockets of the clothes hanging in the closet. As it happened, he began with the inside pocket of a suit that contained a long, folded document. It was a subpoena for the defence from the firm of Pomerant, Pomerant and Greenspan.

"When I saw it," said Terdik later, "you could have knocked me down with a feather."

18. The Dawes Road Plot

Once down at Station No. 11 in Mississauga, it took Stark less than two hours to confess. He didn't confess to anything as irrevocable as the murder of Christine, though. What he confessed to — given a suitably charitable interpretation — was a plot to defraud Peter Demeter.

Still reeling from the surprise of finding Pomerant's subpoena in Stark's pocket, Terdik had a hurried meeting with Chris O'Toole and Jimmy Wingate at 9:40 P.M. The other two had just returned to Mississauga from downtown Toronto, where they had been trying (as yet unsuccessfully) to flush "Foxy" out of the Hungarian underbrush. They decided to handle Stark firmly but carefully. In spite of the blueprints and Maria's story, the detectives couldn't imagine Pomerant calling the ex-legionary to appear at the trial if he didn't have something useful to contribute to Peter's defence.

O'Toole began Stark's interrogation at 9:50 P.M. Although the earnest detective-sergeant was possibly the last cop on the entire Mississauga force who would ever employ strong-arm tactics, suspects encountering him for the first time might easily have thought he would be the first. What they would see would be a one-time miner, well over six feet tall, with shoulders and arms sculpted to unsettling proportions, and calm eyes behind horn-rimmed tortoiseshell glasses that invited no trifling. All his early-morning workouts at the Regency Racket Club, his hand-grip lying casually on the table of his bachelor quarters (next to a copy of Dostoyevski and some essays on criminology), combined with O'Toole's silvery hair to make him a figure of respect. When he asked questions, people were loath to make him wait long for an answer.

"Mr. Stark seemed a bit concerned about being arrested," O'Toole would remember later. "I immediately suspected he was labouring under some burden. He looked so thoroughly wretched I knew here was a guy who was pretty low."

Still, the thoroughly wretched Mr. Stark would not immediately reveal the burden under which he was labouring. He murmured something about having been advised by Joseph Pomerant that he was "under the protection" of his office.

"A law firm can't place you under any kind of protection," said O'Toole mildly. "If you know something about this murder you should tell us."

Stark thought about this for a few seconds. "Well, what position does that put me in?" he asked finally. "Can you guys help me out?"

This sounded like the familiar approach of a crook trying to make a deal. O'Toole knew he had to play this very carefully. If he refused, Stark might tell him nothing. At the same time the detective-sergeant had no right to make any promises. Doing so could, in fact, invalidate anything Stark might reveal, as much as twisting his arm would. Under the law both threats and promises can render a statement worthless and inadmissible. That, of course, has never stopped some policemen from using either or both, but Chris O'Toole always made a point of flying by the book. In practice this required him to reply in riddles, like the Oracle of Delphi.

"We can't promise you anything, Frank," O'Toole said, "but we can talk to the Crown Attorney. We can't promise you immunity. However, we can talk to the Crown and see what we can do."

This bit of hypocrisy evidently satisfied both the law and Ferenc Stark. Still shaking, he asked for a glass of water, which was brought to him as snappily as though he were in an expensive restaurant. He drank it and calmed down.

"Okay," he said, "I'll tell you the truth."

The truth, according to Stark, was the following. One evening, possibly in 1972 (dates were not Stark's strong point), he received a phone call from Peter Demeter. This was perhaps seven or eight months *after* Christine's strange request for a gun and an alibi for Csaba. Now Peter told Stark he wanted to look at the remodelling job Stark was doing on a house, but his car was out of order. Could Stark drive out to Dundas Crescent and pick him up?

Stark picked Peter up, Peter looked at the house, then they drove back to Mississauga. Christine wasn't at home, only the Chinese maid Gigi who, Stark said, fixed him a sandwich. Then Peter asked him if he might know anybody who would do a "special job".

"I did not know what kind of special job he meant," Stark told O'Toole. "What I remember he said was that he would like to have an accident happen somehow, but he didn't mention anything at all. When you put a question like that, I don't know, I going to look around. I ask him what kind of accident, he didn't answer me directly just started to, like, you change the subject. He started to talk about his wife, how she is cheating on him and how miserable he is, and he cannot stand it any longer and names she is calling him. Then we stopped talking about it and I excused myself and said I had to go back to the job. I had all the intention of forgetting about the whole thing. . . . "

The grammar was doubtful, but the meaning seemed clear enough. If Stark could be believed, he must have been in a strange quandary. There was the Demeter couple, people he barely knew (and who knew him only as a small tradesman), suddenly turning to him for rifles, alibis, and accidents. This would be an unusual experience for the average plumber. Still he claimed that, just as he had said nothing to Peter about Christine's earlier request, he now said nothing to Christine about Peter's. He just intended to "forget about the whole thing".

But, Stark continued, Peter kept calling and pestering him from that point on. Finally, just to get him off his back, he promised he would look around for someone. The "someone" he then started looking around for was none other than The Duck. Not knowing where to get in touch with Kacsa, said Stark, he just left word in various restaurants and pool-halls around the Spadina-College district that he wanted to talk to him. A week or so later The Duck telephoned. He agreed to meet with Stark at a place on Bloor Street named The Blue Orchid.

As nearly as Stark could remember, all this happened around March 1973. (Christine and Peter would, at that time, just have returned from their brief holiday in Acapulco.) After setting up the meeting with Kacsa, Stark said, "I called up Demeter and told him that I had located the guy . . . I ask him what should I tell him. He said just for him [Kacsa] to be at Dawes Road and you tell him what to do."

Stark knew "what to do" because he had discussed this with Peter at one of their earlier meetings, sitting in Peter's grey Cadillac, the car beside which Christine's lifeless body would be found four months later. Accordingly, Stark told The Duck that "a person" would drive up to a vacant property on 52 Dawes Road in Toronto's east end. This person would be carrying a roll of architectural drawings inside which there would be money. (Kacsa wanted to know how much money, but Stark claimed he couldn't say because all Demeter told him was that there would be "enough". This assurance, according to Stark, satisfied both him and Kacsa.) In any case, The Duck was to push that person down the basement stairs of the house, making sure that the person "didn't get up". The whole thing had to look like an accident. The Duck agreed.

A few days later, continued Stark, he drove The Duck (who never had a car) out to Dawes Road to show him the house in question. The latch on the back door of the empty, semi-detached townhouse was broken, so Kacsa would have no difficulty getting in and waiting for "the person" on the night the accident was supposed to happen. However, Kacsa and Stark looked at the building only from the outside. After casing the place they started talking about a Hungarian boxer named Joe Dinardo, so they decided to drive out to the Lansdowne Gym (Stark called it the Lonsdale Club in his statement) where Kacsa had a little talk with Dinardo, while Stark watched heavyweight champion George Chuvalo box a few rounds in the ring. Then they parted and, Stark said, he never saw The Duck again.

About a week later, on the evening of what Stark called "the appointed day", Stark was working with one or two other men at a job on Carlton Street. Stark knew that the murder plot called for Peter and Christine to attend a Committee of Adjustment meeting together in the city's Cabbagetown ward. The meeting would start at 8:00 P.M. An hour or so later Christine would be sent out to Dawes Road to show the property to a prospective buyer. Peter, of course, would stay at the meeting. The Duck would be waiting in the Dawes Road house from nine o'clock on.

What in fact happened, Stark said, was that around 10:00 P.M. Peter showed up at the Carlton Street job where Stark was working on some piano benches. He signalled Stark through the front door to come outside. The two men started walking up and down on Carlton Street.

"She came back," said Peter.

"Who came back?"

"Christine."

(The fact that Peter and Stark would be talking to one another in Hungarian made this exchange sound quite believable. The Hungarian language knows no gender, and implied subjects need not be expressed in declarative sentences. In this language, tailor-made for conspirators, Peter could simply have said "came back", leaving it up to Stark to guess whether he was referring to a man, a woman, or a parcel.)

"What happened?" asked Stark. But, as he told O'Toole, he knew the answer anyway. The Duck was a crook, a thief, a con-man. He was bad news. On the street he had the reputation of being a man who would cheat his own grandmother out of her old-age pension. But he was no killer. Though he had discussed nothing with Kacsa and had simply told him what Demeter wanted done, Stark said he had known all along that The Duck wouldn't do it. What he would do, though, was take the money.

"Christine said there was a green Mustang parked on the other side of the road," explained Peter, according to Stark. "When she drove up a man got out and met her on the sidewalk. He said, 'Have you brought the plans?' and then took the plans from Christine. She asked him, 'Don't you want to see the building inside?' and he replied, 'No, I've already seen the building.' Then he got into the green Mustang and drove off."

It sounded just like The Duck.

"You might as well forget about it," Stark said he told Peter. Demeter looked at him for a second, then replied: "You're probably right." Then he left, and that, said Stark, "was all for that night."

What happened later, Stark explained, was that Peter kept insisting he find The Duck. He tried, but Kacsa had disappeared. Stark wanted to find him anyway, because Kacsa owed him $350, advanced for some dry-walling job which Kacsa undertook but never finished. Stark wanted to get his money back (plus whatever The Duck was willing to give him from the proceeds of the Demeter rip-off), but even though he managed to trace him to his common-law wife, Maria Visnyiczky, as well as to his best friend, Leslie Link, he could never actually get hold of The Duck himself. Finally the whole thing just lapsed somehow, and he never heard from Peter until the leaky toilet needed fixing on Russell Hill Road.

When he was brought to Joe Pomerant, Stark said, he didn't say a word about Peter's plot against Christine, only about Christine's earlier attempt to buy a rifle and an alibi for Csaba from him. (Stark kept insisting that this story was also true.) Pomerant gave him some thirty dollars for expenses, and a subpoena to appear at the trial for the defence.

By 11:35 that night Ferenc Stark's statement was typed out. The detectives had to scramble to find a magnifying glass for him because Stark had left his reading glasses behind when he was picked up by Joe

Terdik and his men. O'Toole was pleased as he watched the ex-legionary putting his initials next to the typographical errors on the statement form. With Stark the investigation had clearly hit the jackpot.

But there were a couple of flaws. One, unlike Csaba Szilagyi, Stark refused to take a lie detector test. Two, he wouldn't even sign his statement until he could talk to the Crown. As the detectives escorted him to the nearby Cara Inn where he would be held in protective custody, they reflected that Stark would have to be signed, sealed, and delivered before the case against Peter Demeter could remotely be closed.

The point, of course, was that the Mississauga police wanted the case closed, and wanted it closed very badly. By then the trial had been proceeding in London for over a month, and nearly sixteen months had elapsed since Christine's murder. Whereas the suggestion (which would later be made) that the cops had been conducting a "vendetta" against Peter was never substantiated by any evidence, there was little doubt that he was the only suspect whose conviction ever really mattered to the police. There were some legitimate reasons for that. They began with the genuine belief that Bill Teggart and his team had in Peter's guilt and ranged to the natural moral outrage most people have against a husband killing his wife, except perhaps in a drunken argument or a jealous fit. But there were also some other, less lofty reasons, from which policemen are no more immune than the rest of humanity. Christine Demeter's murder was worthy of "extra miles" and "golden slippers" only if her husband Peter was guilty of it: otherwise it was just another dime-a-dozen urban tragedy. ("I knew it would be the most important arrest in my life," Bill Teggart had said, "because he looked so distinguished.") Making sure that distinguished-looking Peter Demeter — a man of swimming pools, Mercedeses, Cadillacs, and big-city lawyers — would get his come-uppance became an overriding consideration for the authorities.

There was nothing intrinsically wrong with this: it is the duty of the police to gather and present evidence against a man they have reason to believe is guilty. Of course, it is also their duty to uncover as much of the evidence, and against as many people, as possible in a given crime. Society employs the police to find out all available facts, not simply to secure a conviction. Looking at police work in any other light would mean surrendering the value judgment of *whose* conviction is the most important to secure.

At this stage of the proceedings, if the allegations against Peter were true, they showed him to be a man who had been plotting against the life of his wife for over five years to absolutely no effect. Whatever one might have thought of his nature and morals, the danger he represented to society seemed very limited as long as he was on his own. The most he seemed capable of doing was inventing rather puerile plots for the benefit of his friend Csaba Szilagyi, who, of course, was even less ready to act on them than Peter himself. A man like Demeter, if the evidence was to be believed, became a potential menace only in conjunction with people like Ferenc Stark or The Duck. Yet even while Stark was resting in the relative luxury of the Cara Inn, the decision was made that no one would delve too deeply into the circumstances of his involvement with Christine's death, as long as he gave evidence against Peter Demeter. That this was not a decision without some moral ambiguity was indicated by the fact that the Crown, and indeed the trial judge, found it necessary later to defend and even deny it before the jury.

Making a "deal" of course is extremely common, and is often defended by the practical consideration that a great many convictions could never be secured without it. Invariably the idea is to give immunity to a lesser crook to convict a greater one, and it always involves a judgment of some kind as to who is the lesser crook. In addition, of course, there are other questions of utility, such as which crook seems more ready to talk. As in any other kind of deal, the aim is to give away as little immunity as possible in return for the greatest possible co-operation. Ultimately — as Stark seemed to have realized quite well — the deal is always made by the Crown, not the police.

In dealing with Stark, John Greenwood might have been labouring under the disadvantage of being "one of the police team" instead of being a Crown attorney of a more distant kind. It is possible that, as one of the boys, he empathized more with the relative lenience cops often extend to their "own" crooks, as well as feeling a greater obligation to honour any agreement they might have made. (Possibly he also believed that if Stark refused to talk, they would have no real evidence against him anyway.) In any event, by the time Stark would arrive to testify in the London courtroom, though originally charged with murder, he would no longer be charged with *any* crime. It was not a bad deal for a man who seemed on the verge of fainting when he was first arrested. If, instead of being sent to the Cara Inn after two or three hours, he had been questioned a little longer by the formidable Detective-Sergeant O'Toole, he might have settled for less or given away more in return.

But time was pressing. The truth was interesting, of course, but everyone seemed satisfied to learn just as much of it as appeared necessary to convict Peter Demeter. People like Stark or The Duck were no real antagonists, and convicting them would earn no promotions or headlines for anyone. Earlier at the trial Joe Pomerant had insisted that the Crown particularize the charges against Peter — originally he had been indicted simply for murder — and Leo McGuigan had come up with a formula that, in light of the new evidence, seemed to satisfy everyone: *Such murder was committed by the said Peter Demeter by having a person or persons unknown kill the said Christine Demeter. . . .* Why spend valuable time pinning down the likes of Stark, if Christine was killed by persons unknown?

Even more to the point, why spend time looking too closely at the holes in Stark's story? After all, some of the contradictions might not even incriminate Demeter. Let Peter's own teams of lawyers do it, for what it's worth, in cross-examination. It will give them something to think about besides bitching about the on-the-scene efficiency of the Mississauga police.

Because, in the meantime, Joe Pomerant had been busy picking holes in the weakest aspect of the investigation: the collection and preservation of physical evidence at 1437 Dundas Crescent. Ex-Ident man Chief Burrows's instincts were right when, on the night of the murder, he circled anxiously around the Demeter garage, wrestling with his hunch that he ought to put in a personal appearance. (In fact, he finally decided against it only when he heard on his radio that Superintendent Teggart himself was taking charge of the investigation.) Now the prosecution was finding itself on tricky grounds with some of the basic Sherlock Holmesian aspects of the mystery.

It was very much a part of the Crown's case that Christine's murder was set up to look like an accident. The lack of murder weapon or fingerprints, the absence of any sign of struggle or any trail of blood, all pointed to a planned, premeditated execution. (Not a drop of blood leading away from the scene seemed especially unusual considering the extreme goriness of the murder. Privately Greenwood speculated that it could best be achieved by a person standing motionless in the pool of blood after the killing, taking off his shoes one by one and handing them to an accomplice.) The question, however, was whether all this evidence was really absent, or whether the police had simply failed to discover it.

Though this question could no longer be answered, Pomerant's methodical cross-examinations did raise some serious doubts about it. Constable Crosson testified that the scene in front of the garage was not preserved. Sergeant Murray was "not aware" that anyone was detailed to guard the scene behind the Demeter home. Only the garage and the nearest portion of the driveway were protected, and Sergeant Murray thought that the back of the house was never given any protection. Constable Foley's tracking dogs from the Ontario Provincial Police — the ones happily sniffing out Beelzebub's old scents — arrived on the scene only twelve hours after the event. Detective-Sergeant Crozier admitted that the house itself was not examined for fingerprints, and that officers had been using doors that had not been fingerprinted. The area across the street was never searched, said Crozier, the presumption being that the murderer went out the back. In the rear, however, the search went only as far as the line of trees on the near side of the ravine. Most importantly, no fingerprints were taken from the door, found ajar, at the rear of the garage. Later events made this admission especially significant.

Detective-Sergeants Forbes and Koeslag, the actual I.D. and photography men on the case, could not completely dispel the feeling that physical evidence might have been disturbed or overlooked at the scene. The impression wasn't exactly of flat-footed police tramping through the garage (though one member of the prosecution team did joke later that the only footprint found came from a policeman's boot on the back of the corpse), but in all good conscience a jury could not dismiss the idea of a burglar or a mad rapist being the killer on the basis of the physical evidence alone. The police work at the scene was just not meticulous enough for that. Chief Burrows, sounding a note no less familiar for being probably true, would later say that given more budget and training facilities, his force could have done better.

But that was not all. The prosecution could field the accident theory easily enough, but other aspects of the medical evidence were more disturbing. If Christine's body showed any signs of recent sexual intercourse or molestation, it might suggest to the jury that she could have died at the hands of a maniac or an angry lover. Greenwood knew for a fact that Pomerant would be raising the possibility that Christine might have been killed by Williams, the self-confessed murderer of Constance Dickey and Neda Novak. Therefore, the presence of semen in Christine's vagina as well as certain marks on her legs became of special significance.

While the body was still in the garage some of the detectives observed a few small marks on the thighs. They referred to them as
"bruises", this being a logical term of description, but by the time Dr.
Fekete began his autopsy the next day he couldn't see them at all. Real
bruises, of course, would not have disappeared overnight, but blotches
caused by uncirculating blood settling near the surface of the skin
would have. This condition, known as "lividity", draws the blood to the
lowest portion of the body by the normal effects of gravity, and dis-
perses when the body is turned. What worried John Greenwood was
that Dr. Hillsdon-Smith, the other Crown pathologist, himself agreed to
the word "bruises" at the preliminary hearing, even though he saw the
body only on the autopsy table. Greenwood heaved a sight of relief
when, at the actual trial, Dr. Hillsdon-Smith could recall only one old,
yellowing bruise, and confirmed his colleague's view that the rest of the
marks seen by the detectives must have been due to lividity.

The next area explored at length by Pomerant had to do with the sim-
ilarities between the victims of the Williams murders and Christine. According to Dr. Hillsdon-Smith, the only similarity between them was
that they were all women. The Crown, however, still had to contend
with the problem that none of Williams's known victims were killed or
injured in exactly the same manner. The jury might have concluded
that the confessed rapist's *modus operandi* changed from victim to victim.

This brought up the next question: was the presence of semen in
Christine's female organs the result of rape or, at least, recent
intercourse? The prosecution contended, of course, that it wasn't rape.
Peter, by his own admission, had intercourse with his wife in the morning of the day of her murder. Forensic analyst Francis Charles Pinto testified that, in his opinion, the act of intercourse occurred twelve to
twenty-four hours — rather than immediately — before Christine's
death. However, under Pomerant's skilful cross-examination, Pinto conceded that the sexual act *could* have taken place just an hour or so before
Christine's heart stopped beating in the evening of July 18. It was an important concession. It meant that the jury could rely neither on the
physical evidence at the scene nor on the views of the medical experts
to rule out a lovers' quarrel or a rape-murder with absolute certainty.

Ironically, if Peter had said *nothing* to the police on the night of the
murder, the presence of semen might have channelled suspicion away
from him at the time, or at least helped him at his trial. Male sperm in a
murdered woman's body always raises the spectre of rape or some vio-

lent extra-marital affair. No doubt Peter volunteered the information about making love to Christine just to indicate the normal nature of their relationship. But whether he did it calculatingly or in all innocence, it would now boomerang on him in the worst possible way. It proved again that Joe Pomerant's initial advice — *say nothing to anyone* — would alone have been worth the price of his retainer.

Pomerant, of course, was now earning his retainer in other ways. He was raising doubt after doubt, including some that seemed reasonable enough. But that created its own problems. Though the strategy of raising doubts could not be faulted in a legal system that gives the benefit of doubt to the accused, it was still possible that by raising too many Pomerant might leave the jury confused rather than dubious. They might think: *What is the defence trying to prove? Are they saying that Mrs. Demeter, having died in an accidental fall, then fought a pitched battle with her lover, only to end up being raped and bashed over the head by a maniac who happened to be in the neighbourhood?* Although Pomerant was merely questioning the Crown's evidence, his lengthy, detailed cross-examinations seemed to subtly shift the burden of proof to the defence. They created the expectation that, as in a fictional courtroom-drama on television, the defence would finally produce some neat twist that would explain everything. This expectation, of course, could not be fulfilled. In real life, experts or witnesses seldom break down in tears on the stand and admit to having been lying or mistaken — or the murderer.

At this point, though, knowing nothing about Mr. X, The Duck, or the other half of Ferenc Stark's evidence, the defence still seemed to have the winning hand. With a judgment that was probably quite sound, Pomerant offered little challenge to the string of agents who testified about the million-dollar insurance policies that Peter and Christine had on each other's lives. John Greenwood, leaving no stone unturned, called one expert to say that Christine was over-insured, but Justice Grant ruled this evidence inadmissible. Very naturally the defence wanted to spend as little time as possible on the big insurance, the fact of which could not be denied, and which they considered extremely prejudicial to Peter's case. (Cousin Steven would later say in a jaundiced moment that the verdict was a foregone conclusion the minute the jury learned about the million dollars, because anybody on the panel would have killed for less. This opinion seemed sweeping enough to tell more about a Budapest view of humanity than about the ethics of London, Ontario.) But, in fact, even the Crown regarded the million dollars as something of a two-edged sword: if it provided a motive for Peter, it also gave one to Christine.

This mattered, since John Greenwood knew that Viveca Esso, the next person to be called to the stand, might repeat under cross-examination Christine's remark, made only the day before her death, that it would be nice to "knock Peter off and get his money". Viveca did repeat it and, joke or not, Christine's *bon mot* cut too close to the bone. Viveca also stated that the trip to Yorkdale Shopping Centre on the evening of the murder was initiated by Dr. Sybille Brewer; that it was not even discussed until they were returning to Mississauga from their morning trip; and that Peter never expressly directed Christine to remain at home. Less useful to the defence was Viveca's statement that she would have preferred to stay with Christine had Peter not asked her to accompany the party to Yorkdale, and that the dog was taken along at Peter's insistence, against the wishes of Christine. Most damaging of all, of course, was her interpretation of Peter's initial gesture to her while he was on the telephone at Birks. Viveca thought he was waving her away, as though he didn't want her to hear what he was saying to his wife, before calling her over to the extension phone to exchange good-byes with Christine.

This was vital. If Viveca was right, Peter could have been shooing her away because he was just in the process of instructing Christine to go out and fetch something for him from the garage. (A set of car keys was found on the front seat of the Cadillac, and the interior of the car showed some smearing and spattering of blood, indicating that at one point during the attack Christine must have been inside it.) Viveca also told about her going ahead to the jewellery store alone while Peter was taking Beelzebub, who was not permitted inside the plaza, back to the car. This again would have given him the few minutes needed to make a phone call and launch the assassins. All in all, Viveca's testimony provided one element necessary for any circumstantial case: evidence of opportunity.

Dr. Sybille Brewer supported Viveca's story in all major details about the last day of Christine's life. Neither of these two Crown witnesses seemed antagonistic to Peter; Dr. Brewer, if anything, was friendly. Both women might have been shocked not only by the murder, but by the idea that Peter had anything to do with it, and both appeared to make sincere efforts to recall events as accurately as they could. The very fact that they differed on minor points lent credibility to their evidence.

In some respects Dr. Brewer's testimony was slightly more favourable to the defence. Perhaps the most favourable, in a technical sense, was her firm recollection that Peter seemed ready to leave the shopping centre a good half-hour before the agreed time, and it was because she herself and the other girls were not yet finished that they stayed on a bit longer. As it was, they arrived back at Dundas Crescent fifteen minutes earlier than initially planned, and had it been up to Peter they might have been a half-hour earlier still. Clearly, if Peter had arranged for a murder, he ought to have been anxious to linger as long as possible. This was important, and for once Pomerant didn't meander in his cross-examination but brought the fact home to the jury in a direct and forceful way.

John Greenwood would have liked to get Dr. Brewer, an articulate and precise witness, to describe the Demeters' marriage as strained and unhappy, but Justice Grant ruled him out of order. The judge probably did the prosecution a favour, because they might not have liked Dr. Brewer's answer. In fact, on cross-examination Sybille explained the marriage to the jury this way:

"I always had the feeling that there must be some strong bond between Peter and Christine that they stayed together all this time and I, as a matter of fact, on occasion put the question to Peter when he seemed to be particularly unhappy. 'Well, why don't you — you are both grown up people and liberal people, why don't you separate, why do you stay together?' I could only come up with the conclusion, from what he would say, that there was more to it than appeared."

Justice Grant also stopped the Crown as Greenwood tried to get Dr. Brewer to describe Peter's reaction when, years earlier, his old cocker spaniel Miro was killed. (Apparently Peter was extremely upset at the time, blaming Christine in some way for Miro's death. Friends would even suggest later, only half in jest, that if Peter did arrange Christine's murder, it wasn't for Marina's love or the million dollars as much as in revenge for not taking better care of the cocker spaniel.) But if Justice Grant had anything in common with Peter at all, it was an affection for dogs; the judge's own schnauzer, Baron, was even getting greeting cards from his master on his birthday. Though Peter regularly accompanied his lawyers to the judge's chambers — where the atmosphere was more informal and relaxed than in the courtroom — His Lordship would never exchange any words with the accused. Once, however, the two men found themselves in an animated and warm discussion about dogs for a minute or two, before remembering their roles and lapsing back into silence again. Now Justice Grant would not allow the Crown to use Peter's fondness for his old dog against him. "Mr. Greenwood, I think you should probably not pursue that any further," said the judge sternly, and that ended the matter.

Pomerant also scored by having Dr. Brewer recount her treatment at the police station on the night of the murder. It seemed she was taken down to the station around 11:00 P.M., then kept until 3:00 A.M. before her statement was taken. During her four-hour wait the police would not permit her to make a phone call to her husband in Connecticut or make arrangements to have someone take care of the three little girls, Katja, Silja, and Anne, who were in her charge. With Viveca, Peter, and Dr. Brewer held at the station, the three youngsters (two of whom could speak little English) were in fact left alone in the house practically all night, while their hostess's blood dried on the garage floor. This seemed not only pointless and insensitive on the part of the police, but it raised doubts about their claim that Peter started defending himself long before he was accused of anything. If the police treated witnesses the way they seemed to have treated Dr. Brewer, it was hardly surprising that Peter would be defensive, antagonistic, and ready to hire a whole flock of lawyers by the next day.

This was important because (as Greenwood would relate later) the jury seemed almost to gasp audibly when they heard that Peter was surrounded by lawyers less than twenty-four hours after his wife's death. The Crown Attorney knew that this is how the average person, for whom hiring a lawyer is almost tantamount to an admission of guilt, might react to Peter's sophisticated precaution, and he made a point of bringing it out during Dr. Brewer's testimony. On the other hand, he made nothing of a potentially far more damaging part of Dr. Brewer's evidence, for the simple reason that he could not appreciate its significance until a few hours later.

Sybille Brewer related how Peter, on the day of the murder, drove them all to the area of the Riverdale Zoo twice, first before and then after lunch, because he had to talk to some contractor working in the vicinity. The second time he managed to find his man and, while they all waited in the Mercedes, he had a brief conversation with him. Greenwood spent no time exploring this further: it was hardly unusual for Demeter, a developer and builder, to have a discussion with some contractor during the working day.

Dr. Brewer happened to testify on October 30. Greenwood finished his examination-in-chief by lunch, then excused himself from the afternoon session. Even while Joe Pomerant began scoring points for the defence, back in Mississauga Joe Terdik's team was getting ready to hit Ferenc Balint Stark, and Greenwood wanted to be around when it happened. Before the night was out he would learn about the Dawes Road Plot. A little later he would also know that in the weeks preceding and following Christine's murder in July 1973, Ferenc Stark had been working on a house *right around the corner from the old Riverdale Zoo.*

Two days later "Foxy" was found. He turned out to be the first non-Hungarian so far, though (reassuringly for the police's view of the case) he was married to one. The red-haired young man had some previous convictions, though none for crimes of violence. His real name was Joseph Robert Jones. He knew The Duck through The Duck's good friend Gaby Kecskes, whose wife was Foxy's wife's sister. He was cool and ever so helpful when O'Toole's men finally located him after a considerable expenditure of effort. "What can I do for you gentlemen?" Foxy asked. Like Stark, he seemed ready to do just about anything.

Foxy's deposition, taken on the day of his arrest, read as follows:

I have known Jimmy [The Duck] for about a year. I think it was some time in the Spring of last year that I was drinking with Jimmy and Gaby. . . . Some time during the evening Jimmy asked me if I wanted to make a Hundred Dollars to drive him down to the Danforth. He said he had to pick up something for Frank. I didn't know who Frank was.

We went down the Danforth and I parked the car and he went up to the house and knocked on the door. He did not get an answer but all the lights were up in the house. There was a "For Sale" sign on the house — the houses were just being built. He came back and got into the car and he said that there was no one home, and that we would have to wait.

We waited about Fifteen Minutes and a Mercedes Benz came around the corner — I think it was grey. He said, "Well, that's them coming now." The car parked in the alleyway and a woman got out on the passenger side and went into the house, so Jimmy went down and knocked on the door and went in too. I did not see anyone else in the car. . . .

So he wasn't gone too long and he came back to the car. . . . As he was getting into the car he took out this long roll of paper that he had under his raglan coat. He held the roll in his hand between his knees. It was wrapped in an elastic band.

Foxy said he only got forty dollars for his efforts from the clever Duck, even though he did another little chore for him the same night. Apparently, having picked up the roll of paper, "Jimmy" had a long telephone talk with this guy named Frank which, Foxy said, he only half listened to. But The Duck was kind of worried about the conversation. "Jimmy said he was in shit with Frank because he was supposed to do something that he didn't do." In any case, he asked Foxy to drop in at some restaurant where Frank was sitting and tell him that he, Jimmy, would meet him the next day at the Blue Orchid. Foxy did as asked. "Frank was mad and swore at Jimmy when I met him at the restaurant." (Presumably Frank would have been even angrier if he had known that The Duck was at home, packing his suitcase in a hurry.)

Foxy Jones also added that he was driving a green 1969 Mustang when he took Kacsa to his rendezvous.

While this story didn't put Stark in such a relatively innocent light as his own — The Duck said he was in shit *with Frank* because he was supposed to do something he didn't do — it confirmed enough of his statement to tighten the noose further around Peter's neck. This, after all, was the point of the exercise. In fact, Greenwood would not even wait for Foxy to be apprehended to make his move. On Thursday, October 31, at 11:30 in the morning, he entered Justice Grant's chambers with a synopsis of Stark's statement in his hand. He was flanked by Leo McGuigan, Chris O'Toole, and Jimmy Wingate. Joe Pomerant and Eddie Greenspan were already in the room, as was Peter.

Though Greenspan had been uneasy about the senior prosecutor's sudden departure from the afternoon session the previous day, his hunch that something might be up was not shared by Peter. Things had not been going too badly so far. Wednesday, October 30, seemed a particularly good day for the defence, with the Crown's big theory about "the isolation of Christine" on the day of the murder hardly having been proved beyond a reasonable doubt. Peter had felt sufficiently confident, in fact, to take Sybille Brewer to lunch right after her examination-in-chief, before she had even been cross-examined by Pomerant. It was a somewhat impudent — and imprudent — gesture for a man accused of murder. It seemed to publicly state: nothing can touch me when even the Crown's witness is my friend. Once again, it was not the kind of thing calculated to put Peter in a favourable light with anyone who knew about it, and most people seemed to know, including Justice Grant.

Wingate and O'Toole handed copies of Stark's statement to everyone in the judge's chambers. For a few minutes there was silence. Justice Grant leaned slightly forward as he was turning the pages. In a few seconds Joe Pomerant got up and started pacing the room. But Wingate was mainly looking at Peter. He was reading the synopsis with a smile on his face which did not change even when the tears started coming into his eyes.

19. The Trial Continues

Until that Thursday morning in his chambers Justice Grant did not think much of the Crown's chances. He might even have considered (though he'd never confirm this) directing a verdict of acquittal if Greenwood couldn't come up with anything better. "It didn't look too strong," the trial judge would say later of the prosecution's case. "They didn't have very much except the tapes which in themselves were, I thought, inconclusive. . . . They had some motive, but they had no evidence at all of Demeter having approached anyone."

Now there was evidence in the most unequivocal form. This was no vague series of conversations about dime-novel plots, such as Csaba Szilagyi alleged he had been having with Peter for years. If true, Stark's statement told of a real conspiracy, with all details arranged and money paid out, at the end of which Peter could realistically expect to find his wife murdered. The conspiracy happened, moreover, only three and a half months before she actually was. It may not have been direct evidence of Peter's guilt, but it had changed mushy suspicion into a strong circumstantial case.

Greenwood didn't hesitate. From having virtually no hand (after all, Justice Grant hadn't even ruled on the admissibility of the tapes yet), he suddenly found himself holding, if not a royal flush, at least a full house. Immediately the Crown Attorney decided to raise the stakes. Having gone through the synopsis of Stark's deposition, he presented two applications to the judge. The first one was to add the names of Ferenc Stark, Maria Visnyiczky, and Joseph Robert Jones to the back of the indictment. The second was a motion to revoke Peter Demeter's bail.

Naturally the defence countered by asking Justice Grant to declare a mistrial.

Adding the new names to the indictment meant that the Crown was changing, or at least expanding, its theory of the case. It was, in effect, presenting the defence with a new set of circumstances. Pomerant and Greenspan argued that expecting an accused to respond to them virtually overnight would deprive him of his lawful right to give full answer and defence. It was nothing short of being unfair to Peter Demeter.

That there was more than a little validity to this argument was indicated by the fact that not only prolix Joe Pomerant but even concise Eddie Greenspan had some difficulty in presenting it. The surprise was simply too great, and it caught the defence off balance. It was not a moment conducive to great coherence. Even the Crown, which had exploded the charge, seemed somewhat startled by its noise. When Justice Grant asked whether the prosecution really wished to add the names to the *back* rather than the front of the indictment (the difference being whether they would be witnesses or, possibly, co-accused) Greenwood seemed genuinely startled by the novel possibility. "I would like to consider that, My Lord," he said. "That had not crossed my mind, but . . . we certainly will look into that." Apart from any deal that might have been made with Stark, Greenwood very probably had no inkling himself at this stage whom he might wish to proceed against or how. The Crown seemed to know little more about the implications of the new developments than the defence, and they had just begun looking into the possibilities of extraditing The Duck from Hungary. There had been neither time to investigate nor a willingness to hold everything until the new evidence could be explored in detail. Whoever killed Christine, the point was to nail Peter Demeter as the man behind it. The whole truth could wait.

Seeing both opponents slightly dazed in his chambers, Justice Grant must have decided that it was time to gather the reins of the trial very firmly in his hands. It was also time for certain due bills to be presented to Joe Pomerant, who would now have to pay the penalty for having cried wolf too often. The mistrial motion about to be presented was the fourth since the trial began, the previous three (on September 24, October 18, and October 21) having been brought on the ground of prejudicial coverage of the trial in the news media. The problem was not with the motions' having been brought, but that they were brought, in the trial judge's view, on grounds ranging from the flimsy to the self-inflicted. Justice Grant considered Peter and his lawyer very much the authors of their own misfortunes in media affairs. He made it clear on more than one occasion that the accused and his counsel seemed far too accessible to the press, and not nearly careful enough to ensure the confidentiality of defence requests or other matters they did not wish to see reported. The trial judge had no sympathy with what he saw as first seeking publicity and then complaining about the results. He seems to have especially resented the idea of locking up twelve true citizens for months just so that Peter should suffer no restriction in his free movement and speech. Though he never said so, Justice Grant might have found the very idea of a murder suspect's being free on bail incongruous. The spirit of the generation that shaped Campbell Grant's values, though liberal enough, did draw the line at certain things, and sharing a Holiday Inn dining room every night with an accused wife-killer and his mistress may have been one of them.

Even if not actual resentment, the feeling in the judge's chambers might well have boiled down to a question of trust. Had he encountered another defence lawyer in the same situation, Justice Grant might have taken his word that this new blow was below the belt. But while from a counsel whom he trusted more the judge might have accepted generalities, from Joe Pomerant he demanded particulars. It was all very well to complain about difficulties but, said His Lordship, "difficulty is not a reason for a mistrial unless you are not getting a fair trial. Difficulties in themselves are not sufficient, you know. The evidence . . . may be a lot more damning than when we started, but this is not a reason for a new trial unless it deprives you of a fair trial."

Though Justice Grant was unquestionably right in this, the line that divides "difficulty" from "unfairness" still is a matter of interpretation. In the circumstances, a motion for mistrial was pretty much a discretionary matter for the trial judge to grant or refuse as he saw fit. Some people in the legal community — including David Watt, the eminent young lawyer who would later argue the appeal on behalf of the Crown — would see the dramatic shift in the prosecution's case as not merely difficult, but probably unfair to the defence. Some lawyers would agree (in David Watt's case only unofficially, of course) with the argument presented on the following Monday by Eddie Greenspan — who had by that time recovered his customary lucidity — that, in effect, the Crown had virtually brought a new charge against Peter Demeter. In this view the better decision would be to halt the proceedings until the police and the prosecution could properly evaluate their own evidence, decide what their actual case against Peter was going to be, permit the defence sufficient time for discovery, and then start a new trial from scratch.

32. The Prosecution: Crown Attorney John Greenwood and Assistant Crown
    Attorney Leo McGuigan

33. The Defence: Joe Pomerant and Eddie Greenspan with their client, Peter
    Demeter

34. The Honourable Justice
    Campbell Grant

35. Justice Campbell Grant with his dog,
    Baron

36. A portion of the notes Peter Demeter passed to his attorney during the
    Preliminary Hearing

All I had to do to be home at 10 p.m., or later, is to go with Vivica for an ice-cream at Yorkdale and keep the 9:30 p.m. appointment at the car-parking lot, as the trip is 35 to 40 minutes home!!!

I was the one wishing to get home earlier — Chr. was expecting us at 10 p.m.

37. Gabor Magosztovics, a.k.a. Joe Dinardo, a.k.a. The Tractor

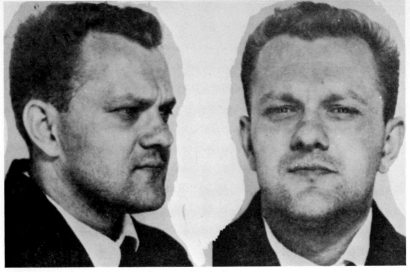

38. Laszlo Eper, the Santa Claus of Shaw Street

39. Scrawled in Eper's handwriting on one side of the paper, "Peter Demeter, ACR Associates", and on the other side, "Police Superintendent William Teggart"

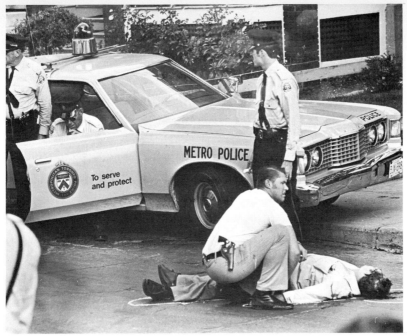

40, Bloor Street, August 29, 1973: Finis for Laszlo Eper

41. "I thought I had died and woke up in a policeman's paradise." Superintendent William Teggart and Detective Terdik in Vienna, en route to Hungary to
investigate the whereabouts of The Duck

42. Maria Visnyiczky and her daughter: "A petunia in a bed of weeds"

43. Joseph Robert Jones: "In this trial, 'Foxy' Jones seemed practically like a breath of fresh air."

F. John Greenwood, Q.C., Crown Attorney, Judicial District of Peel, now Assistant Deputy Attorney General— Criminal Law

Assistant Crown Attorney Leo J. McGuigan, now Crown Attorney

Chief Douglas K. Burrows, now Chief of Police (Region of Peel)

Superintendent William J. Teggart, now Deputy Chief of Police

Detective-Sergeant Christopher N. O'Toole, now Inspector.

Detective-Sergeant Joseph Terdik, now Inspector

Detective James R. Wingate, now Detective-Sergeant

Detective William Koeslag, now Detective-Sergeant

Detective Barry V. King, now Inspector

Justice Grant (and eventually the higher courts) did not see it that way. On Monday, November 4 — having given both sides the weekend to catch their breath and marshal their arguments — the trial judge ruled on all the motions in front of him. (They had by that time included one additional motion for a mistrial by the defence on the grounds that the media had reported many of the discussions that transpired in the judge's chambers, including rumours of the startling new evidence and the Crown's attempt to revoke Peter's bail.) Justice Grant responded by giving the Crown permission to add Stark's, Visnyiczky's, and Jones's names to the back of the indictment, denying all defence motions for a mistrial, and, last but not least, revoking Peter Demeter's bail.

In five days — from his confident luncheon with Sybille Brewer on Wednesday to the judge's order revoking his bail on Monday — Peter Demeter's world had changed completely. In personal terms it might have been a far more fundamental change than any in his life before. Even being charged with murder might have appeared not much more than a game to begin with. People experience their own existence in a day-to-day fashion, and even the most cataclysmic shifts are only really brought home by changes in small personal circumstances. War is just a word until it becomes ration cards, blackout curtains, air-raid sirens, and bombs. Peter was now finding out that being accused of murder was no longer a game, something to be smoothed out or negotiated between clever lawyers and not-so-clever policemen, while his own daily routine continued virtually unchanged. This was no longer a polite disagreement between two teams of gentlemen staying for a few weeks at the Holiday Inn.

On his last weekend of freedom — already deprived of Marina's company by Justice Grant's order, since she was scheduled to take the stand — it must have crossed Peter's mind what it would be like to exist without everything that until now constituted the points of his compass. Far more than just swimming pools and Cadillacs, he had risked his life to be free, free to deal, free to reach for the top, free to be admired and envied. For a man anxious not to be confined by any circumstances in his life, whether it be tyranny, poverty, or unrequited love; who would refuse to take "no" for an answer from geography, the law, the glands of reluctant females, and (possibly) even from that basic animal instinct that generally stops most of us from doing injury to our own kind, the blanket, all-embracing prohibitions of prison must have been an unbearable idea to contemplate. He might have dealt with it by refusing to believe it. Driving back from Toronto to London with Eddie Greenspan on the morning of Monday, November 4, Peter missed the exit from Highway 401 and had to continue driving for a while in the direction of Windsor, Ontario, beyond which lay the United States. Both men had driven to London a dozen times but this had never happened to them before. That morning they were engrossed in conversation, of course, but it might have been other, less conscious reasons that made the car pass by London in a headlong rush for the border. They even joked about being arrested before they could reach the next cut-off and turn back towards the city of Justice Grant's jurisdiction.

The same evening Peter Demeter was in jail.

From the Holiday Inn to prison would have been a startling change in any event, but the London Jail was not just any prison. With the possible exception of the old Don Jail in Toronto, there was no penal institution in English Canada more closely resembling the classic, story-book concept of gaol. The ancient structure — unlike the new courthouse next door — was untouched by any architectural idea less than a hundred years old. Peter's own cell (it was said) had housed someone involved in the bloody and infamous Donnelly feud a hundred years ago. It had the length of a man's body lying down and the width of one extended arm. Its walls were made of dank field-stone. Its only furniture, not surprisingly, was a bunk. The Count of Monte Cristo's cell in the Château d'If would have appeared palatial in comparison. Being locked up here was being in *jail*; there was nothing symbolic about it. But, said Bill Teggart, Peter could always console himself with the thought that there was more room in it than in Christine's coffin.

But Peter, of course, was not admitting guilt any more than before. On the contrary, Stark's evidence only caused Joe Pomerant to voice, on that Thursday morning in the judge's chambers, the defence's alternate theory. Although this theory had been floating around before, it was the first time it was expressed in so many words. Christine, if not the victim of an accident, sex-maniac, et cetera, must have died at the hands of some "unsavory characters" with whom she had been plotting against Peter Demeter's life.

There was evidence for such conspiracy, in the defence lawyer's view, in the first part of the deposition of the Crown's own witness. Ferenc Stark kept stoutly insisting on the truth of his story about Christine's attempt to buy a gun and an alibi for Csaba. To conclude from this that

Christine wanted to get rid of Peter and then somehow died as a result of her own plot was, of course, still quite a few jumps away, but Pomerant wasn't troubled by this. His task wasn't to prove Christine guilty, only to raise a reasonable doubt about Peter's guilt. The Crown wanted the jury to believe Stark, and, whether the Crown liked it or not, the gun-and-alibi plot was part of Stark's story. Pomerant would have no doubt been happier in some other jurisdiction, such as Texas for instance, where calling a witness means vouching for his total veracity. In Ontario Greenwood could say to the jury: though this is my witness, you don't have to believe *everything* he says. I want you to believe only that Demeter tried to conspire against his wife. But the gun story was still evidence, and, from the defence's point of view, much better than nothing. If the jury couldn't quite make up their minds who wanted to kill whom, Peter could be home free.

What if, for instance, the Dawes Road Plot had been the other way around, with Christine meeting The Duck on her own volition to pay him an advance for killing Peter ? This could have been set up through Stark in much the same way. Then, somehow, the conspirators quarrelled a few months later (maybe they wanted more money from her) and Christine got killed. The informer, Mr. X, could have got wind of the murder, told the police "The Duck did it", and when the police found Stark, it would have been in his interest to tell them what they obviously wanted to hear. After all, this seemed to have got him immunity, whereas if he had told the police he had been conspiring *with* Christine *against* Peter, it could have meant a conspiracy charge as well as suspicion of murder. It would have been in Stark's interest to tell his story, changing the characters around.

(In fact, Peter did mention in a taped telephone conversation with Eddie Greenspan fifteen months earlier that Christine used to keep the few thousand dollars she got from the sale of her old Mercedes *rolled up inside some architectural plans*. But at the time the information seemed of no importance, and now no one would remember it.)

The trial having taken this turn, Pomerant must have been itching to get at the ex-legionary on the witness stand, but this could not happen for a few days yet. Since Justice Grant ordered things to proceed in the normal way, there were other scheduled witnesses to get through first. They included the former maid Gigi, now living with Csaba Szilagyi in a fine harmony that testified to Peter's ability as a matchmaker — as opposed to his questionable skill at picking his own women. Gigi, who saw herself as something of a friend and companion as well as a maid to Christine, seemed rather antagonistic to the defence. Since she was now Csaba's girlfriend, this could probably not influence the jury too much. Otherwise, her evidence made little difference either way. The Demeters used to quarrel a lot, she said. Peter never took the dog with him in the car as far as she could recall. A couple of times a man named Nicholas Van Berkel came to the house. (Greenwood was careful to bring out the name of Van Berkel himself, since he knew that Christine had been having a brief fling with the friendly management consultant in 1971, and he didn't want the defence to spring this as a surprise on the jury.)

Inspector Peter Veillard of the Vienna police testified about the arrest of Marina on July 24, 1973, six days after Christine's murder. Though she was held in custody for less than two days, it was very ironic that she was the first person to be arrested in the case. Joe Pomerant used the opportunity very skilfully to demonstrate to the jury how the police can pull big boners and jump to wrong conclusions on the evidence. It was a mystery why Bill Teggart's team would interpret the tiny sum Peter was sending through Marina to an elderly, penniless refugee as a pay-off to the murderer, the more so since Peter made both arrangements right on Joe Terdik's wiretap. Possibly Bill Teggart decided that a bit of harassment might cause Peter to let the cat out of the bag. Still, the error reduced the police's credibility and made them look somewhat foolish in court. The affair also indicated another side of Peter's complex character. Normally even an unselfish person might forget to make a gift of money to some distant mendicant just after his wife's murder of which he himself is being accused. Yet Peter, who would bitterly fight with a Mexican waiter over four dollars on his holiday, seemed unable to miss the opportunity even in these circumstances to act as the Don to his less fortunate friends.

The next witness was Marina herself. Normally her testimony ought to have been the high point of the trial, the moment for which all the reporters, cameramen, and crowds surging around the London courthouse would have waited. As it was, Justice Grant had to order all cameras and tape recorders removed from the floor on which the trial was held. But though necks craned and a hush descended as Marina, looking both enticing and demure, mounted the witness stand, the fact was that the latest developments in the case had stolen her thunder. By Friday, November 1, the trial was abuzz with rumours about mysterious Foreign Legionnaires and creatures named The Duck. The crunchy Miss Hundt was delicious to look at, but after all, what could she say?

Not much, as it turned out. She recounted a relationship between Peter and herself which, by that time, was common knowledge to most people with any interest in the case. Prior to her appearance at the trial, Marina had been living at 1437 Dundas Crescent for more than half a year and in a sense she was no longer news. Greenwood had the good judgment to be very friendly and gentle with her as he led her through the evidence, which consisted mainly of reading the scores of letters she had been exchanging with Peter over the years. They were fascinating letters, but they shed no light on Christine's murder. In cross-examination she said that she was in love with Peter, which she wouldn't be if she had thought he had been involved in Christine's death in any way. It was easy to believe her, and the jury probably did. All the same, having chosen to occupy Christine's "dream-home" in Mississauga with Peter, she couldn't very well be expected to say anything else. By this time Marina's opinion just didn't matter.

What mattered more was that, with Peter locked up in jail, Marina remained on her own at the Holiday Inn in London. Looking after the gregarious model was not easy, and in any case there was nobody to look after her. Pomerant and Greenspan were far too busy with the trial, and their social habits didn't coincide with Marina's. The two lawyers didn't drink or dance if they could help it, while the easy-going Viennese Fräulein was rather fond of good cheer and fellowship. The city of London was crawling with young journalists and photographers from all parts of Canada. Many of them were acquainted with Marina by now, and many of them had similar tastes. A twenty-eight-year-old girl, whose Canadian trip hadn't been much fun so far, couldn't be expected to hold a nightly vigil underneath the window of her lover's cell. Marina certainly didn't. It wouldn't have mattered, except that London was a small town and the jury was still unsequestered. Soon Miss Hundt definitely stopped projecting the cloistered and virginal image in which the defence would have preferred her to be seen.

It was at this point that the relationship between Joe Pomerant and his client began taking a less friendly turn. The pressure on Pomerant must have been immense, of course. He was conducting a trial which had made front-page news in the Canadian press, and was being followed in the United States and in Europe. He was very much on the spot, yet he had not been doing too well. Joe must have sensed (indeed, it didn't require much perception) that he was not enjoying the fullest sympathy of the trial judge. He obviously had to notice that his own partner was having serious reservations about his tactics. But more than anything else, things were coming to light about his client, time and time again, that were making his job more difficult. What started out as an easy case of defending an obviously innocent man against wild accusations from a bumbling and overzealous suburban police force had turned into a legal nightmare.

When it comes to murder, Joe Pomerant had said, a spotless record of victories is often just a matter of choosing your cases wisely. Possibly Joe had accepted Peter's assurances in the beginning that no surprise evidence could come to light against him because there *was* none. Possibly he had chosen his defence strategy on that basis. Possibly he felt no need to provide for the contingency that his client might not be innocent. By now, however, it must have been plain to Joe that Peter either had misled him or happened to be the unluckiest man in the world. First, there was his best friend Szilagyi. Then Peter's own bewildering words on tape. Finally, with Joe already committed to a line of defence halfway through the trial, came Ferenc Stark, the same man Pomerant had been counting on as a defence witness. It was like a stab in the back. This was Pomerant's case as much as Peter's, and Peter was spoiling it for him.

Demeter, for his part, might have started losing faith in Pomerant's magic. There was all the shiny, expensive paraphernalia, but the rabbits were not coming out of the hat. With all his black cloaks, assistants, equipment, Houdini couldn't seem to escape from a wet paper-bag. His cleverest challenges, his boldest motions were being rejected by the bench one after the other. The final act was rapidly approaching and Perry Mason was still being ruled out of order. Peter's costs were mounting (reportedly they would reach $200,000 by the end of the trial) and the results did not seem worth a red nickel so far. Since his original bail hearing (handled by Eddie Greenspan), his fortieth-floor lawyer with the slub-textured ivory tuxedo couch in his office hadn't won a single battle for him. It might have seemed to Peter that throwing himself at the mercy of the court could have been as effective, and certainly far cheaper. Now, with all his airs and chauffeur-driven limousines, his Forest Hill lawyer had landed him in possibly the oldest jail in Canada, in a clammy cell that Peter didn't even think had existed since the storming of the Bastille.

Joe's airs, in fact, might have grated on Peter in a worse way than all the other things. Peter was rather proud of his own brains and fond of taking the floor in any gathering of men. Now Joe would hush him as though he were a child. Joe had also acquired the irksome habit of hold-ing forth after the trial each day in the room reserved for the defence — after he had taken off his lawyer's gown, but before putting on his shirt. At times he would pace up and down in the little room, naked to the waist, talking non-stop for an hour or more. The sweating, hairy chest, of which Joe seemed rather proud, would irritate Peter, a fastidious man in his personal habits, beyond endurance. Turning the London consult-ing room into a Spadina Avenue "shvitz" in which the needle-trade boys gather after a hard day of selling dry goods, letting it all hang out in the delicious hot steam, did not work for Peter at all. In fact, it nau-seated him. In his culture people didn't sit around naked delivering long Talmudic lectures to each other's armpits. Peter would normally see the exposed skin of his friends, carefully tanned and taut, only on a sandy beach or around a swimming pool.

On one occasion, after Joe had rather rudely told Peter to shut up when he tried asking him a question while Joe was talking with a re-porter, Eddie steered their red-faced client to the little consulting room. Before the door would close, someone in the corridor overheard Peter saying a few words to Eddie with deep intensity. "I hate that man," Pe-ter said.

People's nerves were, of course, taut to the point of snapping by that time at the trial. Many of the participants had been away from their families for nearly a month and a half. Some lawyers don't mind when wives or children attend their courtrooms once in a while (on one occa-sion Eddie Greenspan's pretty wife spent a morning in the public benches), but John Greenwood would try to veto all visits from mem-bers of his family. Joe Pomerant, as it happened, was in the process of separation from his own wife just around that time, which probably did little for his disposition and concentration. Justice Grant, though a much younger man might have envied his general health, suffered from a condition of the gall bladder that required him to be on a certain diet. The kitchen at the Holiday Inn had instructions to prepare his dishes accordingly, but one day a new waitress poured some butter over his potatoes that brought on an acute attack, with agonizing pain. Though the trial judge never complained and no one became aware of the inci-dent, he probably had little patience with lengthy and repetitious argu-ments in court on the day that followed his sleepless night.

An incident of macabre irony occurred just around that time, also in-volving the trial judge. His wife, Mrs. Grace Grant, was alone in their

Port Elgin home for the duration of the trial. This was not unusual, since Justice Grant's profession often required him to be away from home for weeks at a time while he travelled the Ontario Supreme Court circuit. Mrs. Grant's arthritis made longer walks a bit difficult for her, so arrangements were made with a neighbour to take the judge's dog, Baron, for a run once in a while. The good schnauzer was always looking forward to these occasions. The neighbour was surprised when one evening, instead of dashing out the front door as usual, Baron refused to leave the house and sat whimpering in front of the door leading to the cellar. Mrs. Grant didn't seem to be in, but Baron's antics were so puzzling that the neighbour decided to investigate. Mrs. Grant lay at the bottom of the cellar stairs with a broken hip, which she had suffered in a fall in the morning. Had Baron been a dog of a more casual nature, the accident could easily have become fatal. Once Justice Grant got over the shock and assured himself that his wife would be all right, he couldn't help reflecting perhaps that the man he was trying was accused of plotting exactly this kind of household accident.

The next matter of evidence was Ferenc Balint Stark. Joe Pomerant got his first chance at cross-questioning his erstwhile "defence witness" in the absence of the jury on a *voir dire* regarding Peter's bail application, which of course had been renewed as soon as Justice Grant had revoked the existing bail on November 4. Then, a few days later, Pomerant had a go at Stark again in front of the jury.

Joe was faced with the very difficult task of examining a witness of whose testimony ten per cent would be quite favourable to the defence, while ninety per cent would be totally devastating. The lawyer could obviously not suggest that everything Stark said was a lie. What he did suggest was that the one-time mercenary was turning the truth inside out to save his own skin. Since Stark admitted that Christine *tried* plotting with him, Pomerant kept suggesting that they did in fact plot together against Peter, until things went sour and Christine got killed.

Stark said no. The only person he plotted with was Peter, and of course he, Stark, didn't really mean that either. He knew the honest Duck would simply take Peter's money without harming Christine.

Pomerant caught the small-job contractor in two discrepancies in his testimony. The first was that, on the *voir dire*, Stark said he had visited Christine on the gun-and-alibi occasion around ten at night. In front of the jury he said it was around five in the afternoon. Pomerant hammered away at this (at the risk of discrediting Stark on the only bit of evidence favourable to the defence) because he wanted the jury to feel that Stark had changed night to afternoon to avoid admitting that he would visit Christine at night. After all, Christine had been *killed* at night. If Stark hadn't dreaded the connotation of "night", why would he have changed his story? It was a subtle point, and the jury might have preferred to believe that Stark could not tell night from afternoon simply because the gun-and-alibi story was in fact cock-and-bull.

The other hole in Stark's story could have been vital, since it fitted in perfectly with the defence theory. If Pomerant could convey it to the jury forcefully enough, it might have raised the reasonable doubt needed to save the day.

The point was this: Stark testified he had known The Duck as Kacsa, Cutlip, and eventually by his real name, Imre Olejnyik. But he insisted that he had never known him as Jimmy Orr.

Demeter, said Stark, didn't know Olejnyik's name at all. He never wanted to know the name of the killer. When Stark first used the name "Kacsa", Peter allegedly replied, "Don't tell me any names."

Yet in Christine's diary for April 2, 1973, in what was apparently Christine's own handwriting, there was the name *Jimmy Or*. April 2 was the date of the Committee of Adjustment meeting in Cabbagetown, from which Christine was supposed to have been sent to the house on Dawes Road.

Stark said he didn't know The Duck as Jimmy Orr.

Stark said Peter didn't know The Duck as Jimmy Orr.

How, then, did the name Jimmy Or(r) get into Christine's diary?

If Stark was conspiring with Peter, as the Crown alleged, it simply couldn't. *But if Christine had been conspiring on her own with Stark and The Duck (as alleged by the defence), the mystery was solved.* The Duck might well have introduced himself to her as Jimmy Orr, even if Stark only knew him by other names.

It seemed of no benefit to Stark to deny knowing this particular alias of The Duck's if he did know it. What possible difference could it make to his involvement? The only explanation was that he made a slip and told the truth, not realizing its significance. Pomerant could have zeroed in on it and hammered it home.

By this time, of course, points needed a lot of hammering. For nearly four weeks the jury (who could make no notes) had been bombarded by scores of outlandish names. Even Justice Grant would have trouble keeping them straight at times, while Dr. Brewer seemed not to realize on the stand that "Csaba" and "Szilagyi" were the same man until it was explained to her. Among all the names, plots, counter-plots, scraps of evidence and the rest, twelve ordinary citizens unused to this type of work couldn't be expected to understand at the drop of a name what was important and what wasn't. Having to think quickly on his feet, with very little time to prepare for the onslaught of Stark's surprise evidence, Pomerant himself might not have fully realized the significance of his point. He needed to focus it for the jury, yet it might have been unfocused in his own mind. It was a good example of how the defence might have been short-changed by not being granted, if not a mistrial, at least an adjournment to prepare for the Crown's new evidence.

In any case, unfortunately for the defence, Pomerant allowed the impact to dissipate by bringing in the fact that Stark's girlfriend happened to be named Gloria Orr. Though there was no connection whatever established between Gloria and Jimmy Orr, it gave Stark a more or less innocent reason for not wanting to know The Duck by this name. The jury might have assumed that he knew "Jimmy Orr" all right, and was denying it only to keep his lady's name out of the whole mess. It would certainly give those on the panel who were inclined to find Peter guilty a chance to dismiss what would otherwise be a very puzzling episode that was clearly in his favour.

By the time Ferenc Stark testified (under the protection of the Canada Evidence Act, which meant that nothing he said in court could later be used against him) a very big change had taken place at the trial. On November 12 Justice Grant decided to sequester the jury.

The defence had been urging sequestration literally since the first day. A month later, on October 22, even the Crown indicated that it would support the defence's application to separate the jury. Pomerant (who by that time had three mistrial motions before the court on the grounds of prejudicial stories in the news media) refused Greenwood's support, saying that all the harm had been done and it was too late to sequester. Later in the same day, however, when Justice Grant refused to declare a mistrial, the defence renewed its application. This was then promptly refused by the trial judge.

There was reason behind this seeming madness. Since separation invariably means a great deal of inconvenience for the jury, neither of the adversaries wish to be known (if they can help it) as the side that wants the jury to be locked up. True or not, the feeling exists that the jury might decide against the sequestering side out of sheer spite. At the same time neither side wishes to be too bloody-minded in opposing sequestration, because it may cost them the case on appeal. The ultimate decision, of course, is up to the judge. Sequestration is a rather dramatic move, and judges are often reluctant to employ it. Among other reasons, some judges feel that it tends to inflame a jury against the accused no matter which side requests it, and that it should only be done if there is no other way of ensuring a fair trial. Some say that lawyers often ask for it for no better reason than that they want to collect Brownie points towards an eventual appeal. If they can find nothing else wrong with the trial, they can always say the judge ought to have sequestered the jury. There seemed no doubt that Justice Grant thought little of holding twelve good men and women under lock and key for months.

Still, a few more mistrial motions later (including one brought on November 6 on the grounds of a newspaper photo showing Peter being escorted to the London Jail by a police officer), Justice Grant gave the order for the jury to separate. For the next four weeks the twelve men and women would live under guard in a nearby motel. They could hear or watch only pre-selected programs on radio and television. They would be permitted to talk with no one except each other. It was an order Justice Grant did not enjoy giving and he gave it with evident distaste. Yet the practice of sequestration is founded on solid reasons. During a long and sensational trial rumours are rampant, and people are often influenced by what they read or hear. What they read or hear, of course, may be untrue. This can happen not only to ordinary jurors, but even to wise and experienced jurists.

Justice Campbell Grant himself was a meticulous jurist. No one could have been wiser or more experienced. He set great store by judicial propriety and decorum. He would have social contact with no one from either side of the case. If he permitted any person to sit at his table, it would be only his own law student or the court reporter. Though by nature a kind man, not in the least stiff or unfriendly, he would prefer to appear somewhat distant and forbidding rather than permit himself to be engaged in any conversation about the trial outside his chambers or the courtroom.

Yet even Justice Grant was a human being, with the ordinary need to say "Nice day" to another person once in a while. And so it happened that someone, somehow, somewhere, mentioned something to him that obviously stuck in the trial judge's mind. It was just a rumour and, as it happened, it was untrue. Yet had it been a fact, it would have made Peter pretty obviously guilty. It would also have made Joe Pomerant something of a shyster.

The trial judge evidently believed that Stark and Foxy Jones were discovered because Peter had been under surveillance and he had led the police to them. "They followed Demeter, you know, from London to Toronto," Justice Grant was to say later, "and that's how they found them. Someone said to me in the lobby of the hotel, Demeter's going to skip the country across the border tonight, and I said, don't be foolish, I said, he's got no reason to skip the country. . . . The Crown hasn't had a good fight with him yet, and there he was paying his bill and away he went. The police were right behind him. . . . The story was he went to Mr. Pomerant's office, and the police waited outside and as these people came out they picked them up. Now I'm not sure about that, that's the story I hear."

No doubt Justice Grant would not act on anything he wasn't sure about and, while on the bench, would dismiss any story he might have heard as just a story. But this story suggested that Demeter and Pomerant were having a meeting, not just with Stark about the gun-and-alibi thing, but with Foxy, the man who drove The Duck. The implications were considerable. If this was true, the Dawes Road Plot would hardly have been a surprise to the defence, as they claimed it was, with some passion. And while the trial judge could separate evidence from rumour, there were many rumours in London and in the press, and the average juror might not have had Justice Grant's discernment. Sequestering the jury in the seventh week of the trial might well have been locking the barn door after the horse had gone. Eventually this would become one of only two points of appeal that the Supreme Court of Canada would give Eddie Greenspan leave to argue.

20. A Man Named Williams

On November 14 Justice Grant ruled the tape recordings between Demeter and Szilagyi admissible.

This was a major victory for the prosecution. The tapes, no matter how ambiguous, meant that it would now be Peter's word against himself. Yesteryear's conversation between the Chief and his Superintendent under the sumach and aspen trees had borne fruit. Daring or dirty pool, Bill Teggart's snoop-scoop had been judged fit to be received by a court of law.

The tapes were admitted, of course, only after Justice Grant heard arguments from counsel for both sides. The game was now for big stakes, and both defence and prosecution were anxious to play it well. John Greenwood led off for the Crown.

Greenwood's argument occupied more than twenty-five transcript pages in the record. For the pithy Crown that was a long argument. In essence he stated that the tapes should be let in because 1) there is no enforceable right to privacy in common law, 2) the tapes conform to the common-law requirement of being accurate and complete, 3) the 1974 Protection of Privacy Act was not retroactive in any of its provisions; and 4) that even if the new Act *were* retroactive, the body-pack tapes complied with it because one party to the conversation, Szilagyi, consented. Lastly Greenwood argued that Szilagyi was not a person in authority *vis-à-vis* Demeter, and even if he had been, Peter had made his statements to him voluntarily.

Greenwood's arguments were clear and covered a whole range of possible objections. He delivered them fluently and concisely. He indulged in no showy fireworks and, as throughout the trial, he was careful not to waste the judge's time. Now came his moment to be rewarded: Justice

Grant saw a possible loophole in his argument and tried to make sure that the Crown Attorney would cover it. He might or might not have done it for any other lawyer.

His Lordship was worried about Greenwood's argument that the new Protection of Privacy Act was not retroactive. Frankly, he thought it might well be. But the Crown could still get the tapes in by using the alternative argument that the interception was lawful at the time it was made. Justice Grant just wanted to make sure Greenwood realized this.

The Crown Attorney seemed a bit slow on this one. "I must be candid," he said, "and I must indicate, in my view, that the legislation cannot be retroactive because it would be a ridiculous situation. . . . "

"I recognize that is your first argument," said the judge patiently. "But if I rule against you, I wondered what you thought of my suggestion."

The coin dropped.

"I would adopt the suggestion," said Greenwood quickly.

Though Eddie Greenspan must have realized it would be an uphill struggle, he was determined not to go down without giving a good account of himself. His argument against letting the tapes in was a masterpiece of ingenuity, and though it made a number of points that (to the layman, at least) seemed very valid, it ought to have succeeded on sheer nerve alone. Eddie had the knack of making complex and lengthy arguments sound simple and brief. Though his submissions were three times the length of Greenwood's, when Eddie apologized in chambers to the judge for taking so long, Justice Grant merely said: "No, I did not think you were taking too much time today." Joe Pomerant might have had his head snapped off after the same performance.

Of course Eddie's discourse was a delight for anyone who, like Justice Grant, had an ear for the music of legal logic. It was not necessary to agree with him to appreciate the cadences and harmonies he created.

"So that your Lordship will understand the position that is being advanced," Eddie began, "I would like to state at the outset that it is my submission that retroactivity is not a legal concept. . . . Alternatively, if it is, I have a number of submissions to make, as well."

Greenspan's first argument was that the law of Canada was simply what the law of Canada said. Since June 30, 1974, the law of Canada said that there can be no surreptitious electronic surveillance without a court order authorizing it, and nothing can be admissible in court that has been obtained in contravention of this law. The Act came into force on a certain date; if it were to apply only to evidence obtained after that date, Parliament would have said so. In Canada there are no implied exceptions to the law.

Eddie's second argument was that Szilagyi's consent was not sufficient to admit tapes against Demeter. Only Demeter could consent to tapes being admitted against him. Szilagyi could only consent to tapes being admitted against Szilagyi.

If the English version of the Act did not make this clear enough, said Eddie, he had a French professor waiting in the wings to testify that in the French version there was no ambiguity. If the law was clear in French but not in English, the two should be read together and the French should prevail because of the equality of status of the two languages in the Official Languages Act of Canada. It was an argument to warm the cockles of Prime Minister Trudeau's heart.

And so it continued. The tapes were defective, misleading, and unreliable. There were 49 inaudible parts in the first tape, 67 in the second, 28 in the third. The fourth, the tape made in November between Csaba and Peter at Mr. Pizza, had 141 inaudible portions. It was dangerous to put evidence of such poor quality before a jury. Demeter said many things that were gravely prejudicial to him, yet which were of trivial probative value. The judge had the discretion to exclude them. The law does not wish a jury to find a man guilty of murder because they resent his business dealings or social views.

Finally, Greenspan said, the way the police conducted the investigation constituted a major abuse of due process. It was precisely to prevent such intrusions into privacy and solicitor-client communications that Parliament found it necessary to change the law less than a year after Demeter had been charged. He urged the trial judge not to reward police tactics that bring the administration of justice into disrepute.

Justice Grant listened seriously and sympathetically, but even from his occasional questions and interjections it seemed probable that in his mind arguments along the more abstract lines of civil rights and liberties would not outweigh the issue of the particular guilt or innocence of the prisoner at the bar. To some extent, of course, the trial judge was bound by the famous 1970 decision of the Supreme Court of Canada in *The Queen* v. *Wray*, in which the majority of the judges held: "Even if the evidence has been obtained unfairly in the opinion of the trial judge it is not his duty to exclude it if its probative value is unimpeachable. . . . There is no judicial discretion permitting the exclusion of relevant evidence on the ground of unfairness to the accused." But even if he had not been bound by *Wray*, Justice Grant might not have shared the sentiments of dissenting Judge Spence in the same case: "If the trial judge had *not* excluded the evidence it would not only have brought the administration of justice into disrepute but would have been a disregard of the principle that a man should not be made to testify against himself." It seemed clear that Justice Grant's spirit was guided by different principles. Later he would say: "I myself don't see any harm in the police using means like that to ascertain the truth in their prosecution. The purpose of these trials is to ascertain the truth. And a person who had committed a crime by some devious means, I don't think he has any particular right to complain if the police do something that obtains the truth from them without their knowledge." So Peter Demeter would be made to testify against himself by the sound of his own voice.

Following this Greenwood decided to plug various potential holes in his case. Big John smelled victory after the judge's decision on the tapes and he was taking no chances. He called a workman and a home-owner to testify that they had seen Stark and Peter together on several occasions. He called Foxy Jones and Maria Visnyiczky, who repeated their stories for the jury. He called Judith Welch, owner of the well-known model agency in Toronto, to show that Christine had earned less than $2000 as a model in her best year and could hardly indulge in the luxury of hiring assassins. Greenwood even called a highly reluctant and discomfited Mississauga journalist by the name of James Bruce Robinson, who had gone to 1437 Dundas Crescent during the summer to obtain a picture of Marina. Apparently Peter gave the man a cup of coffee and told him something about the authorities needing " . . . in the case of my late wife, two or three people in the chair . . . and they don't have them." It seemed that Greenwood considered this an incriminating remark. The witness himself did not.

Little Rose Papastamos, one of the neighbour girls from up the street who occasionally babysat Andrea, testified that after her noon-hour swim on July 18 Christine asked her to return and stay with her in the evening. John Greenwood wanted the jury to know this in case the defence claimed Christine was planning to meet a lover or co-conspirator after Peter's party had left for Yorkdale. Had she had such plans, she would hardly have asked Rose to come back. This fact was potentially a two-edged weapon (though Pomerant made nothing of it) because it meant that killer Peter hadn't even taken the elementary precaution of asking Christine if she was expecting someone in the evening. Had he done so — if Rose was to be believed — Christine would have answered, yes, the little Papastamos girl. This made Peter a careless conspirator indeed.

The Crown also called Mr. and Mrs. Henri Galle. Henri Galle, of course, was the man Peter had always suspected of having been Christine's lover and the possible father of Andrea. The Galles testified that they had been friendly with the Demeters at one time, but Henri had never spent more than five minutes with Christine alone. Joe Pomerant, with eminently good sense, did not pursue the point.

Then, like dank decay from an open grave, an aura of senseless evil ascended over the London courtroom.

When Chief Burrows had first looked at the body of Constance Dickey on the Erindale campus across the ravine from the Demeter garage, he had the feeling that the girl's remains had been moved. Someone must have come around, the Chief thought, and dragged her a little distance, maybe just a few yards, after she was dead. One-time Identman Burrows was right. When Henry Joseph Robert Williams was arrested ten months later he told a grim Chris O'Toole about going back to the campus at night to look at his victim's body and make sure she was no longer alive. He had run into her earlier in the day, having taken time off from his job of putting bricks into a kiln at the Canada Brick Company in nearby Streetsville. He wanted to do something, to drive around, to relieve the pressure. Mainly, perhaps, he just wanted to get away from work.

"Where did you find Miss Dickey?" asked Pomerant.

"She was walking along Mississauga Road."

"Had you ever seen her before?"

"No."

"Had you any idea as to what kind of woman she was, or girl she was?"

"No, I did not." Almost impatiently, Williams shrugged his shoulders.

"You were driving, and you were feeling some impulse, and you stopped the car?"

"I wasn't driving," replied Williams.

"Oh I see," said Pomerant. "Well, I thought you said you wanted to drive around?"

"That is what I said."

"Did you drive around?"

"Yes."

"And then what did you do?"

"I was on my way back to work and I stopped . . . "

"Yes?"

"To relieve myself."

"Yes?"

"She asked me," said Williams, "if it was a short cut to the campus."

Constance Dickey died of strangulation caused by a wire around her neck. Later Neda Novak would die of two stab wounds in her back. Judith Sheldon would survive a knife plunged into her side and being hit over the head with rocks. Williams didn't quite know why any of these things happened. He supposed he panicked. He maintained he never raped anyone; all these girls made love to him voluntarily, though yes, he did threaten them first with a knife. He did get this pressure, these urges, around the time his first child was born, and then again when his next child came along about a year and a half later. The first time would be, yes, around the spring of 1973. He could get off work, his time card wouldn't have to show that. He did it twice, no, only once. He had heard of Christine Demeter's murder on the news. Of Constance Dickey's too, yes. Of Neda Novak's, yes. No, not of Judy Sheldon's. He did have a hunting knife in his car. It was there because he did a lot of fishing. He drove a '72 Charger. New? Brand new. His wife had a car as well. Salary, maybe $180 a week. Yes, he was in debt. He was not here voluntarily, that's right, he didn't want anyone to know what he had done, would you? (No, said Pomerant, not that.)

Williams admitted he did not give himself up to the police. He was arrested because of information given by his one surviving victim. Yes, he knew she was in hospital for a long time. Yes, the police did question him about the murder of Christine. For how long? Maybe three-quarters of an hour. Yes, he did kill Constance Dickey. Yes, he did kill Neda Novak. Yes, he did try to kill Judy Sheldon.

No.

He did not kill Christine Demeter.

It was hard to tell how much the defence might achieve by dragging this ghoul into the courtroom. True, the hair-raising simplicity of his sadistic-moronic crimes was in chilling contrast with the almost humorous Hungarian sting The Duck was said to have pulled on Dawes Road. Williams seemed better suited to the mood of the bloody scene at Dundas Crescent. Apparently he had been on the rampage just around the time Christine was murdered, and he had been prowling in the general vicinity of the Demeter residence. He certainly had no iron-clad alibi. He would kill women every which way, he would stab, strangle, or bash them over the head. But he would always prey on girls walking or hitch-hiking in lonely spots. Going into homes or garages didn't seem to be Williams's style. Since he had admitted to some horrible murders, the jury might feel he would admit to Christine's as well if he had, in fact, done it. (Though this was not necessarily true: Teggart himself half-suspected Williams of one other murder, which he indignantly denied.) Pomerant made much of the fact that Williams was questioned about Christine's death by the police, indicating that they themselves weren't so sure about Peter's guilt. Surely if Teggart's boys were having doubts, so should the jury. (O'Toole would later say he questioned Williams about Christine only because he knew the point would be raised in Peter's defence; otherwise he wouldn't have bothered. This only went to show that with lawyers one couldn't win.) But the real question was: would the earnest exploration of one more alternative increase the doubt in the jurors' minds or, on the contrary, would it make them lose faith in a scattergun, grasping-at-straws defence?

Justice Grant thought that "Williams was very, very badly treated in our case. He was charged with several murders, undoubtedly he was guilty of them, probably the only defence he had was insanity, but during the trial he was subjected to the most vigorous cross-examination after having divulged to counsel everything he knew. I think they were very unfair to him." It was undeniable that civil-rights-conscious Joe Pomerant seemed to pay little heed to Williams's civil rights — since he, after all, had not yet been tried and had the same right as everyone else to a presumption of innocence before an unbiased jury. Dragging out details of his crimes in open court to be reported lavishly by the press might have jeopardized his later chances for a fair trial. True, to reverse one of Justice Grant's earlier remarks, Joe was not the judge but counsel for the defence and his first duty was to his own client.

John Greenwood left Williams for Leo McGuigan to handle. Perhaps he wanted to minimize Williams's importance to the case by palming him off on the Assistant Crown. But it was equally possible that he just couldn't bring himself to exchange words with the Dracula of Streetsville. There was a hush in the courtroom while Williams was in the stand. With much wickedness and human imperfection common to all, he was still a glimpse of something beyond the line that separates the merely sinful from the damned.

21. A Flower at the Racetrack

Since October 1 when he had first talked with Detective-Sergeant O'Toole, Mr. X must have been thinking. Thinking, as is well known, improves the memory. Mr. X started remembering things.

Julius Norman Virag — whose last name meant "flower" in Hungarian — told O'Toole at their initial meeting that all he knew about Christine's murder was the street-rumour that she was killed by someone called Kacsa or The Duck. He couldn't help the police with Kacsa's real name, address, or any other details. Consequently it took O'Toole's men three weeks and a lot of shoe-leather to track The Duck to Maria Visnyiczky's apartment on Denison Avenue.

By the end of the month, however, The Flower's powers of recall had undergone a remarkable change. In his sworn deposition, signed early in November before a judge of the Provincial Court, Virag attributed this to the fact that " . . . last week I heard on the news that Demeter had a Million Dollars Insurance on his wife and I just never liked greedy people." Since this bit of news did not hit the media until around October 28, The Flower must have finished remembering things just before the arrest of Stark.

His new, enriched story was the following: July 18, 1973, the day of Christine's murder, had been a memorable date for Virag because it happened to be the day on which he had been deported from the United States for illegal entry. Having landed at Toronto Airport, Virag said, he immediately visited the nearby Woodbine Race Track. He arrived there before the first race, that is, around 1:30 in the afternoon. In the clubhouse bar he ran into his old acquaintance The Duck.

The Duck seemed happy. He was certainly spending money like water. He showed Virag a bunch of fifty-dollar tickets. When Virag asked him where he got all that money from The Duck said he won it playing cards — which Virag said he knew was bullshit. By the time they left Woodbine to go their separate ways, related the snitch, The Duck must have dropped about $3000.

The next day, July 19, Virag said he walked into The Silver Dollar on the corner of Spadina and College. In the lounge he saw The Duck again. This time he seemed very depressed. The Flower stood him a rum-and-coke.

"What's wrong? You broke?"

"No, I still got $4000," replied Kacsa.

"Where did you get it?"

"Never mind."

Virag said he bought Kacsa a few more drinks and kept asking him about the money. Finally The Duck said: "We did the most stupidest and terrible thing in my life. We killed Demeter's wife."

Virag knew what his friend meant, he said, because he had read about it in the papers. "There were three of us," continued the unhappy Duck. "We made a mess of her in the garage and my share was $10,000." Then Kacsa stood up, gave the snitch a dirty look, said "My God", and ran out of the lounge. Later Virag heard that he had gone back to Hungary. End of story.

Short of a schoolboyish eagerness to put the lid on Peter Demeter, there was nothing to justify a decision by police and prosecution to offer evidence from such a dubious source to the court. Even the dumbest crooks don't usually go around confessing murder to bar-room acquaintances who don't know them well enough to know their names, and Virag didn't know The Duck either as Imre Olejnyik or as Jimmy Orr. Crooks especially don't confess to drinking buddies known to be snitches, which The Flower was. And even if the Crown could vault over this barrier to Virag's credibility, there was still the formidable obstacle that it took Mr. X about a month to "remember" his story. Of course his memory may have been jogged by his disgust over the million dollars he had heard Peter stood to gain. But it is just as likely that his recall was prompted much more by the $2000 reward that was reportedly paid to him by the police.

Of course, in fairness to the authorities, Virag did tell them about Kacsa in the first place, and they had no idea whether The Duck did or did not return from Hungary to finish the job he was alleged to have been paid for on Dawes Road. Maria Visnyiczky thought he didn't come back until October, but she couldn't be certain. Stark said he gave up on The Duck after just a little pressure, but then Stark would have his own reasons for not saying otherwise. Extradition proceedings to get The Duck back from Hungary might take forever. But it's an adversary system. If Virag says what he says, why should the prosecution argue? The defence can cross-examine and the jury can decide.

And so it happened that on November 15 John Greenwood made the somewhat dramatic announcement that the informer, Mr. X, had now become available and the Crown had just received his statement. He asked the trial judge to order the courtroom cleared of spectators and permit him to testify under a pseudonym to protect his identity.

Justice Grant read Virag's statement (a copy of which was handed to Joe Pomerant at the same time), and ruled that he could not repeat on the stand the hearsay conversations he said he had had with The Duck. The judge also ruled against the theatricals of having the courtroom cleared, though he permitted the snitch to wear a hood over his head while in the stand. Then he christened Virag "Tom Smith" and permitted him to testify before the jury about his July 18 and July 19 meetings with Kacsa at Woodbine and The Silver Dollar, except for the dialogue between them.

"My Lord," said Pomerant somewhat desperately. "Again I was given the statement possibly two minutes ago, and I assure your Lordship it is difficult to deal with evidence on this basis."

"I know," replied His Lordship. "But sometimes . . . It may be in this case. In respect of the last witness [Williams] you had every opportunity months ago to see him, and I'm told you interviewed him and spent a great deal of time. And his counsel is here, and told me you could have had [his] time cards if you wanted them. And that is what worries me."

"That is absolutely not so," said Pomerant. (He had previously claimed that the Crown wouldn't make the killer's time cards for July 18 available for examination.)

Justice Grant grew forceful.

"Counsel is here in Court," he said, "with his gown on. And he saw those cards and you could have seen them, too. And you made statements to the Court that bother me."

The tense exchange with its foregone conclusion went on for a few minutes. It was the old story. In this instance (as in some others) the defence seemed shortchanged. But in many other instances throughout the trial Pomerant himself had employed tactics the trial judge had come to view as dubious. Just when Joe might have needed and deserved it most, his reservoir of goodwill had run out.

The Flower, a.k.a. Mr. X, a.k.a. Tom Smith, took the oath and told the jury about his two meetings with The Duck. Even without the hearsay "confession", the story tied the man who was tied to Peter Demeter through the affair on Dawes Road to the murder of Christine. All other evidence — Stark, Szilagyi — was about old, unsuccessful plots. But now Tom Smith said that The Duck was seen spending thousands on the day of Christine's murder, and seemed upset the next day. It was a clincher. Pomerant, having just been handed the statement, had no basis on which to cross-examine. He would later claim that the police wouldn't even give him Virag's criminal record, though according to Detective Wingate he had it in his hand. In any case, Pomerant didn't know about the one month it took The Flower to remember his story. He didn't know how little Virag seemed to know about The Duck when he first informed on him to Chris O'Toole. He didn't know that Virag hadn't even been aware of Kacsa's names.

And nobody knew one other thing: that the Woodbine Race Track was not even operating on July 18, 1973.

22. Portrait of a Friend

The next witness was Csaba Szilagyi.

Time and thought, of course, had also improved Csaba's memory. There seemed little doubt that he, too, had spent the intervening months fine-tuning his tale. Though in *substance* his testimony did not change from the preliminary hearing, it now had more fluency, texture, and detail. Certain things sounded just a little more plausible. But they were small matters and they might have been due to genuine recollection. The basic story — and its basic ambiguities — remained.

The jury, hearing it for the first time, must have been fascinated and astounded by this account of a young man quietly listening to the ruminations of his good friend about murder plots over a period of five years. How, in the beginning, while they were still in Austria, it began dawning on Csaba that Peter's intended victim must be his beautiful young bride. How Peter would say this was ridiculous, then would blithely continue talking about it. How Csaba understood he would be the person to do it for Peter, and how Peter implied he might be paid $10,000 for the job. How, knowing all this, Csaba accepted Peter's invitation and came to Toronto to share a home with scheming husband and victim wife for seventeen months.

Then the unbelievable plots: the fall down the stairs on Burnaby Boulevard and Dawes Road, the electrocution in the swimming pool, the hit-and-run on Dundas highway while chasing the dog, the gasoline fumes exploding in the garage, the fake break-in with the Mexican rifle. (Szilagyi remembered one more plot he didn't mention at the preliminary, which called for him to park some heavy construction equipment next to the roadway in such a manner that Peter could crash the passenger-side of the car into it and decapitate Christine.) It was mind-boggling.

Mind-boggling enough, perhaps, for the jury to reject it, had it come at an earlier point in the trial. There's a healthy defence mechanism in ordinary human minds that, somewhat like a fuse, disconnects certain overloads of experience from the normal circuits of belief. Lawyers are aware of the tendency jurors have to look, whenever possible, for common-sense explanations more in keeping with their own everyday notions of truth. Once in a while counsel will not submit useful evidence out of fear that it might shock the jury into total incredulity. For instance, a malicious ex-friend perjuring himself might be more within the range of the London jury's experience of human behaviour than the steely callousness of two friends coldly discussing the ways and means of killing a beautiful woman who is living with them in the house, making their beds, cooking their meals, and washing their socks. People are prepared to believe the worst about other people only up to a point. It was Greenwood's shrewdness (and good luck) that he could offer Csaba Szilagyi as the last witness to a jury primed by earlier adventures with The Duck, Stark, Foxy Jones, "Tom Smith", and the ghastly Williams. By then the jury might have believed anything.

Then, of course, there were the tapes. On November 19 Csaba's testimony was interrupted while Justice Grant, Eddie Greenspan, and John Greenwood met in the board room of the Holiday Inn to review the many hours of chatter between Csabaschek and Papitschek and excise irrelevant or prejudicial material. Later Justice Grant would remember this occasion as the only one in the long trial that was even vaguely amusing. "The night we went over the tapes with Eddie Greenspan was the best night we had," His Lordship would say. No doubt, in addition to many grave and important ones, the conversations on the tapes contained some very funny sections. At times the humour was quite unintentional. The trial judge kept coming back to an expression Peter used about a man, whom he called a "registered homosexual". The whole bit was irrelevant and everyone agreed to delete it, but Justice Grant was puzzled by what Peter could possibly have meant by this curious expression. (It was, of course, simply an all-too-literal translation of the Hungarian idiom for someone no longer in the closet.) Then there was the bit where Peter explained to Csaba that his lawyer, who at first thought he was an idiot, now had a higher opinion of him. Eddie wanted the remark out and His Lordship agreed: lawyers have a right to remain silent on what they think of their clients. References to "fat old Jew" and "Jewish Forest Hill" and "Jewish lawyer" were deleted. So was one where Peter referred to himself and Csaba as "central European". For some reason Justice Grant thought that this might be prejudicial to him and, after all, the judge must have known the jurors in his own neck of the woods. The recurring references to Cousin Steven by his Hungarian nickname "Pista" had Justice Grant stymied. By that time there were altogether too many strange names cropping up in the case. On the tape Peter was explaining to Csaba that "Pista too would be able to prove that our marriage was better than average."

"What has Pista got to do with marriage?" asked His Lordship.

"He is a social worker, marriage counsellor," said Greenwood.

"I thought," said Justice Grant thoughtfully, "he was a restaurant fellow."

Then there was the bit where Peter referred to Gigi's being lonely and ready for a liaison prior to her meeting Csaba. The trouble was that Peter described Gigi's ripeness for male companionship in purely physical terms. The two lawyers and the trial judge spent some time trying to render Peter's expressive Hungarian into more decorous English before settling on "gaping pussy" as the mildest possible alternative.

Szilagyi resumed the stand the next day. Instead of playing the tapes, which, being in Hungarian, would have been totally meaningless to the jury, Greenwood had Csaba read aloud the entire English translation on the stand. This, clearly, was a practical solution but it immediately gave rise to a problem.

Peter's manner of speaking was convoluted at the best of times. When talking in a short-hand fashion to an old friend, under pressure, his conversation became nearly incoherent. The poor recording quality, passing trucks, and translation into another language added to the difficulty. Csaba, however, obviously had an interpretation of almost every oblique reference, pause, gap, or meaningless jumble of words. Where these occurred, Greenwood called on him to tell the jury what he thought Peter meant.

Very naturally, Pomerant objected. If Csaba were to do the interpretation, whenever Peter said "whatchamacallit" Csaba could interpret it to mean "I killed her." It was a valid point, and Justice Grant accepted it. Even so, Csaba could say what he himself meant, and often Greenwood was able to sneak the odd interpretive remark into his reading of the tapes. A fairer method might have been to have the entire transcript read without interruption by one of the court reporters, letting the jury draw their own conclusions from the words themselves. (Chances are, of course, that halfway through the jury would have been asleep.)

As it was the jury seemed wide awake as Greenwood extracted the incriminating bits from the masses of rambling dialogue. The Crown Attorney took good care that all the juicy bits would sink in as fully as possible. *You are the only one who knows. Csaba, the hell I don't know. If that person doesn't know me and doesn't even speak our language, and there is no, we don't even have contact . . .* And on the telephone: *You remember we had a Mexican topic, just don't say about what.* And many more.

Then it was Pomerant's turn. If The Flower was an example of evidence for which the defence was unprepared, Csaba was clearly the witness for whom they had been ready for over eight months. Not surprisingly, Pomerant's cross-examination showed the difference good preparation makes in meeting damaging testimony. With Csaba on the stand, Joe didn't miss a trick.

Of course when Pomerant first drew up his battle plans, demolishing Csaba was central to the strategy of the defence. Like King Henry's knights at Agincourt, Csaba was the only visible enemy force. When all the English archers — Stark, The Duck, Mr. X — came up from the wings, Joe Pomerant, like the French, could no longer change the direction of his assault. Now his dilemma wasn't whether he could carry the day against Csaba, but whether, if he did, it would make any difference to the outcome of the engagement.

But at this point Joe was committed and must have decided to keep on fighting. Whether or not Csaba was still the all-important key, he was the enemy Pomerant seemed to have been waiting to meet. At his best Joe could be formidable, and Csaba appeared to draw back for an instant on the stand as the defence counsel approached him.

A very cool man of considerable reserve strength, Csaba must have been fairly exhausted at this point. His examination-in-chief had lasted for days. The ordeal that was to come, which he must have expected would be carried out on the most personal level, delving into his every failure and inadequacy, could have filled him with apprehension, perhaps even dread. There can be little question that it filled him with resentment. In his hours to come on the stand Pomerant would be Peter's surrogate, accusing Csaba of every ingratitude, indecency, and betrayal. In this respect it made little difference whether he was maliciously inventing his accusations against his one-time mentor, or merely dishonouring the trust that his lonely, only friend had for some reason chosen to place in him. As a man who seemed to have faith in no one, Peter was likely to have viewed Csaba in a very special light. Csaba did not seem to have had many friends himself. The bond that must have existed between them, even if in perversion or iniquity, could not have been breached without distress.

Of course for Csaba it might have been revenge. This emotion, according to Lord Byron, does have a sweet taste. It might also have been a rather courageous act, the culmination of a task to which his last number of years had been devoted. This, ultimately, was what Csaba suggested in his own testimony.

Obviously Csaba had to come up with some kind of an answer for his own part in his relationship with Peter over the years. After all, by his own admission, he did listen to his plots. He followed him to Canada. He must have behaved in a manner, according to his own evidence, that would indicate to Peter that he was a man with whom such plans could be discussed. You don't chat about murder with just anyone. Csaba must have invited his trust in some way. Why?

Because, said Csaba, he wanted to save the life of Christine. When he had realized what Peter was bent on doing, he had decided to offer himself to Peter as his sounding board, his foil. As long as Peter was plotting with *him*, he wouldn't plot with anyone else, and Christine would be safe. A mission? Yes, a mission. It wasn't his word but if Pomerant wanted to use it, Csaba would agree.

Oh really? Why wouldn't he go to the police? Because the police wouldn't believe him, and it would be just his word against Peter's, anyway. (True, but while no action could be taken against Peter, being reported might dissuade him from murder in a hurry.) Why didn't Csaba simply go away, have nothing to do with Peter any further? Because if he didn't seem to co-operate, once Peter had told him about his intentions, Csaba's own life would be in danger. It was safer for him to stick close to his friend, listen to him, object to each new plot on purely technical grounds, and hope that in time Peter would just forget about the whole thing. Didn't sticking close to Peter have other advantages, such as room, board, laundry, a chance to come to Canada, the hope of future favours? These were, Csaba said, fringe benefits, yes.

But if it was a matter of sticking close to Peter, Pomerant asked, why did Csaba, in fact, move out of his house after seventeen months, disrupt the relationship for a long time, except for one Christmas phone call? That call at Christmas was enough, Csaba replied. Peter would know he was still around. And what about the last time, the last plot, when Peter demanded an answer, and Csaba (according to his evidence) went down to the Lakeshore to think about it all and then didn't call his friend back? Wasn't that an implied "no", a final indication that he would not murder for him? Wouldn't that have freed Peter to go to someone else? Wouldn't that have been a refusal endangering Csaba's own life?

Not really. Things didn't work in such a straight yes-or-no fashion between Csaba and Peter.

All right, then what *did* he do to ensure the success of his "mission"? What did he do after Peter's alleged call on July 16 when Peter asked him to keep Gigi away from Christine for the afternoon? After he phoned and told Csaba his non-cooperation had just cost him $10,000 because the guy said the deal was for one girl, not two? By that time, if Csaba's story was true, it must have been sickeningly clear to him that "sticking close" to Peter and objecting to his plots wasn't enough any more. His friend was obviously going through with his plans through others. What did Csaba do? Nothing?

Well, not exactly nothing. He was just in the process, Csaba said, of working out a scheme whereby he would deposit his story in two parts, with two different lawyers, and instructions to forward them to the police if anything happened to him or Christine. Having done this he would have told Peter about it and this would have been enough.

How old was Csaba at this time, in his teens, twenties? Oh, in his early thirties. Yes.

Did he ever think of telling Christine? While he lived in the same house with her? While they were going shopping, or for ice cream, or the movies? While she was serving him lunch, breakfast, dinner? Or much later, the time Peter was having his fling with Marina in Montreal, and Csaba was spending the odd night with Gigi and the desolate Christine in the house on Dundas Crescent? No? What about Tuesday, July 17, the day before Christine's death, when she dropped by their place to talk with Gigi?

No.

Did he like Christine? He didn't dislike her, Csaba said. When he was at the funeral home with the hidden microphone taped to his chest, did he stop for a moment of mourning in front of her casket? He did not.

Pomerant changed the subject. Csaba had testified to nearly a dozen different murder plots. There were schemes with electrocution, gasoline, Mexican rifles. There was talk about carbon monoxide from car exhausts and about shoving Christine down a flight of stairs. Then, after

Christine's death, Csaba taped four lengthy conversations with Peter. Where, in all the hours and hours of tape, was there any confirmation of any of the specific things they were supposed to have been plotting about? The fire, the rifle, the car crash, the decapitation? Could Csaba point out an exchange in the tapes, any of them, that would refer to any of these topics? Something, that is, that did not depend on *his* interpretation that "Mexican theme" really meant fake break-in and murder. Something that an uninitiated person reading Peter's actual words might regard as corroboration.

Csaba tried. Pomerant suggested that he take the transcripts with him overnight, study them carefully, and try again the next day. The next day Csaba tried again. There was still nothing. Every incriminating remark depended on Csaba's explanation for its supposed meaning.

It was at this point, with Csaba faltering on the stand, that Greenwood made the error that (in his own opinion) could have cost him the whole trial. All along the cautious Crown Attorney had been meticulous — perhaps mindful of Justice Grant's view that "the prosecution owes a greater duty to be fair" — not to be carried away and not to lose his temper in the heat of battle. This once, however, he did. It happened when he anxiously suggested that Csaba should, perhaps, have the transcript in his hand while being questioned, and Pomerant replied that it would be of some help to the defence if he could conduct the examination in his own way.

"I am," replied Greenwood, "*not interested in the defence; I am interested in the truth.*"

He could have bitten his tongue off the minute he said it.

"I have something to say in the absence of the jury," said Pomerant.

"No. Keep on cross-examining, please," said His Lordship.

Pomerant did, but at the end of the day he moved for a mistrial. He considered the Crown Attorney's words unfair and gravely prejudicial to the defence. For some reason Greenwood was convinced that this time the judge would rule in the defence's favour. There he was, with victory in his grasp, and he blew it by one careless, dumb remark in the ninth week of the trial. Actually, it was an interesting indication of how John Greenwood could be mortified by what he regarded as his own gaucherie. At times the senior Crown could still not help seeing himself in the awkward image of his youth when he thought he was all knuckles and fumbles. The fact that nobody else saw him that way — and if they had it would have made no difference — didn't help.

Needless to say, Justice Grant hadn't the slightest intention of declaring a mistrial because of Greenwood's gaffe. As far as the judge was concerned, the remark was quite trivial. Later Eddie Greenspan would argue the motion, very dutifully, but without much conviction. Worse things have been said by counsel in many a courtroom.

When Joe Pomerant let go of Csaba at the end of the next day he must have felt a sense of real accomplishment. The strange, reserved, highly-bred Hungarian was not an easy opponent. He had a way with words even in a language still somewhat foreign to him. He could jab quickly, then tuck his nose between his feet like an armadillo. But Pomerant had handled him, reduced him, put him in his place. Short of making Csaba confess, there was not much more he could have done with him. It was Joe's finest hour. His cross-examination of the Crown's star witness showed why he was regarded by many of his peers as a fine, major-league lawyer. If Csaba Szilagyi had been charged with anything, Joe would probably have convicted him.

But Csaba Szilagyi wasn't charged. Peter Demeter was. With murder.

Worried as Greenwood must have been, his instinct suggested he should not try to rehabilitate Csaba in his re-examination. By now he had been on the stand for days and, no matter how he may have hardened himself for his ordeal, the cracks were beginning to show in his armour. In trying to patch them up, Greenwood might inadvertently widen them even more. However badly Pomerant might have hurt him, Szilagyi wasn't on trial. There had to be a way of putting the Crown's case back into focus for the jury.

Greenwood wasn't quite sure what the best way would be, even as he rose. He started saying something to Csaba and Pomerant immediately objected. The prosecutor was making a remark, Joe said, instead of asking a question. It was true, but Greenwood hardly listened as Joe argued the point with the judge. An idea was crossing his mind. Like most good ideas, it was simple.

Justice Grant was speaking to him. "Well, leave out the remark," the trial judge yielded to the defence. "Let's hear your question."

"Only one question, my Lord," said Greenwood. "Is Christine Demeter dead?"

"Yes," replied Csaba.

It was all over.

23. Meanwhile, Maloney

Chris O'Toole was an honest cop.

Being a good, straightforward, conscientious man, not content to let sleeping dogs lie, he came close to losing the Crown's case against Peter Demeter. Simply by doing his duty, he helped the defence stage a comeback from which the prosecution might not have recovered. It was in no way Chris O'Toole's fault. He just did what detectives are paid to do: investigate. He couldn't let things well enough alone.

Thinking about matters, O'Toole noted that, in spite of all the evidence against Demeter, the police still did not have the actual killer or killers of Christine. O'Toole did not for one moment doubt the validity of the evidence. After all, he was the man who had gathered much of it. He did not doubt that Christine had been killed at the instruction and instigation of her husband. He merely wished to know who did it. Finding the men who, for a few bucks, would go into a garage and beat the brains out of a young woman seemed a matter of some importance to Detective-Sergeant O'Toole.

Incidentally, finding the killer would also clinch matters against Demeter. Once found, the man would talk and implicate him as such men almost invariably do. This would change the Crown's case from circumstantial to direct evidence. O'Toole, who had no more questions about Peter's guilt than the rest of the police, thought it might be nice to prove it not just beyond a reasonable doubt, but beyond any doubt at all.

His mind kept going back to one Gabor Magosztovics, a.k.a. Joe Dinardo. The hapless firebug of Burlington. The sometime boxer. The Hungarian lad who would break arms and legs for a little bit of money. The closest friend of the late Laszlo Eper.

Of course the police had questioned Dinardo about Eper after they had found the piece of paper with the words *The President, Peter Demeter* on one side, and *Superintendent William Teggart* on the other, in the slain man's room. But Dinardo, recovering from his burns in hospital, had said he knew nothing about his departed pal's activities. He had no idea what his old friend might have been up to. While the "Tractor" did not share Eper's murderous hatred for cops — as far as Dinardo was concerned they were just doing their thing, as he was doing his — he would certainly not cross the street to help them out. What did Eper have to do with Peter Demeter? He didn't know. He knew nothing.

But then Dinardo's name came up again on the night of October 31, when O'Toole was taking down Stark's statement. After driving The Duck to look over the house on Dawes Road, Stark said, "We talked about a Hungarian fighter Joe Dinardo and then I drove Kacsa to Lonsdale Club and he said George Chuvalo would be there. When we got there Kacsa talked to Joe who was in the ring."

Interesting. Of course The Duck, though he'd get into fights, wasn't really known as an enforcer. Dinardo was. Were they perhaps trying to sub-contract Dinardo to do the job? He was not known to have ever been a hit-man, but the gap between breaking arms and legs and breaking heads could perhaps be bridged for the right amount. Stark seemed very careful in saying that *he* didn't talk to Dinardo; Kacsa did. He, Stark, just stood around watching George Chuvalo do three practice rounds in the ring. Was there perhaps a reason for Stark to emphasize this? Of course nothing happened on Dawes Road, so Dinardo probably wasn't involved (unlike Kacsa, the honest Tractor was no con-man: if he undertook a job, he'd probably finish it), but maybe they just chatted about it. O'Toole couldn't get rid of the feeling that Dinardo must know *something*.

Now Dinardo didn't have much going for him. He didn't have a high reputation for matters of the mind even in boxing circles. Apparently he couldn't torch a garage without blowing himself up. His financial assets seemed limited. Huge and powerful as he was, people in the know would later chuckle at his claim that he'd get $1000 sometimes to throw a fight. "Pay *Joe* to throw a fight?" asked one old-timer around the Lansdowne Gym. "Maybe you'd pay the other fellow." Success in the ring is not just a matter of native muscle, and training had always seemed too much like work to Joe Dinardo. Nor was he exactly Mr. Big in crime. But people in the Toronto-Hamilton axis of the Organization seemed to kind of like having him around. He was not unpopular with girls who didn't care if a fellow was a champion, as long as he looked like one. And there was one other thing. Dinardo had exquisite taste in lawyers.

Arthur Maloney was not just another one of Her Majesty's Counsel in the Judicial District of York in the City of Toronto. Before he became the first ombudsman for Ontario, Arthur Maloney had been, along with such legendary figures as J. J. Robinette and G. A. Martin, *the* top criminal lawyer in the province. It wasn't just a matter of skill, learning or public-spiritedness; if the word "unimpeachable" could without exaggeration be connected with anyone's reputation, it would be with Arthur Maloney's. His appointment as ombudsman was looked at as a self-evident choice when the Conservative government first established this office in Ontario. All this was no reason, of course, why he should not have been The Tractor's lawyer, and so he was.

Around the first week of November Detective-Sergeant O'Toole decided to pick up the telephone and ask for an appointment with Mr. Maloney. He figured that if Dinardo knew something — about Eper, Stark, The Duck, anybody — perhaps he could be persuaded to tell the authorities if he were approached through his lawyer. Somewhat reluctantly, Maloney agreed. Naturally he made it a condition that he'd tell his client he was conveying this request for information on behalf of the police.

Dinardo was held in the Guelph Jail at the time, awaiting trial on assorted charges ranging from theft to possession of counterfeit money, in addition to awaiting sentence on a conviction of arson, and it was there that his lawyer visited him on Sunday, November 19. (By that time Peter had already been languishing in his London Jail cell for about a week.) Dinardo seemed at first "extremely hostile to the suggestion that he become involved", Arthur Maloney was to state later. "He indicated that he had information relating to the case which he would have divulged to me long before had I been the defence counsel for Mr. Demeter but since I was not, he kept it to himself. . . . I made no serious effort to dissuade him."

But hardly had Mr. Maloney arrived back home ("home" in this case being a farm not far from Guelph) than his telephone rang. It was a jail official conveying a message from Dinardo. Apparently The Tractor wanted his lawyer to return and discuss the matter with him a little further. Maloney agreed to go back the next day. Later when Chris O'Toole phoned him at the farm the lawyer told the anxious policeman about his " . . . abortive visit to Dinardo and the subsequent telephone call . . . and undertook to report to him after my second meeting with Dinardo." There might have been some rejoicing back in London's Holiday Inn. Apparently Dinardo was going to talk.

Dinardo did, the next day, when his lawyer returned to the Guelph Jail. The information he gave to Arthur Maloney amounted to this: The Tractor knew who killed Christine Demeter. He also knew that the man who did it *had nothing to do with Peter Demeter at all.*

Leo McGuigan learned about the news on Saturday, November 16. Csaba Szilagyi had already begun his testimony on the stand. Arthur Maloney told the gist of Dinardo's story to the Assistant Crown at his farm, to which Leo had driven out with Chris O'Toole. There is no record of what "Tiger" McGuigan said to the unhappy Detective-Sergeant during their drive back to London.

24. The Whole Truth and Nothing But

Having a client like Dinardo did nothing to diminish Arthur Maloney's credibility. If one is a criminal lawyer, some of one's clients may be criminals. There is nothing unusual about it.

Having a lawyer like Maloney, on the other hand, did quite a bit to enhance Dinardo's credibility. Had some local enforcer picked up the phone to tell a story to O'Toole or McGuigan, it would have meant little. But Dinardo did nothing of the sort: he confessed to his lawyer. Under pressure. In confidence. Not just any lawyer, either, but Arthur Maloney. And it was this eminent lawyer who, apparently, encouraged him that he should do the right thing for once in his life, come forward, assist the cause of justice, tell his story to the authorities. Then, only then, did Dinardo very reluctantly agree. A whole different situation from that of some petty crook telling tall tales.

Not only that, but how did Dinardo's distinguished lawyer get to him in the first place? At the request of the police, that's how. They asked him to see if he could persuade his client to tell the truth. He did, and now the prosecution didn't like it. Well, wasn't that just too bad.

John Greenwood could already hear Joe Pomerant's closing argument for the defence.

If Dinardo testified and the jury believed him Demeter would be acquitted. It was as simple as that. He could be acquitted if the jury *half*-believed Dinardo. The doctrine of reasonable doubt, by law, operated in the accused's favour. There were no ifs and buts about it.

Stunning.

And this, dammit, had happened just at a time when Greenwood had not only established a solid case for the Crown from some initial pieces of gossip and gossamer, but had pretty much dotted the i's and crossed the t's on Peter's guilt. Bill Teggart's team had been flying all this time, flinging tentacles all over the place. Now they had come up with the Fancsiks and the Links.

Magda and Laszlo Link were friends of Mr. and Mrs. Duck. So were Helen and George Fancsik. They had all known The Duck for many years. They had known him by all his names. (In fact, Mrs. Link added *Andy* Orr to the roster, which apparently had also been employed at times by Kacsa-Cutlip-Duck-Imre Olejnyik-Jimmy Orr.) It was Laszlo Link who drove The Duck to the airport in April 1973, when he was trying to leave in a hurry, with his bulging wallet.

Having a social relationship with The Duck, of course, did entail certain risks. George Fancsik found this out to his peril when, some time earlier, he had been charged with assault after The Duck got involved in an altercation with a man named Turan in the parking lot of the St. Elisabeth Church on Spadina. It was a Girl Guides meeting and they were picking up their wives, but Kacsa managed to get into a fight and Fancsik got charged in his place.

The point of the Links' testimony was this: after The Duck absconded in the spring of 1973 the Links were approached by two different men trying to locate him. One of the men left his card, which read *Stark Construction,* and offered Link "ten per cent" to help him find Kacsa. The next day another man came and said to Link: "I gave Kacsa money and I either want it back or the work done."

Link identified this man in the courtroom as the accused, Peter Demeter.

Mrs. Link identified him.

George and Helen Fancsik said that at Fancsik's trial on the assault charge a man was sitting in the courtroom taking notes. In the recess this man approached them and said: "Why are you hiding Kacsa?"

George and Helen also identified this man as the accused, Peter Demeter.

After this testimony, it clearly wasn't simply Stark's word against Peter's any more. The Dawes Road affair couldn't be a conspiracy between Christine and Stark, as the defence had been suggesting, if Peter was seen all over town clamouring to find The Duck. If the defence's theory was right, Peter shouldn't have even known that The Duck existed. The Links and the Fancsiks seemed to have no reason to lie. It was also unlikely that all four of them would be mistaken.

After their testimony, the best thing that could be said in Peter's favour was that to do what the Links and Fancsiks said he did was so stupid as to be unbelievable. The whole point of hiring middlemen in a murder plot is to keep one's own hands clean. Peter was not retarded. Why keep a Stark and bark himself? Was this not an incredible way for anyone to behave, let alone a man who, according to Stark, was so careful that he didn't even want to know the name of the killer?

On the other hand, why would the four Hungarians say what they did? For money? Who on earth would pay them? They could certainly not hope to get any of Demeter's own $10,000 reward (which was never officially withdrawn), and there was never any suggestion that they were offered or received any of the $3,000 put up by the Mississauga police. (Peter's own theory — or obsession — about who would pay them didn't come to light until later.)

"The jury," John Greenwood remembered, "was extremely impressed by these four, especially Fancsik. They were simple people with no reason to lie. They settled it for the jury." The best Joe Pomerant could do in cross-examination was to get Link to describe his visitor's Mercedes as "white", which the Demeters' car wasn't. It was oyster-grey. (It probably wouldn't have made much difference if Joe had known that "link" was a Budapest slang expression for somebody lying or unreliable and pointed it out to the jury. For those in the courtroom who spoke Hungarian it was kind of ironic, though, as it would be for an English speaker to listen to the evidence of someone named "Mr. Cheat".)

In any event, this was it. In essence this completed the case for the Crown. There were some minor loose ends to be tied up, the only one of even passing interest being Stark's girlfriend's evidence that although she had lived in the same apartment building as Csaba Szilagyi, the two of them were not acquainted. After this, under normal circumstances, the prosecution could rest.

But circumstances were not normal. There was Dinardo.

The Crown had to do some very hard and fast thinking when they learned the gist of Dinardo's evidence on November 16 from Arthur Maloney. Even though the defence lawyer had gone to Dinardo at the request of the police, the solicitor-client privilege attached to their meeting required him to observe certain legal niceties when imparting its essence to McGuigan and O'Toole. "I made it clear to them," Maloney would state later, "that Dinardo had evidence of the utmost importance to give that would have the effect of exonerating Mr. Demeter. I prefaced my remarks to Messrs. McGuigan and O'Toole with such a statement as: 'What if there were a witness whose evidence would be to the following effect?' "

The Crown listened. They couldn't help agreeing with Maloney that the evidence would have the effect of exonerating Peter. They had equally little doubt that it was a perfect lie. (Not, of course, on Maloney's part, but on Dinardo's.) The question was what to do about it. Quite naturally, as The Tractor's lawyer, Arthur Maloney would not permit them to interrogate Dinardo on his story. The only thing that he would allow was for Dinardo to go on the witness stand and tell his version of the truth to the court, under the protection of the Canada Evidence Act. Some of it, Greenwood thought, would probably not be admissible anyway, thank God, but the rest might be enough to demolish his case against Demeter if the jury believed it.

The weekend must have been a mad scramble for the Crown. Their possibilities ranged from the totally improper to the extremely gentlemanly. Totally improper would have been to simply shrug and forget about the whole thing, saying that the defence didn't know of Dinardo and he was lying anyway. Had Dinardo's story come to light in the privacy of some interrogation room in a police station that possibility would have actually been open to the prosecution, though there's no reason to suppose that Greenwood would ever have contemplated it. As it was, of course, he could not even be tempted by it. Ombudsman-to-be Arthur Maloney knew about Dinardo, and the Crown could never get away with simply writing off The Tractor's story as so unworthy of belief as to be kept hidden in the Guelph Jail.

At the other end of the scale, Greenwood could have been the perfect gentleman and undertaken to call Dinardo as a witness for the Crown. There's a view that the authorities investigate — as O'Toole in fact did — then live with whatever evidence they discover. Whether it goes against the thrust of their case or not shouldn't matter. In fact, they should bend over backward to be impartial. "The Crown never loses as long as justice triumphs," held Leo McGuigan, speaking in the abstract, of course. "The prosecution has a greater duty to be absolutely fair," said Justice Campbell Grant. Or Lord Chief Justice Parker in his well-known dictum: "The prosecution do not, of course, put forward every witness as a witness of truth, but where the witness' evidence is capable of belief, then it is their duty, well recognized, that he should be called, even though the evidence that he is going to give is inconsistent with the case sought to be proved."

Arthur Maloney was also inclined toward this opinion under the circumstances. "I was of the view that the prosecution should call Dinardo as a witness," he stated, "and suggested this course to Mr. McGuigan, reminding him that he would not be obliged to vouch for the credibility of what such witness was saying."

Between the improper and the ultra-fair lay a third course. The defence could be informed of Dinardo's story. Then, if they wished, they could call him as a defence witness after the close of the prosecution's case. Greenwood was not a vindictive prosecutor and would not do anything improper, but he was not bucking for sainthood, either. He clearly had no discretion to simply bury the enforcer's story, but he had, he felt, a discretion whether or not to call him for the Crown. Would calling him be more *just*, seeing that it was in fact the prosecution that uncovered his evidence? That depended on one's philosophy. "I have no concept of justice in the abstract sense," Greenwood had said. "I think the crown attorney is there to get the evidence, evaluate it, and get a conviction."

But perhaps Dinardo could be discredited even before the prosecution would have to decide what to do with him. After listening to Maloney, McGuigan had asked him to give the Crown a little breathing space to consider the new development. They would have to inform Joe Pomerant in a day or two, of course, but maybe in the meantime . . .

Tuesdays weren't visiting days but Joe Dinardo acquired a surprise visitor in the Guelph Jail. (Nobody knew just how this was arranged, but there were rumours of some really good contacts that gold-slippered Bill Teggart had in the Correctional Services.) Dinardo's unexpected friend had more wires and batteries than the Six-Million-Dollar Man. But, unlike The Duck, Dinardo could recognize a snitch when he saw one. The luckless Flower (who else?) brought back nothing from his suicide mission but a string of choice invective in two languages. Mr. X must have had the instincts of a kamikaze to undertake the assignment in the first place. Alternatively, he must have been broker than hell. (Later the police came to believe that Virag played it safe in the Guelph Jail: he pointed to his chest where the microphone was hidden when he saw Dinardo.)

The Crown had far more luck with another person in the Guelph Jail. That, however, would not come to light for a little while yet.

Greenwood broke the story to the defence on that Tuesday, November 19. As it happened, it was while they were reviewing the tapes with

Justice Grant in the boardroom at the Holiday Inn. This was one of the few occasions when Peter Demeter himself wasn't around, and perhaps Greenwood timed his information precisely for this reason. (Normally Peter was present even in the judge's chambers because Justice Grant made a point of never discussing any aspect of the case outside of the accused's presence, not even purely legal arguments.) The Crown Attorney revealed the gist of what The Firebug was expected to say on the stand, should anybody ask him to appear. The prosecution, said Greenwood, wasn't going to. They regarded Dinardo's story as a lie.

What's more, warned the senior Crown, they could prove it. If the defence still wanted to call Dinardo, it was their look-out.

The game was clearly getting rough, and all pretence of clubman-like behaviour was going out the window. This was no longer cricket, but a battle between openly antagonistic forces with big rewards and big ambitions at stake. On Peter's part, of course, it was virtually life and death: Joe Terdik remembered that as soon as the really damaging evidence against him came to light, Peter stopped all his smiling and light-hearted banter with the police officers. Instead, he would thrust his face into Terdik's during recess in the corridor and look into his eyes wordlessly for ten or twenty seconds at a time. (A great many of Peter's social friends were still Hungarians even after twenty years in Canada. He must have especially disliked the Hungarian police officer, whose actions he might have viewed in a special light of betrayal. For his part, Terdik reciprocated the feeling. After all, he had been the one who had listened for months to Peter's telephone chats full of subtle and no-so-subtle indications of class superiority over people like Terdik's own parents.) But Peter's or Terdik's feelings didn't matter much at this stage. The lawyers' did.

Greenwood believed that Dinardo's story was a lie. He also suspected that Demeter's attorneys knew it.

When he first mentioned Dinardo's name, Greenwood would say later, the two lawyers for the defence exchanged glances and smiled. Why would they do that if the name meant nothing to them?

Simple, Eddie Greenspan would say after the trial. They had *another* client named Dinardo. He and Joe had merely raised eyebrows at the amusing coincidence. Joe Pomerant would later also confirm this.

But the mood between the opponents, at this stage, wasn't conducive to such misunderstandings being cleared up over a cup of coffee. While the pugnacious Crown Attorneys might not have gone as far in their suspicions as to assume that their legal friends were conniving in actually manufacturing evidence to get their client off, they did think the defence lawyers were at least *aware* of such an attempt. If so, behaving like King Arthur's knights would make the prosecutors plain fools. They, too, could play it close to the edge if it came to that. The Crown is under no obligation to reveal the actual evidence it may have in rebuttal. True, it will usually do so, because it is regarded as fair practice. But if the defence is playing it rough, so can they.

Clearly the ball was now in Justice Campbell Grant's court. Having heard of Dinardo's evidence, the defence moved that the Crown not be allowed to close its case before calling the muscle-man to the stand. If the prosecution wouldn't, they were petitioning the judge to use the powers invested in the court and call Dinardo himself. Calling Dinardo as part of the defence's case was not enough, Eddie argued. The duty lay with the prosecution to introduce the evidence it had discovered. It could make a world of difference in the eyes of the jury. This was certainly true and was, in fact, the reason why Greenwood had no desire to do it. Nor would he reveal the evidence he said he had in rebuttal.

Eddie's plea to the judge, never without lucidity and style, now had the fine edge of passion. This was the first real break the defence had had in ten weeks or more. Surely they should be allowed to make the most of it. Since the beginning of the trial two and a half months ago the Crown had been allowed to change or expand its theory, Eddie said, several times. The judge had permitted them to add 43 names to the original indictment, 43 new witnesses who, on the whole, had testimony unfavourable to Demeter. Now that they had stumbled on one witness, one man whose evidence would favour the defence, the Crown was saying that they wouldn't call him because they considered him a liar. This was the decision of the very Crown Attorney who seemed so interested in the truth. The same Crown who thought nothing of blurting out his passion for verity in front of the jury.

Not only that, Eddie continued, but Greenwood was even threatening the defence that if it called Dinardo as part of *its* case, the Crown had evidence to discredit him. But the prosecutor wouldn't reveal what that evidence was. How, then, could the defence make a decision? How could they make up their minds whether or not to call this witness?

"Let the defence, " said Greenspan, "ten weeks into the trial, let them call a witness so they [the Crown] can lay a trap, that is a wrong and improper abuse of the prosecutorial process."

"Neither must the Crown be led into a trap," remarked Justice Grant, "and I take it that is what they are guarding against."

The implication was clear enough. If Greenwood revealed his hand to Pomerant and Greenspan, his Lordship seemed to say, it might *change* Dinardo's evidence. There was no suggestion, of course, that the lawyers would tamper with the witness themselves, but . . . Said Eddie: "With respect, if it is told to Mr. Pomerant and myself, then it is told as it must be told to our client. Only one of the three of us are in a position to use that information. Mr. Demeter is in custody."

"That doesn't keep Mr. Demeter from talking to people because he is in custody," said Justice Grant mildly, "does it?"

The day was spent in argument, then the judge ruled. He ruled that the Crown did not have to call Dinardo. He ruled that they did not have to disclose the nature of their rebuttal evidence.

The judge also rejected the motion that the Crown be compelled to call The Duck as a witness for the prosecution. He dismissed the plea that Greenwood should send a commission to take evidence from Kacsa in Hungary before continuing the trial. The charge against Peter was murder by a person or persons unknown. Olejnyik's presence and evidence were not essential to the case as it stood, and Justice Grant saw no reason for further delays.

There seemed to be no question that the judge's rulings were meticulously in line with the requirements of the law. Whether they were in line with his own view that " . . . the crown owes a greater duty to be absolutely fair" was a different matter. The highest-flown and most deeply felt sentiments have a way, in all human beings, of adjusting themselves to the discernible merits of a given situation. *Inter arma silent Musae.* There have been few people in recorded history who could choose their abstract principles over their considered judgments. Some who have, have been canonized. Some, like Pontius Pilate, ended up releasing Barabbas and crucifying Jesus; for choosing principles over judgments is not always the better part of wisdom, either.

On a much more mundane level, Justice Grant might simply have remembered the rumour he had heard in the lobby of the Holiday Inn about Stark and Foxy being arrested coming out of Joe Pomerant's office. And he knew that Peter chatted with reporters and Crown witnesses in court because he had seen it with his own eyes, and had warned Joe and Eddie about it several times. It was, once again, a question of trust. Under the circumstances, the flamboyant Demeter defence could only expect the benefits to which they were entitled by law. The benefits of discretion would be more likely to go to a Crown that, generally, managed to look as if butter wouldn't melt in its mouth.

The defence began putting on its case in the morning of Tuesday, November 26.

Pomerant did, of course, have the choice of putting on no defence at all. He could have said to the jury, *it's for the prosecution to prove their case beyond a reasonable doubt and, in our view, they have not done so.* This choice would have given the defence the advantage of being last to address the jury. Such a choice is not infrequently exercised in purely circumstantial cases, which the Crown's case against Peter Demeter still was. If Greenwood had not been able to offer anything more than what he thought he had at the start of the trial — that is, Szilagyi's story and maybe the tapes — Pomerant might well have elected to proceed on this basis. As it was, he could and did not.

The first witnesses were very brief. A lady court reporter testified that she never saw Peter Demeter at George Fancsik's trial. John Turan, the complainant in the same case, never saw Demeter either. Jimmy Wingate of the Mississauga police was called to identify a receipt showing that Peter had checked into a Montreal motel with Christine on the night before the Fancsik trial in Toronto. This would have barely given him time to appear at the trial and ask Fancsik and his wife why they were hiding Kacsa. Though not conclusive, these were good and valid points.

Then Pomerant tried, for some reason, calling a lady to testify that on the night of Christine's murder she received a call at her home, in the vicinity of 1437 Dundas Crescent, on the other side of the ravine. The caller requested her to stand at the window dressed only in her négligé. Justice Grant ruled her evidence irrelevant and inadmissible, which it certainly seemed to be. It only served to put the trial judge in a somewhat testy mood and give further proof of his doubts about the approach of the defence. At the same time Joe chose not to call Peter's architect, Leslie Wagner, who (allegedly) could have confirmed that Peter *was* in Montreal on the day of George Fancsik's trial. He did call Nicholas Van Berkel, who told about having spent a few nights with Christine in 1971. It seemed a small affair.

The next witness was a Toronto police officer relating how the piece of paper with Peter Demeter's name had been discovered in the slain Eper's room on Shaw Street. Though the jury had heard that before from Bill Teggart, Pomerant wisely wanted to emphasize its importance to the defence. He'd need it for what was to follow.

Joe Dinardo.

The appearance of the sometime boxer was preceded by a little conference in the judge's chambers. Apparently one of the police officers had sent a note to Justice Grant suggesting that the enforcer should be handcuffed on the witness stand. The trial judge had an intense dislike of dramatics and no desire to prejudice the defence's case by having their key witness appear in chains before the jury. At the same time he did not wish to have torn and bleeding lawyers scattered all over his courtroom. Joe Pomerant was experiencing a conflict himself: he seemed to feel a little more comfortable with the idea of a handcuffed Dinardo but didn't like the effect this might have on his client's case.

The judge tried to encourage the courtroom officers. "The two of you can handle him," he said. The officers seemed more dubious.

"Hopefully," said one. "He's very big. Six six."

"A professional," added the other.

Though Dinardo was only six feet four inches, at 230 pounds and with the effects of his adventure in the exploding garage still visible on his scarred face, he seemed a formidable figure when he finally made his appearance in the courtroom. (The handcuffs were scrapped in favour of a third officer standing directly behind him.) But the precautions were unnecessary. Dinardo was, in fact, far more chilling for being perfectly polite and well-behaved.

Equally chilling was his story, which he first told to the court in the absence of the jury.

Dinardo said that he had known Laszlo Eper ever since he and Laszlo were in their teens. They had "scored" together, been in jail together. They were friends. One day in June 1973, Eper telephoned him at the Lansdowne Athletic Club. By then they hadn't seen each other for nearly three years.

They met at a restaurant where Eper told his old friend that he had a big score set up. Dinardo learned some of the details at a later meeting when he drove down to the shore of Lake Ontario at Sunnyside to meet Eper, who was sitting in a car with a strange man. Dinardo never liked discussing scores in front of third parties, so he and Eper left the man in Eper's car. The description Dinardo gave of the man fitted Csaba Szilagyi. For good measure, Dinardo also identified Csaba from his newspaper photo.

Then, said Dinardo, he and Eper drove to the Sherway Shopping Plaza. They parked the car, and Eper went inside. In a little while he returned with a good-looking woman of around thirty. She wore a kerchief over her hair, which Dinardo described as blonde, and had dark glasses on. Later Dinardo would identify her as Christine Demeter.

Christine got into the car next to Dinardo; Eper sat in the back seat. She said, related Dinardo, right off the bat: "You look every bit like your friend described you to me."

"Never mind the preliminaries," Dinardo said he replied, gallantly. "Let's get down to the money."

"Would you like to make $10,000?" the lady asked.

Dinardo said he agreed, hopefully, that yes, he'd like to make ten thousand. What's the deal?

The lady said the deal was to kill her husband.

"I say," continued Dinardo on the *voir dire*, " 'No, I don't go that far. I put men in the hospital; I'll break his hands or legs, but I'll not go far to beat him to death. I will beat him and rob him, but not to death.' So I turned around to my friend Eper and said to him in Hungarian, I said, 'This girl is not only crazy, she is dangerous and I don't like her act.' He said to me, he says to shut my mouth."

At this point Dinardo said he got out of the car and walked into the plaza. On returning maybe twenty minutes later the woman was just waving good-bye to Eper, her parting words being, "Call me, dear," to which Eper replied, "I will, baby." Then Eper and himself, Dinardo said, got into a bit of an argument over the fact that Dinardo had been unpleasant to Christine. The deal, Eper told him, was very sensible. The girl would put some sleeping pills or knock-out drops in her husband's drink, have a friend witness the fact that he was asleep, then go and have dinner with this friend. Eper would arrive, shoot the sleeping husband, rob the house of jewellery, and that would be it. Christine's friend, who would provide her with her alibi, Eper said, would be " . . . him; the idiot in the car." Meaning, of course, Csaba Szilagyi.

Dinardo's advice to Eper, he said, was to forget about it. Csaba and Christine were not their own kind, and they would only double-cross them. So Eper gave him five $20 bills (though he seemed to have only five bucks before meeting Christine) and then they parted. Dinardo didn't hear from Eper for about two weeks.

One evening, in the middle of July, Dinardo was at home in his eleventh-floor apartment on Lawrence Avenue. It was a little after ten P.M.

when his intercom rang. It was Eper. When Dinardo let him in he saw that his friend's shoes and trousers were covered with blood, right up to his crotch. Eper was hysterical, Dinardo said, " . . . screaming, hollering, calling her 'Pig, pig, pig.' I didn't say nothing to him until he finished changing clothes. I said, 'What happened?' He said to shut the pig up. [sic] He went to see her for money. He says he called her, went to see her for money. He said an argument started. She made a threatening remark to him. I said, 'What did you do? Did you blow her away?' I asked him that, and when I see the gun in his side he say, no, he bar her."

To "bar" someone, Dinardo explained, was jail slang for hitting someone over the head with some weapon.

Eper finished changing his clothes. Before leaving he told Dinardo he did not think anyone had seen him; he did not rob Christine because a car was just coming to a stop in the driveway and he barely had time to escape through the back door. The only thing that worried him was that he might have left his print on the door knob. (The back door of the garage, according to earlier police evidence, had not been checked for fingerprints.) This, Dinardo told the court, was all he said. Then Eper left and " . . . I never seen the man no more."

This was Dinardo's story. It was perfect. It fitted the defence's theory immaculately and it exonerated Peter completely. It engendered only one suspicion.

John Greenwood had expressed this suspicion to Leo McGuigan long before he had ever heard of Dinardo. He said so right after he had learned of the defence's subpoena in Ferenc Stark's pocket. "The next defence witness for Peter Demeter," said Greenwood, "will be the killer."

25. The Curious Jailguard

Whether he was or not, six-foot-four Dinardo, who casually admitted to breaking arms and legs for a few hundred dollars, certainly fitted many people's idea of what Christine's killer would look like. Given the Crown's assumption that he was lying, there seemed to be only two logical reasons for him to do so. One, he was paid by Demeter. Two, Demeter had something on him, such as the knowledge that he, in fact, was the killer. A combination of both reasons could not be ruled out either.

There were only two problems with the Crown's assumption. First, Dinardo did not exactly come forward on his own as a paid perjurer might be expected to do. He was dragged into the case, practically kicking and screaming, at the request of the police. "So far as I am aware," Arthur Maloney would state later, "Dinardo gave evidence at the Demeter trial only because of what arose out of his discussions with me — discussions that were initiated solely by me at the request of Detective-Sergeant O'Toole. It was apparent to me that Dinardo was reluctant to become involved."

Second, Dinardo (a person of less than nimble mind) told a complex, elaborate story that fitted the theory of the defence like a glove. If it wasn't the truth, somebody must have coached him in it. Who would have done so, and when?

Dinardo had been in one jail; Peter in another. True, prisoners in Canada are not galley slaves, and Canadian penal institutions are hardly the Gulag Archipelago. People in custody receive visitors and so forth. There's jailhouse scuttlebutt. But, if it was a lie, Dinardo's story had to be constructed to mesh in many fine details with known facts — right down to Szilagyi's habit of seeking solitude at the Lakeshore — and coaching Dinardo must have taken some doing. Who? When? The police couldn't, then or later, bring forward any person with known contacts to both Peter and Dinardo, and it couldn't have been for want of trying. Discrediting Dinardo was obviously the key to the Crown's case. Bill Teggart's men must have researched all traffic between the jails of London and Guelph in minute particulars. Had they found anything — *anything* — they would have said so. Loud and clear.

The way the Crown eventually went about suggesting to the jury that The Tractor had, in fact, been coached became one of the touchiest (though least known) controversies in the trial.

Before this would come up, however, the jury still had to hear Dinardo's testimony, or as much of it as Justice Grant would rule admissible. Initially the Unfriendly Giant had only told his story on the *voir dire.* The next question was, how much could he tell to the jury according to the rules of evidence? It was a vital issue.

Clearly Dinardo's alleged conversations with Eper, Christine, or Szilagyi were hearsay. Hearsay (with some exceptions) is not admissible in court. Some lawyers are fond of putting the rule the other way around and say that hearsay is admissible in court — with some exceptions. In any case, everyone agrees that not *all* hearsay is admissible.

Justice Grant was inclined, without much argument, to let in all conversations Dinardo said he had with Christine, or in Christine's presence. The judge felt that proving Christine's state of mind was an integral part of the defence's case, and there was clearly no other way of doing it — Christine being dead — than by letting others repeat what they had heard her say. That was why he had permitted Viveca Esso to repeat the "it would be nice to knock him off and get his money" crack Christine had made just before her death.

Eddie Greenspan could think of two reasons why the trial judge should also admit the conversations Dinardo said he had with Eper. The first was an argument of general principle. Though hearsay, this evidence would have favoured the accused. Eddie quoted authorities to the effect that evidentiary rules should never be interpreted as strictly against the defence as against the prosecution. No technical rule, argued Eddie, should prevent a man charged with a serious offence from letting the jury know things that might exonerate him. Speaking once again with much passion, Greenspan said that standing on the letter of the law in such a grave and notorious case would forever "haunt" the judge and the administration of justice in Canada. If the jury convicted Peter without hearing Eper's confession, it would create an eternal question mark in the annals of judicial history. But just in case the sober Scottish-Canadian judge remained unmoved by this appeal to posterity (as he seemed to) Eddie was ready with his second argument. This one was very ingenious.

Admissions of a deceased person against his own pecuniary interests are an exception to the hearsay rule and can be heard by a jury. The reason for this is said to be that no one would make an admission against the interests of his own pocket-book unless it were true.

Eddie argued that admissions against a person's own *penal* interests should also be admissible. Though this did not seem to be the law at present, it would be open for Justice Grant to set a precedent. Judges in other countries had done so. The principle, after all, was the same: why should a person admit to an offence for which he could be locked up for life unless it were true?

Justice Grant listened carefully. He no doubt thought about it overnight. The next morning he said that though Eddie's argument was interesting, his answer was no. Eddie's argument was very interesting, the judge said and he noted that Eddie had argued the exact opposite, with equal eloquence, when it was a question of letting in the "confession" The Duck had made to Mr. X. That was the same kind of hearsay, and the judge didn't let that one in. Now he wouldn't let in Eper's. Though Justice Grant didn't put it this way, what was sauce for the gander, in his mind, was obviously sauce for the goose.

As a result, all the jury heard Joe Dinardo say on the stand was that he had met his old friend Eper in the company of a man he identified as Csaba Szilagyi; he then described the scene between Eper, Christine, and himself at the Sherway Gardens Shopping Plaza, dialogue and all, and finally he told about the blood-stained Eper's visit to his apartment two weeks later. He was not permitted to quote Eper's confession.

The cross-questioning was done by Leo "Tiger" McGuigan. Greenwood might, once again, have let his co-pilot have the landing to minimize Dinardo's importance to the jury, though he might also have wished to utilize the psychological effect that resulted from the difference between McGuigan's skill and pugnacity as a cross-examiner and his physical stature. Greenwood himself was nearly as big as Dinardo. McGuigan versus Dinardo, on the other hand, was clearly a contest between David and Goliath.

Just as in the biblical story, the little guy won the day. It was actually as easy as shooting fish in a barrel for McGuigan, because no matter how fast Dinardo might have been on his feet in the ring, in a court-room he was hardly a match for any competent lawyer. McGuigan was more than competent, and he fastened on to the many inconsistencies of detail in Dinardo's story. Dinardo seemed to have no idea how to get from the Lakeshore to Sherway Gardens by car; where the gas station he was supposed to have filled his tank was; or that turning left where he said he did would have made him drive into a stone wall. McGuigan also made the most of the inherent outlandishness of an Eper, dripping with blood, arriving at Dinardo's apartment, having taken the elevator to the eleventh floor, and carrying a change of clothes with him on a hanger. In the end McGuigan had reduced Dinardo to sullen stares and shrugs. So there's no gas station on the Queensway, he seemed to say. Who the fuck knows? And who the fuck cares?

Yet — just like Csaba Szilagyi when questioned by Pomerant — Di-nardo did not cave in completely. He insisted to the end that his story was true. He wasn't put up to it by anyone. He had never set eyes on Demeter in his life. Mr. Maloney, his lawyer, told him to do the right thing for once in his life, and that's why he was here. "Then I will ask you one final question, sir," said McGuigan. "How much were you paid to give your testimony in this case?"

"I was not paid anything."

Dinardo left the stand. The defence rested. It was impossible to tell how much or how little the jury might have believed their last witness.

Greenwood was not taking any chances. He called his first witness for his Evidence-in-Reply: William Illerbrun, Custodial Officer at the Guelph Jail.

The jail guard's testimony was very brief, compared with evidence of much less significance; it occupied only five pages out of more than 5000 in the transcripts of the trial. Yet this not quite one-tenth of one per cent of all the material the two sides saw fit to put on the record of the Demeter murder indicated more than anything else how high the stakes were at that point for the Crown. (That they were high for the defence went without saying.) It indicated what John Greenwood would never deny: that in the adversary system, a lawyer's job is to *win*.

William Illerbrun said he was on duty at the Guelph Jail on Saturday, November 16. He and another guard were told to take Dinardo from his cell to the visiting room. Dinardo's visitor was his lawyer, Arthur Malo-ney. Illerbrun said he recognized the lawyer from his pictures in the pa-pers and television. The jail guard thought it peculiar that such a fa-

mous man would come down on a Saturday and sit and talk to a man
. . .

"Never mind what you thought," interrupted Justice Grant, "tell us what happened."

What happened, said the guard, was that from the other side of the bars he observed Dinardo and his lawyer looking at a copy of the Friday, November 15, issue of *The Toronto Sun*. They were looking at the inside page of the paper, Illerbrun said, and from the movements of their lips he could see that they were talking. They did that for about fifteen or twenty minutes. That particular issue of the newspaper contained some facts about the Demeter case. Dinardo did not have a copy of the paper when he went down to the visiting room, said the guard, not even in his pocket, as he was dressed only in his undershirt and some blue denim pants. That was it. Thank you.

The Crown's insinuation through their surprise rebuttal witness was clear. Dinardo had been coached in his testimony by Arthur Maloney, Q.C.

Generally, lawyers guard each other's reputation more jealously than members of the medical profession. This attitude of professional protection normally extends even to their most recently admitted friends at the bar, but questioning (even by implication) the conduct of Arthur Maloney was somewhat like questioning the catholicity of the pope. It mattered little that, once the guard had testified, Greenwood had immediately cast himself in the role of the champion of Maloney's reputation, saying (seconded by Justice Grant) that he was prepared to admit " . . . that Mr. Maloney is the most ethical and/or prominent lawyer in the Dominion of Canada." The prosecution could protest all they wanted: it was perfectly clear what it was they wanted the jury to infer from Illerbrun's evidence. Actions speak louder than words.

That Maloney himself thought so was obvious from the pained tone of the affidavit he later gave to the defence:

> [Illerbrun's] evidence that Dinardo and I looked at a copy of the Toronto Sun dated Friday, November 15, 1974, for a period of fifteeen or twenty minutes and the implication that I brought the copy of the Toronto Sun into the jail with me and that Dinardo and I reviewed the facts of the case with reference to that paper is totally and completely at variance with the truth.

At no time did I bring a newspaper into the jail — the Toronto Sun or any other newpaper — during the times of my interviews with Dinardo and any suggestion that I was preparing Dinardo for his testimony in the Demeter trial by referring to the Toronto Sun or any newspaper is totally groundless.

I very much regret Mr. Greenwood and Mr. McGuigan did not contact me before making the decision to call Mr. Illerbrun as a witness. If they had alerted me as to the evidence he was to give I would have explained to them how totally incorrect it was and would have urged them to call me as a witness also so that the jury would then hear both versions of what transpired between me and Dinardo.

The Crown would claim later that they certainly tried contacting Maloney but he was not to be found. In his affidavit Maloney disagreed:

On the day the evidence of Mr. Illerbrun was given I was in Calgary, Alberta. I was there in connection with a Review I was conducting on behalf of the Metropolitan Toronto Board of Police Commissioners about Police Complaint Procedures. My itinerary was well known to my secretary and the staff in my office.

In the unthinkable event that Maloney *had* coached Dinardo, of course, the mystery of how the dim heavyweight knew exactly what to say to fit in with the theory of Peter's defence would have been solved. (There seemed little doubt that the six-foot-four boxer's personality must have had some attraction for the famous defence lawyer, if it was true — as Dinardo had testified — that Maloney visited him in jail once every week. Conscientious as Ontario's ombudsman undoubtedly was in his role as defence counsel, the complexity of Dinardo's own case, at least on the face of it, would not seem to have warranted visits of such frequency. Having an interest in one's client, however, is hardly unethical.) Furthermore, since Maloney had no contact with Peter Demeter, he could not have prepared Dinardo for his testimony in the Demeter case unless he himself had been prepared by one of Peter's lawyers. To sugges this would amount to suggesting that two officers of the court, two of Her Majesty's Counsels, had conspired to tamper with evidence and pervert the course of justice. Once Illerbrun had testified, of course, the

Crown did everything to dispel even the shadow of this monstrous suggestion.

But the fact remained that they had first called Illerbrun to testify, knowing what he would say.

The Custodial Officer himself was very reluctant later to talk about his experiences in the Demeter case. "I have no comment," he would say. "I know what I saw. If I had known then what I know now I wouldn't have testified at all."

Whatever that means.

26. The Verdict

The court adjourned on Thursday, November 28, at three o'clock in the afternoon. The first part of the trial was over. Next Monday, December 2, the final arguments would begin.

Though Justice Grant set great store by speed and efficiency — especially with a sequestered jury — this once it was he who suggested the long weekend. In part he wished to make sure Joe Pomerant would have enough time to prepare his closing address to the jury, but he probably also wanted everyone to have a few days in which to cool down. In the last week things were wound tighter than a drum in his courtroom. The police actually went to the length of bringing the well-known underworld chieftain Johnny Papalia into court just so McGuigan could ask Dinardo on the stand if he knew this man. (Bill Teggart and his cops were evidently hoping that even a staid London jury would realize who Papalia was, which may or may not have been too optimistic.) The incident certainly showed that the Mississauga lawmen were not, to put it mildly, indifferent to the outcome of their most notorious case. (A less prominent mobster would later say he had told Bill Teggart when he was subpoenaed: "Sure, I'll testify. Why, I saw Dinardo and Eper together dozens of times. Will that help you?" Needless to say, the mobster was not called.) Greenwood himself would comment later: "When some lawyers talk about the power of the state trying to convict their poor little client, well, that always struck me as a pile of baloney. Usually it's just one ordinary police officer who may or may not have done his homework. But in the Demeter case it was the power of the state in every sense of the word. The help I had was unbelievable. The number of detectives assigned to the case was unlimited." Greenwood's comment would certainly have been a good lesson to every lawyer who was ever tempted to defend his case in the press. A lot of publicity, it seemed, made the police anxious to put their best foot forward as well.

Perhaps nothing characterized more the mood of mistrust that had, by that time, developed in the London courtroom than Justice Grant's order to eject a spectator for — as it seemed to the judge — nodding his head during Dinardo's testimony. It turned out that the unfortunate gentleman was a totally innocent visitor, one of hundreds attracted to the trial, who got so caught up with Dinardo's story that he kept inclining his head after every one of Joe Pomerant's questions. It was his bad luck that he happened to sit in the front row and directly in the trial judge's line of vision. Later, of course, Justice Grant explained the misunderstanding to the jury very carefully, so that they should not be left with the wrong impression. Nevertheless, it was a clear indication of the suspicions the trial judge himself must have had about Dinardo and, by logical extension, about the defence. Even though the nodder happened to be innocent, the judge's mistrust could not have escaped the notice of the jury.

But the most important thing was that after Dinardo's testimony the defence rested.

Peter Demeter would not testify in his own behalf.

The law doesn't require any accused ever to stand up in court and say: "I'm innocent." This is something that the law presumes in any case. The burden of proof is on the prosecution. They have to satisfy a jury beyond a reasonable doubt that the defendant is guilty; they can't ask the defendant to explain himself. They can't even comment on the fact that he doesn't choose to do so, if he doesn't. The jury is not permitted to draw the slightest inference of guilt from a defendant's silence. This, undoubtedly, is one of the most majestic things about our law.

In practice, however, explaining one's own side of the story may make good common sense. There's no rule about it; it changes from case to case, depending on the circumstances. Knowing when to put one's client on the stand and when not to is one of a defence lawyer's great arts. It requires judgment and intuition. Unlike many other things about the practice of litigation, it cannot be learned from books.

Joe Pomerant, apparently, had decided to keep the option of whether or not to call Peter on his own behalf open right until the end. The reason for this, in all likelihood, was not indecision. No doubt, Pomerant wanted to see how things were progressing for his side. Putting Peter on the stand meant exposing him to a gruelling cross-examination by the Crown — something Greenwood had been looking forward to since the beginning of the trial. No lawyer would want to submit his client to such an experience unless he had to. A skilled cross-examination by an experienced, aggressive prosecutor can reduce a perfectly innocent man to a confused glob of apparent guilt. It can shore up a buckling case for the Crown.

Conversely, it can also tear a big hole in a very strong web of suspicion.

Pomerant's dilemma must have been considerable.

Until now, whenever Peter had opened his mouth, he had managed to talk himself into trouble. Regardless of whether he was guilty or innocent, the Crown would have had no case against him at all if he had taken his lawyer's initial advice and talked to no one. Had he sat in stunned silence at the police station after Christine's death, shaking his head in silent grief, he might not even have been suspected. Half of the prosecution's case against Joe's client consisted of things he had said after his wife's murder. In the beginning that was the whole case against him. He was a complex, convoluted man, stamped with a culture quite alien to a jury of local citizens. He could make the truth sound like a lie. He might have been smarter than a lot of people, but he might not have been nearly as smart as he thought. No doubt Pomerant remembered that, traditionally, people enamoured with their own brains make the most vulnerable witnesses. In normal circumstances Peter seemed the very man to keep away from the stand at all costs.

But were circumstances normal?

With things as they stood, could the defence possibly win without an explanation from Peter?

Pomerant could say in his closing argument to the jury: *why believe Csaba Szilagyi, why believe Stark? They are people of a character no more sterling than Dinardo. Listen to Dinardo, think of the reasonable doubt.* Saying that required no explanations from Peter at all.

But could Pomerant say, *Don't believe Peter's own words on tape?* Could he say, *His words are ambiguous?*

Who on the jury (whatever their understanding of the defendant's rights to silence) would not reply: *if his words are ambiguous, why doesn't he explain them?*

Why doesn't he tell us what he meant when Szilagyi said: "You don't know yourself?" and he replied: "Csaba, the hell I don't know." Was he thinking Csaba's question referred to something else, not the killer? Maybe, but why doesn't he tell us? Why doesn't he give us a chance to resolve the doubt in his favour?

It was an unenviable dilemma. After ten hours of discussions Pomerant was said to have solved it by leaving it up to Peter. It's a fifty-fifty chance, the lawyer reportedly said, whether it can help you or hurt you. Fifty-fifty. It might make things better, it might make things worse. It's fifty-fifty.

Accurate as this legal advice may have been, under the circumstances it may not have been sufficient. But there was more than a little poetic justice in it, making as it did Peter once again the captain of his fate. As a man who preferred conducting his own affairs; as a man who had trusted (according to his own words on tape) no one except Csaba — and that to his peril — he might well have wanted it this way. Certainly, if he hadn't, he could have told Pomerant that he would be guided by his advice, which would have forced the most reluctant lawyer to decide, and Pomerant wasn't a reluctant lawyer. But, with a man as difficult as Peter for a client, he could be understood (if not necessarily applauded) for not wanting the decision to rest on him alone.

There were a number of people — lawyers and relatives — in the consulting room when Peter finally drew himself up to his full size and said, "I elect not to testify." Some said he had never looked more like an officer and gentleman from the old Prussian army. Marina exclaimed: "Liebchen!" It was said to have been an exclamation of surprise. Up until this moment, whatever shortcomings Marina might have had, doubting her lover was not among them. If she did now, it showed the accuracy of Wigmore's classic remark that the right to silence is a matter of policy rather than logic. The jury might feel the same way.

Joe Pomerant addressed the jury on behalf of the defence at 10:23 in the morning of Monday, December 2.

The preceding eleven weeks had taken their toll on the defence lawyer. He must have been psychologically drained, no matter how often he told himself (as he'd later say he did) that a case is just a case: you do your damndest, then forget about it. There's little doubt that in his years as a criminal lawyer, Pomerant had never had a case like this. Few lawyers ever had. All eyes were on him, he was being watched by his peers, by the press, by millions of interested laymen, and it mattered very little at this point whether his high profile was due partly to his own choice or not. Though Pomerant didn't have as much at stake as Peter — no one did — he had as much as he could afford to have. It was not a case of simply doing one's best then, win or lose, going home and forgetting about it. His jury address for the defence had to be ten out of ten. Better still, a miracle.

Pomerant began with the presumption of innocence. He called it the thirteenth juror. And, he said, " . . . you don't do Peter Demeter a favour by giving him the presumption of innocence. You become [sic] armed with that. Our society makes you put that on, each one of you." He also talked about reasonable doubt, and the responsibility of the jury. He talked aptly and forcefully, though with little grace. His standard opening admonitions to the jury seemed eloquent rather than elegant.

Then, addressing himself to the first particulars, Joe Pomerant said that the Crown " . . . alleges in this case that a man . . . because of classic motives caused the death of his wife." He listed the motives: a less than satisfactory marriage, a love affair, a million-dollar insurance. Then he pointed out that " . . . this case in no way determines in law whether or not Peter Demeter will recover any of the insurance monies. . . . That question does not go with you when you go to make your decision." It was perfectly true, but perhaps less than tactful. Another lawyer might not have chosen to remind the jury of what Peter would stand to gain, not even in negation.

Then Pomerant analyzed Peter's alleged strange behaviour on the night of Christine's death. He did it well and convincingly, with just the right touch of sarcasm. He created the feeling, without actually saying so, that any one of the jurors might have behaved in much the same way under the same circumstances. He listed some of the things Peter did *not* do, though a guilty man might or indeed would have. "How easy it would have been for Peter Demeter to say anything is missing, a clock, a radio, let alone thousands of dollars in cash or jewels or furs, if he wanted to point suspicion away from himself," said Pomerant. This, too, was true.

Then the defence lawyer attacked the weak link in the prosecution's circumstantial chain: opportunity. The evening trip to Yorkdale Plaza, which was clearly *not* Peter's idea. The little German girls wanted moccasins; it was their last day in Canada; Sybille Brewer decided to take them to the shopping centre after dinner. They were out-of-town people; as a good host Peter had offered to drive them. He had driven them everywhere else in the preceding two days of their visit, too. The dog: so he took his dog. He liked his dog. The dog was in the habit of jumping into the swimming pool after Christine if there was no one around to hold him back, and the chlorinated water tended to give him a rash. (There was some evidence for that.) The dog was a friendly cocker spaniel, not a watchdog, not a Doberman Pinscher. The Crown made much of the fact that dogs were not permitted inside the shopping plaza, Pomerant said, and taking him back to the car gave Peter an opportunity to make a phone call. Surely he didn't need the dog for that; surely he could have used any other excuse. The telephone call at Birks: Viveca said Peter had waved her away first, told her to keep looking for the name-day gift, the locket, before calling her back to the phone to talk to Andrea and Christine. Even if Viveca didn't misunderstand him when she thought he was waving her away, couldn't there be many things between a husband and wife, innocent things, that they might want to discuss in private? Then, when Viveca said good-bye to Christine on the phone, did Peter try to find out what they had talked about, did he ask, "What did she say to you?" No. If Peter had made any suggestions to his wife, Pomerant implied, such as go to the garage, get my keys, my wallet, anything, he would have been eager to find out if she might have mentioned it to Viveca. But he wasn't.

Pomerant covered many of the other areas, such as the broken garage door which the Crown implied but couldn't prove was sabotaged, commenting sarcastically on the uncanny skill Demeter would have needed to make the old door break down from normal wear and tear just in time for the murder. (He failed to mention some areas, such as Dr. Brewer's evidence that if it had been up to Peter, they might have been back half an hour *earlier* at the house, or the fact that Demeter took Beelzebub with him in the car in the morning as well, which showed that taking the dog might not have been such an unusual thing for him to do.) Still, the defence lawyer did, as it seemed, quite well in this vital area. The jury couldn't but ponder that if Peter did set up his wife under the uncontrolled and uncontrollable circumstances of that Wednesday in July — a spur-of-the-moment shopping trip with four women, three of them kids, any of whom could have changed her mind about anything at any time — he must have been cutting it pretty close. If the real-estate people had left sooner in the afternoon (as expected), the trip to Yorkdale would have been completed in broad daylight. In this one respect, at least, any doubts about Peter's guilt need not have been altogether fanciful. His opportunity to commit the crime seemed touch and go at best.

Then Pomerant chose to take the whip to the near-dead horse of Henry Williams, the Streetsville killer. "When a man like that passes through the neighbourhood," the lawyer suggested, "it can never be said with certainty what he has done." From the defence's point of view the best thing about Williams was that when he was arrested, a year after Peter had been charged, the police felt the need to question him about Christine's murder for three-quarters of an hour. Why? If they had no doubt of Peter Demeter's guilt, Pomerant asked, why question Williams at all?

Csaba Szilagyi. Now there was something for Pomerant to get his teeth into, and he did, with passion, irony, conviction, and force. He pointed out the inherent weaknesses, contradictions, and improbabilities in Csaba's story in great detail. He highlighted the failings in Csaba's character with perfect logic. He called him one-tenth of a man. There was no doubt, when Pomerant was finished, that no one on the jury would have felt inclined to take Szilagyi home for dinner. But the problem that had been there from the outset still remained: was Szilagyi lying? The jury might not have cared much whether he was a nice man or not, a good friend or a traitor; they might not even have worried about Szilagyi's own role in the murder plot discussions. What difference did it make if he was not as innocent as he claimed to be, if he was more than just a passive listener, or a saviour with a mission? What if he seriously contemplated helping Peter all along and chickened out only in the last minute? The questions was, was he telling the truth *now*? Did Peter try to get him to kill Christine over the years?

No, of course not, Pomerant suggested. There was Stark's evidence that it was Christine who wanted a gun and an alibi for Csaba. There was Dinardo's evidence about meeting Csaba on the Lakeshore in Eper's company. Szilagyi *lived* with Christine and Peter for seventeen months. Christine had as much insurance on Peter's life as he had on hers; she had even more to gain, considering that Peter was worth nearly half a million, with all his assets in his own name. Christine had already lost one custody battle earlier in her life: would she risk another one in a divorce action? She had had at least one known affair during her marriage, according to the testimony of Van Berkel; it was at least conceivable she might have had others. Look at this photograph, this little photograph of Christine, Csaba, and Peter together, Pomerant suggested. "Look at the faces. It will tell you more about who was plotting the murder with who for what."

Pomerant asked for a recess while the jury looked at the snapshot, then continued. On Monday, two days before the murder, Szilagyi claims Demeter calls him: "Keep Gigi away." He is living with Gigi; they're in love; does he keep her away? No. Does he say anything to her when, in the afternoon, Demeter supposedly calls again to say, "The deal was for one girl, not two"? No again. Does he warn Christine the next day, the day before she dies, when she comes to their place for a secret visit? No, no, no. Is this credible, is this believable?

Does Christine have murder on her mind? Who is to say? She does remark to Viveca: "It would be nice to knock him off and get his money." A joke? Maybe. But Dinardo's story is no joke. The defence doesn't find Dinardo: it's the police who find him. The defence doesn't ask for Eper's car to be examined for bloodstains: the police do that on their own. It's the police who are puzzled by the piece of paper with Peter Demeter's name in Eper's room; it's they who keep after Dinardo, and finally turn to his lawyer to get him to talk. Then, when Dinardo talks, the Crown doesn't like it. He is lying, they say. Is Stark lying, too, about the gun and the alibi for Csaba? Is everybody lying except when they testify against Demeter? Is it just a coincidence in a city of two million people that Stark's girlfriend Gloria Orr lives in the same apartment building as Csaba?

Hiding pay-off money in a roll of blueprints: isn't *that* incredible? Does it not make more sense for Christine to meet The Duck herself, to give him money for Peter's murder? All those people who now claim to "recognize" Peter as the man asking for the Duck, the Links, the Fancsiks, are they not all The Duck's friends, on their own evidence? The independent witnesses, the court reporter, and the complainant do not remember seeing Demeter at the trial. The receipt from the Montreal motel places him four hundred miles away the night before; isn't that the more credible evidence? Is that not sufficient for a reasonable doubt?

"Peter Demeter," said Pomerant in closing, "has a little girl and that little girl will grow up and I suggest to you that the test that you apply is this: you convict Peter Demeter, if you can look this girl in the eye when she grows up and say, 'I was satisfied to a moral certainty that your father committed this crime.' "

It was a strong pitch. The question was, was it strong enough? This address was the defence's last shot at the trial. Once Joe Pomerant had sat down nothing more could be said to the jury on Peter's behalf. Did Pomerant say everything? Did he say it as well as he might have or, indeed, as anybody might have said it? Would it have been possible to turn the tide of the prosecution's case at this point in the trial? Would a stronger, better address for the defence have done it? Some other trial lawyers thought so:

The tapes. Of course Pomerant mentioned the tapes but, just as at the preliminary hearing, he chose not to come to grips with them. It was impossible to say whether this was because he thought of them as relatively weak evidence or, on the contrary, as so strong that he wanted to stay as far away from them as possible. Maybe he found the very idea so offensive that he simply couldn't bear to touch it. Perhaps he thought that by not paying the tapes much attention, they would somehow just go away. Why did Csaba have to go back *four* times, he told the jury, if the tapes really proved anything? Wasn't the first one enough, the second, the third? Why couldn't Csaba get his unsuspecting friend to commit himself, not even once, not even obliquely? It would have been so easy, Pomerant said, to ask, "Was it the same people who called you on Monday, Peter?" He reminded the jury that Csaba couldn't pick out one spot in the hours and hours of conversations that would have directly supported any of his stories about the various murder plots.

All this was true, of course, but the problem still remained that concentrating on what the tapes didn't say couldn't quite gloss over what they did say. Why did Peter seem so glad that a private detective had him under observation only " . . . in the completely neutral first days . . . " and not " . . . in the vital last days . . . ?" Going ostrich about things like that might not have been sufficient defence.

Nor was it pointed out to the jury that once Maria Visnyiczky's story became known, Stark could be implicated in two different crimes if he admitted plotting with Christine against Peter: first, conspiracy against Demeter; second, suspicion of murder of Christine. It would be far more self-serving for Stark (Pomerant might have said) to invent a non-existent plot with Peter against Christine. This would get rid of one crime — the conspiracy against the husband — and would create a suspect other than Stark for the second, the murder of the wife. (Pomerant did skirt this idea, but he failed to bring it into focus for the jury. They might not have understood right to the end why Stark would, even in theory, say what he said unless it was true. There was the suggestion of immunity, of course, but that might have sounded too bald for the jury.)

There was also a total lack of focus on the vital point: how did

"Jimmy Or" get into Christine's diary? If Stark did not know Kacsa by the name of Jimmy Orr, there was no way for the name to get into Christine's black book *through Peter*. If Stark himself didn't know Kacsa's alias, how on earth would Peter have known it? According to Stark, Peter had no direct contact with The Duck. If Pomerant simply hadn't said anything about this to the jury it could be imagined that he just happened to overlook one thing in a very complex case. But he did mention it. He said, " . . . and remember what Stark did in the witness box. I put to him twenty times 'Jimmy'. He said 'Why do you call him Jimmy?' Well, if you look at Christine's diary for April 2 you will see." Then, having spent maybe twenty seconds out of three and a half hours on one of the key puzzles in the Crown's case, Pomerant went on to talk about something else.

Though Pomerant didn't linger on Williams too much, it might have been an error to bring him in at all once Dinardo had "solved" the murder of Christine. If in the end it was Williams who had killed Christine, what happened to all the murder plots between Stark, Olejnyik, Eper, and Szilagyi that the defence took so much time and effort to establish? Even raising the possibility — other than to illustrate the police's own doubts — meant discrediting Dinardo, the strongest defence witness. Christine, unless particularly unlucky, couldn't have been killed by both Eper and Williams the same evening. The very suggestion, instead of raising one more doubt, might have tempted the jury to conclude that she wasn't killed by either.

The real problem might have been Pomerant's style — a somewhat rambling, discursive, and diffuse style — that tended to confuse matters even more in this complicated case. Instead of doubts, reasonable or not, the jurors by this time might have been yearning for some clarity. They seemed ready to listen to whoever would give it to them. They wished to know which one of the many far-fetched stories was worthy of their belief, instead of being urged to give to one side the benefit of their unresolvable doubts. At times Joe sounded as though he were thinking out loud, an honest and bewildered man trying to resolve some uncertainties of his own. How could all this have happened, he seemed to be saying, how could this simple case of an innocently suspected husband turn into such a wicked conundrum? Rather than convincing the jury, it almost appeared as though he were trying to find answers to his own nagging questions and, having failed, chose to vote for acquittal simply as a good liberal. But the nine men and three women facing him might have prefered to acquit on some more down-to-earth grounds, such as a solid chance of the accused's innocence. They were hoping for fewer rhymes and more reasons.

Hindsight, of course, is always very sharp. Justice Grant himself had no patience with it. "It's easy to look back," the judge would later say, "on what's been done and say it should have been done this way or that way or this should not have been done. It's easy to do that."

Campbell Grant, the former defence lawyer, appreciated the difficulties Pomerant had to face. In the end so did others, though some thought the judge was part of Pomerant's problems. "An impossible client," said one lawyer, "a bloodthirsty police, and a judge who can't bear the sight of you. How could anyone win?"

The Crown tried to make sure Pomerant didn't, when it was their turn. In complete contrast to his opponent, John Greenwood tended to be all reason and hardly any rhymes. He elected to meet his biggest problem head-on, right from the beginning. If you believe Dinardo, he said to the jury, you have to acquit Peter Demeter. You have to forget about all other evidence as if you had never heard it and set Peter Demeter free.

If you think he is lying, on the other hand, then Dinardo becomes the best witness for the prosecution. Because why would Dinardo lie?

Before setting out to tear The Tractor apart, Greenwood detoured for a minute or two on the subject of his own high regard for the competence and integrity of Arthur Maloney. Then slowly, methodically, point by point he destroyed Maloney's client's evidence. It showed, at the very least, that the Crown took Dinardo seriously. Greenwood paid him the compliment of not even touching on his own accumulated evidence of eleven weeks until the Firebug's story was out of the way.

Then, starting from the beginning, the senior prosecutor went through the Crown's evidence. He spoke with no more elegance than his colleague for the defence, but he spoke without pretensions. He attempted no irony, no metaphors, no rhetorical devices, no flights of fancy or language. Unless, of course, this very absence of frills, this very insistence on logic and sequence, was in itself a rhetorical device.

The prosecutor took his time, though he was careful not to waste it. He began with motive: the insurance and Marina Hundt. He did not have to cross the obstacle of Peter, allegedly talking murder as early as 1968, long *before* the million-dollar insurance or the renewal of the Marina-affair, since Pomerant didn't bring up this aspect of Szilagyi's evidence in his jury address. Instead, Greenwood was able to talk in terms of a simple motive: another woman and a lot of bucks. Even if all the jurors would not have killed for a million dollars as Steven Demeter assumed, probably all the jurors could imagine somebody else killing for it. Then the Crown lingered over the setting-up of the murder on July 18, and on what Greenwood called "the isolation of Christine". (The prosecutor came up with this catchy phrase at the trial. It was certainly a great improvement on his original phrase, "the abandonment of the premises", which he used at the preliminary hearing.) But whatever he called it, Big John had to make sure that the jurors would read malicious intent into a set of rather ordinary actions and events, such as asking a gardener not to spray for weeds while the house was full of guests; driving a bunch of girls to a shopping plaza at their own request; having a dog hop into the car; having a stuck garage door; or phoning one's wife to make sure one didn't buy the wrong thing for her. This was important, since, in all likelihood, there was no one in the jury box who might not have gone through exactly the same series of events the week before the trial — except for finding their wives dead at the end of it. To show that all these things could have been done by Peter for the purpose of isolating Christine was not enough. Obviously they could have; but Greenwood had to show that they *were*. It was not easy.

Nor was it easy to show that Peter's behaviour, at the scene or down at the police station, was that of a guilty man. Greenwood tackled this problem next, perhaps more to justify the subsequent investigative techniques employed by the police than for any other reason. Certainly by summation-time the Crown had far better evidence of Peter's guilt than his defensive prickliness with Chris O'Toole and his colleagues on the night of July 18. Dwelling on this subject might, in fact, have created a feeling of perverse sympathy in some jurors. Anyone who has ever been a complainant or victim in a criminal matter knows how, in some cases, the behaviour of the police only adds insult to his injuries. Greenwood's question: " . . . what possibly could lead Mr. Demeter to the suggestion that he was being treated as a murderer . . . ?" sounded a bit hollow in light of the evidence before the court. Even Bill Teggart would say later, referring to one of the investigators Demeter had to deal with that night: "Well, some of our people are a little less tactful than others. . . . But, remember, there was one very dead lady."

There was indeed, and Greenwood continued his submissions of proof that she died because of her husband. Now he was talking about the real stuff: Stark and his story of the plot at 52 Dawes Road. Some of it was easy, since all the Crown Attorney had to do was to reiterate the evidence and urge the jury to believe it, adding that in some respects it was supported by the evidence of Maria Visnyiczky and "Foxy" Jones. Some of it was not easy, such as Stark's story about the gun and alibi Christine wanted to buy from him for Csaba. Greenwood, as always, dealt with this in very simple terms. It was a lie, he said, made up under pressure from Peter. Once Stark had told it to Joe Pomerant he was stuck with it.

Why Stark would be "stuck" with anything was not enlarged upon by the Crown. The authorities, no doubt, would have been only too glad if he had admitted that his gun-and-alibi story was a lie. Conversely, he couldn't have expected to buy Peter's goodwill by doing him one small favour after demolishing him with the rest of his evidence. Though Stark might well have preferred playing both ends against the middle, Greenwood's suggestion that he had actually accomplished this by sticking to his original story strained credulity. Still, it was a simple explanation and the prosecutor was probably right in feeling that it was simple explanations that the jury wanted to hear.

Then there was the evidence of the trusty Flower, a.k.a. Tom Smith, which Greenwood had to offer very carefully indeed. By claiming that The Duck was the actual killer of Christine he could have boxed the Crown into a very bad corner. At the same time it was such a clincher — in fact the *only* thing linking Peter directly to the death of Christine and not just some abortive plot — that the prosecutor couldn't resist using it. What he himself must have thought of the evidence was obvious from the cautious way he put it to the jury: "Now, again I am not suggesting to you that you accept in totality the evidence of Mr. Smith," said Greenwood. "I suggest it is quite reasonable, however, that Olejnyik did return to Canada for the murder of Mrs. Demeter under extreme pressure of Mr. Stark and Mr. Demeter. . . . However, Olejnyik's participation in the murder of Mrs. Demeter is not in issue in this case. . . . The only issue you have to decide is whether Demeter counselled a person or persons unknown to kill his wife and as a result Christine Demeter was in fact murdered."

Now this was playing both ends against the middle by a master. Stark could have learned from it.

Then Greenwood turned his attention to Szilagyi. Unlike, of course, counsel for the defence, he spent very little time on Csaba's character.

What Greenwood talked about, at length and in great detail, were the tapes. As he was reading excerpt after excerpt for the jury one could feel great sympathy with Joe Pomerant for not wanting to tackle the tapes directly. It seemed to matter little what they didn't contain in light of what they did. *Don't take a lie detector test. Stick to the truth in everything except that we ever discussed this. . . . How would that person know you if he doesn't know me? Why do you think I can offer my own $10,000 reward?* Et cetera.

Greenwood returned briefly to the events of July 18. Peter, he reminded the jury, wanted to speak badly enough to a "contractor" in the Riverdale Zoo area on that day to go there twice. Viveca said so, Dr. Brewer said so. Now who was doing a construction job in that area? Stark, Ferenc Stark.

Another thing: why was Dinardo lying, as Greenwood asked the jury to believe he was? There was medical testimony that Christine's skull was broken in three places *at the base*, that is, not just the top of her head from the direct impact, but at the bottom from the transmitted force of the blows. It no doubt required a very powerful man to wield a weapon with such a force. It was not the jury's task to solve the puzzle of the actual killer, but they might well ask themselves *why* would Dinardo lie for Demeter?

"I have no comment to suggest to you," said Greenwood, "other than ask you to do your duty as you have sworn to do it."

The time was a quarter to seven in the evening. The Crown Attorney sat down. His job was finished. Now it would be the turn of the trial judge, Justice Campbell Grant.

After more than forty years at the bar and on the bench Campbell Grant was neither naïve nor easily scandalized. As a judge he had seen wickedness before. As a lawyer he had defended a dozen murderers himself. Still — as he'd say later — he had never encountered a whole string of Epers, Dinardos, Ducks, Starks, or Williamses in any one case in his court. Why, in this trial, "Foxy" Jones seemed almost like a breath of fresh air. When it came to people like Peter, Christine, Marina, or Csaba Szilagyi — regardless of who had been plotting against whom — well, they were something pretty much outside the judge's personal experience. It was not a lack of worldly wisdom, but Justice and Mrs. Campbell Grant were still living in the same house in Walkerton, Ontario, that Grant had built as a young lawyer for his bride over forty years ago. They'd been to Europe, oh, maybe twice in forty years, the first time just before the outbreak of the war. They toured Germany and France, and then on the first Sunday back in Canada they heard on the radio that the ship they took on the way over, the *Athenia*, had been torpedoed in the Atlantic. They didn't go to the movies or the theatre (television had taken the place of that, Justice Grant would say), though Mrs. Grant still had a season's ticket for matinées at the O'Keefe Centre in Toronto. Now there were people, it appeared, who'd move into a different house every year, like gypsies, to avoid paying capital gains taxes, yet they'd jet their way across the ocean at the drop of a hat. Or, more likely, at the click of a fashion photographer's camera. At the same time they'd put Connecticut licence plates on their Cadillacs to save on parking tickets and demand discounts from the florist for the wilted wreaths at their wives' funerals. It had nothing to do with guilt or innocence, of course, but it was pretty strange. Pretty strange. Justice Grant appreciated the value of money himself — he'd chuckle at the thought that he had paid more in taxes as a lawyer than his first year's salary as a Supreme Court judge — but all the same he "just never got around to" increasing the rent on a house he had been leasing to some people for the last thirty years or so. He knew it was foolish, but those people had lived there for a long time. Yet, it seemed, there were people of other kinds in this world. Here today, gone tomorrow people. Kick over a stone, and they would come crawling out like maggots.

In his charge to the jury Justice Grant would be faced with the difficult task of dismissing any and all such thoughts from his mind and purging them from his emotions. Though the jurors were the sole judges of the facts — as he'd point it out to them — they would still hang on every one of his words, even his pauses or inflections while he was delivering his charge. They'd be guided by him, not only on the law as they had to be, but on everything else as well. The authority of a judge on the bench was immense, and in Justice Grant's case the authority of his personality would be added to that of his office. Though he'd never say so himself, he'd know it very well and weigh every one of his words accordingly. Justice was no game or abstraction for Campbell Grant: it was something he wanted to see done in his court in the individual case at the bar. It didn't mean imbuing the jury with his own views of the merits of the case, but it didn't mean bending over backwards in some misleading display of impartiality either. The blindness of justice, for the trial judge, meant blindness to irrelevant sympathies only. It didn't mean blindness to the truth.

Like any other human being, the judge had his own view on what the proper verdict ought to be in the case on the basis of the evidence, and he hoped that the jury would arrive at it, but it was his duty to see that they would arrive at it on their own and without undue influence from him or anyone else. In his charge he would — literally — have to lay down the law for them. He would have to establish the guidelines, show them the scale on which the evidence ought to be weighed. He would have to take great care not to put his own weight into the scales on either side, but without making the jury think that it was therefore *his view* that the scales were evenly balanced. That, too, could be an improper influence.

Justice Grant took four hours to deliver his charge on Tuesday, December 3. It had taken him many weeks to to sketch it out, working each night for a few hours after adjournment as the evidence unfolded before him. He reviewed the whole mass of it now, explaining the law as it pertained to each item before the jury. Being a patient, courteous man, he spoke patiently and courteously. Having the rare ability to make plain the most complex points of law, he spoke simply but without condescension. He used metaphors sparingly, but when he used them they seemed right, as in likening circumstantial evidence to a man's knowledge of rain having fallen at night, though he had neither seen nor heard it, from the moisture on the ground and the flowers standing straight and firm. Speaking of Maria, The Duck's common-law wife, he reminded the jurors that they might sometimes see a petunia growing in a bed of weeds. Though he spoke without gestures, emphasis, and in something of a monotone, there was not the slightest doubt, that he had the complete attention of the jury. At the end, had he seemed to suggest that Peter Demeter ought to be acquitted, the jury might have acquitted him.

Justice Grant seemed to make no such suggestion.

As soon as the jury left the courtroom, the defence objected to the charge. Justice Grant had spent 225 minutes on his instructions to the jury, said Eddie Greenspan, but only 5 minutes of it on the defence. He did not outline the defence's theory. He stated as facts things that were not, in fact, facts. Greenspan requested that the judge revise the entire charge.

Greenwood objected to Greenspan's objections. Justice Grant sent word to the jury not to begin deliberations until he had listened to the arguments of both counsel. Then he called back the jury and gave them some additional instructions.

He may have been wrong, the judge said to the jury, in saying that Dinardo's description of Christine's hair colour probably discredited Dinardo. (Justice Grant *was* wrong in that: Dinardo described Christine as a blonde, which Christine could appear to be at times.)

He may have been wrong in saying that Csaba Szilagyi came forward to the police very soon after the murder; there was little evidence as to when he came forward. (In fact, Szilagyi didn't come forward at all. The police picked him up after Rita Jefferies' statement.)

He may have been in error saying that Dinardo sent for Maloney. (The judge was in error, at least as regards the initial approach, which was made by the police to Arthur Maloney.)

In his recharge Justice Grant also made references to a few bits of defence evidence he had omitted in his original charge: Van Berkel's testimony about his affair with Christine; Link's description of the Mercedes as "white"; and the Montreal motel receipt that threw some doubt on whether Peter could have been at Fancsik's trial around the same time. Finally Justice Grant told the jury that the defence had asked him to indicate that, in their view, it was Eper who was the killer of Christine. "I thought we had dealt with that in the light I saw it," said the judge. "But it is in the light that you see that. And if you can draw any such conclusions from that evidence, and it raises any reasonable doubt in your mind, however, I think I have already said to you that the accused is entitled to the benefit of that."

Indeed. While the jury deliberated, someone asked Peter what he had thought of the judge's charge. "A directed verdict of acquittal — in reverse," Peter is said to have replied. Even while the judge was delivering his instructions, Joe Pomerant (reportedly) threw his pencil in the air, then turned his back to the bench. Later Justice Grant would comment: "I am advised that during my charge to the jury there was constant interruption from the defence table, and so on. I myself did not notice it. But I understand that the jury were very displeased at the attitude of the defence counsel during the charge. It affected them to some extent. If the judge is trying to be fair in the minds of the jury, they don't want counsel irritating the judge; it has a great backlash to it. . . . Now don't misunderstand me: I don't mean for a moment that throughout the trial either defence counsel ever did anything to antagonize the judge."

The next morning, on December 4, the jury sent in a request to the court. They wanted to have some evidence reread to them: Viveca's and

Dr. Brewer's, with regard to some of the events on July 18; Stark's evidence; Gigi's evidence about the trip to Dawes Road with Christine on the Monday before her death; and, mainly, the tapes. The taped conversations between Csaba Szilagyi and Peter Demeter.

The tapes.

The original evidence with which the Crown decided to go to trial. Peter Demeter's own words. The initial design patterned by Bill Teggart. If there was ever a justification for bold, unorthodox police work — all the policemen on the case would later say — it was in this request of the jury's. Twelve ordinary men and women in London, Ontario, wished to base their decision on what Peter himself had to say. What could be fairer than that?

The evidence was reread by court reporter William Cathcart. The tapes were reread by Justice Grant. The jury retired from the courtroom at 12:35 P.M. Three hours later, at 3:49, they reported that they were ready with their verdict. It was one of the shortest deliberations for one of the longest murder trials on record.

"Members of the Jury," said the registrar, "do you find the accused guilty or not guilty as charged?"

"We find him guilty as charged," replied the lady foreman.

Exactly twenty years earlier, on December 5, 1954, Peter Demeter had crossed the Iron Curtain into the free west. Now, on a mandatory sentence of life imprisonment for non-capital murder, he would be first eligible for parole after ten years. In ten years it would be 1984. By that time, if George Orwell's prophecy came true, he would be stepping out into the same kind of world from which he had risked his life to escape. In any case, he would be fifty-one years old.

27. Justice versus the Law

Flashbulbs popped when Peter Demeter was convicted. In the next few days there would be many photographs and stories in the newspapers. Some of them would be straight reportage, some colourful and spicy, some salacious and sensationalist. But none would raise any questions of principle. No journalist in Canada would feel that there were any to be raised. This wealthy, shrewd, conspiratorial, sophisticated foreigner seemed no underdog. There was nothing about him to engage sentimental sympathies. He was no politicized university student, no downtrodden Indian, no abandoned farm wife.

There would be no editorials.

Yet Peter Demeter's conviction did raise three questions.

1) Was he in fact guilty as charged? No matter what, this question is always raised in a complex case when a man leaves the courtroom protesting his innocence.

2) Whether he was guilty or not, was he lawfully convicted? This question, of course, would be eventually reviewed by the higher courts.

3) Whether or not he was lawfully convicted, was his conviction just? Higher courts may or may not address themselves to this question. In practice they seldom do. But this is very much a question for the public, at least in a free society. Because a trial can be a model of lawfulness and still be a travesty of justice.

The law is a quest for the Holy Grail of justice; the law is not justice itself. This is why it changes from country to country, from time to time, from one session of Parliament or the Supreme Court to the next. The law is only the means by which men try to achieve the ends of justice. Like other ends and means, law and justice may come into conflict. At such times one may be attained only by bending or breaking the other. Unlawful justice is done and lawful injustice is committed somewhere in the world every day.

One of the things with which the law concerns itself is due process.

Due process is simply the way in which justice is administered and the laws are enforced. The law requires this process to be *due* — that is rightful, dignified, and fair — on the rather common-sense principle that you can't sweep a house clean with a filthy broom. At its crudest, this is the principle that would have prevented Superintendent Teggart from putting a thumbscrew on Peter Demeter and turning it until he confessed to his crimes. There's no reason to suppose, of course, that Bill Teggart would have done that even if the law had allowed him this option, but as it was, he couldn't even consider it. Had he tried it, the confession would have been worthless (even if other evidence had shown it to be true), and Peter Demeter would have gone free. Free, even if guilty of premeditated murder.

At least he would have gone free in the United States. Probably, also, in Great Britain. Could he have been certain of going free in Canada?

In the last quarter-century the law in Canada has taken a direction that has alarmed many thoughtful people, not all of them reflex-liberals. While in the United States due process has been elevated to the point where strict observation of the accused's rights seems to have superseded most other considerations of justice, in Canada other considerations of justice — or even utility — seem to have increasingly superseded the basic rights of people accused of criminal acts. While in the United States the cases of some of the most obviously guilty and reprehensible criminals — ferret-like little crooks with records a mile long, like Miranda or Escobedo — have served to establish the highest principles of due process (such as right to counsel, guarantees against self-incrimination and the rest), Canadian courts during the same period tended to put general principles second to the urge of not letting the guilty escape punishment. This resulted in the curious situation where, while many civil-liberties-minded Canadian lawyers like Joe Pomerant were looking to due process in the United States for an enlightened social model, some Americans — faced with an ever-increasing crime rate that began to threaten the very existence of major cities like New York, Philadelphia, or Detroit — started looking to Canada for a solution. This was true especially of those American sociologists and legal thinkers who had begun to question environment and economics as the sole causes of crime, and felt that if crime rates were rising in the United

States *in spite* of a notable increase in general prosperity and social justice, this had to have something to do with the law itself. Perhaps procedural rules had become impossibly lax. Perhaps Canada — where a man could *lawfully* be tricked into incriminating himself on tape; where the police could *lawfully* listen in on solicitor-client conversations, then destroy evidence they didn't consider "relevant"; where the prosecution could *lawfully* present a defendant with a whole new case to answer in the middle of a trial, or offer testimony from as dubious a source as "Tom Smith", but refuse to call a witness turned up by their own investigation, like Joe Dinardo — had the right answer. Maybe things should be made a bit tougher for the accused and easier for the police in the United States, too.

One of the most important decisions in this respect was made by the Supreme Court of Canada on June 26, 1970, involving a man by the name of John Wray.

On March 23, 1968, a service station attendant was shot through the heart and robbed of fifty-five dollars near Peterborough, Ontario. The Ontario Provincial Police investigated, and on the morning of June 4 picked up a suspect named John Wray. For the next nine hours Wray was interrogated at the police station in Peterborough. At a few minutes past 7:00 P.M. he confessed, and even told the police the location of the swamp in which he had thrown the murder weapon. There was evidence, presented at Wray's trial, that his confession was *not* voluntary and that he was denied access to legal counsel. The investigating officer admitted at the trial that he was worried Wray wouldn't show the police where the gun was if he had permitted him to speak to his lawyer. The trial judge threw out the confession, including the part that had to do with finding the gun in the swamp. There being no other evidence, the jury acquitted. The Crown appealed; the Ontario Court of Appeal agreed with the trial judge. Then the Crown appealed to the Supreme Court of Canada.

A majority of six justices upset the decision of the lower courts and ordered Wray to stand trial again on the charge against him. Speaking for the majority, Justice Martland wrote: "The admission of admissible evidence relevant to the issue before the Court and of substantial probative value may operate unfortunately against the accused, but not unfairly. . . . If a trial Judge did have a broad general discretion to exclude otherwise relevant and admissible evidence there would be difficulty in achieving any sort of uniformity in the application of the law." Added

Justice Judson, also for the majority: "There is no judicial discretion permitting the exclusion of relevant evidence on the ground of unfairness to the accused. . . . "

A minority of three judges dissented, including Chief Justice Cartwright. Their opinion was that the methods used by the police were sufficiently offensive to the spirit of justice to permit the trial judge to exercise his judicial discretion as he did. "It is the duty of every trial Judge to guard against bringing the administration of justice into disrepute . . . " wrote Justice Spence. He argued that judges should be free to reject evidence procured by trickery or duress. Also, said Justice Spence, "If the trial Judge had not excluded the evidence it . . . would have been a disregard of the principle that a man should not be made to testify against himself." The Chief Justice echoed this view. He disliked involuntary confessions, not only for the obvious reason that they may be untrue — a man under a thumbscrew might say anything — but also because they offended the maxim of *nemo tenetur se ipsum accusare*, the principle opposing self-incrimination. "It would be a strange result indeed," wrote Chief Justice Cartwright, "if it being the law that no accused is bound to incriminate himself . . . he could none the less be forced by the police or others in authority to make a statement which could then be given in evidence against him." Evidence need not be extracted through force to be involuntary; it could be obtained by deceit. The Chief Justice quoted a decision by the Lord Chief Justice Goddard: "If, for instance, some admission of some piece of evidence, e.g., a document, had been obtained from a defendant by a trick, no doubt the judge might properly rule it out."

Canada's Chief Justice also quoted another Chief Justice of England, Lord Parker: " . . . in every criminal case a judge has a discretion to disallow evidence, even if in law relevant and therefore admissible, if admissibility would operate unfairly against the defendant. I would add that in considering [unfairness] one would certainly consider whether it had been obtained in an oppressive manner by force or against the wishes of the accused person. That is the general principle."

If this had been the general principle in force during Peter Demeter's trial, Justice Grant might have considered whether the tapes obtained from Peter through Csaba constituted "trickery", or whether they were obtained "against the wishes of the accused person". If this had been the law, the trial judge might have thought that admitting the damaging statements on the tapes would be "a disregard of the principle that a man should not be made to testify against himself". Campbell Grant might also have agreed that instructing a witness, as the police did instruct Csaba Szilagyi, to secretly tape a conversation with a lawyer (and also telling him to mislead this officer of the court, as Csaba Szilagyi was told to mislead Greenspan) could be construed as "bringing the administration of justice into disrepute". Taping telephones, then arbitrarily throwing out most of the evidence as "irrelevant", might have seemed even more objectionable. Here the police, instead of simply collecting evidence, were usurping the functions of Crown, defence, judge, and jury. In addition, Joe Terdik's tapes picked up dozens of conversations with Pomerant or Greenspan after (as well as before) Demeter had been charged with murder. There's little doubt that in the United States this could have been viewed as denial of right to counsel, and sufficient reason to halt the proceedings as an abuse of due process. In *Coplon* versus *U.S.* the Appeal Court for the District of Columbia " . . . flatly held that the prosecution is not entitled to have a representative present to hear the conversations of accused and counsel." The same court also said that " . . . interception of supposedly private telephone consultations between accused and counsel, before and during trial, denies accused his constitutional right to effective assistance to counsel. . . . " (*Caldwell* versus *U.S.*) In Canada, even if the *Wray* decision had gone the other way, it would probably have only meant that Justice Grant in his judicial discretion could, if he so desired, come to the same conclusion. He would not have been obliged to do so and maybe he would not have.

As it was, however, he probably couldn't have, even if he had wanted to. In 1974 *The Queen* versus *Wray* was the best law of Canada, the decision a trial judge was pretty much obliged to follow. If a man was guilty, as John Wray obviously was, he could no longer look to the courts for the protection of his rights. The police forces of the country were practically invited to use deceit, trickery, subterfuge, and perhaps even improper inducements or duress to secure evidence and a conviction. The Supreme Court seemed to say that as long as the evidence went to the heart of the issue — as John Wray's rifle or Peter Demeter's words did — it couldn't be said to operate unfairly against the accused, only unfortunately. How it was gathered seemed to matter no longer. If, in the past, the police had to be careful because *some* judge might disallow their best piece of evidence if he thought they had acquired it in an objectionable way, they could stop worrying. Judges would seem to have this discretion no more.

In the United States, of course, an excess of a different kind appeared to have developed during the same period of time. There judges were pretty nearly obliged to throw out highly relevant evidence if it failed to satisfy the smallest technical protection the accused might enjoy in law. Justice is hardly being served when vicious criminals go unpunished on the most tenuous of grounds.

Part of the problem in both countries seemed to be a limitation placed on judicial discretion. Though it had gone in the direction of super-liberalism in the United States and perhaps super-conservatism in Canada, it was really the same thing. Judges seemed more and more curtailed in their ability to look at the circumstances of each case and decide accordingly. Streamlined efficiency, "uniformity in the application of the law", began to take precedence over the premise of judicial discretion. The wise, common-law acknowledgement of life's diversity, with decisions, like merits, varying from case to case, started giving way to rigid rulings and increasing statutory provisions. Principles taken from the Harvard School of Business began intruding into the administration of justice. The trend went in the direction of confining the art of lawyers and the perceptions of judges and juries. (Indeed, in 1976 Canada's Minister of Justice started flirting with the idea of abolishing juries as "inefficient".) As in many other aspects of life, centralization, uniformity, federalism were the watchwords of the day. *Égalité* was winning another round in its age-old battle with *liberté*. To reduce the risk of equal cases being treated unequally, the risk was taken that unequal cases might receive equal treatment. It was, apparently, not seen that this could lead to new heights of inequality.

Not that it was a simple problem, admitting of simple solutions. Some lawyers (and even judges) actually welcomed the curtailing of judicial discretion, and made it clear that they would like to see an even stronger shift in this direction. Judges, they pointed out, are only human beings, and it is dangerous to rely on their fallible and often idiosyncratic assessments in the administration of justice. Why should anything turn on whether Campbell Grant trusts Joe Pomerant or not, or whether he is irked by Peter Demeter clicking his heels? Why should the judge himself be burdened by the weight of his own views and sympathies? It would be fairer if the rules pertaining to evidence, procedure, and sentencing were rigid, uniform, and unequivocal, and trial judges simply saw to it that they were properly enforced. In this respect the model should be the United States, where the judge is not much more than an umpire between two contesting teams.

But this still left open the question of what the rules should be. In most states south of the 49th parallel much of the evidence against Peter Demeter would almost certainly not have been admitted in a court of law. In Canada the *Wray* decision, which seemed to substitute the *weight* of the evidence for most other criteria of admissibility, in effect decreed that there should be one due process for those regarded as guilty, and another for those viewed as possibly innocent.

While there was no reason for assuming that in the Demeter case Justice Grant would have chosen to exclude any of the evidence had he not been bound by *The Queen* v. *Wray* — after all, Bill Teggart did not use any thumbscrews — the *Wray* decision did not really leave him any choice. It would only be a small overstatement to say that after *Wray*, the police might as well have saved themselves the time, trouble, and expense of an investigation and gone straight to the torture chamber. (Of course the *Wray* decision did not go that far, but it was nevertheless the direction in which it seemed to be heading. The principle, quoted with approval by Justice Martland, was that any evidence relevant to the matters in issue is admissible, *and the court is not concerned with how the evidence was obtained*.) There might have been no problem with constructing such an inflexible net, as long as it was catching only the guilty, which John Wray undoubtedly was. No public outcry could be expected over the retrial and conviction of someone who had shot a man in broad daylight for fifty-five dollars. It is not a Canadian tradition to crusade for the rights of Escobedos and Mirandas. If they are tricked, taped, interfered with in their right to counsel, or given less than adequate time to answer new charges brought against them, nobody cares all that much. They are obviously guilty anyway. Unpleasant people have few champions. Railroading guilty men does not seem as bad somehow as railroading the innocent.

But it is.

And the same liberties taken with due process that snare the guilty can, and one day will, snare the innocent.

And Peter Demeter's guilt already seemed a shade, or more than a shade, less obvious than John Wray's.

In order to convict a person on circumstantial evidence alone (as Peter was, unless one construed his own words on tape as direct evidence, a confession, which the trial judge did not), the evidence against him must not only be consistent with his guilt, but inconsistent with any other rational explanation. Was there no other rational explanation for the sequence of events that led to Christine Demeter's body being found in the darkened garage on 1437 Dundas Crescent on July 18?

Christine Demeter, as John Greenwood had Csaba Szilagyi point out on the witness stand, *was* dead. To say that she might have died of an accident or at the hands of a sex maniac seemed frivolous and unsupported or contradicted by the evidence. But could Christine, in fact, have been a victim of her own plot against her husband? Bizarre and distasteful though the suggestion was, it did become the main defence theory in the end. It was supported by part of Stark's evidence and by the evidence of Dinardo, whatever one might have thought about the reliability of either. Peter Demeter's name, found on a piece of paper in Eper's apartment, was capable of supporting it, at least in the continuing absence of any evidence connecting Eper with Demeter. Christine's remark — "It would be nice to knock him off and get his money" — might also lend the theory some slender support. Motive, in so far as it existed on Peter's part, existed equally on Christine's: a bad marriage cuts both ways, and so does a million-dollar life insurance. The name "Jimmy Or(r)", which Stark claimed not to know, and which therefore Peter couldn't have known either, *was* found in Christine's notebook. So was the name "Samson", referring to no known person, but which was strongly descriptive of The Duck's friend Joe Dinardo. Finally, what was known of Christine's earlier lives and loves (including at least one affair during her marriage to Peter) did not indicate such loyalty and high moral standards as to place her completely above the suspicion that she might involve herself in a conspiracy against Peter's life. The jump between extra-marital affairs and murder is, of course, a very long one, but courts have traditionally regarded such evidence as relevant enough to meet the test of admissibility, which is why Justice Grant permitted Van Berkel's evidence to be placed before the jury. In fact, had Peter been found dead, this combined evidence might have been enough to commit Christine to trial, though it very likely would have ended in her acquittal, and rightly so. But what about the rest of the evidence?

Whatever there was seemed to point to Peter, not Christine, as the guilty party. There was Szilagyi's story. There was Stark's. There were the Links and the Fancsiks. (Maria Visnyiczky and "Foxy" Jones only corroborated that a plot existed, but could not indicate whose plot it might have been.) There was also Flower the Snitch, dubious as his role seemed to be. But even if the Flower lied and everyone else told only part of the truth, there were still the tapes, with Peter's own incredibly suspicious statements. Was there a rational explanation with which all this evidence could have been consistent other than Demeter's guilt?

After the jury had brought in the verdict, Justice Grant asked the defendant if he wished to make any statement before sentence was passed. Though Peter had been warned by all his lawyers that he should say nothing when this question was asked — in fact, the normally quiet and cool Eddie Greenspan screamed at him loudly enough to be overheard in the corridors — when the moment came, Peter said in a voice of apparent surprise: "Oh, am I allowed to say something?" and then he did. In ten rambling, emotional minutes he absolved the jury from all blame for his conviction. He reassured them that they need not have any second thoughts because they could not have arrived at any other conclusion on the basis of what they had heard in court. But, Peter said, they hadn't heard everything. Then he half-stated, half-intimated that he had instructed his lawyers not to reveal, out of respect for Christine's memory, the plot in which she had been engaged with Szilagyi, Eper, and a certain Dr. Bende, now dead, to have Peter murdered. Thinking he'd be acquitted anyway, Peter implied, he did not wish this to be known about his wife.

Now, of course, it seemed too late, both Eper and Dr. Bende being dead and Szilagyi — in Peter's words — "living off the avails of prosecution" with a valid Austrian passport in his pocket. This, said Peter, was what Christine's famous secret visit to the Szilagyi apartment was all about, on the day before her death. She was informing Csaba on that Tuesday that she wanted to pull out of the whole thing, that " . . . she is not able to go through with the plans and she wants to settle everything, and do everything in her power to avoid that I leave her." Then, continued Peter, when Eper was told " . . . she is going to renege, and she wants to get her money back . . . " he killed her. She was going to expose him as a fugitive unless he paid her money back, and so he killed her. The jury would read in the newspapers, said Peter — neatly revealing the confession reported by Dinardo that Justice Grant had ruled inadmissible — that Eper had "barred" her. He had learned all this from Dr. Charles Bende, Peter said, before their one-time friend died.

Of course none of this grotesque, embarrassing outburst dispelled any of the existing evidence against Peter, nor did it support any that might have existed against Christine. But it did raise the possibility of a game for armchair-detectives.

All evidence against Peter seemed to point only to old, intended, attempted, unsuccessful plots. Much of it appeared quite contradictory. Could there be any one hypothesis resolving the conflicts and self-contradictions in the evidence of all the witnesses, as well as in some of the material evidence? A single thesis that might be in line with the known personalities of the characters, and might introduce some logic to their otherwise inexplicable statements and behaviour?

Possibly, yes. Such a theory would make Peter innocent of murder, though it would make both Peter and Christine guilty of conspiracy. If it were postulated that both husband and wife had been plotting against each other's life, many (if not all) of the apparent contradictions could be cleared up. It would explain the inconsistencies in the testimony of all key witnesses. It would make the case even more bizarre perhaps, but slightly less inexplicable. Needless to say, such a theory would be purely speculative. Still, it would account for more of the evidence than either the prosecution's or the defence's theories at the trial.

The key to this hypothesis would be held by the special dynamics between Csaba and Peter that might have developed at a very early stage of their relationship. This bond might have been a "philosophy", elevating the powers of merciless, cold intellect into some position of superiority. This somewhat romantic, semi-Nietzschean idea might have suggested to a couple of poor, prospectless, déclassé boys in confused, post-war Europe that in this hard, unfair world a special bond between two clever, ruthless friends, owing loyalty to nothing but each other and the idea of success, could overcome all obstacles. Injustices had been perpetrated against both; all the old standards had disappeared; and the only thing that seemed real was the survival of the fittest. This could have been understood between Csabaschek and Papitschek without having to be spelled out.

It might even have appeared to them that on the other side of the Atlantic, in the "Wild West" of popular European imagination, the ordinary rules didn't apply anyway. On that faraway, unreal continent of cowboys, Indians, and Chicago gangsters there would be no holds barred. Though this might well sound ridiculous to North Americans, to a generation of European youths raised on the cheapest clichés of the cinema and pulp literature (and Peter had always been very fond of both) our part of the world had always appeared romantically lawless. This can be better understood by remembering how the Balkans and the world of the Orient Express might seem to simpler-minded North Americans. It is the other side of the same coin.

Now Peter had always seemed to be something of a misogynist. His attitude towards women had been ambivalent, his experiences often unhappy. Like many people, he had a vulnerable ego. Like some, he could hold a grudge for a long time. No doubt he was attracted to Christine because of her striking looks, but women of striking looks often draw men like flies. Some men can cope with the competition better than others. Right after his humiliation by Marina in 1966, Peter might not have been able to cope very well. When Christine did whatever she did with the handsome soccer player in the summer of '67 in Canada, Peter might have started toying with the idea of revenge. Some men, of course, would have contented themselves by kicking her out, perhaps after having slapped her around a bit.

For Peter, however, this might not have been enough to assuage his hurt and humiliation. Female infidelity is not viewed quite as casually in some cultures as in North America. Though very, very few Hungarians would actually kill their unfaithful wives or lovers — and some native Canadians might — the statistical tendency to take such things seriously is greater in Peter's part of the world. So is a tendency to act with slow, cruel deliberation rather than impulsively and on the spot. (In his classic take-off on *Cavalleria Rusticana*, Hungarian style, the author Karinthy describes two enemies sitting side by side on a bench wordlessly smoking their pipes all day, until one says, "Well, then," and thrusts his knife to the hilt into the other's stomach.) Taking one's time in extracting vengeance, while not an exclusively Hungarian trait, has been nurtured in the character of a nation playing the underdog for so many centuries. Success for a small, powerless people could not be hoped for without some cunning, stealth, and patience.

In any case, the idea need not have been fully formed in Peter's mind when he started his vague conversations with Csaba in the first year of his marriage in 1968. But there was this woman who had betrayed and humiliated him, who seemed to want him only for her own ends. Was it going to be like this forever: he earning, she spending, *and* playing around with other men? It wasn't the question of Marina or a million dollars, but getting his own back on a world that had bombed, confined, and cheated him since the age of twelve. At the same time he was so much smarter than this world, so much more cautious and patient. He could bide his time. He could even derive some benefit from it: spouses *could* eventually be insured for large amounts of money. Peter's own father had been an insurance executive, he knew all about these things.

Csabaschek, for his part, might have felt much the same way about the world that had reduced his class and family in a similar way. In any case, it was just talk, an exciting, romantic idea with which two close friends could toy. Feeding and reinforcing the notion in Peter's mind also had some practical advantages for Csaba (later he would call them "fringe benefits" on the witness stand), such as being brought out to Canada by his better-to-do friend. But mainly it was such a clever, superior concept. Together they could devise a gradual, cool, perfect murder.

The tapes between Peter and Csaba, when read in context, make it abundantly clear that some such *folie à deux* must have existed between them; it would seem sheer frivolous obstinacy to deny it. "Remember we talked at the Park Plaza, the subject there was the accident . . . " said Csaba to Peter in their taped conversation on August 16. "Don't say what we talked about, just that we met," replied Peter. But even if the tapes failed to prove it, a statement Peter made to a certain Constable Shaw (which the prosecution either forgot or chose not to rely on), suggesting that *the killer must have dropped the murder weapon off the Burlington Skyway*, would. Csaba stated in court that their so-called Mexican plot called for getting rid of the rifle by throwing it off the Burlington Skyway. The chances that both Csaba and Peter would, independently of one another, invent the Burlington Skyway of all places in the immensity of southern Ontario as the best spot to get rid of a murder weapon would be far too small to credit. The two of them must have talked about it.

Now, for the purpose of the theory under discussion, it's immaterial how serious Csaba might have been in his intent to help kill Christine, or indeed how serious Peter himself might have been in the beginning. It would make no difference if Csaba's word were accepted that he was always the passive, discouraging listener, or even the man with the mission of saving Christine. The question is, did he ever *tell* Christine about it?

Csaba testified that he didn't, ever, not even the day before Christine's death, when she came to visit at the apartment he shared with Gigi. He had said nothing, even though, on his evidence, on the previous day Peter had requested him to help set Christine up to be killed, then bawled him out when Csaba failed to do so. This, of course, is the hardest part to credit in Csaba's entire testimony.

There are many reasons to suspect that Christine knew her life was in danger. There was her letter, in May 1973, to her parents: " . . . sometimes I have this feeling I'm not going to live for long." There were her statements to Mrs. Tennant and Judy Markovich. "They're going to get rid of me, you'll see," she had sobbed while Peter was in Montreal with Marina. All this, moreover, while Csaba was right there in the house on Dundas Crescent, spending his first nights with Gigi. For Csaba to have said nothing to the distraught Christine even under those circumstances would have been unlikely for any man, let alone a man with a mission. In fact, it was far more likely that Christine could be so specific about her fears to Judy Markovich only because Csaba did say something.

When someone believes her life to be in danger, there are three logical things she can do about it. One is to pack up and go away. Christine didn't do that. The second is to convince herself that the whole thing is ridiculous and dismiss it from her mind. Christine certainly didn't dismiss it, according to her letters and statements. The third is to take some counter-action of her own. Did Christine choose this latter course?

There is little doubt that Szilagyi had eventually come to dislike his dominant, bountiful, overbearing friend Peter; the question is when? And what did *he* do about it? Did he in fact have a greater affection for Christine than he would later admit? Did they have an affair? (According to Bill Teggart, this was the only point on which the results of Csaba's lie detector test were a bit ambivalent.) Did he tell her that Peter was hardly worthy of her fidelity and love? And did he tell her why?

There are no answers to these questions, of course, but it's possible to look at the evidence. Frightened as he was of the authorities, eager to save his own skin as he might have been, Ferenc Stark stuck all along to his story about Christine wanting a rifle and an alibi for Csaba. It would have been quite possible for the ex-legionary, who was no doubt fond of dropping the odd hint about his military exploits in Indochina in the right company, to have been approached separately by both the wife and the husband. In this case he needn't have lied under oath: it would be a simple case of both his stories being true. It could be true that he had rejected Christine's offer without ever telling Peter about it until they met beside the leaking toilet on Russell Hill Road. But it is equally possible that he merrily went along conspiring with both, as long as both seemed to be a source of some money for him. In this event The Duck might have been sent to Dawes Road by Stark on Peter's behalf, but with Christine's full knowledge. (Later a very interesting bit of evidence would come to light which, if true, would tend to support this:

apparently the honest Duck did not find all the money he had counted on in his roll of plans. Of course Peter might have felt like shortchanging his hit-man, but then again it might have appealed to Christine's sense of humour to expropriate a third or so of her own blood-money. Her husband was a notorious tightwad, and this would beat scrounging for old receipts on the floors of supermarkets.) This could also explain the mystery of how "Jimmy Or" (spelled with one "r" — very much in line with Christine's native German orthography) got into Mrs. Demeter's notebook, even though Stark didn't know this alias of Kacsa himself.

Of course Stark, no matter how much he double-crossed the scheming Demeters, would not have bargained on being double-crossed himself. As for Kacsa, while ripping off Peter would be pretty safe (after all, he could hardly go to the police and, not being a mobster, would not be likely to send thugs after him), ripping off Stark was a different matter. This could well have made The Duck waddle off to Hungary with Stark and possibly even Peter in mad pursuit. In that case the Links and the Fancsiks could have been telling the truth as well when they spoke of Peter looking for Kacsa. In spite of the much vaunted smartness of his convoluted mind, Peter was a bit of an amateur in these matters and might have thrown caution to the winds when chasing after his hard-earned cash, for which he had received no value. But what would Csaba do during this merry-go-round?

On his own evidence, supported by bits and pieces on the tapes, Csaba was in touch with Peter and might well have continued being apprised of his plans and frustrations. If — and that of course is pure conjecture, supported by nothing but Peter's outburst in the courtroom, and one statement by another person that did not come to light until later — if Csaba played the *agent provocateur*, he could have used Christine's emotional state during Peter's fling with Marina in Montreal to involve her in a counter-plot of a more realistic kind. Csaba, unlike the highly-strung, impressionable Christine, was very cool and intelligent. (That Szilagyi could play a double role very capably was shown by his body-pack conversations with Peter and Eddie Greenspan: Detective Joe Terdik often commented with approbation on the quality of Csaba's nerve and coolness during the intelligence operation.) At any rate, Christine seems to have undergone a very remarkable change after Peter's return.

Gone were the scenes, the recriminations, the fights. Everybody commented on how well the couple appeared to get along in the last six weeks of Christine's life. Though Christine had never been as hurtful and caustic as Peter, in the past she too had been capable of disparaging remarks (such as saying when she had received her first Mercedes from her husband: "Too bad it's not a Ferrari") and was not reticent in making her feelings and desires known in public. It's quite possible, of course, that she became all sweetness and light solely because of marriage counsellor Dr. Steven Demeter's good advice, but she might also have had another reason. It was a fact, for instance, that after her one interview with divorce lawyer Biderman in June 1973, she sought no further legal advice. Was she possibly receiving advice of a different kind?

She might have been, and she might have died because of it, if Dinardo's evidence was to be believed. The jury evidently didn't believe it, and that was no surprise: the story did sound utterly incredible. Yet so did many of the other stories, including Szilagyi's, that *were* believed at the trial. Dinardo would be easier to dismiss if it weren't for the fact that he would not have been in the witness stand at all if the police hadn't pressured him into testifying through his lawyer. Whether Peter had him paid or coached somehow, the fact is that he did not come forward by himself. According to Arthur Maloney, Dinardo seemed very reluctant even when he first approached him. Though Greenwood accused Dinardo of perjury in open court (from which the Canada Evidence Act wouldn't protect him), no moves were later made to charge him with this grave offence. In fact, there is a tiny chance that he could have been telling something like the truth.

But if he did, if Christine had indeed decided that killing spouses was a game at which two could play, if she had got into some conspiracy with Szilagyi and Eper, how could that ever explain Peter's own words on the tapes? After all, his conversation implied more than just old plots; no matter how obliquely, he also hinted to Csaba that he *knew* how Christine was actually killed. How could that possibly mesh with the theory that Christine died of her own plot?

Tenuous as it is, there would be one answer. The Link-Fancsik evidence indicated that Peter wasn't giving up on The Duck, that he wanted to "get his money back or the job done". He was obviously pressing Stark as well. Whether or not Stark was really trying to get Kacsa — or anyone else — to "finish the job", he might well have told Peter that he was. After all, he would prefer to keep Peter off his back.

He might even have suggested to him to sit tight; he, Stark, was looking after the deal, and Peter would get his money's worth one day soon. Peter liked having all his conversations in a convoluted, conspiratorial fashion, and who knows how he might have interpreted the oblique, whispery half-tones in which Stark and he would have communicated. When finally he did find Christine dead on the floor of the garage, he might have simply assumed that it was his own doing.

If this sounds very far-fetched, there is some evidence for it in the tapes themselves. Throughout the conversations, Peter repeatedly indicated to Csaba that he'd give anything to know exactly what happened. It was *such* a puzzle to him, he told Csaba, adding that Csaba knew, of course, what was and what wasn't a puzzle. The intimation throughout seemed to be that Peter knew what happened in a general kind of way, but the whole thing was nevertheless a big surprise to him, and there was nobody he could ask to explain it. "Is that man an idiot or what?" asked Csaba, and Peter replied: "Look, this, in short, Csaba, if I had an answer to this today I wouldn't give my left arm, I'd give up my right arm. Can't you understand?" The Crown urged the jury to interpret this and similar remarks to mean that Peter was furious that the fake accident he had bought turned out to be an obvious murder. Of course, it could have meant no more than that. But it could also have indicated that Peter was so removed from the details of what he assumed to be his plot that he simply accepted that what had happened to Christine was somehow the result of his own conspiracy.

Knowing this, Csaba could count on Peter's absolving him of all involvement in Christine's death, which of course Peter did, repeatedly, right on the tapes. (Csaba would, of course, have been technically innocent in any case, if Dinardo's story was right.) In this case, by volunteering to act for the police as an *agent provocateur* Szilagyi could kill two birds with one stone: establish his own innocence and Peter's guilt. He could also prove that he was, in fact, smarter than his pompous, overbearing, one-time friend.

There was one final piece in the evidence that could support the double-conspiracy theory. Szilagyi testified that on Tuesday, July 17, the day before her death, Christine paid a brief visit to the apartment he shared with Gigi. Christine came, said Csaba, to discuss something with Gigi, not with him. Gigi, however, couldn't recall this visit. Being visited by the victim of a murder the day before her death is not something most people would forget. Christine kept the visit confidential from her house guests: neither Sybille Brewer nor Viveca seemed to know anything about it. It is not all that far-fetched to suggest that the object of her visit might have been Csaba himself. It could be conjectured that he admitted the visit on the witness stand only because he had no way of knowing whether someone had seen Christine, or whether she had mentioned to someone that she was going to drop in at the Szilagyis'. But, he said, the visit was for Gigi, not for him. Gigi didn't remember the visit. What could Christine have been visiting Szilagyi for that he did not wish to talk about in court?

In his post-conviction speech Peter claimed that Christine went to see Csaba to tell him she no longer wanted her husband killed. The next evening she was killed herself. Possible?

Certainly not in the way that Peter would have wanted the jury to believe it: his own words on tape make it clear that Christine's death did not come as a total surprise to him, as it would have, had it been purely the result of a plot between Christine, Csaba, and maybe Eper. To maintain this line of defence in face of the tapes seemed merely stubborn, unless the defence claimed that Peter, though entirely innocent, for some pathological reason wanted his friend Csaba to think that he wasn't. (Even as a remote possibility, this could only be entertained if Peter admitted that he and Csaba had discussed murdering Christine over the years as some kind of a sick game.) But the evidence need not be twisted at all to support the theory that Csaba used his knowledge of Peter's plot to kill his wife to involve Christine in a counter-plot that somehow went wrong in the end. Such a theory would, in fact, account for all the evidence — including most of Csaba's own — except for the story told by the redoubtable Mr. X, which later events would in any case prove to be an almost certain lie.

While this reading of the evidence would not be remotely sufficient to accuse Christine and Szilagyi of conspiracy in a court of law, it might raise a not altogether unreasonable doubt about Peter's guilt of the actual murder. It would, of course, still support a charge of conspiracy to cause his wife's death, and morally it might make little difference whether she died as a result of Peter's or her own plot. It would, however, make a legal difference. Though the penalty for conspiracy could be just as severe as the penalty for non-capital murder, a life-sentence is not mandatory. Convicted of this lesser charge, Peter could have been free on parole after five to seven years.

This would have been the tack Leo "Tiger" McGuigan would have taken had he been defending Demeter. "If I had been defending the case," remarked the Assistant Crown afterwards, "I would have said: Yes, I'm a rotten bugger and I talked to Szilagyi about it, but ladies and gentlemen it was my good fortune to come home on the night of July 18 and find her dead. I intended to kill her. I wanted her dead, but I didn't do it."

There was only one thing that this approach would have required: Peter's agreement. There is no indication that Peter would have agreed. As far as he was concerned, he was completely, totally innocent — and convicted only because of the trial judge's numerous errors in law.

Which was the basis on which the defence launched its appeal against Peter Demeter's conviction to the Court of Appeal for the Province of Ontario.

28. Brothers on the Bench

It was an old, close community to which Peter Demeter would have to raise his voice in appeal.

The town of Port Elgin nestles snugly on the eastern shore of Lake Huron, just at the foot of the Bruce Peninsula. In pioneer days Port Elgin did a flourishing business in beer and buckshot, as hardier ancestors, intent on land and liberty, stopped off for supplies before heading into virgin forest and Indian territory. Today the great-grandsons of Scottish, British, and German forefathers keep their summer homes in Port Elgin. The neat stone or clapboard homes line unpaved meandering streets filled with children and dogs. In one such home, directly overlooking the lake and with a confused clutter of wooden stairs inching perilously down to the beach below, the Honourable Justice Campbell Grant and Mrs. Grant pass their summers. Set back from the road and fronted with tall trees of oak and maple, the house is barely visible to outsiders. "But if you can't find it," confided Justice Grant to a first-time visitor, "just ask anyone in town where Campbell Grant lives. They'll help you."

Up past the marina and just a mile or so along the shore road in Southampton is the summer home of Justice Grant's good friend and brother judge, Ontario Chief Justice (as he then was) George Arthur Gale. Along the road a little farther, towards the Saugeen Golf and Country Club, as he ambles in that direction for a lunch of fresh whitefish, Justice Campbell Grant will wave to summer neighbour John Josiah Robinette, the prestigious Ontario lawyer, founding member of the Advocates Society and influential bencher of the Canadian Bar Association and the Law Society of Upper Canada.

This is Bruce County, part of the great triangle of Western Ontario that is bounded, roughly, by the three cities of Niagara Falls, London, and, at its northern point, Owen Sound. In between are the counties whose names reflect the settlers of more than a hundred years ago: Elgin, Grey, Bruce, Simcoe. From this rich farmland that gave substance to the ambitions of Upper Canada came the men who moulded the law and ritual of justice in Ontario.

They were Englishmen at first, distinguished patriots bent on preserving a little bit of England in the rough-hewn land of the New World. King George III sent them abroad to ensure that in Upper Canada, at least, British jurisprudence would prevail. If Lower Canada had to be sacrificed to the rigid abominations of the Napoleonic code, well, that was the lookout of the French Canadians. In 1792 Colonel John Graves Simcoe, first Lieutenant-Governor of Canada and personal emissary of His Majesty, King of Great Britain, France, and Ireland, opened the Parliament of Upper Canada with a clarion call:

"This province is singularly blessed," intoned Simcoe, "not with a mutilated constitution, but with a constitution which has stood the test of experience and is the very image and transcript of that of Great Britain."

And, by God, Simcoe and his successors were determined to keep it that way. The administration of justice in Canada took on a decidedly Inner Temple air. The court calendar was divided into Easter, Trinity, Hilary, and Michaelmas terms. The Law Society of Upper Canada was formed with the proposition that, as in England, there be a separation between the professions of Barrister and Solicitor. But the parliament at Niagara was a long way from Westminster, and a new breed of men were being shaped by the rigours and needs of a country that could fit Great Britain into its vest pocket but lacked, in those early years, enough men and women to populate even the boroughs of London.

So, ritual had to be modified in favour of pragmatism. The snobbish nicety of separating barrister and solicitor scarcely made sense when all of Upper Canada had less than half a dozen lawyers. Gradually the system evolved. The impulse and much of the letter of British law was retained, together with the special mystique and obligation conferred on members of the Bar. The near-divine status of the judiciary was reinforced by avoiding the vulgarities of the American election system in favour of discreet appointments quietly made by the government. The decorum of the judiciary was maintained by an intricate web of courtesies beginning with the habitual inclination of lawyers' heads and the mumblings of "M'Lord" whenever a Judge appeared on the horizon. Professional associations, luncheon clubs, and the self-regulation of members of the Bar by their own elected Benchers all combined to create a tightly woven group of men related by politics, temperament, and a strong sense of *noblesse oblige*. By the middle of the nineteenth century, as Englishmen were augmented by the Scots and then the Irish, the list of Judges in Upper Canada was spotted with names that would reappear on the Bench right through to the 1970s — Cartwright, Jessup, Kerr, Osler, Evans, Grant, Campbell. But this was a new kind of élite, some members still with calluses on their hands from felling trees or riding old farm horses across the snow to the nearest school. The pomp and circumstance, the stiff wigs of the British courtroom, would sit awkwardly on these heads. The frills were reduced to sensible Canadian proportions.

They named the clubhouse after the Honourable William Osgoode, the first Chief Justice of Canada. When it was built in 1829, complete with Corinthian columns and Doric arches, it was necessary to install fences around it with iron gates large enough to let (slim) members of the Bar past, and narrow enough to discourage the cows that were pastured near by. Today Osgoode Hall, home of the Ontario High Courts and the Law Society of Upper Canada, faces the 750 bedrooms of downtown Toronto's new Sheraton Centre; the eighth floor of the hotel conveniently houses the plush sports facilities of the Cambridge Club, which enables lawyers to nip across the road during court recess for a quick game of squash before lunch. Tucked away in the west wing of Osgoode Hall, behind electrically operated and camera-monitored doors, are the chambers of the Supreme Court Judges. Here, in one corner, is their dining room. Until three years ago a head table was reserved for the judiciary in the main eating room of the Law Society, but now they dine in private splendour with one another, inaccessible at lunch time even to their secretaries.

An underground tunnel connects the chambers with the new courthouse. In the maze of backroom corridors, guarded and scrutinized by security men, courtroom gossip flows within the magic circle of electronic surveillance systems and careful insulations of privilege. Crown attorneys, clerks, and recording secretaries move freely along these halls, relaying pertinent information to the members of the Bench and occasionally easing a trying morning in court with a little light banter for His Lordship. This is home for both the Supreme Court of Ontario (of which Justice Campbell Grant was a senior member) and the Ontario Court of Appeal. In a purely legal sense the trial and appellate courts function quite separately, each with its own Chief Justice and slate of judges. On a personal level, trial and appeal court judges maintain understandably close contact, many of the appeal court members having been at one time in the trial division and often shared a passing opinion on counsels and cases.

It would be a particularly distinguished court that would hear the appeal of Peter Demeter. Chief Justice George Arthur Gale himself, it was whispered in the Great Library of the Law Society of Upper Canada, had postponed the date of the appeal to make absolutely certain that he would be available for it. "I wouldn't miss this one for anything," he was quoted as saying. The Demeter case might be the last major trial of Gale's good friend Campbell Grant — now that Grant was approaching the supernumerary age of seventy — and, as everyone knew, it had been a particularly long and arduous affair for Campbell. Of course, his Lordship Chief Justice Gale would not dream of bending the law just so his neighbour could retire in a blaze of glory, but he would be certain to put any lawyer through his paces before overturning the decision of the man with whom Gale had sat on trial court for ten years and shared many a pleasant meal in the warm ambience of the University Club, to which they both belonged. Fellow University Club member Justice Arthur R. Jessup would be the second member of the Appeal Court. A man of considerable personal courage and a soldier of distinction, he had served in Europe in the Canadian army, winning the Croix de Guerre from the French, and the Order of Leopold II from the Belgians. An active Anglican, like Chief Justice George Gale, he shared with Gale and Campbell Grant the easy hobbies of summer people with access to boats, clubs, and stocked wildlife preserves. There was nothing Jessup liked better than relaxing on the golf course or wading hip-deep into good fishing streams. Justice Gregory Thomas Evans, the third member of the Appeal Court, had come down from the northern Ontario town of Timmins to become class president of Osgoode Hall and secretary of the Roman Catholic Newman Club. By the time he was first elected to the Council of the Canadian Bar Association (on which Chief Justice George Gale also served), he had twenty-five murder trials behind him and a distinguished record of acquittals. Still, his record paled beside that of the eminent Justice Goldwin Arthur Martin, the fourth member of the Appeal Court, and, in his day, one of the most respected advocates in Canada. In the more than sixty murder cases he had defended, G. Arthur Martin had *never* had a client convicted of that charge. His rise in the legal establishment was punctuated by a series of honours: gold medallist at Osgoode Hall; K.C. less than eight years later; Treasurer of the Law Society of Upper Canada and, like Gale and Evans, a member of that decidedly select group, the Council of the Canadian Bar Association, which informally advises the federal Minister of Justice on all judicial appointments. So esteemed and popular indeed was the bachelor Justice Martin that on the thirty-sixth anniversary of his call to the Bar, in June 1974, some fifty leading members of the Bar and judiciary attended a testimonial dinner for him thrown at Toronto's Royal York Hotel by his longtime friend Ontario Ombudsman Arthur Maloney, with guests including the Chief Justice of Canada, Bora Laskin, and Martin's close associate, Ontario Chief Justice George A. Gale.

He had been labelled a progressive throughout his many years at the Bar, where he consistently fought for the abolition of capital punishment, the establishment of legal aid in Ontario, and the Bail Reform Act. And the words of then defence attorney G. A. Martin to a gathering of Osgoode Hall law students might have given appellant Peter Demeter some comfort: "If we only defend those we love," said Martin, "who defends the unloved? No matter how obnoxious a client may be, he has the right to a defence by a capable advocate." (Perhaps if Peter had remembered his history lessons at the Cistercian Gymnasium, he might also have called to mind that an office puts a stamp on a man much more readily than a man puts his stamp on an office. By the time G. Arthur Martin donned his judicial robes he ran a ship so conservative that his staff would refuse to give out as much as his printed biography to journalists. There were no other members of the Bench who would carry judicial reserve to such an extent.)

The last member of the five-man Court of Appeal which would hear *Regina* v. *Peter Demeter* was Justice Lloyd William Houlden, a kindly faced, grey-haired man who established in his courts a sympathetic air as much by his habit of leaning forward to catch counsel's every last word as by the questions he occasionally asked. Though primarily a bankruptcy expert, he had dramatically established his concern with due process in a controversial decision some years earlier, which had forced the Thunder Bay Police Commission to reinstate twenty-one demoted officers. Wrote Justice Houlden: "The Commission had deprived the men of their ranks without a hearing in a manner that leaves much to be desired." Now the most junior member on the Demeter appeal court, at fifty-three years of age Justice Houlden had been on the appellate bench for only nine months and had little experience in hearing criminal cases. Observers concluded, perhaps unfairly, that he would be strongly guided by the two criminal law heavyweights seated beside him: Chief Justice George Alexander Gale and Justice G. Arthur Martin. The defence, noting the make-up of the appeal court and remembering Martin's concern with ensuring due process and the civil liberties of all defendants, had pinned much of their hopes on him.

If the five men on the appeal court shared anything apart from their solid Anglo-Canadian roots, distinguished careers at the Bar, and club memberships, it was a confidence in the openness and equality of the system of justice at whose pinnacle they now presided. They would have noted that back in 1956 Justice Abraham Lieff was appointed to the Supreme Court of Ontario, the first Jew on the High Bench in its two-hundred-year history, and in Justice Grant's words "a capital fellow, very well-liked". On the other hand, had they occasion to read a 1975 doctoral thesis on the recruitment of judges in Ontario, they might have noted that there seemed to be over-representation of judicial appointments among lawyers with political connections and, most especially, those holding positions as Benchers. Still, they might have replied, accurately, that Benchers were elected, which meant that the office was a vote of confidence by their peers.

Nevertheless, the election of Benchers, long a contentious issue, was viewed by some as little more than a self-perpetuating oligarchy of the WASP Establishment. Since would-be Benchers are not allowed to indulge in any crass campaigning for the office, members of Establishment firms clearly have the advantage when they are proposed for office; and members of Establishment firms tend, not surprisingly, to be WASP themselves. Independent lawyers arouse shock waves in the legal community when, on rare occasions, they make a "fuss" about election procedures. The rarity of "ethnic" Canadians on the Ontario High Bench is never more forcefully demonstrated than by the waves of self-congratulation that sweep the marble corridors of Osgoode Hall whenever such an appointment is made.

Of course, this in no way precludes fairness and justice from the High Courts of Ontario as indeed quotas of representative "ethnic" appointments might, should excellence give way to the reverse injustice of "affirmative action". But the court's homogeneity does reinforce a system of values and a shared belief in a traditional way of life. Like their British forefathers, the WASP members of the Ontario High Court might view "foreigners" as people to be treated justly and courteously, but whose drinking water should always be boiled before being ingested. For a defendant who wished to rely on an inside track of natural sympathy in addition to the merits of his case and the legal skills of his lawyer, the logical route should have been to hire a defence counsel at home in the golf-links-and-roast-beef territory of Upper Canada.

At twenty-seven years of age John David Watt was doing very nicely in his legal career. Handling the Demeter appeal for the Crown was a prestigious assignment, although one that would involve a great deal of work. Still, he assumed that the retroactivity of the wiretap legislation would be a major point in the defence argument, and it just so happened that Watt had already argued — and won — a not dissimilar point in an earlier appeal held in front of Justices Martin, Jessup, and Houlden.

Almost all of Watt's legal career had been spent in the Ontario Court of Appeal. In fact, he had only argued two cases at trial before he was seconded into appeal work. He felt at home in the bright, neon-lit halls of the New City Courthouse, riding up the escalators along with the gawking law students and worried wives waiting to see if their loved ones would get off. It was curious, Watt reflected, how he had ended up specializing in criminal appeals. At law school he had wanted to practise corporate law and make a lot of money, but corporate law classes were scheduled on Fridays and Mondays, and Watt had other commitments. Hockey was his first course, and during his law school years he commuted every weekend from Queen's University in Kingston to cities between Houston and Halifax to play pro hockey in the Central League. He couldn't afford to tie himself up with classes on a Friday or a Monday in case he got snowed in and missed a game, and so in the end he found himself specializing in criminal law, which fitted around his hockey timetable much better. He still played amateur hockey in between appeals, and if there was one thing the Supreme Court Justices shared besides a dining room and sense of decorum, it was an overwhelming interest in Canada's national sport. It was a safe bet that should David Watt wander down the long corridors behind the courtrooms, one or another of His Lordships would corner him on a point of law and continue on the finer aspects of body-checking or stick-handling. After the last Canada-Russia hockey series — which he had watched from the press box — David scarcely had a moment to himself. It seemed that every member of the Bench wanted to get down to serious talk in Chambers about exactly what had happened on the Benches of Team Canada.

Still, he didn't begrudge the time spent chatting in Chambers. These were men of his own kind, much like his own family, three generations Canadian-born out of Edinburgh. Shipbuilding was the family business, and up in Owen Sound where David went to high school — at the foot of the Bruce Peninsula directly across from Port Elgin — his father's firm had turned out some of the best ferry boats Canada ever made. In fact, for four years while he was still at school, David had spent his summers as mate aboard the S.S. *Norisle* on the Tobermory–South Bay ferry service. He knew those waters and that land of spruce and pine almost as well as he knew the contours of a hockey rink or the gentlemanly procedures of the High Court of Ontario.

There was never any doubt about who would handle the appeal for the defence. At the law firm of Pomerant, Pomerant, and Greenspan the technical virtuosity necessary for excellence in the Court of Appeal belonged to Edward L. Greenspan. The choice was further reinforced by the feelings existing between Peter Demeter and Joe Pomerant, which by now, to put it generously, were strained.

Eddie Greenspan was not to the legal manor born but he was born to the legal manner. His father had studied to be a lawyer himself, but when his own father suffered a heart attack, the luxury of further schooling was out of the question. Instead he took over the family scrap metal business and passed his ambition and love of the law on to his son. From the moment Eddie Greenspan managed his first declarative sentence his intention never wavered: he would be a criminal lawyer.

Though the legal profession in Canada is wide open to Jews — indeed the Chief Justice of Canada, the Dean of the University of Toronto Law School, and the Dean of Osgoode Hall are Jewish — the profession is most certainly not *run* by Jews. The distinction is subtle but important. Academic achievement and excellence in jurisprudence are rewarded with positions of honour but not influence. The Chief Justice has one vote on the court like everyone else. The Dean of a Law School does not regulate the profession. Still, without consciously trying, Greenspan had begun to work his way up the ladder of the Legal Establishment. His climb was motivated by a genuine and consuming fascination with the law rather than any social ambitions. Very soon he was assistant editor of *Canadian Criminal Cases*, a weekly summary of selected cases of special legal interest. This gave him a small position of patronage. He had some say in which cases (which points of law, which judges, and which lawyers) should be singled out from dozens each week as noteworthy. His Editor-in-Chief was Horace A. Krever, a figure of significance in the legal establishment. When appointed to the Supreme Court, Krever recommended Greenspan as his successor. (The in-joke of the changeover became Greenspan's announcement that his first decision as new editor would be to exclude reporting the just-lost Demeter case. "Wrong," Krever is said to have replied. "My last decision as out-going editor is to include it.")

Greenspan knew nothing of fishing, little about hockey, and when it came to White Anglo-Saxon Protestantism, all he could manage was to be white; but his prodigious legal knowledge, puritan work ethic (eighteen-hour days, six days a week), and wry, self-deprecating sense of humour had won him a fair measure of respect in the High Court. His portly figure straining in three-piece suits never matched the careful nattiness of Joe Pomerant, but was less offensive to the homespun values of the Bench. He was young, of course, only thirty when he argued the Demeter case, but never disrespectful. And at the occasional legal cocktail party where Greenspan would meet Chief Justice Gale or Deputy Attorney General Frank Callaghan he could entertain them with a pleasing mixture of levity and law.

But he was still only a guest in a house where his opponent was at home. When David Watt was eight years old, a close friend of his father's took the young boy on a tour of the local prison. Putting him in a tiny cell, he told the youngster to climb up on a bench and look out of the window. Then the family friend slipped out of the cell and locked David in. If he wanted to be a lawyer, he later explained, he ought to have an idea of what it was like to be in prison. The friend was himself a lawyer from the nearby town of Walkerton, Ontario. His name was Campbell Grant.

29. Habeas Corpus

"I thought I had died," said Deputy Chief William Teggart, "and woke up in a policeman's paradise."

Bill Teggart and Joe Terdik were in the People's Republic of Hungary.

The two Canadian policemen touched down at Budapest's Ferihegy Airport on August 25, 1975, just about two years to the day after Peter Demeter had been charged with murder, and roughly eight months after he had been convicted of it. Teggart and Terdik were in Budapest to listen to the story of The Duck. To listen, at least, to the official Hungarian version made available by the People's Ministry of Justice. Made available after due and leisurely deliberation. Made available nearly half a year after the unfortunate Duck himself was no longer among the living.

This is what happened.

On October 31, 1974, Chris O'Toole swore out an information in which he stated he had "reasonable and probable grounds to believe" that one Imre Olejnyik, presently residing in the town of Miskolc, Hungary, did, on or about the eighteenth day of July, unlawfully murder Christine Demeter, a human being. The same day a warrant was issued for The Duck's arrest. At the same time, through the appropriate diplomatic channels in Ottawa, extradition proceedings were initiated against Kacsa. The Canadian Department of External Affairs (availing themselves of the opportunity to express their sentiments of the highest esteem for the Foreign Ministry of The People's Republic of Hungary) requested their assistance in making Imre Olejnyik available to the authorities in Canada to answer the charges brought against him. The People's Republic of Hungary (seizing the opportunity to renew their assurances of the highest consideration for the Department of External

Affairs of Canada) replied that they would certainly think about it. Would the deeply honoured Foreign Ministry permit a Canadian commission of inquiry to take a statement from Imre Olejnyik in Hungary? This interesting suggestion by the venerated Department of External Affairs would also be taken under advisement.

On February 8, 1975, The Duck (having apparently been arrested at some earlier point) made a statement in interrogation room Number 17 at the headquarters of the Chief Prosecuting Attorney's Department, Investigation Branch, in the town of Miskolc, Hungary. He stated that his name was Imre Olejnyik, also known as Kacsa or The Duck. He had four years of elementary school education. His occupation was unskilled workman; his present employer the Miskolc Livestock Trading and Meat Processing Enterprise, where he was making eleven *forints* (about thirty-five cents) an hour. He had held the military rank of private and had no membership in any social organization. Personal effects and real property: one automobile. He further stated that he was laying no complaints against his interrogation as a suspect, and did not wish to be represented by defence counsel.

As regards the charges, said Imre Olejnyik, he did not feel guilty; he did not commit any crime; he did not know a person by the name of Demeter or his wife; he did not remember any person named Virag. Leslie Link was his friend, and he did know "Foxy" Jones as the brother-in-law of his other friend Gaby Kecskes. He was acquainted with Ferenc Stark, a small contractor, but he never had any conversations with him about any accidents and he did not go on any assignments and did not take any roll of plans containing any $10,000 from anybody. He owed Stark no money. He had returned to Hungary, having previously applied for permanent residence while visiting between April and October, 1973, because he had trouble with his common-law wife and he felt homesick. He had nothing else to add.

Six days later, on February 14, The Duck was taken to the interrogation room again. He stated that he had changed his mind; in fact, he had changed it right after his first interrogation and had asked to be taken to " . . . the appropriate interrogation officer because I wanted to tell the truth. This was not possible at the time and on the subsequent day I put down what happened using the stationery given to me for that purpose."

On the stationery the Hungarian authorities reserve for the purposes of the truth, The Duck put down that he had first met Ferenc Stark when he was in his employ as a casual labourer for a few days in March 1973. The first day he started working for him, The Duck said, Stark looked up from the newspaper he was reading and said: "I see where in America they kill people for $10,000." Replied The Duck: "For $10,000 or $5,000 I'd kill the whole of America." Having thus informed one another of their feelings regarding humankind, The Duck said Stark offered him a job the very next day where he could make $5,000. It involved waiting for a lady in a house, who would arrive around 8:00 P.M. in a Mercedes and carry a roll of plans in her hand. Inside the plans there would be $3,000. Kacsa was to hit the lady on the head in such a manner as to create the impression that she had fallen down a flight of stairs. The next day Kacsa would get an additional $2,000. The Duck said he pretended to agree.

It wasn't true, continued Kacsa, that Stark had driven him to 52 Dawes Road to show him the house. Stark didn't have to do that, said The Duck, since the job for which Stark had employed him was to clean the empty house on Dawes Road, which Kacsa had been doing at the rate of one or two hours a day for several days. It was on the last evening, The Duck said, that Stark told him: "The woman is coming tonight at 8."

He had no idea who the woman was, stated The Duck, and he didn't care, as he hadn't the slightest intention of hitting her on the head anyway. He went to "Foxy" Jones and told him the whole story, including what he was supposed to do for the $3,000 and that he wouldn't actually do it. Then he asked Foxy to drive him out to Dawes Road. Foxy did, in his green Mustang. The woman came and Kacsa told her he was sent by Frank and could he please have the plans. She seemed surprised that he wasn't interested in looking at the house, but she gave him the plans anyway. "I must add," stated Kacsa, "that she asked me what my name was and I gave her my name as Jimmy Olnik [sic] by which I was known in Canada."

(Instead of resolving the mystery, this deepened it. Stark didn't know Kacsa as Jimmy Orr. This meant Peter couldn't have known him by this name either. Kacsa himself told Christine his name was Jimmy Olnik. How did the name "Jimmy Or" get into Christine's diary?)

At home, The Duck said, he and Foxy inspected the roll which had been sealed with scotch tape. There was a thing that looked like a cardboard cylinder inside and it did contain money. However, it did not contain $3,000, only $1,810 or maybe $1,820. That was all. Foxy, said

The Duck, got $500 of it, not $40 as he stated. Kacsa said he then tried calling Stark to tell him he didn't kill the woman and there was only $1,820 in the roll anyway and that he'd work this amount off for him or repay him in some other way. However, Stark did not seem to go home that night. The person who answered the phone would only tell Kacsa that "daddy wasn't in." The next morning Kacsa did talk to Stark, but Stark didn't want to have a long conversation on the telephone; he wanted to meet The Duck in a restaurant. The Duck sent Foxy instead (who, said Kacsa, seemed eager to meet "Frank", the man who had such fabulous deals up his sleeve), and he himself skipped the country the following day or the day after.

Olejnyik was next interrogated on March 5. This time he told the Hungarian authorities in detail what he did between April and October 1973 in Hungary. He denied knowing anybody named Virag and said that any statements by the latter about any meetings in July must be a lie: he couldn't be at the Woodbine racetrack or The Silver Dollar because he had been in Hungary all along. He had residence permits and passports and other documents, Kacsa said, and they could all be checked out to support his story. He never got back to Canada until October 1973, three months after Christine had been murdered.

The Duck was interrogated for the final time on March 24, 1975. According to the official record, he repeated his stories about the events on Dawes Road, as well as his alleged stay in Hungary between April and October. He added a few minor details but nothing new. He acknowledged that he had been issued a new passport for his final return to Hungary, but he did not know where it was or what had happened to it. His old, original passport on which he had always travelled except for his very last trip in 1974 was in his possession at the time of his arrest. He had thrown it into the garbage when his new passport had been issued, but then he had fished it out again because he wanted to save the picture. Some kids had been playing with it and this was why one page seemed to be missing: it must have been the children who tore it out. Except for whatever might have been on the missing page, it listed every one of his trips, including the entry into Hungary in April 1973, and his exit in October.

"I have nothing else to submit. I agree with the record and am setting my hand to it."

The Duck never set his hand to another record after that. At 1:05 A.M. on the night of March 31 he was taken by ambulance to the Elisabeth

Hospital of Miskolc "due to loss of consciousness". Later on the same day he died.

Kacsa's post-mortem examination was conducted at the hospital named for Dr. Semmelweiss, the discoverer of the cure for puerperal fever, on April 2, 1975. It was two years to the day after he took the plans from Christine at 52 Dawes Road. Drs. Kiss and Hegyi, forensic pathologists, viewed the handiwork of Istvan Hideg, Master Dissector. They saw a man of average height and muscular development, of a general appearance commensurate with his age of thirty-nine years, with forehead bent backward, eyeballs slightly protruded, chin bristly, teeth normal, chest deep, pubic hair manlike, penis flaccid, testicles descended. The colour of the skin under the nails of the hands was purple-blue, on the feet pale.

On the lower third of the left arm a tattoo showed a heart-shaped design with a wreath of branches and the words "My dear mother and father". On the chest near the sternum two similar designs showed the words "Eva and Imre" in one, and "I love you" in the other, both encircled by stylized leaves and flowers. On the right arm the same heart-shape took on a more ominous aspect, with a snake wound around a sword and a cross behind it. The words inside the heart were illegible.

The Duck's head and body showed no signs of external injuries. His brain, however, gave evidence of a massive, continuous haemorrhage. It followed the direction of the middle brain vessels. It extended to both frontal lobes in the membraneous pia mater, forward to the olfactory tubercles and backward to the myelencephalon on the back pole. The brain substance seemed oedematous and swollen everywhere. In the right temporal lobe there was evidence of a destructive cerebral explosion described as "the size of a woman's fist".

A woman's fist. If Christine's ghost struck back, it did about the same amount of damage to Kacsa's brain as the killer did to Christine's. Of course a bloody brain stroke can do a great deal of injury to cerebral matter, and this was given as Imre Olejnyik's official cause of death. At the same time people with little faith — and some experience — in the investigative methods of the police in the People's Republic of Hungary would not rule out repeated trauma with soft, heavy objects such as sandbags or the telephone directory for Greater Miskolc and Region. In any case, The Duck could answer no more questions. He had finally skipped beyond the reach of even Bill Teggart's golden slippers.

So it was the Hungarian officials who answered the Deputy Chief's questions over tiny cups of steaming black coffee in the fifty-foot-long conference room at 10 Apaczai Csere Janos Street, underneath a hammered-copper portrait of Lenin. There was the Chief Prosecutor of the People's Republic himself, Dr. Daniel Froma, with his neat, severe, attractive assistant, Dr. Marta Brayer. Later Bill Teggart would be very impressed with the calibre of the Hungarian prosecutors ("he had piercing grey eyes; her eyes were a very strong blue") and also the kind of co-operation that would make some of the top officials of the country available to a couple of investigating officers, even if high-ranking ones, from a regional police force in Canada. Teggart was also intrigued by their hosts' descriptions of due process in this policeman's paradise: the accused having no right to cross-examine the police, and no right to have a lawyer present when questioned by the police, though he could have a lawyer in court. It sounded very neat. Bill Teggart also noted that in socialist Hungary murder was punishable by death. For good measure, so was conspiracy to commit murder. Pretty Marta Brayer, of the neat blue dress and matching eyes, careful hairdo, and well manicured hands, had herself prosecuted several men who were hanged. No compunctions, recalled Bill Teggart admiringly: she would have swung on their feet. She could have done so with vigour, too, because in her spare time Marta rowed a skiff on the blue Danube. She couldn't understand, Teggart said, how murderers could possibly get *bail* in Canada. Olejnyik, for instance, did not " . . . talk to anyone after he was arrested. No relatives. Just us."

Bill Teggart never thought he would have any liking for socialism or communism. The few socialists he had met in Canada certainly didn't seem to be his kind of people. But these men and women were no long-haired freaks, no sandal-wearing, soppy, bearded weirdos. In fact, they seemed people pretty much after the Deputy Chief's own heart. They were very responsible. He might have a lot in common with them. Funny thing was, they did seem perhaps a bit too *conservative* for his taste. Bill Teggart didn't mind being cross-questioned by the accused's lawyer on the stand; actually, he rather enjoyed it. Maybe these Hungarians were a little bit too strict. Perhaps we didn't need that much law and order.

In any case the Hungarians seemed very thorough. They investigated the late Duck as much as possible, and it did not seem to them as though he could have gone back to Canada between April and October 1973. He had, for instance, signed and dated a snapshot for a girl on July

21. He was registered at a hotel on July 14. He had appeared as a witness in the case of a woman charged with prostitution on August 9. All of these events definitely took place in Hungary. In spite of one missing passport — and a missing page in the other one — they were pretty satisfied that Kacsa never left his native country during the critical months.

But, said the Hungarians, they couldn't guarantee it.

On the face of it Bill Teggart and Joe Terdik's trip to Hungary — five and a half months after the prime suspect's death — seemed to make little sense. No evidence gathered under the peculiar rules of the Hungarian law enforcement authorities would be admissible in any Canadian court. They themselves clearly couldn't interview a dead man — and the possibility always existed that he was dead so that no Canadian policeman should be able to interview him. (This was not necessarily true, and there was no evidence to support even the suspicion, except for the less than spotless record of the People's Administration of Justice in Hungary.) Kacsa, in his statements before he died, seemed to have confirmed all the major contentions of the Crown against Peter Demeter. The task for which he was hired was to kill Christine, not Peter. The relatively minor discrepancies between his story and those of Stark and Foxy could be explained by the attempts of the latter to put themselves in a better light. (There was certainly nothing in Kacsa's statements to support Stark's contention that he *knew* The Duck would never kill Christine; at best, he seemed unconcerned whether he did or not, which would have been enough to support a murder charge against Stark, too, if Christine had met her death on Dawes Road.) But there was one problem with Kacsa's evidence.

The Hungarian authorities didn't simply ask The Duck to tell them everything he knew. They interrogated him — as is clear from their own official records — on the basis of the material gathered by the investigators in Canada. They didn't say to him: What happened? They said: This is what Stark (or Foxy Jones or Virag) said happened; is it true? The Hungarian police knew what theories The Duck was supposed to confirm. They knew what the Canadian authorities *hoped* he would confirm. So Kacsa conveniently confirmed them all and then, before anybody else could talk to him, he died. Good; but perhaps not quite good enough.

Because the authorities in Hungary had a reason for wanting to please the Canadians and have their prisoner tell just the things that would suit their case. Teggart and Terdik received the red-carpet treatment, at least in a minor way, because the Hungarians wanted a little reciprocity. They dined the Canadian policemen (and would have wined them if Bill hadn't been such a confirmed non-drinker) because, as Teggart said later, "they want information on their Hungarian nationals in Canada." The Deputy Chief himself did not make this cause-and-effect connection, but he recalled the talk over the veal paprikash and apple strudel on beautiful Margaret Island repeatedly turning to subjects of this nature. Everything was scrumptious; everyone was gracious. "They gave us complete access to their information," remembered Teggart, "and asked us about getting access to our information. They asked if I thought this could be the start of some reciprocal agreements whereby they could get information on their nationals."

Yes indeed. With good instincts (and also having been thoroughly briefed by the requisite Canadian officials, who might have been worried about some bond — Policemen-Of-The-World-Unite — developing between Bill, Joe, and their socialist counterparts) Teggart replied that all co-operation could no doubt be arranged as long as it was done through official channels. In spite of all this good-fellowship, the Lieutenant Columbo of Mississauga was not about to open his files to the attractive blue eyes of the Chief Prosecutor's assistant in Hungary. It was just as well.

Because, in fact, there is a great gulf between countries that understand the principle of *habeas corpus* and those that do not. No sympathy between even the best-meaning policemen can bridge it. This principle, first codified in 1679 by Charles II of England, requires any authority holding a person to bring him before an independent judge so that the lawfulness of his restraint may be reviewed. Failing this, he cannot be held, questioned, or investigated. Kacsa the miserable Duck " . . . did not talk to anyone after he was arrested. No relatives. Just us."

Habeas corpus: you must have the body. The words are understood by many who can't conceive of the principle. If anyone had said them to the authorities in Hungary, they might have replied: *Habemus corpus?* Yes, sir, we sure do.

30. Her Majesty the Queen, Respondent

When Eddie Greenspan gathered his black gown around his girth and approached the high bench in Toronto's spacious new courtroom 20, it was somewhat like a sacrificial calf entering the lions' den. This feeling was reinforced within five minutes of the commencement of his address. Chief Justice George Gale, flanked on either side by Appeal Court Justices Evans, Jessup, Martin, and Houlden, could only be described, with all due respect to their high office, as ill-tempered. The Appeal Court resembled nothing more than a pride of elderly, moody, male lions whose afternoon nap had been disturbed by some immature, gawking water-buffalo. What was more, the innocent young bovine continued to stand there mooing at the snapping and growling kings of the desert instead of recognizing the mortal danger and getting the hell out. It was nothing short of awesome. Throughout the first two days of the appeal lawyers and law-students kept nipping in and out of the courtroom to enjoy the slaughter and, perhaps, be edified by it. In the back benches what seemed to be the entire Peel Regional Police Force were solemnly watching the spectacle. Bill Teggart was there, Joe Terdik, Chief Burrows, Chris O'Toole.

Flushed, battered, at times visibly pulling himself together, Greenspan continued. Once in a while, when his address was interrupted by some particularly slashing remark by the Chief Justice or one of his brothers on the bench, the young lawyer's ears would turn a delicate shade of pink. However, he would never lose his temper and never relinquish the thread of his argument. Polite and seemingly undaunted, he would go on. He would employ few oratorical devices except surprising reserves of coherence and logic even when supporting somewhat tenuous points. But often his points — to the layman at least — would not seem tenuous at all. By the second day he would be interrupted less and less frequently. His stern seniors would begin to listen to him attentively and in silence. Even the caustic, cutting, formidable Chief Justice would accord him the odd nod of agreement or half-smile of grudging respect.

Eddie Greenspan had entered the arena armed with twenty-six points of appeal and three pieces of new evidence. The new evidence was in the form of three affidavits. In the end only one of the three would be used. The second would not be led by either the defence or the Crown. The third would be led by the defence, but the Court of Appeal, after hearing the evidence in a closed session, would refuse to consider it and would order the press not to divulge it in any form.

The one affidavit that became part of the appeal was a minor bombshell, though in a sense it only confirmed what everybody suspected anyway — except, possibly, the jury that convicted Peter Demeter. The Flower's evidence was worthless. Robert D. Midgley, a Toronto barrister and solicitor, Secretary to the Ontario Jockey Club since 1972, stated in a sworn deposition that on July 18, 1973, the day of Christine's murder, there was no racing conducted at the Woodbine Race Track or any other Toronto race track in the afternoon. Therefore, the part of Tom Smith-Virag-Flower's testimony where he had met Olejnyik spending money like water at Woodbine on the day of the murder must have been a lie.

Why the defence chose not to lead the second piece of new evidence could only be a matter of conjecture. Perhaps they felt that the story was so utterly far-fetched and incredible — almost like an opera plot or a nineteenth-century melodrama — that it would only confirm the Appeal Court's idea of Peter's guilt. The story supported, in many of its background aspects, Dinardo's evidence; but the person deposing it under oath seemed to be as unlike Dinardo as another member of the human race could possibly be. It was fifty-six-year-old Klara Majerszky, the Demeters' former housekeeper.

Ms. Majerszky seemed a perfectly ordinary, middle-aged, middle-class, widowed lady who emigrated from Hungary to Canada in 1970 and, through some mutual acquaintances, was taken on as a housekeeper by Peter and Christine. The idea was that Ms. Majerszky would stay with them until she could familiarize herself with the language and get a job in her own profession as a graduate pharmacist. By and by, this was what happened. When Peter and Christine moved to Mississauga Klara stopped working for them altogether, though she would continue to be a welcome visitor and companion to Christine and little Andrea. In fact, she had been spending part of her holidays with them on Dundas Crescent from June 22 to July 10, 1973 — that is, until just about a week before Christine's death.

The gist of Klara's affidavit was that during this last period Christine borrowed small amounts of money — $50 or $100 — from her, ostensibly for a ticket to bring her parents to Canada, even though Peter had already given her money for that purpose. Christine also mentioned to her that she was seeing a man " . . . who was a very good lover and [who] had not had a woman for a very long time . . . " but without telling Klara the man's name. In this period Christine also went out of the house wearing a blonde wig, kerchief, and sunglasses on at least two occasions. (This, of course, would completely match the description Dinardo gave of the woman he and Eper met at the shopping plaza, while "the lover who hadn't had a woman for a long time" would be strongly suggestive of the escaped convict Eper.)

Ms. Majerszky further stated that she had been well acquainted with a mutual friend of the Demeters whose name was Dr. Bende. This gentleman was a dentist who, according to Klara's affidavit, became seriously ill and eventually died in the spring of 1974. In the spring of 1973, however, while helping out in his office, Klara saw that he was being visited by Csaba Szilagyi and a man she later recognized from his newspaper photo as the fugitive Laszlo Eper. She also stated that very shortly before Dr. Bende died he had visited her in her apartment on Sherbourne Street and asked for Peter's phone number. Having obtained it, Klara stated, he used her phone to call Peter and tell him — in a conversation parts of which Klara overheard — that being a very sick man, he wished to unburden himself to Peter and tell him that two days before Christine's death she called to ask Dr. Bende to tell Csaba that she no longer wanted "the deal". Dr. Bende gave that message to Csaba, who replied that he wanted to see Christine in his apartment the next day. (Presumably this would have been the Tuesday when Christine did visit the Szilagyi apartment in the afternoon.)

Klara then asked Dr. Bende "what was going on" and received the reply that Christine, Csaba, and Laszlo Eper had wanted to get rid of Peter Demeter. He, Dr. Bende, would have gone to the police earlier, but Csaba had been blackmailing him because as a fugitive Eper had used his (Dr. Bende's) island in Georgian Bay as a hideout in 1973. Then Dr. Bende left, and shortly afterwards Klara heard that he had died.

"I talked to Peter Demeter about this conversation," concluded Klara Majerszky's sworn statement, "the next time I saw him and he made me swear on the life of my children and Andrea's life that I would never tell anyone of these things because he did not want Andrea to grow up knowing these things about her mother. Peter Demeter told me he was certain he would be acquitted on the charge of murder. . . . I came forward with this information only after Peter Demeter sent word through Marina Hundt that I was released from my vow. . . . "

There it was; and one could hardly blame Eddie Greenspan for not wishing to tender it to Chief Justice Gale and his fellow justices. This story, though it only became available to Peter's lawyers in the spring of 1975, some months after their client's conviction, would have been available to Peter himself since the winter of 1974. According to Klara's affidavit, he would have learned about it somewhere between his preliminary hearing and his indictment by the grand jury. Though some of Peter's codes of honour seemed not to be of this century, the sacred vow was a little too much to swallow. It *could* have been the truth — anything is possible — but for all its practical value to the defence, it might as well have been a lie.

Because, hard as it was to conceive of an ordinary, law-abiding, middle-aged, middle-class lady perjuring herself in a matter as grave as murder, it was even harder to believe that Peter refused to call her as a defence witness at his trial just to preserve Christine's good name. After all, what else did his defence consist of in the end but the suggestion that Christine died as a result of her own plot? In what way did relying on Stark's gun-and-alibi story or Dinardo's evidence preserve Christine's reputation? And if her reputation was being attacked in open court anyway, why not use the best, most trustworthy witness, the one witness whose testimony might have done Peter some good in front of the jury?

Why the Crown chose not to lead Klara's belated evidence was, of course, a different question. The affidavit was available to them and, no doubt, they had investigated it pretty thoroughly. Had they been able to *prove* it a lie, they would probably have been only too glad to present it to the Court of Appeal. As a proven falsehood, it would have become new evidence of Peter's guilt. As it was, it was just nothing. Like an unreliable old grenade, neither side wanted to touch it for fear it might blow up in their faces.

Greenspan did his best to get in the last piece of new evidence, also an affidavit, or rather two, by a certain Mr. N. and his wife. The N's were a Hungarian couple living somewhere in Ontario. There was no known connection established between them and Peter Demeter; on the face of it they seemed disinterested bystanders. Their name and the details of their story could not — and presumably still cannot — be revealed because of Chief Justice Gale's order of prohibition.

Suffice it to say that, after hearing it, the Chief Justice started referring to Eper as "Eper the Confessor". That is, when he was not referring to him as "Leper", much to the restrained mirth of his fellow justices.

Other than the new evidence, Greenspan's twenty-six grounds of appeal all had to do with alleged errors made by Justice Grant in the course of the trial. After several days of listening to Eddie's argument, the Court requested Crown Counsel David Watt to reply to nine of them. In the view of the five justices these had sufficient merit to deserve a reply.

Some of the nine points had to do with niceties of legal language and minor evidentiary rules. But the main points were the following:

Did Justice Grant err in weighting his charge to the jury in favour of the Crown? (The Appeal Court didn't quite put it that way.)

Did Justice Grant err in excluding the alleged confession of Eper, as reported by Dinardo?

Should Justice Grant have been required to declare a mistrial when the Crown changed the thrust of its case after discovering the Stark conspiracy, or when the media revealed the motion for sequestration and the order for revoking the accused's bail?

Should a new trial be ordered because of the new evidence casting doubt on the testimony of the witness "Tom Smith"?

The Court of Appeal requested no reply from the Crown with reference to the wiretaps, body-packs, or any other aspect of the investigation. Bill Teggart's police work had been vindicated once more.

David Watt spoke for the prosecution with dry, nonchalant erudition. He too eschewed devices of oratory. He had the ability of seeming to coast even when he was probably going pretty near full steam. Still, there was a great difference between his approach to the High Court and Eddie Greenspan's. The defence lawyer was always trying, with respectful persistence, to draw the justices along his own line of argument, somewhat like a tug-boat steering huge ocean-liners into the harbour. David Watt seemed to prefer going with the tide. He would be scanning the faces of the five appeal court judges nearly as frequently as his own notes. His radar appeared to be on the alert for invisible, intangible signals of agreement. When he sensed any — it could be a nod, an encouraging question — Watt would steer his own argument in the direction of least resistance. He seemed to have an athlete's or a general's ability to drift with the momentum of things instead of fighting them. He threw off few sparks but he was easy and graceful. Whatever his own views on the merits of the Crown's case for whose side he argued, in court he would concede nothing. Later, privately, he would use the word "circus" to describe Peter's trial in London. David Watt felt it ought to have been stopped the minute the new evidence became available; or at least the defence should have been given a postponement, a chance to gather their wits.

After two weeks of listening to arguments the Court of Appeal for Ontario reserved judgment. The day the decision was finally announced Eddie Greenspan happened to be in Ottawa, arguing a case before the Supreme Court. He got the news on the telephone from one of his partners, Allen Gold.

"Oh, an appeal came down," said Gold. "Something called Deme . . . Demer . . . "

"You're kidding, Demeter?" asked Eddie. "Well?"

"I don't think you won," said Gold, tactfully.

Eddie swallowed. "How many dissents?" he asked.

"I don't think you have any," answered his partner, throwing tact to the wind.

Greenspan said he simply couldn't believe it. Not that he expected to win, necessarily, though one always hopes, but he had really thought the Court of Appeal might honour his arguments for the cause of Peter Demeter with at least one dissent. It wasn't just a matter of making the defeat honourable. No dissents meant that the decision could not automatically be appealed to the Supreme Court of Canada. Unless that august body gave Greenspan leave to appeal, which was by no means certain, all legal avenues would have been closed to Peter Demeter. It could have been the end of the road.

As far as Chief Justice Gale and Justices Evans, Jessup, Martin, and Houlden were concerned, it clearly ought to have been. They began by rapping the defence on the knuckles rather severely: "The massive evidence of conspiracies could have been contradicted only by the appellant and he did not testify. . . . The address to the jury of senior counsel for the defence does not disclose the theory of the defence with any clarity. . . . [The trial's] conduct was marked by shifting and inconsistent defence theories, some of which would require great astuteness to appreciate. . . . " But this was almost by the by.

The main reason for the Court of Appeal's unanimous decision, handed down on December 1, 1975, was that, in the justices' view, the evidence for Peter Demeter's guilt was so overwhelming that whatever small irregularities might have occurred during his trial they could not have affected the verdict and did not constitute a substantial miscarriage of justice. Should a dead person's statement against his own penal interest, for instance, be made admissible? The law seemed to say no, and this was the basis for the exclusion of Eper's alleged confession. The Appeal Court judges seemed to feel that, while the law may not be all that perfect, they were not about to change it for an obviously guilty man. ("However, because of its facts, we do not think it is necessary or propitious to attempt to settle the law for this Province in this case and we refrain from doing so.") They would not hear new evidence, tendered by the defence in the form of affidavits, because such evidence "must be well capable of belief". This principle of the law, of course, is another one that depends almost entirely on interpretation: other courts have held that anything that isn't a physical impossibility or doesn't involve little green men from Mars is *capable* of belief, which doesn't mean that a court or jury has to believe it, but they should be allowed to hear it and make up their own minds. The defence might have been squeezed a little for time with all the new evidence the Crown was piling on but " . . . we are unable to say that it was so short as to deprive the accused of a fair trial." Added the justices: "It is not inappropriate to observe in this connection that the appellant was defended by two experienced defence counsel who had available to them the services of a trained investigator employed by their firm." It was another indication that Peter might have been no worse off being defended by a young storefront lawyer from legal aid. At least, in this instance, the one law that is supposed to be for the rich did not seem to operate in his favour. The justices did find the publicity surrounding Peter's revocation of bail deplorable, and rapped the Crown on the knuckles for taking no immediate action against the offending parties. However " . . . unless the violation has resulted in a miscarriage of justice . . . " such a violation " . . . does not warrant an appellate court setting aside the verdict of the jury. . . . " In this instance "miscarriage of justice" clearly seemed to mean an outcome with which the Court of Appeal might not have agreed. The same was true of the affidavit of the Jockey Club official discrediting "Tom Smith's" evidence.

Regarding the snitch's story, the five judges conceded that it was reasonable to assume that the jury would have rejected Mr. X's evidence in its entirety if it had known about there being no races at Woodbine on July 18. But would they have acquitted Peter as a result of this?

No and a thousand times no, the Court of Appeal seemed to say. There were the *tapes* clearly indicating that the man was guilty. It wasn't just a question of the tapes tending to confirm Szilagyi's story. They were virtually confessions. They were virtually direct evidence. They were the statements of a guilty man. Peter's innocence, even as a hypothesis, " . . . ceases to be a rational one when considered in the light of the appellant's statements in his taped conversations with Szilagyi."

This view of five distinguished high court judges was final confirmation of the importance of the initial evidence. The tapes, with which Greenwood chose to enter the fray, and which seemed to be regarded as of less than crucial significance by Joe Pomerant: the tapes, that could have been explained only — if at all — by Demeter on the witness stand. The jury wanted to hear the tapes again before rendering their verdict; the Appeal Court regarded them as admissions of guilt. Trickery? "I think I'd want to see the extent of trickery, I'd want to see the nature of it," Justice Grant had said, "even though we're bound by the *Wray* case. . . . I don't think the *Wray* case goes exactly that far." Admissions of guilt? "Szilagyi was a very, very clever person," Justice Grant had said, "and I was never convinced that everything he said was entirely correct." The tapes, of course, were Szilagyi's assignment to get as much support as he could from Demeter for his own story. Did he?

"Well, I think the Court of Appeal took more out of the tapes than I did," commented Justice Grant. "They attached to them a greater indication of guilt on the part of the accused than I had. I saw Demeter and I knew the type of man he was and I may have, because of that, I may have thought there was more opportunity of his, to some extent, talking loosely and all that. The Court of Appeal didn't attach that consideration to it at all. They went by what was in the tapes, quite properly. And as I read their judgement, I recognize I probably ought to have attached more weight to them than I actually did."

It seemed quite clear that the Court of Appeal dealt with Peter as a *confessed* murderer, not merely one who had been convicted by solid circumstantial evidence. This understanding of the weight of the tapes might well have dwarfed all other possible considerations. This reading gave room for no dissents and no questions about any miscarriage of justice, substantial or otherwise. Dinardo, "Smith", Eper, penal interest, sequestration, postponement, the five justices seemed to say, what did they matter? Having heard the tapes, the jury couldn't *help* but find Peter Demeter guilty.

Perhaps the five justices were right.

After the appeal was turned down, Eddie Greenspan and civil lawyer Phil Epstein drove down to Millhaven Penitentiary. By that time Demeter had spent nearly a year in the maximum-security institution. The two lawyers expected him to be upset, but Peter took the news very calmly. He seemed, in fact, strangely calm, resigned in the way of a man who has more important things on his mind. In prison, of course, even the walls have ears and everybody knew that by now Peter seemed to believe that his conviction was due to a conspiracy against him between the insurance companies, trying to save a million dollars, and the police. Also his own lawyer, Joe Pomerant. The loss of the appeal, yes, he could see the hands of Joe through all this. ("What are you talking about," said Greenspan, "I lost this one all on my own.") In any case, Peter wasn't terribly interested. It was more important to make a new deal, to start again, to pick up the threads of business. Having lost a murder appeal was one thing, but it could wait. The deal that was on Peter's mind was urgent, it had to be completed before the end of the fiscal year.

Visiting time was over, the two lawyers were already walking towards the front gate, but Peter was still talking. He had a piece of paper in his hand with all the details worked out, tax benefits, deferrals, loopholes. He remembered that Eddie always liked Christine's Mercedes; once when he had missed his plane he had driven it to Toronto from London and back. The guards were already peeking out of the room where Peter would be frisked at the end of the visiting period; the electronic door letting out the two lawyers would not open until the other door had closed behind Peter. But Peter had a deal to close. "You loved my car." He continued talking about the wheels, the engine; a persuasive, magnificent sales pitch. "Buy it before December 31, no tax advantage otherwise." Murder appeals aside, Peter was selling his car. Obstacles were only obstacles; borders, borders; it was bootstraps time again. No matter how high the bar would go, he'd jump over it. The Crown has a new witness: fine, he would have a new witness too. He would match the authorities plot for plot, the insurance companies story for story;

there would be no defeat. If an innocently convicted man could wish for anything, what piece of evidence should he wish for? (The real killer, a friend replied once, and Peter was indignant: the killer was Eper. It's easier to have a live man dead than a dead man alive.) But it was one thing at a time, and now it was the car. It was a good deal, a chance for a bargain. (Bill Teggart, talking of Peter: "It probably all goes back to the colour of the spots on his hobby horse, but as far as I'm concerned he should be in his grave.") The heavy electronic door moving slowly; the guards waiting. Magnificent car. A discontinued series, a classic. Giving up on Eddie Greenspan, Peter turned to his other lawyer, "Maybe you'd like it."

Then the steel door closed.

Epilogue

Everybody got his medal.

The man who was not afraid to go the Extra Mile, Superintendent William James Teggart, advanced first to Staff Superintendent, then to Deputy Chief. (Teggart himself said nothing to his opponents, but Leo McGuigan couldn't resist leaning over to the defence table after the verdict, and asking on Bill's behalf: "Well, how's the paper route now?") Detective-Sergeant Christopher O'Toole made it to Inspector, as did Joe Terdik. Officers Wingate, King, and Koeslag were specially commended after the trial by the Crown. "As a personal observer, I wish to add my congratulations on a professional job, well done! As you know I am extremely proud of all of you," wrote Chief Burrows. The Town of Mississauga itself had been promoted to the City of Mississauga, and the Mississauga Police Force became the Peel Regional Police Force, comprising the former municipal forces of Mississauga, Brampton, Chinguacousy, Port Credit, and Streetsville. Chief Douglas Kenneth Burrows now headed one of the six or seven largest police forces in Canada.

John Greenwood, Q.C., became Director of Crown Attorneys for the Province of Ontario, and later Assistant Deputy Attorney General. Leo McGuigan was appointed Senior Counsel for the Crown in the Judicial District of Peel.

"He who laughs last laughs loudest," Peter had remarked at one point to Detective-Sergeant Joe Terdik during recess in the London courthouse. "No, Peter," replied Terdik, "he who laughs last laughs *best*." On one of his last nights at the Holiday Inn before his bail was revoked Peter spoke to Teggart and Terdik in the hallway; it was the day that the Crown had revealed Stark's statements for the first time. "I hope," said Peter, with fine ambiguity, "you get the sleep you deserve."

There were other developments.

In the spring of 1976 three justices of the Supreme Court of Canada (including Canada's Chief Justice, Bora Laskin) listened to Eddie Greenspan's arguments requesting leave to appeal the decision of the Ontario Court of Appeal to the highest court of the country. Eddie argued valiantly as always, but without much hope for success. When leave was actually granted (limiting the appeal to two grounds: sequestration and penal interest) Greenspan would not admit to being pleasantly surprised, but he was. The case of Peter Demeter would be heard by the Supreme Court of Canada. Should the appeal succeed, a new trial would be ordered. When word of the Court's permission reached the defence lawyer's office a flurry of activity ensued. Should Peter's subscription to the *Globe and Mail* at the penitentiary be renewed for one more year, a secretary wanted to know. "Good question," Greenspan replied. "If I renew it for another *year* he'll go berserk. Better make it six months."

Though being permitted to appeal to the Supreme Court of Canada was good news for the defence, it must have created a special dilemma for Peter. Just around the time the Supreme Court granted its leave to appeal, in the summer of 1976, Parliament passed a bill abolishing capital punishment, but increasing the time convicted murderers were to spend in jail before becoming eligible for parole from ten to twenty-five years. The Liberal government, bent on abolishing the death penalty, threw in the twenty-five-year-minimum clause as a sop to retentionists, without making adequate provisions for those men and women whose cases were still pending in the appellate courts. In a case like Peter's, it meant that a prisoner either had to acquiesce in what he regarded as a wrongful conviction, or run the risk of winning his appeal, getting a new trial, then, if convicted again, spending twenty-five years in prison instead of ten. It seemed like a monstrous choice.

Peter was shaking it rough in jail. (Older inmates would have called it "doing hard time".) Still, after a while things settled down. Peter had lost a good deal of his hair (for reasons that were not entirely clear; the stories ranged from a nervous condition to acid being thrown on his head). But eventually he found his niche in his new environment. When he took charge of the prison's print shop, it was reported that this enterprise started showing a profit for the first time in the institution's history.

There were other changes: on December 17, 1975, a few weeks after

Peter's appeal had been dismissed in Ontario, the partnership of Joe Pomerant and Eddie Greenspan came to an end. The offices in the Toronto-Dominion Centre were retained by the new law firm of Greenspan, Gold, and Moldaver, while Joe Pomerant decided to take some time off, perhaps go on a sabbatical. Pomerant had interests outside the law: travel, teaching, literature, even broadcasting. Few people doubted, however, that he would eventually return to his legal practice, which he did in early 1977.

Little Andrea Demeter stayed with Peter's cousin and his wife, who had looked after her ever since the night of July 18. She was growing into an exceptionally beautiful child, with an almost uncanny physical resemblance to Christine. She seemed a happy little girl, with no bad memories of anything she might have seen or heard during the seventy-five minutes that elapsed between the telephone conversation at Birks and the arrival of the Mercedes in the driveway at 1437 Dundas Crescent. True, in the beginning of her stay at Steven and Marjorie's there were episodes of bad skin rashes, which the dermatologists attributed to nerves, but a child-psychiatrist who talked with her soon after the event found her equilibrium quite normal. She seemed to realize that her Mommy "got broken". It didn't prevent her from asking Marjorie for some nail polish during the week of her arrival and, for a three-and-a-half-year-old, doing a surprisingly professional job of manicuring her hands.

Life was going on. Psychologist and marriage counsellor Dr. Steven Demeter, perhaps discouraged by his signal failure as counsellor for Christine and Peter's marriage, began doing less and less work in his own profession and more and more as a developer and builder. He seemed to have as much of a knack for it as his cousin, and his partnership with Peter's former architect, Leslie Wagner, appeared to flourish. Lovely Marina Hundt returned to her native Vienna, taking Peter's spaniel with her. The years must have taken their toll on poor Beelzebub (who, in Bill Teggart's view, always smelled like a rhinoceros) because the thrifty Viennese lady began complaining in her letters to Peter after a while that the dog had to be taken to the vet constantly and unless Peter paid for the treatment she would have him destroyed. Marina seemed to have survived her traumatic separation from her lover well enough otherwise, and was running a chic and fashionable boutique in the old Kaiserstadt. *Omnia vincit amor*, according to Vergil. *Sed tempus et distantia*, he might have added; except time and distance.

Justice Campbell Grant, though he had reached the compulsory age of retirement, was still hearing cases as a supernumarary judge of the Supreme Court. Both John Greenwood and Eddie Greenspan would plead before him after the Demeter case — and win. The trial judge had received a great many congratulatory notes after the Demeter verdict. "As I am recalling a memorable day in Court," wrote one Crown witness, a former friend of the Demeters, "I am deeply moved by your display of seemingly inexhaustible patience, strength and wisdom in this bizarre affair." Some letters came from cranks ("Mr. Judge, I still not satisfied with this case, this blady jew Peter Demeter should be hang to day") but quite a few were written by leaders of the community, the clergy, and even fellow justices. "Dear Campbell, you did a terrific job on a most difficult and trying case," wrote a judge from the trial division of the High Court. "It is very fortunate that a man of your ability and extensive experience was designated to try it." One of the retired Chief Justices of the Supreme Court was even more explicit. "Now that the Demeter case is over today," he wrote, "I want to congratulate you on the manner in which you have conducted a most difficult case — probably the most difficult criminal case that has been before the courts during this century. The difficulties of the case were obviously not mitigated by the conduct of defence counsel." Another judicial note said: "Congratulations. Everyone here was thinking of you knowing the strain you were undergoing. I may tell you at this time that there are two Supreme Court Judges who are 10¢ each poorer and I am 20¢ richer. They were betting on circumstantial evidence and I was betting on you."

Chief Justice George Gale, after an exceptionally long service on the Bench, would retire in 1976 with great and well deserved honours. Like Justice Grant, Chief Justice Gale had also laboured under a small misapprehension due to corridor gossip during his hearing of the Demeter case. The Chief Justice seemed to be under the impression that not only The Duck and Eper the Confessor had departed this vale of tears but also Flower the Snitch. In fact, the Flower was sitting, enthralled, right there in Justice Gale's courtroom during the appeal. It seemed that the good Mr. X could not stay away from the Demeter case, and was especially fond of seeking out journalists with little bits of "inside" information. To one reporter, who took him out to lunch during the appeal, he gave the names of three men who he said were the killers, though later he would not confirm these names to the police. (Virag's names were no surprise to the police anyway; they were all people who figured in the trial, one dead and two still alive, who were always suspected, but against whom there was never sufficient evidence.) Then, in the winter of 1977, Virag "confessed" to a reporter named Peter Moon that he had lied on the witness stand when he said that he had met the late Duck at the Woodbine Race Track on the day of Christine's murder.

Though this confession came as a surprise to no one, Peter Moon duly interviewed six of the jurors in London, Ontario, who told him that since they had never believed Mr. X's story anyway, it made no difference to their views about Peter Demeter's guilt. Since Virag also mentioned to Peter Moon that he knew who the actual killers were (though he wouldn't name them), the reporter printed this information. Virag allegedly told the reporter that the killers had nothing to do with Peter, but the way the news-story appeared, the killers were supposed to have been paid $40,000 for the job — and there was certainly no one but Peter to whom Christine's death, even in theory, would have been worth $40,000. Peter reportedly suffered a mild attack of angina pectoris — heart spasm — the day on which he read this news in the Toronto *Globe and Mail*.

Though public interest in the Demeter case had not abated, at least three women made it a rule that the case must never again be mentioned in their presence. The request was understandable, since Mrs. William Teggart, Mrs. John Greenwood, and Mrs. Edward Greenspan had heard about little else from their husbands since 1973. Mrs. Csaba Szilagyi — Gigi — had also had enough of the "demented Demeters". Csaba and Gigi got married not long after the trial: they now have a child.

A few loose ends remained. In spite of the congratulatory notes rained on the police team by members of the judiciary and the public (including some of Peter's former friends), as well as fellow law enforcement officers — like Criminal Investigation Bureau Inspector W. J. Harding who wrote: " . . . the courage required to authorize and undertake some aspects of the investigation defy adequate plaudits and praise. . . . " — the embarrassing fact was that the person or persons who actually killed Christine Demeter were as unknown as ever. If it wasn't Eper or the Duck; if Stark and Dinardo were accused by the Crown in court but never charged, who wielded the crowbar or tire-iron in the garage at Dundas Crescent?

Of course, the fact that Stark, Dinardo, or, for that matter, Eper had not been charged hardly eliminated them as suspects. Assuming that the jury's finding of fact — that Peter Demeter hired some people to kill his wife — was correct, the most logical candidates for carrying out the crime had to be these three, along perhaps with one or two more persons. By his own admission, Stark was not above a murder conspiracy, and Peter did seem to try to get in touch with a "contractor" in the area of the Riverdale Zoo where Stark worked on the day of Christine's murder. As for Dinardo, if Peter was the man behind the crime, his story couldn't be true, and therefore he had to have *some* reason for perjuring himself. The reason, of course, could be nothing more than a sum of money, but people like Dinardo don't enjoy getting involved in murder trials, are not likely to do it just for money, and would be much too difficult to coach in a series of events that they knew nothing about. On the other hand, if Dinardo had been telling the truth — except, to use Demeter's favorite expression, for the vital point — he might easily have met *someone other than Christine* at the shopping plaza with his friend Eper to arrange the murder plot. This someone could have been Stark (who made a big point of *not* having talked with Dinardo when he and The Duck went to see him at the Lansdowne Athletic Club), or it could have been Peter himself. There also had to be some reason for Eper finding it worthwhile to jot down Peter Demeter's name — and even Teggart's — on a piece of paper. Eper did own a Volkswagen car, and real estate man Rick Varep did observe a Volkswagen with three men pull up in front of the Demeter garage, park for about thirty seconds, then drive away, just a few hours before Christine's death. Both Dinardo and Eper had been involved in crimes of violence — Eper, as a fugitive from a life sentence, had especially little to lose — and were perfect choices to carry out a brutal killing. Stark himself is less likely to have been at the scene, whatever his role in the murder plot, but it would not be difficult to find a third person to act as look-out or to drive the car. Finally, if Peter was guilty, involving Eper would be very much in line with his method of "always sticking to the truth" when telling a lie.

But there were other suspects, too. On the night of July 16, 1976, two dead men were pulled out of an overturned car close to the intersection of Steeles Avenue and Dixie Road in an area patrolled by the Peel Regional Police. Apparently the car in which they were travelling crashed into a ditch while being chased by a patrol car driven by uniformed police. Unknown to the uniformed men, the car was under surveillance at the same time by some plainclothes detectives from Bill Teggart's force. Since there was no radio communication between the two police vehicles, the observers couldn't call off the pursuers. It was regrettable, for more than one reason.

One of the men, dead on the spot of cardial tamponade secondary to severe chest trauma, was a sometime enforcer named Paul (Charles) Horvath. His name had appeared in the transcripts of the Demeter trial, though completely out of the blue, in a totally inexplicable way. Joe Pomerant had begun his cross-examination of Csaba Szilagyi by asking him if he knew a man by this name. Csaba replied that Paul Horvath was a common enough name (it is, in Hungarian) and professed not to recognize the photograph Pomerant had showed him of this particular Paul Horvath. Then the whole subject was dropped.

But why was it brought up in the first place? It seemed to have nothing to do with anything.

Bill Teggart had some suspicions. He was in the process of trying to confirm them when fate intervened in the shape of his own highway patrol. After Eper and The Duck, now one more name in the Demeter trial would belong to a dead man. Killed by, or while in custody of, or while being chased by the police. Pity.

But Bill Teggart wouldn't give up. It was nothing personal; murder is murder; if Peter Demeter were killed he wouldn't give up either. Crimes were to be solved, even if it meant whacking asses to get them solved. Some were easy, some were tough; some were smoking guns, some were mysteries. The Deputy Chief couldn't walk on water but he could go a long way on the ground. This murder was solvable.

Way back in July 1973, Bill Teggart had promised Peter Demeter he'd solve it.

But in spite of the continuing investigation, the person who wielded the weapon that killed Christine Demeter was still unknown on February 28, 1977, when the Supreme Court of Canada began hearing Peter Demeter's final appeal against his conviction. Rumours, as usual, were rampant in Ottawa's Skyline Hotel, a slightly toned-up version of London's Holiday Inn but with much the same mock-rustic coffee shop where, as in the days of the trial, many of the participants gathered. In addition to Eddie Greenspan and his assistant Mark Rosenberg — who was Pomerant's articling student at the time of the trial — Chris O'Toole, Joe Terdik, Leo McGuigan, and Steven Demeter were staying in the hotel, trying to dodge the reporters and photographers who still did not seem to have had enough of the Demeter case. On the evening before the appeal began, the tables at the coffee shop were carefully selected. Adversaries did not actually sit at the same table. The police and Crown Attorney Leo McGuigan chatted comfortably over cups of coffee within elbow distance of the next table where the defence team were prepping themselves with milk shakes and french fries. It took only a slight swivel of a chair to make conversation between the two tables possible without violating unspoken feelings of propriety and legal antagonism. Steven Demeter watched the interplay from a table spaced discreetly across the room. It was not until all appeal arguments had been heard that the entire group would sit together in the luxurious dining room atop the Skyline Hotel where, fortified with beverages a little stronger than coffee and milk shakes, the Demeterites — police, Crown, defence, press, and lone relative — would dine together, enjoying a natural ebbing of tension. The bill for that dinner would be in excess of three hundred dollars and very carefully divided up between the participants. No one was going to be in the pocket of either side when it came to a social evening.

Crown Attorney David Watt, who had been promoted to Deputy Director Crown Law Office (Criminal), was the only active participant in the appeal who chose not to stay at the Skyline Hotel but took his two-man team to the classier trappings of Ottawa's Carlton Towers. On the morning of the second day of the hearing John Greenwood showed up, trying to look as inconspicuous as is possible for a man of his size and stature. He was accompanied by a very dapper and jovial Deputy Chief Teggart. There was no official reason for people like Teggart and Greenwood or indeed any of the police force to be at the appeal, but by now the case was more than a file not yet quite closed. The months and years of judicial proceedings, filled alternately with confusion and periods of quiet, had in some curious way forced almost everyone involved to their mirrors. What was on the face of it a fairly straightforward murder case had come to reflect the careers, the values, and even the concept of justice of all those involved. They may not have consciously put it that way, but still the force of the case drew them relentlessly to Ottawa. Only the glamour was missing: Marina did not come over from Vienna where she was said to be living with her newest boyfriend, and Peter himself remained locked up in the penitentiary at Millhaven. The rumours, therefore, were restricted to the dispositions of the nine Supreme Court justices, and the theory that the Crown was not going to put up much of a fight: they would *prefer* Peter to get a new trial so that they could make sure he was put away for twenty-five years under the new law.

That Eddie Greenspan himself doubted that the Crown would, for whatever reason, hand the decision to the defence on a silver platter was clear from the remark he made to his opponent David Watt on the Saturday before the appeal. The two young lawyers, having worked all day preparing their arguments, apparently decided to take in a late movie. They happened to choose the same show playing around the corner from their respective hotels. The film was about a boxer named Rocky who gets a chance to fight the champion and, though hopelessly outclassed, decides at least to stay on his feet until the final bell. Clearly, Eddie Greenspan identified with the underdog. "I only want to go the distance," he said to David Watt plaintively, quoting Rocky's line from the show.

The next day it seemed as though he might. Unlike the arguments before the Ontario Court of Appeal, the arguments before Chief Justice Bora Laskin and his fellow justices took less than two days. Greenspan, citing excellent authorities from exhaustive and ingenious legal research, argued brilliantly that the jury ought to have been sequestered earlier at Peter's trial, and that Eper's confession should have been admitted. David Watt argued in reply that the trial judge was right in doing neither, and in any case it would have made no difference to the verdict of the jury.

The Supreme Court of Canada reserved its decision.

In a well-kept cemetery on the outskirts of Toronto Christine lies in her grave. Next to Peter's mother. Peter wanted the two Mrs. Demeters to be buried close together.